THE AMERICAN EXPERIENCE: NONFICTION

THE AMERICAN EXPERIENCE: FICTION

THE AMERICAN EXPERIENCE: NONFICTION

THE AMERICAN EXPERIENCE: POETRY

THE AMERICAN EXPERIENCE: DRAMA

THE AMERICAN EXPERIENCE: NONFICTION

Marjorie Wescott Barrows

Formerly, General Editor
Macmillan Literary Heritage

H. Lincoln Foster

Housatonic Valley Regional High School
Falls River, Connecticut

Frank E. Ross

Professor of English
Eastern Michigan University
Ypsilanti, Michigan

Eva Marie Van Houten

Formerly, Head of English Department
Mumford High School
Detroit, Michigan

Clarence W. Wachner

Formerly, Divisional Director
Language Education Department
Detroit Public Schools

A revision of *The Early Years of American Literature, The Changing Years of American Literature,* and *Contemporary American Prose,* previously published by Macmillan Publishing Co., Inc.

MACMILLAN PUBLISHING COMPANY
NEW YORK

COLLIER MACMILLAN PUBLISHERS
LONDON

ACKNOWLEDGMENTS

For permission to use material in this book, grateful acknowledgment is made to the following:

Basic Books: For "Mark Twain: The Adventures of Huckleberry Finn," by Henry Nash Smith, Chapter 6 of *The American Novel,* edited by Wallace Stegner, © 1965 by Basic Books, Inc., Publishers, New York.

The Dial Press: For "My Dungeon Shook" reprinted from *The Fire Next Time* by James Baldwin. Copyright © 1963, 1962 by James Baldwin and used by permission of the publisher, The Dial Press, Inc.

Harcourt Brace Jovanovich, Inc.: For "Philadelphia" from *The Autobiography of Lincoln Steffens,* copyright, 1931, by Harcourt Brace Jovanovich, Inc.; renewed, 1959, by Peter Steffens. Reprinted by permission of the publishers. For "The Funeral Train" abridged from *Abraham Lincoln: The War Years,* Volume 4 by Carl Sandburg, copyright, 1939, by Harcourt Brace Jovanovich, Inc.; renewed, 1967 by Carl Sandburg and reprinted by permission of the publishers.

Harper & Row, Publishers: For "The Age of Dust" (pp. 115-116) *The Second Tree from the Corner* by E. B. White. Copyright 1950 by E. B. White. Originally appeared in *The New Yorker,* and reprinted by permission of Harper & Row, Publishers. For pp. 96-115 from *Mark Twain's Autobiography,* copyright 1924 by Clara Gabrilowitsch; renewed 1952 by Clara Clemens Samossoud. Reprinted by permission of Harper & Row, Publishers.

Holt, Rinehart, and Winston, Inc.: For "Mountain Fighting" from *Brave Men* by Ernie Pyle. Copyright 1943, 1944 by Scripps-Howard Newspaper Alliance and Holt, Rinehart and Winston, Inc. For portions of letters from *Selected Letters of Robert Frost* edited by Lawrence Thompson. Copyright ©

Cover design by Leo and Diane Dillon

Macmillan Publishing Company
866 Third Avenue, New York, New York 10022
Collier Macmillan Canada, Inc.
Printed in the United States of America
ISBN 0-02-194100-9
9 8 7 6 5 4 3 2 1

ACKNOWLEDGMENTS (*continued*)

1964 by Holt, Rinehart and Winston, Inc. Reprinted by permission of the Estate of Robert Frost and Holt, Rinehart and Winston, Inc.

Houghton Mifflin Company: For "The Spirit of the New Frontier" from *A Thousand Days* by Arthur M. Schlesinger, Jr. Copyright © 1965 by Arthur M. Schlesinger, Jr. For "Harvard College" from *The Education of Henry Adams* by Henry Adams. Copyright 1946 by Charles F. Adams.

Alfred A. Knopf, Inc.: For "Journey Toward a Sense of Being Treated Well" from *Here to Stay* by John Hersey. Copyright © 1957 by John Hersey. Reprinted by permission of Alfred A. Knopf, Inc. This article was first published in slightly different form in *The New Yorker*. For "On Being an American" from *Prejudices*, Third Series, by H. L. Mencken. Copyright 1922 by Alfred A. Knopf, Inc. Renewed 1950 by H. L. Mencken. Reprinted by permission of Alfred A. Knopf, Inc.

Macmillan Publishing Co., Inc.: For "The Poverty of the Bowery" by Michael Harrington, reprinted with permission of Macmillan Publishing Co., Inc. from *The Other America* by Michael Harrington. Copyright © Michael Harrington, 1962.

William Morris Agency, Inc.: For "Why Do We Read Fiction?" by Robert Penn Warren. Copyright © 1962 by Robert Penn Warren.

World Journal Tribune: For "A Farewell to the Last Harvard 'Dandy' " by Malcolm Cowley, as published in the *New York Herald Tribune* Book Review Section of July 9, 1962. Reprinted by permission of the *World Journal Tribune*.

G. P. Putnam's Sons: For "Why Don't We Complain?" by William F. Buckley, Jr. Reprinted by permission of G. P. Putnam's Sons from *Rumbles Left and Right* by William F. Buckley, Jr.; © 1963 by William F. Buckley, Jr.

Acknowledgments *(continued)*

Random House, Inc.: For selections from *I Know Why the Caged Bird Sings* by Maya Angelou. Copyright © 1969 by Maya Angelou. Reprinted by permission of Random House, Inc. For William Faulkner's "Speech of Acceptance, Nobel Prize for Literature." Reprinted from *The Faulkner Reader* (Random House, 1954).

Charles Scribner's Sons: For "Circus at Dawn," reprinted with slight deletions with the permission of Charles Scribner's Sons from *From Death to Morning* by Thomas Wolfe. Copyright 1935 Charles Scribner's Sons; renewal copyright © 1963 by Paul Gitlin. For letter on *The Great Gatsby* dated November 20, 1924, reprinted with the permission of Charles Scribner's Sons from *Editor to Author: The Letters of Maxwell E. Perkins,* edited John Hall Wheelock. Copyright 1950 Charles Scribner's Sons. For "A Good Café on the Place St. Michel," reprinted with the permission of Charles Scribner's Sons from *A Moveable Feast* by Ernest Hemingway. Copyright © 1964 Ernest Hemingway, Ltd.

Mrs. Helen Thurber: For "University Days." Copyright © 1933, 1961 James Thurber. From *My Life and Hard Times,* published by Harper and Row. Originally printed in *The New Yorker.*

The Viking Press, Inc.: For the William Faulkner interview from *Writers at Work* edited by Malcolm Cowley. Copyright © 1957, 1958 by The Paris Review, Inc. Reprinted by permission of The Viking Press, Inc. For "The Texas of the Mind" from *Travels with Charley In Search of America* by John Steinbeck. Copyright © 1961, 1962 by The Curtis Publishing Company, Inc., copyright © 1962 by John Steinbeck. Reprinted by permission of The Viking Press, Inc. For "What's Happening to America?" from *America and Americans* by John Steinbeck. Copyright © 1946 John Steinbeck. All rights reserved.

Contents

The Individual Experience 128

Introduction

If fiction is "an 'illusion of life' projected through language," as the novelist Robert Penn Warren suggests, then nonfiction is the reality of life preserved through language. Nonfiction is an entertainment of the intellect rather than an "imaginative enactment." Through a nation's nonfiction, we learn about its principles, its government, and its people. Writers of American nonfiction have described America's history, literature, social life and attitudes. In this book, you will find a selection of nonfiction that explores the forces, events, and influences that shaped the American character.

The opening essays by St. John de Crèvecoeur and John Steinbeck present two views of the American character which are quite different. Crèvecoeur eloquently extols the virtues of the new American. According to him, "The American is a new man, who acts upon principles . . ." Steinbeck, on the other hand, says we are a people "who proceed to break every law we can if we can get away with it." While Crèvecoeur depicts America as a great melting pot where there are no prejudices against newcomers, he is sharply contradicted by Steinbeck's statement that Americans are quick to "release the mechanisms of oppression" against any newcomers who are "poor, weak in numbers and unprotected."

What then is the true character of the American people? Are we a nation of restless, dissatisfied searching people, or are we "the western pilgrims" moving forward with vigor and industry? The questions at the end of each selection will focus your attention on the salient points of each essay and help you understand the author's message. As you read, evaluate not only what the author states but also what he implies and expects you to infer. If you examine each author's perspective as well as his purpose and explore the variety of ideas and comments presented in the various essays, you will no doubt form your own opinion of the American character.

TWO BASIC QUESTIONS

DE CRÈVECOEUR AND STEINBECK

This book will explore two questions: "What does it mean to be an American?" and "What is America's destiny?" The following essays, written two centuries apart, are designed to introduce these two questions and to aid both our pursuit of that elusive creature, the typical American, and our search for his past and his future.

Before coming to this country in 1754, St. John de Crèvecoeur lived in England seven years, where he learned the language and became familiar with the English way of life. Thus he could view this country and its people both as they appeared to him, a "new American," and as he thought they would appear to "an enlightened Englishman." Though he tended to idealize the simple American life and was occasionally sentimental, he wrote with a charm and grace that caught the fancy of his European readers. He also pleased American readers who enjoyed seeing themselves portrayed in such an attractive light. His way of seeing Americans is evident in the essay "What Is an American?" from his book, *Letters from an American Farmer.*

Today's America is full of disturbing contradictions. In the midst of plenty, there is poverty. A sense of well-being is constantly being shattered by anger and violence. John Steinbeck, winner of both a Pulitzer Prize and the Nobel Prize, draws from his extensive knowledge of the American people in his analysis of our perturbed contemporary mood in "What's Happening to America?"

What Is an American?

ST. JOHN de CRÈVECOEUR

I wish I could be acquainted with the feelings and thoughts which must agitate the heart and present themselves to the mind of an enlightened Englishman, when he first lands on this continent. He must greatly rejoice that he lived at a time to see this fair country discovered and settled; he must necessarily feel a share of national pride, when he views the chain of settlements which embellishes these extended shores; when he says to himself, this is the work of my countrymen, who, when convulsed by factions, afflicted by a variety of miseries and wants, restless and impatient, took refuge here. They brought along with them their national genius, to which they principally owe what liberty they enjoy, and what substance they possess. Here he sees the industry of his native country displayed in a new manner, and traces in their works the embryos of all the arts, sciences, and ingenuity, which flourish in Europe. Here he beholds fair cities, substantial villages, extensive fields, an immense country filled with recent houses, good roads, orchards, meadows, and bridges, where an hundred years ago all was wild, woody, and uncultivated! What a train of pleasing ideas this fair spectacle must suggest;

it is a prospect which must inspire a good citizen with the most heartfelt pleasure.

The difficulty consists in the manner of viewing so extensive a scene. He is arrived on a new continent; a modern society offers itself to his contemplation, different from what he had hitherto seen. It is not composed, as in Europe, of great lords who possess every thing, and of a herd of people who have nothing. Here are no aristocratical families, no courts, no kings, no bishops, no ecclesiastical dominion, no invisible power giving to a few a very visible one; no great manufacturers employing thousands, no great refinements of luxury. The rich and the poor are not so far removed from each other as they are in Europe. Some few towns excepted, we are all tillers of the earth, from Nova Scotia to West Florida. We are a people of cultivators, scattered over an immense territory, communicating with each other by means of good roads and navigable rivers, united by the silken bands of mild government, all respecting the laws, without dreading their power, because they are equitable. We are all animated with the spirit of an industry which is unfettered and unrestrained, because each person works for himself. If he travels through our rural districts he views not the hostile castle, and the haughty mansion, contrasted with the clay-built hut and miserable cabin, where cattle and men help to keep each other warm, and dwell in meanness, smoke, and indigence.[1] A pleasing uniformity of decent competence appears throughout our habitations. The meanest of our log-houses is a dry and comfortable habitation. Lawyer or merchant are the fairest titles our towns can afford; that of a farmer is the only appellation of the rural inhabitants of our country. It must take some time ere he can reconcile himself to our dictionary, which is but short in words of dignity, and names of honor. There, on a Sunday, he sees a congregation of respectable farmers and their wives, all clad in neat homespun, well mounted, or riding in their own humble wagons. There is not among them an esquire, saving the unlettered magistrate. There he sees a parson as simple as his flock, a farmer who does not riot on the labor of others. We have no princes, for whom we toil, starve, and bleed; we are

[1] *indigence:* poverty

the most perfect society now existing in the world. Here man is free as he ought to be; nor is this pleasing equality so transitory as many others are. Many ages will not see the shores of our great lakes replenished with inland nations, nor the unknown bounds of North America entirely peopled. Who can tell how far it extends? Who can tell the millions of men whom it will feed and contain? For no European foot has as yet traveled half the extent of this mighty continent!

The next wish of this traveler will be to know whence came all these people. They are a mixture of English, Scotch, Irish, French, Dutch, Germans, and Swedes. From this promiscuous[2] breed, that race now called Americans have arisen. The eastern provinces must indeed be excepted, as being the unmixed descendants of Englishmen. I have heard many wish that they had been more intermixed also: for my part, I am no wisher, and think it much better as it has happened. They exhibit a most conspicuous figure in this great and variegated picture; they too enter for a great share in the pleasing perspective displayed in these thirteen provinces. I know it is fashionable to reflect on them, but I respect them for what they have done; for the accuracy and wisdom with which they have settled their territory; for the decency of their manners; for their early love of letters; their ancient college,[3] the first in this hemisphere; for their industry; which to me who am but a farmer, is the criterion of everything. There never was a people, situated as they are, who with so ungrateful a soil have done more in so short a time. Do you think that the monarchical ingredients which are more prevalent in other governments, have purged them from all foul stains? Their histories assert the contrary.

In this great American asylum,[4] the poor of Europe have by some means met together, and in consequence of various causes; to what purpose should they ask one another what countrymen they are? Alas, two thirds of them had no country. Can a wretch who wanders about, who works and starves, whose life is a continual scene of sore affliction or pinching penury—can that man call England or any other kingdom his

[2] *promiscuous:* mixed
[3] *ancient college:* Harvard
[4] *asylum:* refuge

country? A country that had no bread for him, whose fields procured him no harvest, who met with nothing but the frowns of the rich, the severity of the laws, with jails and punishments; who owned not a single foot of the extensive surface of this planet? No! Urged by a variety of motives, here they came. Every thing has tended to regenerate them; new laws, a new mode of living, a new social system; here they are become men. In Europe they were as so many useless plants, wanting vegetative mold, and refreshing showers; they withered, and were mowed down by want, hunger, and war; but now by the power of transplantation, like all other plants they have taken root and flourished! Formerly they were not numbered in any civil lists of their country, except in those of the poor; here they rank as citizens. By what invisible power has this surprising metamorphosis[5] been performed? By that of the laws and that of their industry. The laws, the indulgent laws, protect them as they arrive, stamping on them the symbol of adoption; they receive ample rewards for their labors; these accumulated rewards procure them lands; those lands confer on them the title of freemen, and to that title every benefit is affixed which men can possibly require. This is the great operation daily performed by our laws. From whence proceed these laws? From our government. Whence the government? It is derived from the original genius and strong desire of the people ratified and confirmed by the crown. This is the great chain which links us all, this is the picture which every province exhibits, Nova Scotia excepted. There the crown has done all; either there were no people who had genius, or it was not much attended to: the consequence is, that the province is very thinly inhabited indeed; the power of the crown in conjunction with the musketos[6] has prevented men from settling there. Yet some parts of it flourished once, and it contained a mild harmless set of people. But for the fault of a few leaders, the whole were banished. The greatest political error the crown ever committed in America was to cut off men from a country which wanted nothing but men!

[5]*metamorphosis:* basic change
[6]*musketos:* mosquitoes

What attachment can a poor European emigrant have for a country where he had nothing? The knowledge of a language, the love of a few kindred as poor as himself, were the only cords that tied him: his country is now that which gives him land, bread, protection, and consequence. *Ubi panis ibi patria,*[7] is the motto of all emigrants. What then is the American, this new man? He is either an European, or the descendant of an European; hence that strange mixture of blood, which you will find in no other country. I could point out to you a family whose grandfather was an Englishman, whose wife was Dutch, whose son married a French woman, and whose present four sons have now four wives of different nations. *He* is an American, who leaving behind him all his ancient prejudices and manners, receives new ones from the new mode of life he has embraced, the new government he obeys, and the new rank he holds. He becomes an American by being received in the broad lap of our great *Alma Mater.*Here individuals of all nations are melted into a new race of men, whose labors and posterity[8] will one day cause great changes in the world. Americans are the western pilgrims, who are carrying along with them that great mass of arts, sciences, vigor, and industry which began long since in the east; they will finish the great circle. The Americans were once scattered all over Europe; here they are incorporated into one of the finest systems of population which has ever appeared, and which will hereafter become distinct by the power of the different climates they inhabit. The American ought therefore to love this country much better than that wherein either he or his forefathers were born. Here the rewards of his industry follow with equal steps the progress of his labor; his labor is founded on the basis of nature, *self-interest;* can it want a stronger allurement? Wives and children, who before in vain demanded of him a morsel of bread, now fat and frolicsome, gladly help their father to clear those fields whence exuberant crops are to arise to feed and to clothe them all, without any part being claimed, either by a despotic prince, a rich abbot, or a mightly lord. Here religion demands but little of him; a small volun-

[7]*Ubi panis ibi patria:* Where bread is, there is a fatherland.
[8]*posterity:* descendants

tary salary to the minister, and gratitude to God; can he refuse these? The American is a new man, who acts upon new principles; he must therefore entertain new ideas, and form new opinions. From involuntary idleness, servile dependence, penury, and useless labor, he has passed to toils of a very different nature, rewarded by ample subsistence.—This is an American.

FOR DISCUSSION

1. In the closing lines of this "Letter," Crèvecoeur answers the question stated in the title. In your opinion, was his definition accurate at the time he wrote it? How accurate is it today? Does this country still offer people from other countries as much as, or more than, it did in 1782? Explain.
2. What would an "enlightened Englishman" find in this country that would fill him with pride and would "inspire a good citizen"?
3. Crèvecoeur suggests that a visitor from the Old World might have difficulty in viewing "so extensive a scene." Why? In what ways was life in the New World different? What were some of the basic reasons for these differences?
4. Like many newcomers to this country, Crèvecoeur appreciated what America had to offer "the poor of Europe." Why does he say that two thirds of them had no country? To what does he compare them? What "invisible power" performed this "surprising metamorphosis"?
5. The eastern provinces receive special mention. Why? What does Crèvecoeur admire them for? Why does he say that all Americans were once scattered all over Europe? When, and how, did they become Americans?
6. Why ought the American "to love this country much better than that wherein either he or his forefathers were born"? What part did *self-interest* play both in luring him to this country and, later, in his revolt again restrictions by England?
7. What qualities does this "Letter" have which are characteristic of the informal essay? What impression did you gain of the writer as a person? In what ways did he appeal to the emotions of his readers? Point out evidences of the grace and charm of his style, and also of the effectiveness of his use of specific detail and concise, graphic words in his descriptions.

FOR COMPOSITION

Early in this essay, Crèvecoeur points out what the visitor from England would observe in America that was different from what he observed at home. Write a short essay in which you point out what Crèvecoeur would observe in present-day America that is different from what he observed back in 1782. Base your essay on only the second paragraph of Crèvecoeur's essay, following as closely as you can the kinds of things he mentions and his style of writing. You might begin, "The difficulty for the eighteenth-century American consists in the manner of viewing so modern a scene. Where once there were small villages, there are now large cities. Fewer and fewer Americans are tillers of the earth"—and so on.

What's Happening to America?

JOHN STEINBECK

It is customary (indeed, at graduations it is a requirement) for speakers to refer to America as a "precious inheritance"—our heritage, a gift proffered like a sandwich wrapped in plastic on a plastic tray. Our ancestors, so it is implied, gathered to the invitation of a golden land and accepted the sacrament of milk and honey.

This is not so. In the beginning we crept, scuttled, escaped, were driven out of the safe and settled corners of the earth to the fringes of a strange and hostile wilderness, a nameless and hostile continent. Far from welcoming us, it resisted us. This land was no gift. The firstlings worked for it, fought for it, died for it. They stole and cheated and double-crossed for it.

But we built America, and the process made us Americans—a new breed, rooted in all races, stained and tinted with all colors, a seeming ethnic anarchy. Then in a little, little time, we became more alike than we were different—a new society; not great, but fitted by our very faults for greatness: *E Pluribus Unum.*

The whole thing is crazy. Every single man in our emerging country was out for himself. When communities arose, each one defended itself against other communities. All that was required to release the mechanism of oppression was that the newcomers be poor, weak in numbers and unprotected—although it helped if their skin, hair, eyes were different, and if they spoke some language other than English, or worshipped in some church other than Protestant. The Puritans took out after any other faith; the Germans clotted for self-defense until the Irish took the resented place; the Irish became "Americans" against the Poles, the Slavs against the Italians.

It occurs to me that this very cruelty toward newcomers might go far toward explaining the speed with which the ethnic and national strangers merged with the "Americans." In spite of all the pressure the old people could bring to bear, the children of each ethnic group denied their background and their ancestral language. Something was loose in this land, and the new generations wanted to be Americans more than they wanted to be Hungarians or Italians or British. And in one or two, certainly not more than three generations, each ethnic group has clicked into place in the union without losing the *pluribus*.

One of the generalities most often noted about Americans is that we are a restless, a dissatisfied, a searching people. We spend our time searching for security, and hate it when we get it. We are an intemperate people: we eat too much, drink too much, indulge our senses too much. We work too hard, and many die under the strain; and we play with a violence just as suicidal. The result is that we seem to be in a state of turmoil all the time, both physically and mentally. We are able to believe that our government is weak, stupid, overbearing, dishonest and inefficient, and at the same time we are deeply convinced that it is the best government in the world, and we would like to impose it upon everyone else.

Americans seem to live and breathe and function by paradox; but in nothing are we so paradoxical as in our passionate belief in our own myths. We shout that we are a nation of laws, not men—and then proceed to break every law we can if we can get away with it. Our most persistent folktales—constantly retold in books, movies and television shows—concern cowboys, gun-slinging sheriffs and Indian fighters. The brave and honest sheriff who with courage and a six-gun brings law and order to a Western community is perhaps our most familiar hero. And in these moral tales, so deep-set in us, virtue does not arise out of reason or orderly process of law—it is imposed by violence and maintained by the threat of violence.

I wonder whether this folk wisdom is the story of our capability. Are these stories permanent because we know within ourselves that only the threat of violence makes it possible for us to live together in peace?

No one can define the "American Way of Life" or point to any person or group who lives it, but it is real nevertheless.

Our means of governing ourselves, while it derives from European and Asian sources, is unique. That it works at all is astonishing; that it works well is a matter for amazement. In thinking about conferring the blessings of our system on other people, we forget that ours is the product of our own history, which has not been duplicated anywhere else. We have amassed a set of feelings which grew out of our background, but which are just as strongly held when we do not know that background.

For example, Americans almost without exception have a fear and a hatred of any perpetuation of power—political, religious or bureaucratic. Whether this anxiety stems from what amounts to a folk memory of our own revolution against the England of George III, or whether in the family background of all Americans from all parts of the world there is an alert memory of the foreign tyrannies which were the cause of their coming here in the first place, it is hard to say. Regardless, any official with a power potential causes in Americans first a restiveness, then suspicion and finally—if the official remains in office too long—a downright general animosity. Many a public servant has been voted out of office for no other reason than that he has been in too long.

In nothing are the Americans so strange as in their attitudes toward their children. I have studied children in many countries, and I find nothing to approximate the American child-sickness. Before it appeared, parents were delighted to have children at all and content that they might grow up to be exactly like themselves. Farm boys grew up farmers; housewives trained their daughters to be housewives. Population explosions were taken care of by wars, plagues and starvation.

Our child-sickness has developed very rapidly in the last 60 years, and it runs parallel, it would seem, with increasing material plenty and the medical conquest of child-killing diseases. Suddenly it was no longer acceptable that the child should be like his parents and live as they did; he must live better, know more, dress more richly and, if possible, change from his father's trade to a profession. Since it was demanded of the child that he be better than his parents, he must be guided, pushed, admired, disciplined, flattered and forced. But since the parents were and are no better than they are, the rules they propounded were not based on their experience but on their wishes and hopes.

If the hope was not fulfilled, the parents went into a tailspin of guilt, blaming themselves for having done something wrong or at least something not right. This feeling of the parents was happily seized upon by the children, for it allowed them to be failures through no fault of their own. Laziness, sloppiness, indiscipline, selfishness and general piggery, which are the natural talents of children and were once slapped out of them, now became either crimes of the parents or sickness in the children, who would far rather be sick than be disciplined.

Into this confusion the experts entered, and American parents put their troubles, and their children, in the hands of the professionals—doctors, educators, psychologists, neurologists, psychiatrists. The only trouble was and is that few of the professionals agreed with one another except in the belief that the child should always be the center of attention—an attitude which has the full support of the children.

I have been putting off writing about the most serious problem that Americans are faced with, both as a people and as individuals. We discuss it constantly, and yet there is not even a name for it. Immorality does not describe it, nor does lack of integrity, nor does dishonesty. Many people, not able to face the universal spread and danger of the cancerous growth, split off a fragment of the whole to worry about or to try to cure.

But I begin to think that the evil is one thing, not many; that racial unrest, the emotional crazy quilt that drives our people to the psychiatrists, the fallout, dropout, copout insurgency of our children and young people, the rush to stimulant as well as hypnotic drugs, the rise of narrow, ugly and vengeful cults of all kinds, the distrust and revolt against all authority—this in a time of plenty such as has never been known—I think all of these are manifestations of one single cause.

I'm not going to preach about any good old days. By our standards of comfort they were pretty awful. What did they have then that we are losing or have lost? For one thing, they had rules—rules concerning life, limb and property; rules governing deportment and manners; and finally rules defining dishonesty, dishonor, misconduct and crime. The rules were not always obeyed, but they were believed in, and a breaking of them was savagely punished. The rule-breaker knew he was wrong and the others were right. The rules were understood and accepted by everyone.

Adlai Stevenson, speaking of a politician of particularly rancid practices, once said, "If he were a bad man, I wouldn't be so afraid of him. But this man has no principles. He doesn't know the difference." Could this be our difficulty—that gradually we are losing our ability to tell the difference? The rules fall away in chunks, and in the vacant place we have a generality: "It's all right because everybody does it."

We are also poisoned with *things.* Having many things seems to create a desire for more things. Think of the pure horror of Christmases when children tear open package after package and then, when the floor is heaped with wrappings and presents, say, "Is that all?" And two days later the smashed and abandoned "things" are added to our national trash pile, and perhaps the child, having got in trouble, explains, "I didn't have anything to do." And he means exactly that—nothing to do, nowhere to go, no direction, no purpose, and worst of all, no needs.

It is probable that the want of things and the need of things have been the two greatest stimulants toward the change and complication we call progress. And surely we Americans, most of us starting with nothing, have contributed our share of wanting. Wanting is probably a valuable human trait. It is the *means* of getting that can be dangerous.

The evil that threatens us came quickly and quietly, came from many directions and was the more dangerous because it wore the face of good. Almost unlimited new machine power took the place of straining muscles and bent backs. Medicine and hygiene cut down infant mortality almost to the vanishing point, and at the same time extended our life-span. Leisure came to us before we knew what to do with it, and all of these good things falling on us unprepared constitute calamity. We have the things, and we have not had time to develop a way of thinking about them.

I strongly suspect that our moral and spiritual disintegration grows out of our lack of experience with plenty. We had a million years to get used to the idea of fire and only 20 to prepare ourselves for the productive-destructive tidal wave of atomic fission. Our babies live, and we have no work for their hands. We retire men and women at the age of their best service for no other reason than that we need their jobs for younger people. To allow ourselves the illusion of usefulness, we have standby crews for functions which no longer exist.

Why do we act the way we do? I believe it is because we have reached the end of a road and have discovered no new path to take, no duty to carry out, no purpose to fulfill. I think we will find a path to the future, but its direction may be unthinkable to us now.

Something happened in America to create the Americans. Now we face the danger which in the past has been most destructive to the human: success, plenty, comfort and ever-increasing leisure. No dynamic people has ever survived these dangers. If the anesthetic of self-satisfaction were added to our hazards, we would not have a chance of survival—as Americans.

But I expect that we will survive as Americans. A dying people tolerates the present, rejects the future and finds its satisfactions in past greatness and half-remembered glory. It is in the American negation of these symptoms of extinction that my hope and confidence lie. We are not satisfied. Our restlessness is still with us. Young Americans are rebellious, angry, searching. The energy pours out in rumbles, in strikes and causes, even in crime—but it is energy. Wasted energy is only a little problem compared with the lack of it.

The world is open as it has never been before, and for the first time in human experience we have the tools to work with. Three fifths of the world and perhaps four fifths of the world's wealth lie under the sea, and we can get to it. The sky is open at last, and we have the means to rise into it.

We are in the perplexing period of change. We seem to be running in all directions at once—but we are running. And I believe that our history, our experience in America, has endowed us for the change that is coming. We have cut ourselves off from the self-abuse of war by raising it from a sin to an extinction. Far larger experiences are open to our restlessness—the fascinating unknown is everywhere.

How will we Americans act and react to a new set of circumstances for which new rules must be made? We will make mistakes; we always have. But from our beginning, in hindsight at least, our social direction is clear. We have moved to become one people out of many. We have failed sometimes, taken wrong paths, paused for renewal, filled our bellies and licked our wounds. But we have never slipped back—never.

FOR DISCUSSION

1. How does Steinbeck's description of America's early years differ from Crèvecoeur's? Do you think that Steinbeck is cynical, or that Crèvecoeur is unrealistic, or both, or neither? Does the time in which the writer lives affect his interpretation of facts? How do Crèvecoeur and Steinbeck illustrate your answer?
2. When Steinbeck compares the phrase "precious inheritance" to a sandwich wrapped in plastic and served on a plastic tray, what is he saying about the phrase?
3. What is the explanation for the "cruelty toward newcomers" which Steinbeck notices in the American past? Does such cruelty still occur? Explain.
4. Is it true that "Americans almost without exception have a fear and a hatred of any perpetuation of power"? What evidence do you have to support this statement? What evidence can you find which disproves it?

5. What method of child-rearing do you think Steinbeck would advocate? Do you agree with him?
6. Steinbeck suggests that leisure is a powerful calamity. Why? Do you agree that "our moral and spiritual disintegration grows out of our lack of experience with plenty"? What evidence is there of such disintegration?

FOR COMPOSITION

1. Write an essay either agreeing with or disagreeing with the generalization Steinbeck refers to: that "we are a restless, a dissatisfied, a searching people." Support your view of this generalization with proof and documentation. Simply repeating your opinion is not enough.
2. Carefully describe and discuss one paradox by which you feel "Americans live and breathe and function." Try not to repeat Steinbeck's examples.

ON HISTORY AND POLITICS

SMITH AND BRADFORD

The subjects of American nonfiction cover almost any topic about which man has ever wondered. In the course of American history, however, certain topics have frequently reappeared—perhaps because they are matters of human concern. Writing on a topic of widespread human interest can help the writer to define himself as a human being.

One way of defining oneself is through one's history or past. And because the United States of America is a political unit, its political past is of importance in the definition of the term *American*. In the never-ending quest for his own definition, the American writer has examined his country's history and politics for clues to what and who he is. He has also displayed from the beginning a desire to record this history as it was being made. Thus, the line between journalistic reporting of political events and the more "literary" treatment of those events often has been invisible.

The obvious starting point in this search for historical definitions is the beginning—during the first days of the settlers.

Not even at this point, however, do simple definitions appear. America was settled by individuals with different outlooks and methods for facing problems. Nevertheless, out of the enormous variety of people who emigrated and struggled and died here, two particular "types" often seem to recur; and these two types—almost opposites—are well represented in the autobiographical writings of William Bradford of Plymouth and Captain John Smith of Jamestown.

Captain Smith emerges from his own account of the Jamestown settlement, *The Generall Historie of Virginia*, as a romantic hero. He reacts quickly, moves swiftly, and never halts to entertain troublesome doubts or paralyzing thoughts. Smith accepts himself confidently because he finds himself capable of meeting any unexpected emergencies. When surrounded by Indians, he has no scruples about forcing his Indian guide to act as a human shield. Neither does he waste sentimental regrets over the occasional deaths among his men. Above all, his imagination is worldly. He sees himself as the protagonist of a drama, and all events as moving toward comedy or tragedy.

The difference between John Smith's account and that of William Bradford is great. Bradford never forgets, in his *History of Plimmoth Plantation*, that he owes his survival from minute to minute to a watchful and divine Providence which intervenes personally in his behalf. Such Providence brings him safely through the dangers of malevolent Nature and hostile savages. While Smith acts instinctively, Bradford meditates long and finally moves carefully, cautious always not to displease his God, while he is hopeful always of winning His favor. Bradford's is the more terrible experience because he more often experiences terror. And such terror befalls him because he is more aware of the complex implications of his predicament. He is overwhelmed by his personal helplessness in a wild and savage land, and turns for physical, moral, and emotional salvation to a force more powerful than he. While Smith moves, Bradford speculates; while Smith plots, Bradford prays.

Here, then, are two major types who shaped the course of the nation and the character of her people. One is a man of thought, the other a man of action. One is concerned with the moral significance of human events, the other is preoccupied with surviving to tell his tale. One worships, the other explores. From the influence of these two types and the ways of living each represents, came the healthy tension out of which a nation not only could grow, but also could assess her growth with intelligence. Each was essential to the unfolding story of America.

Pocahontas

JOHN SMITH

Our comedies never endured long without a tragedie. Some idle exceptions being muttered against Captaine Smith, for not discovering the head of the Chickahamania river, and taxed by the Councell to be too slow in so worthy an attempt, the next voyage hee proceeded so farre that with much labour by cutting of trees insunder he made his passage; but when his barge could passe no farther, he left her in a broad bay out of danger of shot, commanding none should go ashore till his returne. Himselfe with two English and two salvages went up higher in a canowe. But hee was not long absent, but[1] his men went ashore, whose want of government gave both occasion and opportunity to the salvages to surprise one George Cassen, whom they slew, and much failed not to have cut off the boat and all the rest.

Smith little dreaming of that accident, being got to the marshes at the river's head, twentie myles in the desert, had his two men slaine (as is supposed) sleeping by the canowe, whilst himselfe by fowling sought them victuall. Who finding

[1] *but:* before

he was beset with 200 salvages, two of them he slew, still defending himselfe with the ayd of a salvage his guid, whom he bound to his arme with his garters, and used him as a buckler. Yet he was shot in his thigh a little, and had many arrowes that stuck in his cloathes, but no great hurt till at last they took him prisoner.

When this newes came to James towne, much was their sorrow for his losse, fewe expected what ensued.

Sixe or seven weakes those barbarians kept him prisoner; many strange triumphes and conjurations they made of him. Yet hee so demeaned himselfe amongst them, as he not only diverted them from surprising the fort,[2] but procured his owne libertie, and got himself and his company such estimation amongst them that those salvages admired him more than their owne Quiyouckosucks.

Their order in conducting him was thus. Drawing themselves all in fyle, the King in the middest had all their peeces and swords borne before him. Captaine Smith was led after him by three great salvages, holding him fast by each arme, and on each side went six in fyle with their arrowes nocked.... Smith they conducted to a long house, where thirtie or fortie tall fellowes did guard him; and ere long more bread and venison was brought him than would have served twentie men. I thinke his stomacke at that time was not very good. What he left they put in baskets and tyed over his head. About midnight they set the meate againe before him, till the next morning they brought him as much more, and they did eate all the old, and reserved the new as they had done the other, which made him thinke they would fat him to eat him. Yet in this desperate estate, to defend him from the cold, one Maocasseter brought him his gowne, in requittal of some beads and toyes Smith had given him at his first arrival in Virginia.

At last they brought him to Meronocemoco, where was Powhatan their Emperor. Here more than two hundred of those grim courtiers stood wondering at him, as he had beene a monster, till Powhatan and his trayne had put themselves in their greatest braveries. Before a fire, upon a seat like a bed-

[2]*fort:* Jamestown

stead, he sat covered with a great robe made of rarowcun[3] skinnes, and all the tayles hanging by. On either side did sit a young wench of 16 or 18 yeares, and along on each side the house, two rowes of men, and behind them as many women, with all their heads and shoulders painted red. Many of their heads bedecked with the white downe of birds, but every one with something, and a great chayne of white beads about their necks.

At his[4] entrance before the King, all the people gave a great shout. The Queene of Appamatuck was appointed to bring him water to wash his hands, and another brought him a bunch of feathers in stead of a towell to dry them. Having feasted him after their best barbarous manner they could, a long consultation was held; but the conclusion was, two great stones were brought before Powhatan. Then as many as could, layd hands on him, dragged him to them, and thereon laid his head, and being ready with their clubs to beate out his braines. Pocahontas, the King's dearest daughter, when no intreaty could prevaile, got his head in her armes, and laid her owne upon his to save him from death. Whereat the Emperor was contented he should live to make him hatchets, and her bells, beads, and copper; for they thought him as well of[5] all occupations as themselves. For the King himselfe will make his owne robes, shooes, bowes, arrowes, pots; plant, hunt, or doe any thing as well as the rest.

> They say he bore a pleasant shew,
> But sure his heart was sad.
> For who can pleasant be, and rest,
> That lives in feare and dread,
> And having life suspected, doth
> It still suspected lead.

[3] *rarowcun:* raccoon
[4] *his:* Smith's
[5] *well of:* skillful in

FOR DISCUSSION

1. This account of Captain Smith's rescue by Pocahontas—now an American legend—was first published in England in 1624, fifteen years after the incident took place. Why do you think it would appeal to English readers for whom it was written? What impression would they gain of the New World and of the "salvages" who inhabited it? Why does Smith refer to their braves as courtiers and to their chief as Emperor?
2. Today, the historian is expected to state and interpret his facts accurately and objectively. Assuming that Smith's account is substantially true, what evidence can you find that the facts are, or are not, stated and interpreted objectively? Point out comments, descriptive words, or choice of details which will support your opinion.
3. Who is the "he" referred to in the lines of poetry which conclude this episode? Judging from this short excerpt, what kind of person was the famous Captain Smith?

On Their Safe Arrival at Cape Cod

WILLIAM BRADFORD

Being thus arived in a good harbor and brought safe to land, they [the Pilgrims] fell upon their knees and blessed the God of heaven, who had brought them over the vast and furious ocean, and delivered them from all the periles and miseries thereof, againe to set their feete on the firme and stable earth, their proper elemente. And no marvell if they were thus joyefull. . . .

But hear I cannot but stay and make a pause, and stand half amased at this poore people's presente condition; and so I thinke will the reader too, when he well considers the same. Being thus passed the vast ocean, and a sea of troubles before in their preparation (as may be remembered by that which wente before), they had now no friends to wellcome them, nor inns to entertaine or refresh their weather-beaten bodys, no houses or much less townes to repaire too, to seeke for succoure. It is recorded in scripture as a mercie to the apostle and his shipwraked company, that the barbarians shewed them no smale kindnes in refreshing them;[1] but these savage barbar-

[1] *It is . . . them:* The apostle Paul was being taken as a prisoner from Jerusalem to Rome. The ship ran aground on the island of Malta, where the natives fed the travelers and kindled a fire for them.

ians, when they mette with them (as after will appeare) were readier to fill their sids full of arrows then otherwise. And for the season, it was winter, and they that know the winters of that cuntrie know them to be sharp and violent, and subjecte to cruell and feirce stormes, deangerous to travill to known places, much more to serch an unknown coast.

Besides, what could they see but a hidious and desolate wildernes, full of wild beasts and willd men? And what multituds their might be of them they knew not. . . .

For summer being done, all things stand upon them with a wether beaten face; and the whole countrie full of woods and thickets, represented a wild and savage hiew.[2] If they looked behind them, ther was the mighty ocean which they had passed, and was now as a maine barr and goulfe to separate them from all the civill parts of the world. If it be said they had a ship to succour[3] them, it is trew; but what heard they daly from the master and company, but that with speede they should looke out a place with their shallop,[4] where they would be at some near distance. For the season was shuch as he would not stirr from thence till a safe harbor was discovered by them wher they would be, and he might goe without danger; and that victells consumed apace, but he must and would keepe sufficient for them selves[5] and their returne. Yea, it was muttered by some that if they gott not a place in time, they would turne them and their goods ashore and leave them.

Let it also be considered what weake hopes of supply and succoure they left behinde them, that might bear up their minds in this sade condition and trialls they were under, and they could not but be very smale. It is true, indeed, the affections and love of their brethren at Leyden[6] was cordiall and entire towards them; but they had litle power to help them, or them selves; and how the case stood betweene them and the merchants[7] at their coming away, hath allready been declared.

[2] *hiew:* appearance

[3] *succour:* sustain

[4] *shallop:* small boat

[5] *themselves:* the sailors

[6] *Leyden:* The Puritans had gone to Leyden, Holland, before embarking for America.

[7] *merchants:* The colonists had agreed to give the products of their labor during the first seven years to the London merchants who had provided the money for the trip.

What could not sustaine them but the spirite of God and his Grace? May not and ought not the children of these fathers rightly say: *Our fathers were Englishmen which came over this great ocean, and were ready to perish in this willdernes; but they cried unto the Lord, and he heard their voyce, and looked on their adversitie, etc. Let them therfore praise the Lord, because he is good, and his mercies endure for ever. Yea, let them which have been redeemed of the Lord, shew how he hath delivered them from the hand of the oppressour. When they wandered in the deserte willdernes out of the way, and found no citie to dwell in, both hungrie, and thirstie, their sowle was overwhelmed in them. Let them confess before the Lord his loving kindnes, and his wonderfull works before the sons of men.*

FOR DISCUSSION

1. Bradford's history *Of Plimmoth Plantation,* which was written between the years 1630 and 1648, was discovered in 1855 in the library of the Bishop of London and published. What makes you think it was printed exactly as he had written it down on paper?
2. Some critics have called this history one of the most important of early American documents, not only for its historical significance, but also for its literary style. Which sentences have much the same rhythm as lines from the Bible? Which words would you use to describe the tone of the writing—solemn, dignified, emotional, religious?
3. Point out what you consider the most important differences between this account and John Smith's account in what they chose to record and in the way they recorded it.

FOR COMPOSITION

Write a theme comparing and contrasting John Smith and William Bradford. Point out qualities each had that say something about the American character.

PAINE AND LOWELL

Once the land was settled and the farms planted, it seemed necessary to fight two new kinds of battles. One battle was for political independence, which was won fairly rapidly. The other battle was longer and more difficult, since it was for political—and national—respect from other countries. The first could be won by weapons and tactical superiority. The second must be won by force of character, and, even more difficult, by charm.

In the first battle, a leader of primary importance was Thomas Paine. Paine's exceptionally powerful prose made him a professional inciter to insurrection. Called "the stormbird of the revolutions," he wrote tracts which influenced not only the American but also the French Revolution. A maker of phrases and coiner of watchwords, Paine excelled in producing sentences which could move men to action. He held that "the mind of a living public feels first and reasons afterwards." For Paine, definitions were never a great problem and alternatives were clear. In the famous pamphlet which follows, he defines "those who have suffered in well-doing" as the Whig patriots; that is, those colonists who were for independence. Those who endanger the country are all whose conclusions disagree with his own. Paine had a mind of considerable power. By both his immediate exhortations to support the revolutionary troops, and by his long-range influence on future leaders such as Thomas Jefferson, Paine exerted a decisive influence on the history and political philosophy of the emerging nation.

Once the political union had been formed and the Constitution ratified, the newly born nation turned its attention to its internal growth and development. But like individuals, nations look to their equals for acceptance. During the nineteenth century, as the internal political ties grew stronger, the United States began to long for proper respect from other nations. Of the many representatives sent abroad to encourage such recognition, none acquitted himself with greater distinction than did James Russell Lowell toward the close of the century.

Lowell, American ambassador to England from 1880 to 1885, was a man who, if he did nothing with genius, did many things well. Poet, essayist, satirist, editor, and social critic, he was eminently suited to interpret the American government to England. As he presented his government in *Democracy*, it not only seemed reasonable, admirable, and sound, but also familiar: a refinement of the old British tradition out of which it grew.

The Crisis

Number 1

THOMAS PAINE

These are the times that try men's souls. The summer soldier and the sunshine patriot will, in this crisis, shrink from the service of his country; but he that stands it *now*, deserves the love and thanks of man and woman. Tyranny, like hell, is not easily conquered; yet we have this consolation with us, that the harder the conflict, the more glorious the triumph. What we obtain too cheap, we esteem too lightly: it is dearness[1] only that gives everything its value. Heaven knows how to put a proper price upon its goods; and it would be strange indeed if so celestial an article as FREEDOM should not be highly rated. Britain, with an army to enforce her tyranny, has declared that she has a right (*not only to* TAX) but "to BIND *us* in ALL CASES WHATSOEVER"; and if being *bound in that manner* is not slavery, then is there not such a thing as slavery upon earth. Even the expression is impious; for so unlimited a power can belong only to God.

Whether the independence of the continent was declared too soon, or delayed too long, I will not now enter into as an argument; my own simple opinion is, that had it been eight

[1]*dearness:* expensiveness

months earlier it would have been much better. We did not make a proper use of last winter; neither could we, while we were in a dependent state. However, the fault, if it were one, was all our own; we have none to blame but ourselves. But no great deal is lost yet. All that Howe has been doing for this month past is rather a ravage than a conquest, which the spirit of the Jerseys[2] a year ago would have quickly repulsed, and which time and a little resolution will soon recover.

I have as little superstition in me as any man living; but my secret opinion has ever been, and still is, that God Almighty will not give up a people to military destruction, or leave them unsupportedly to perish, who have so earnestly and so repeatedly sought to avoid the calamities of war, by every decent method which wisdom could invent. Neither have I so much of the infidel in me as to suppose that He has relinquished the government of the world, and given us up to the care of devils; and as I do not, I cannot see on what grounds the king of Britain can look up to heaven for help against us: a common murderer, a highwayman, or a housebreaker, has as good a pretense as he. . . .

I once felt all that kind of anger, which a man ought to feel, against the mean principles that are held by the tories: A noted one, who kept a tavern at Amboy, was standing at his door, with as pretty a child in his hand, about eight or nine years old, as I ever saw, and after speaking his mind as freely as he thought was prudent, finished with this unfatherly expression, "*Well! give me peace in my day.*" Not a man lives on the continent but fully believes that a separation must some time or other finally take place, and a generous parent should have said, "*If there must be trouble, let it be in my day, that my child may have peace;*" and this single reflection, well applied, is sufficient to awaken every man to duty. Not a place upon earth might be so happy as America. Her situation is remote from all the wrangling world, and she has nothing to do but to trade with them. A man can distinguish himself between temper and principle: and I am as confident as I am that God governs the world, that America will never be happy till she gets clear of foreign dominion. Wars, without ceasing, will

[2]*Jerseys:* East and West Jersey

break out till that period arrives, and the continent must in the end be conqueror; for though the flame of liberty may sometimes cease to shine, the coal can never expire.

America did not, nor does not want[3] force; but she wanted a proper application of that force. Wisdom is not the purchase of a day, and it is no wonder that we should err at the first setting off. From an excess of tenderness, we were unwilling to raise an army, and trusted our cause to the temporary defense of a well-meaning militia. A summer's experience has now taught us better; yet with those troops, while they were collected, we were able to set bounds to the progress of the enemy, and thank God! they are again assembling. I always considered militia as the best troops in the world for a sudden exertion, but they will not do for a long campaign. Howe, it is probable, will make an attempt on this city;[4] should he fail on this side the Delaware, he is ruined. If he succeeds, our cause is not ruined. He stakes all on his side against a part on ours; admitting he succeeds, the consequences will be that armies from both ends of the continent will march to assist their suffering friends in the middle states; for he cannot go everywhere—it is impossible. I consider Howe as the greatest enemy the tories have; he is bringing a war into their country, which, had it not been for him and partly for themselves, they had been clear of. Should he now be expelled, I wish with all the devotion of a Christian, that the names of Whig and Tory may never more be mentioned; but should the tories give him encouragement to come, or assistance if he come, I as sincerely wish that our next year's arms may expel them from the continent, and the Congress appropriate their possessions to the relief of those who have suffered in well-doing. A single successful battle next year will settle the whole. America could carry on a two years' war by the confiscation of the property of disaffected[5] persons, and be made happy by their expulsion. Say not that this is revenge; call it rather the soft resentment of a suffering people, who, having no object in view but the *good* of *all*, have staked their *own all* upon a seemingly doubtful

[3]*want:* lack
[4]*city:* Philadelphia
[5]*disaffected:* hostile or disloyal

event. Yet it is folly to argue against determined hardness; eloquence may strike the ear, and the language of sorrow draw forth the tear of compassion, but nothing can reach the heart that is steeled with prejudice.

Quitting this class of men, I turn with the warm ardor of a friend to those who have nobly stood, and are yet determined to stand the matter out: I call not upon a few, but upon all: not on *this* State or *that* State, but on *every* State: up and help us; lay your shoulders to the wheel; better have too much force than too little, when so great an object is at stake. Let it be told to the future world, that in the depth of winter, when nothing but hope and virtue could survive, that the city and the country, alarmed at one common danger, came forth to meet and to repulse it. Say not that thousands are gone—turn out your tens of thousands; throw not the burden of the day upon Providence, but *"show your faith by your works,"* that God may bless you. It matters not where you live, or what rank of life you hold, the evil or the blessing will reach you all. The far and the near, the home counties and the back, the rich and the poor, will suffer or rejoice alike. The heart that feels not now is dead; the blood of his children will curse his cowardice who shrinks back at a time when a little might have saved the whole and made *them* happy. I love the man that can smile in trouble, that can gather strength from distress and grow brave by reflection. It is the business of little minds to shrink; but he whose heart is firm, and whose conscience approves his conduct, will pursue his principles unto death. My own line of reasoning is to myself as straight and clear as a ray of light. Not all the treasures of the world, so far as I believe, could have induced me to support an offensive war, for I think it murder; but if a thief breaks into my house, burns and destroys my property, and kills or threatens to kill me or those that are in it, and to *"bind me in all cases whatsoever"* to his absolute will, am I to suffer it? What signifies it to me whether he who does it is a king or a common man; my countryman or not my countryman; whether it be done by an individual villian; or an army of them? If we reason to the root of things we shall find no difference; neither can any just cause be assigned why we should punish in one case and pardon in the other....

There are cases which cannot be overdone by language, and this is one. There are persons, too, who see not the full extent of the evil which threatens them; they solace themselves with hopes that the enemy, if he succeed, will be merciful. It is the madness of folly, to expect mercy from those who have refused to do justice; and even mercy, where conquest is the object, is only a trick of war. The cunning of the fox is as murderous as the violence of the wolf, and we ought to guard equally against both. Howe's first object is, partly by threats and partly by promises, to terrify or seduce the people to deliver up their arms and receive mercy. The ministry recommended the same plan to Gage,[6] and this is what the tories call making their peace, *"a peace which passeth all understanding," indeed!* A peace which would be the immediate forerunner of a worse ruin than any we have yet thought of. Ye men of Pennsylvania, do reason upon these things! Were the back counties to give up their arms, they would fall an easy prey to the Indians, who are all armed: this perhaps is what some tories would not be sorry for. Were the home counties to deliver up their arms, they would be exposed to the resentment of the back counties, who would then have it in their power to chastise their defection at pleasure. And were any one State to give up its arms, *that* State must be garrisoned by all Howe's army of Britons and Hessians.[7] to preserve it from the anger of the rest. Mutual fear is the principal link in the chain of mutual love; and woe be to that State that breaks the compact. Howe is mercifully inviting you to barbarous destruction, and men must be either rogues or fools that will not see it. I dwell not upon the vapors of imagination; I bring reason to your ears, and, in language as plain as A B C, hold up truth to your eyes.

I thank God that I fear not. I see no real cause for fear. I know our situation well, and can see the way out of it. While our army was collected, Howe dared not risk a battle; and it is no credit to him that he decamped from the White Plains,[8] and waited a mean opportunity to ravage the defenseless Jerseys;

[6] *Gage:* Thomas Gage, (1721-1787), Howe's successor
[7] *Hessians:* German mercenaries hired by the British
[8] *White Plains:* an indecisive battle between Washington and Howe north of New York City

but it is great credit to us, that with a handful of men, we sustained an orderly retreat for near a hundred miles, brought off our ammunition, all our fieldpieces, the greatest part of our stores, and had four rivers to pass. None can say that our retreat was precipitate;[9] for we were near three weeks in performing it, that the country might have time to come in. Twice we marched back to meet the enemy, and remained out till dark. The sign of fear was not seen in our camp, and had not some of the cowardly and disaffected inhabitants spread false alarms through the country, the Jerseys had never been ravaged. Once more we are again collected and collecting, our new army at both ends of the continent is recruiting fast, and we shall be able to open the next campaign with sixty thousand men, well-armed and clothed. This is our situation, and who will may know it. By perseverance and fortitude we have the prospect of a glorious issue; by cowardice and submission, the sad choice of a variety of evils: a ravaged country—a depopulated city—habitations without safety, and slavery without hope—our homes turned into barracks and bawdy-houses for Hessians—and a future race to provide for, whose fathers we shall doubt of. Look on this picture and weep over it! and if there yet remains one thoughtless wretch who believes it not, let him suffer it unlamented.

[9] *precipitate:* hasty

FOR DISCUSSION

1. At the time Paine wrote this pamphlet, what dangers did he feel impelled to point out to the colonists? Why would an immediate peace be the "forerunner of a worse ruin than we [the colonies] had yet thought of"? What was the full extent of the evil that threatened if the colonies gave up their arms?
2. Why does Paine contend that it was not wise for the colonies to win peace too easily? To what does he compare tyranny and freedom? Why does he believe so firmly that God supported the cause of the colonists? What must they do to deserve His blessing?
3. Paine took a firm stand against an offensive war, as has this country many times since. When, in his opinion, is war justified and neces-

sary? Compare his belief that it is better to have "too much force than too little" with the belief held by many statesmen, scientists, and military advisers today.

4. What reasons does Paine give to support his opinion that the colonies should have declared their independence earlier? Also, what reasons does he give to prove that, despite divided loyalties and military defeats, there is "no real cause for fear"?
5. What is the purpose of this editorial? Cite examples from this work that demonstrate (a) Paine's appeal to the reader's feelings, and (b) his references to what matters most to all people—family, property, security, freedom, and the like.
6. In all writing intended to arouse emotion or to persuade, the way the author presents his material is of major importance. Note Paine's use of figurative language in such expressions as "sunshine patriot," "flame of liberty," and "wrangling world." Find other examples, as well as examples of such emotionally charged words as *common murderer, cowardice,* and *barbarous.* Tell why you do, or do not, think that Paine was "candid, simple, clear and bold," both in what he says and the way he says it.

FOR COMPOSITION

1. When Paine writes, "Not a place upon earth might be so happy as America," he sees it as "remote from all the wrangling world." In a short composition tell why this country could *not* remain "remote." Also tell why you think that Paine would, or would not, support this country's present policy of assisting those countries that want to "get clear of foreign domination."
2. Suppose that you are one of those colonists whom Paine hoped to "awaken to duty." In two or three paragraphs, tell why this editorial persuaded you to join the fight for freedom. Refer to specific arguments and appeals which Paine used to support his plea for action.

Democracy

JAMES RUSSELL LOWELL

There can be no doubt that the spectacle of a great and prosperous Democracy on the other side of the Atlantic must react powerfully on the aspirations and political theories of men in the Old World who do not find things to their mind; but, whether for good or evil, it should not be overlooked that the acorn from which it sprang was ripened on the British oak. Every successive swarm that has gone out from this *officina gentium*[1] has, when left to its own instincts—may I not call them hereditary instincts?—assumed a more or less thoroughly democratic form. This would seem to show, what I believe to be the fact, that the British Constitution, under whatever disguises of prudence or decorum, is essentially democratic. England, indeed, may be called a monarchy with democratic tendencies, the United States a democracy with conservative instincts. People are continually saying that America is in the air, and I am glad to think it is, since this means only that a clearer conception of human claims and human duties is beginning to be prevalent. The discontent with

[1] *officina gentium:* workshop of nations

the existing order of things, however, pervaded the atmosphere wherever the conditions were favorable, long before Columbus, seeking the back door of Asia, found himself knocking at the front door of America. I say wherever the conditions were favorable, for it is certain that the germs of disease do not stick or find a prosperous field for their development and noxious activity unless where the simplest sanitary precautions have been neglected. "For this effect defective comes by cause," as Polonius[2] said long ago. It is only by instigation of the wrongs of men that what are called the Rights of Man become turbulent and dangerous. It is then only that they syllogize[3] unwelcome truths. It is not the insurrections of ignorance that are dangerous, but the revolts of intelligence:—

> The wicked and the weak rebel in vain,
> Slaves by their own compulsion....

Few people take the trouble of trying to find out what democracy really is. Yet this would be a great help, for it is our lawless and uncertain thoughts, it is the indefiniteness of our impressions, that fill darkness, whether mental or physical, with specters and hobgoblins. Democracy is nothing more than an experiment in government, most likely to succeed in a new soil, but likely to be tried in all soils, which must stand or fall on its own merits as others have done before it. For there is no trick of perpetual motion in politics any more than in mechanics. President Lincoln defined democracy to be "the government of the people by the people for the people." This is a sufficiently compact statement of it as a political arrangement. Theodore Parker said that "Democracy meant not 'I'm as good as you are,' but 'You're as good as I am.' " And this is the ethical conception of it, necessary as a complement of the other; a conception which, could it be made actual and practical, would easily solve all the riddles that the old sphinx of political and social economy who sits by the roadside has been proposing to mankind from the beginning, and which man-

[2] *Polonius:* character in Shakespeare's *Hamlet*
[3] *syllogize:* formulate

kind have shown such a singular talent for answering wrongly. In this sense Christ was the first true democrat that ever breathed, as the old dramatist Dekker said he was the first true gentleman. The characters may be easily doubled, so strong is the likeness between them. A beautiful and profound parable of the Persian poet Jellaladeen tells us that "One knocked at the Beloved's door, and a voice asked from within 'Who is there?' and he answered 'It is I.' Then the voice said, 'This house will not hold me and thee;' and the door was not opened. Then went the lover into the desert and fasted and prayed in solitude, and after a year he returned and knocked again at the door; and again the voice asked 'Who is there?' and he said 'It is thyself;' and the door was opened to him." But that is idealism, you will say, and this is an only too practical world. I grant it; but I am one of those who believe that the real will never find an irremovable basis till it rests on the ideal. It used to be thought that a democracy was possible only in a small territory, and this is doubtless true of a democracy strictly defined, for in such all the citizens decide directly upon every question of public concern in a general assembly. An example still survives in the tiny Swiss canton of Appenzell. But this immediate intervention of the people in their own affairs is not of the essence of democracy; it is not necessary, nor indeed, in most cases, practicable. Democrats to which Mr. Lincoln's definition would fairly enough apply have existed, and now exist, in which, though the supreme authority reside in the people, yet they can act only indirectly on the national policy. This generation has seen a democracy with an imperial figurehead, and in all that have ever existed the body politic has never embraced all the inhabitants included within its territory; the right to share in the direction of affairs has been confined to citizens, and citizenship has been further restricted by various limitations, sometimes of property, sometimes of nativity, and always of age and sex.

The framers of the American Constitution were far from wishing or intending to found a democracy in the strict sense of the word, though, as was inevitable, every expansion of the scheme of government they elaborated has been in a democratical direction. But this has been generally the slow result of growth, and not the sudden innovation[4] of theory; in fact, they had a profound disbelief in theory, and knew better than to commit the folly of breaking with the past. They were not seduced by the French fallacy that a new system of government could be ordered like a new suit of clothes. They would as soon have thought of ordering a new suit of flesh and skin. It is only on the roaring loom of time that the stuff is woven for such a vesture of their thought and experience as they were meditating. They recognized fully the value of tradition and habit as the great allies of permanence and stability. They all had that distaste for innovation which belonged to their race, and many of them a distrust of human nature derived from their creed. The day of sentiment was over, and no dithyrambic affirmations[5] or fine-drawn analyses of the Rights of Man would serve their present turn. This was a practical question, and they addressed themselves to it as men of knowledge and judgment should. Their problem was how to adapt English principles and precedents to the new conditions of American life, and they solved it with singular discretion. . . .

Has not the trial of democracy in America proved, on the whole, successful? If it had not, would the Old World be vexed with any fears of its proving contagious? . . . We have taken from Europe the poorest, the most ignorant, the most turbulent of her people, and have made them over into good citizens, who have added to our wealth, and who are ready to die in defence of a country and of institutions which they know to be worth dying for. The exceptions have been (and they are lamentable exceptions) where these hordes of ignorance and poverty have coagulated in great cities. But the social system is yet to seek which has not to look the same terrible wolf in the eyes. On the other hand, at this very moment Irish peasants are buying up the wornout farms of Massachusetts, and making them productive again by the same virtues of industry and thrift that once made them profitable to the English ancestors of the men who are deserting them. To have achieved even these prosaic results (if you choose to call them so), and that out of materials the most discordant,—I might say

[4] *innovation:* change
[5] *dithyrambic affirmations:* emotional declarations

the most recalcitrant,[6]—argues a certain beneficent virtue in the system that could do it, and is not to be accounted for by mere luck. Carlyle said scornfully that America meant only roast turkey every day for everybody. He forgot that States, as Bacon said of wars, go on their bellies. As for the security of property, it should be tolerably well secured in a country where every other man hopes to be rich, even though the only property qualification be the ownership of two hands that add to the general wealth. Is it not the best security for anything to interest the largest possible number of persons in its preservation and the smallest in its division? . . .

We are told that the inevitable result of democracy is to sap the foundations of personal independence, to weaken the principle of authority, to lessen the respect due to eminence, whether in station, virtue, or genius. If these things were so, society could not hold together. Perhaps the best forcing-house of robust individuality would be where public opinion is inclined to be most overbearing, as he must be of heroic temper who should walk along Piccadilly at the height of the season in a soft hat.[7] As for authority, it is one of the symptoms of the time that the religious reverence for it is declining everywhere, but this is due partly to the fact that state-craft is no longer looked upon as mystery, but as a business, and partly to the decay of superstition, by which I mean the habit of respecting what we are told to respect rather than what is respectable in itself. There is more rough and tumble in the American democracy than is altogether agreeable to people of sensitive nerves and refined habits, and the people take their political duties lightly and laughingly, as is, perhaps, neither unnatural nor unbecoming in a young giant. Democracies can no more jump away from their own shadows than the rest of us can. They no doubt sometimes make mistakes and pay honor to men who do not deserve it. But they do this because they believe them worthy of it, and though it be true that the idol is the measure of the worshiper, yet the worship has in it the germ of a nobler religion. But is it democracies alone that fall into these errors? I, who have seen it proposed to erect a

[6] *recalcitrant:* uncooperative

[7] *walk . . . hat:* to go against convention. At the height of the "season," a well-dressed London gentleman would wear only a hard bowler or top hat.

statue to Hudson, the railway king, and have heard Louis Napoleon hailed as the savior of society by men who certainly had no democratic associations or leanings, am not ready to think so. But democracies have likewise their finer instincts. I have also seen the wisest statesman and most pregnant[8] speaker of our generation, a man of humble birth and ungainly manners, of little culture beyond what his own genius supplied, become more absolute in power than any monarch of modern times through the reverence of his countrymen for his honesty, his wisdom, his sincerity, his faith in God and man, and the nobly humane simplicity of his character. And I remember another whom popular respect enveloped as with a halo, the least vulgar of men, the most austerely genial, and the most independent of opinion. Wherever he went he never met a stranger, but everywhere neighbors and friends proud of him as their ornament and decoration. Institutions which could bear and breed such men as Lincoln and Emerson had surely some energy for good. No, amid all the fruitless turmoil and miscarriage of the world, if there be one thing steadfast and of favorable omen, one thing to make optimism distrust its own obscure distrust, it is the rooted instinct in men to admire what is better and more beautiful than themselves. The touchstone of political and social institutions is their ability to supply them with worthy objects of this sentiment, which is the very taproot of civilization and progress. There would seem to be no readier way of feeding it with the elements of growth and vigor than such an organization of society as will enable men to respect themselves, and so to justify them in respecting others.

[8] *pregnant:* meaningful

FOR DISCUSSION

1. What comparison and contrast does Lowell draw between England and the United States? What was becoming more prevalent that made people say, "America is in the air"? When do the "Rights of Man become turbulent and dangerous"? Why are the revolts of intelligence dangerous?

2. Why would it be a great help if people knew what democracy is? Why is it more likely to succeed "in a new soil"? How does Theodore Parker's definition differ from Lincoln's, yet complement it? What would happen if Parker's conception could be made actual and practical?
3. Lowell, as well as Lincoln, did not think that a "strictly defined" democracy is either necessary or practical. Is the "right to share in the direction of affairs" still limited in this country? In what ways have these rights been extended?
4. What beliefs and disbeliefs guided the framers of the American Constitution? To what practical problem did they address themselves? Why does Lowell say, "The day of sentiment was over"?
5. What proof does Lowell give that the "trial of democracy in America" has proved successful? Why couldn't the "prosaic results" be accounted for by mere luck? What "terrible wolf" has every social system—including our own—had to look in the eyes? Is that same "wolf" with us today? What progress have we made in getting rid of it?
6. More than a hundred years have passed since other nations and people were practicing "the inevitable result of democracy." In what ways have these predictions proved to be true or false? Do you agree or disagree with Lowell's explanation of the lessening respect for authority? Explain.
7. Why does Lowell refer to this country as "a young giant," react to its "rough and tumble" manners, and regret the "idol" it often worshiped? What proof does he give that democracies have their "finer instincts" as well?
8. In the closing lines of this address, Lowell's eloquence reaches its highest peak. Beginning with the line "No, amid all the fruitless turmoil . . ." discuss both what he says and the way he says it. How well has this country provided the "organization of society" he considers so essential?

FOR COMPOSITION

While Lowell did not write in epigrams, he did make several statements which are memorable both in thought and expression. Select one of the following and, in a short essay, express your thoughts and feelings either about its meaning or the way it was stated.

a. ". . . the real will never find an irremovable basis till it rests on the ideal."

b. "It is only on the roaring loom of time that the stuff is woven for such a vesture of their thought and experience as they were meditating."
c. "Democracies can no more jump away from their own shadows than the rest of us can."
d. "Is it not the best security for anything to interest the largest possible number of persons in its preservation and the smallest in its division? . . ."

DOUGLASS AND LINCOLN

Ideals are always difficult to translate into reality. For that reason, many attempts to make real life fit an ideal seem to end in compromise. Not surprisingly, by the middle of the nineteenth century, when mere survival was no longer a major American problem, the rumblings of discontent began to be audible. For the first time since the nation was founded, large numbers of men concluded that they were not living in an earthly Eden in which events were happily guided by the common will—a will which always chose the greatest good for the greatest number. Social inequities were evident everywhere. Worse, the best interests of some states were not the best interests of others. Nowhere was society as happy as all had assumed it would be. Two constructive reactions are possible when an individual discovers that the conditions in which he lives are defective: he can angrily fight against the intolerable aspects of his situation; or he can concentrate on doing the best he can in whatever circumstances confront him.

Two American writers of historical importance—each accomplished stylists—illustrate these two approaches. The first, the runaway slave Frederick Douglass, became one of the most popular of Abolitionist orators before the Civil War. He was also a journalist of much influence and used his periodical, *Douglass' Monthly,* to sway opinion in favor of the abolition of slavery. The following editorial from the June, 1861, issue of this publication illustrates the Douglass style.

He often berated his audience for permitting the ideals incorporated into the Constitution to be compromised and betrayed. He protested bitterly against the hyprocrisy of a nation which allowed slavery to exist, and was beaten for his charges by Northern audiences. His phrases have the power which comes from an extraordinary combination of passion and talent.

Illustrating the second approach to a problem, Abraham Lincoln seems Douglass' opposite—a man supremely conscious of his own shortcomings, and consequently tolerant of the inadequacies of others. In the selections which follow, we see Lincoln first as the man who hopes to save the Union, then as the man who must somehow guide many jealous factions as they fight for the Union, and finally as the man who must lead the even harder fight to "bind up the nation's wounds." Throughout each of these demanding phases of his presidency, Lincoln remains a practical, humble, and humorous man. The rhythms and phrases of his writings have had a lasting influence on American prose.

Position of the Government Toward Slavery

FREDERICK DOUGLASS

Few things could better illustrate the extent to which the national conscience has been perverted, blinded and depraved by slavery, than the attitude of favor which the American Government has assumed toward it in the present conflict with the slaveholding traitors and rebels. Slavery has drawn the nation to the very verge of destruction. It has turned loose upon the Government an hundred thousand armed men, eager to embrue[1] their rebel hands in the warm blood of loyal citizens. It has inaugurated piracy and murder on the sea, and theft and robbery on the land. It has destroyed credit, repudiated just debts, driven loyal citizens from their homes, ruined business, arrested the majestic wheels of progress, and converted a land of peace and plenty into a land of blood and famine. It has diverted capital, industry and invention from the channels of peace, and filled the land with war and rumors of war, so that the whole people are under a cloud of terror and alarm. It has attempted to supplant Government with anarchy, and the fury of a brutal mob for the beneficent operation of law, and the legally appointed lawmakers.—It has blasted our

[1] *embrue:* drench

peace and prosperity at home, and brought shame and disgrace upon us abroad. It has robbed our treasury, plundered our forts and arsenals, trampled on our Constitution and laws, threatened Washington, and insulted the national flag—and yet how has the Government treated this foul and red-mouthed dragon? Why, thus far, with the utmost deference, tenderness and respect. The President is careful to proclaim his pacific intentions towards it; generals acting under him offer themselves and their men, unasked, to uphold it, and are at the pains of sending back to its blood-thirsty dominion those who have fled from it.

1. It is said the slaves are property and ought to be respected. Let us look at the matter in this its most favorable light. The whole title of slavery to respect, is based upon the idea that the *slave is property.* Beyond this, slavery imposes no obligation, and discharges none. Its one, single, sole, and only merit is that its victims are (so called) property.—The slaves are property, just as horses, sheep and swine are property—just as houses, lands, agricultural and mechanical implements are property. The right to a slave is no more sacred than the right to a horse or cow, or a barrel of flour. In law they are chattels, things, merchandise, and subject to all the conditions and liabilities of sale, transfer and barter, in time of peace, and of seizure and confiscation, like any other property, in time of war. If our Government is bound to respect the rights of property in a slave, it can only be to the extent to which it is bound to respect all other property. It clearly has no right to discriminate in favor of slave property as against any other species of property. If it does so discriminate, special and powerful reasons are demanded for such a policy.—Why should the flour and iron of the non-slaveholding merchant of Richmond be seized and appropriated by the Government, while the slave of the slaveholder, which slaveholder has helped foment this rebellion, is carefully returned to his master, as a piece of property too sacred to lose its character as property, even though its owner is an open traitor to the Government? What is this but punishing the possibly innocent, and rewarding the certainly guilty? What is it but an uncalled for gratuitous and humiliating concession to the very

heart and core of the treason which has placed itself above and opposed to the laws under which those engaged in it might otherwise claim to have this very species of property respected? Viewed, therefore, solely as property, and granting all its sacredness as such, it stands precisely on a footing with all other property recognized as such by the laws of the land. From this clear and incontestable position, it is plain that any plausible argument or rule of action, upon which the present American Government admits special favor to this species of property, must be based upon considerations other than the mere claim of property.

2. If the policy of our Government, in putting down slave insurrections and returning fugitive slaves who escape to our army and our forts, during this war, cannot be defended upon the plea that slaves are property, it certainly cannot be defended on the ground of natural justice. By that law, universal, "unchangeable and eternal," every man is the rightful owner of his own body, and to dispossess him of this right, is, and can only be, among the highest crimes which can be committed against human nature. The only foundation for slavery is positive law against natural law, and the only positive law that binds the national Government in any way to do aught towards supporting slavery, is now cast off, and set at open defiance by the slave-holding traitors and rebels. The Confederate Slave States have flung away the law, and resorted to rebellion for the protection of slave property. Should they not be allowed—nay, should they not be made to feel all the disadvantages of their choice? Why should the strong and swift-sailing ship *Union* follow in the wake of the rotten and rickety slave ship of the Confederate States, to save passengers, property of crew, when dashed to pieces by the storm? Should they not be made to suffer all the consequences of their deliberate folly? They have appealed to Cæsar—should they not be compelled to abide by Cæsar's judgment? They have forsaken the law—why should the law seek after them? The common sense, we say nothing of the humanity of the people, who bear the expense of blood and treasure in putting down this slaveholding rebellion, can and will come to but one, and only one conclusion, namely—that if there ever was any legal obligation rest-

ing upon them to assist in putting down a slave insurrection, or to restore fugitive slaves to their masters, that obligation is inoperative, suspended and void while the rebellion is still in progress, and that to do any such thing as to suppress a rising of slaves, or to return fugitives to their so called masters, is a work of supererogatory[2] servility and wickedness.

3. But the policy of the Government, viewed only in the light of military wisdom, is most wretched. The slaves are not only property, but they are men, capable of love and hate, of gratitude and revenge, of making sacrifices to serve a friend, or to chastise an enemy. It is, therefore, in the circumstances of our Government, the wildest and most wanton folly to teach this element of power, for good or for evil, to hate the American flag. They are the natural friends of all who would check and subdue the malign powers of their masters. But when the Government shall thoroughly convince the slave population that their friendship is to be repaid with enmity—that they have nothing more to expect from the Star-Spangled Banner than from the Confederate flag—they will curse the very earth shaded by the presence of a United States soldier, and welcome any means to rid the South of their unnatural enemies. What they have done already, in building forts, entrenchments, and other drudgery for their Southern masters, under compulsion, they will do as patriotic duty, as a means of escaping evils unseen and mitigating those they already endure. The slave will mingle his curses with those of his master upon the head of the Northern invader and destroyer, and be among the foremost of those to fight for his expulsion. The evils of the war are not to be confined to the master. The slave will suffer in his food and raiment. He will have to make bricks without straw, and perform his task without the incentive of a possible holiday, and a few hours of seeming liberty, for he will be kept under a more rigorous surveillance[3] than ever before. The crafty slaveholders will know how to excuse this increased rigor. It will be cunningly set to the account of these Northern hordes who are come to plunder, destroy and ruin the South. The very best way, therefore, for the Government to give the

[2] *supererogatory:* going beyond the demands of duty
[3] *surveillance:* survey or watch

slaveholders a stick to break its own head, is to take up and cling to a line of policy of favor to slavery.

4. The glaring impolicy of alienating the slave population becomes the more striking in view of the situation of the conflict. "Knowledge is power," and nowhere more than in war. Battles are won by knowledge, rather than by arms; and battles are often lost, rather by the want of knowledge, than the want of arms. To know the movements, the position and the number of the enemy, just where and when they mean to strike, is of first importance. Without this knowledge, we strike in the dark, and as one who beateth the air. To gain knowledge of the situation is one of the simplest dictates of military prudence. Now, by making enemies of the slaves, the Government destroys one means of obtaining valuable information. It might be in the power of a slave, in a given case, to save the lives of thousands, to prevent discomfiture and defeat to a whole army. But what slave would put himself to the least trouble of imparting such information, if made certain before hand that he should be rewarded with slavery and chains? What slave would hesitate to deceive and mislead an army when that army had only brought to him and his, stripes, hunger, nakedness, and an every way more rigorous bondage? The Washington Government, in offering to put down slave insurrections, in sending back to infuriated masters the slaves who may escape to them, enacts the folly of maiming itself before striking down its enemy, of increasing the number of its enemies, and diminishing the number of its friends, of weakening itself while giving strength to the arm that would strike it down, of abusing its allies to please its implacable foes.

5. But while depriving itself of all possible advantage in the conflict with traitors, from their natural allies in the slave States, our Government seems bent upon making those natural allies efficient helps to the traitors.—We are for saving them all danger from sending spies into our camp. The black slave makes his way into our camp, reports himself a runaway slave, seeking his liberty, and asks for protection. While his tongue is busy, his eyes are busy also; and when he has seen just what he was desired to see, and obtained the information

which those who sent him most of all want to know, we magnanimously send away the spy in peace, under military escort, to communicate his valuable information to our enemies. What hinders the Confederate rebels from using their slaves as spies, while they can do so without fear of loss of life or property? This, to be sure, is an idea of our own; but among the excited brains of the South they will not be long in hitting upon it if our Government persists in the gross absurdity of making their army the watch dog of the slave plantation, to guard and protect the rebels from insurrection, and from loss of the very species of property in defense of which they have plunged the nation into all the hardships and horrors of civil war. Instead of retaining them to help uphold the law, by giving valuable information, and building fortifications, we send them back to help the rebels destroy the Government, by imparting information, erecting fortifications, and using arms against the friends of the Government. If this is military sagacity,[4] where shall we look for military insanity?

6. In a moral and humane point of view, the conduct of our Government towards the few slaves coming within their power, would be a disgrace to savages. Even a man in arms against us will be spared when he cries quarter; but we pounce upon the slave who comes, not in arms, but flings himself upon our charity; we bind him with chains, and fling him into the hands of both his, and our deadly enemies, to be tortured and killed, only for the crime of loving liberty better than slavery, disregarding all laws of humanity, asylum and hospitality. Such conduct, in the circumstances, is too monstrous, cruel and brutal, to be fittingly characterized by anything in the English tongue.

Perhaps, when the slaveholders shall have assassinated a few more Ellsworth,[5] poisoned a few more troops, sent out a few more pirates to prey upon our commerce, hanged and shot a few more Union-loving and loyal citizens, shed the blood of a few more soldiers, mobbed a few more loyal troops, our Government will begin to treat them like enemies, and no

[4] *sagacity:* shrewdness

[5] *Ellsworth:* In May, 1861, Colonel Elmer E. Ellsworth, a Union officer, spied a hotel in Alexandria, Virginia, which was flying the Confederate flag. He cut the flag down and was promptly killed by the hotel proprietor.

longer be guilty of the folly and crime of treating them as friends, for whom it may excusably stain its soul with innocent blood, to increase their power for future mischief and murder. But whatever may come to pass after suitable instruction, in this slaveholding revolutionary school through which the nation is passing, the sad truth stares us in the face at every turn, that slavery is still the dominant and master power in the country, and that it has perverted the moral sense, blinded and corrupted the mind and heart of the nation beyond all power of exaggeration, and that overawed by the accursed slave system, our Government is still clinging to the delusion that it can put down treason without putting down their cause; that it can break the power of the slaveholders, without breaking down that in which their power consists.

—At this point of our writing, a statement has reached us which, if true, slightly relieves the picture thus drawn, and shows that our Government is taking a wiser and more humane course towards those of the slaves who succeed in getting within the lines of our army. General Butler, now at Fort Monroe, who a few weeks ago at Annapolis, under circumstances which made the act peculiarly and abominably hateful and shocking, offered, unasked, to suppress a reported rising among the slaves in Anne Arundel county, has now promptly received a number of fugitives into his camp, and set them to work, refusing, on the demand of the rebels, to give them up to their masters.[6] This is as it should be, and shows that better ideas are beginning to control the action of our army officers. The men of our Northern army did not quit their homes and families, and expose themselves to all the hardships and dangers of war, to hunt slaves and put down slave insurrections. They have not gone down there as the guards and watch dogs of the slaveholders, to ferret out the slave in the dismal swamp, and to rivet the fetters more firmly upon the limbs of the bondmen; and to compel them to do it, is a scandalous outrage, which should be exposed, rebuked and abandoned at

[6]*General Butler . . . masters:* When a Confederate officer demanded the return of slaves who had come to the headquarters of General Benjamin F. Butler in eastern Virginia, the General refused to force their return. His explanation was that he could use them to build fortifications as validly as the Confederates could.

once. Gen. Butler has made progress, and that is something.—The end is not yet. He has come to put slaves on a footing with other property, entitled to no more respect than any other—a new thing under the sun of the Old Dominion—but the General will not stop here. He is within the broad and all-controlling current of events, and if the war continues, we shall see him contending for the freedom of all those slaves who have assisted the Government in putting down the slaveholding rebellion. It is our work here to radiate around our army and Government the light and heat of justice and humanity, and make it impossible for them to fling one soul back into the jaws of bondage which has escaped to them for an asylum during this war.

FOR DISCUSSION

1. Douglass often acted—before and during the Civil War—like a proverbial gadfly which stings those in power, thus keeping them alert to internal and external dangers to the state. Judging from the opening section of this editorial, how effective a gadfly do you think he was? How would you have responded to him if you had been a government leader in 1861?
2. What rhetorical techniques and methods of argument does Douglass use in order to persuade others to agree with him? Where do you find examples of emotionally-loaded images or language? of catalogues of horrors? of irony and sarcasm? of exaggeration? Why is each of these things effective in convincing or swaying others?
3. Does the way in which Douglass develops his first point surprise you? When you see the phrase *slave is property*, what idea do you expect him to attack, prove, or disprove? In what direction does his actual argument move?
4. What distinction does Douglass draw between positive law and natural law? Does he think one more valid than the other? What attitude does he take toward the less valid type of law?
5. Why does Douglass fear that slaves may learn to hate the American flag? What evidence does he give that this hatred may already have been implanted among the slaves? What steps would Douglass advocate for arresting such hatred?

6. In his fourth argument, what military possibilities and strategies does Douglass suggest the Union army is failing to take advantage of?
7. In his fifth argument, what tactics does he fear the South may be using? Does this argument strike you as valid or contrived?
8. What government policy towards slaves, carried out for the first year and a half of the Civil War, arouses Douglass' contempt in his sixth argument? What differences does this argument bring out between Northern and Southern reasons for entering the war?
9. What light do Douglass' accusations against the government shed on Lincoln's policies during this time? Do they explain why Lincoln has been a nationally, instead of regionally, popular figure?
10. What evidence does this speech present of Douglass' enormous powers as a public speaker? Judging from the editorial, why might his speeches have been effective?

FOR COMPOSITION

1. Write an editorial such as Douglass', presenting three or four arguments in favor of changing a current government policy. Include in your editorial a preface and a conclusion designed to sway your readers.
2. Write an oration for a national holiday, using as many of Douglass' rhetorical techniques as possible. Give particular attention to your language, sentence structure, and movement toward a stirring climax.

Address in Independence Hall

February 22, 1861

ABRAHAM LINCOLN

I am filled with deep emotion at finding myself standing in this place, where were collected together the wisdom, the patriotism, the devotion to principle, from which sprang the institutions under which we live. You have kindly suggested to me that in my hands is the task of restoring peace to our distracted country. I can say in return, sir, that all the political sentiments I entertain have been drawn, so far as I have been able to draw them, from the sentiments which originated in and were given to the world from this hall. I have never had a feeling, politically, that did not spring from the sentiments embodied in the Declaration of Independence. I have often pondered over the dangers which were incurred by the men who assembled here and framed and adopted that Declaration. I have often pondered over the toils that were endured by the officers and soldiers of the army who achieved that independence. I have often inquired of myself what great principle or idea it was that kept this Confederacy[1] so long to-

[1]*Confederacy:* the union of American colonies that won freedom from Britain

gether. It was not the mere matter of separation of the colonies from the motherland, but that sentiment in the Declaration of Independence which gave liberty, not alone to the people of this country, but, I hope, to the world, for all future time. It was that which gave promise that in due time the weights would be lifted from the shoulders of all men, and that all should have an equal chance. This is the sentiment embodied in the Declaration of Independence. Now, my friends, can this country be saved on that basis? If it can, I will consider myself one of the happiest men in the world if I can help to save it. If it cannot be saved upon that principle, it will be truly awful. But if this country cannot be saved without giving up that principle, I was about to say I would rather be assassinated on this spot than surrender it. Now, in my view of the present aspect of affairs, there is no need of bloodshed and war. There is no necessity for it. I am not in favor of such a course; and I may say in advance that there will be no bloodshed unless it is forced upon the government. The government will not use force, unless force is used against it.

My friends, this is wholly an unprepared speech. I did not expect to be called on to say a word when I came here. I supposed I was merely to do something toward raising a flag. I may, therefore, have said something indiscreet. But I have said nothing but what I am willing to live by, and, if it be the pleasure of Almighty God, to die by.

FOR DISCUSSION

1. Did Lincoln believe war necessary or inevitable? Explain.
2. What effect did the Declaration of Independence have on Lincoln's political thinking?
3. This is a wholly unprepared speech. Do you think it is well organized? Why? Discuss the structure and its effect.

Letter to General Joseph Hooker

Executive Mansion
Washington, January 26, 1863

Major General Hooker:

GENERAL: I have placed you at the head of the Army of the Potomac. Of course I have done this upon what appear to me to be sufficient reasons. And yet I think it best for you to know that there are some things in regard to which I am not quite satisfied with you. I believe you to be a brave and skillful soldier, which of course I like. I also believe you do not mix politics with your profession, in which you are right. You have confidence in yourself, which is a valuable if not an indispensable quality. You are ambitious, which, within reasonable bounds, does good rather than harm; but I think that during General Burnside's command of the Army you have taken counsel of your ambition and thwarted him as much as you could, in which you did a great wrong to the country and to a most meritorious and honorable brother officer. I have heard, in such way as to believe it, of your recently saying that both the Army and the Government needed a Dictator. Of course it was not for this, but in spite of it, that I have given you the command. Only those generals who gain successes can set up dictators. What I now ask of you is military success, and I will risk the dictatorship. The government will support you to the utmost of its ability, which is neither more nor less than it has done and will do for all commanders. I much fear that the spirit which you have aided to infuse into the Army, of criticizing their commander and withholding confidence from him, will now turn upon you. I shall assist you as far as I can to put it down. Neither you nor Napoleon, if he were alive again, could get any good out of an army while such a spirit prevails in it. And now, beware of rashness. Beware of rashness, but with energy and sleepless vigilance go forward and give us victories.

Yours very truly,

A. LINCOLN

FOR DISCUSSION

1. What aspect of Lincoln does this letter reveal?
2. What kind of person does General Hooker seem to be? Does Lincoln trust him? Cite sentences to support your opinion.
3. How does Lincoln show fairness toward the general?

The Gettysburg Address

November 19, 1863

Four score and seven years ago our fathers brought forth on this continent a new nation, conceived in liberty and dedicated to the proposition that all men are created equal.

Now we are engaged in a great civil war, testing whether that nation, or any nation so conceived and so dedicated, can long endure. We are met on a great battlefield of that war. We have come to dedicate a portion of that field as a final resting place for those who here gave their lives that that nation might live. It is altogether fitting and proper that we should do this.

But in a larger sense we cannot dedicate, we cannot consecrate, we cannot hallow this ground. The brave men, living and dead, who struggled here, have consecrated it far above our poor power to add or detract. The world will little note nor long remember what we say here, but it can never forget what they did here. It is for us, the living, rather to be dedicated here to the unfinished work which they who fought here have thus far so nobly advanced. It is rather for us to be here dedicated to the great task remaining before us—that from these honored dead we take increased devotion to that cause for which they gave the last full measure of devotion; that we here highly resolve that these dead shall not have died in vain; that this nation, under God, shall have a new birth of freedom; and that government of the people, by the people, for the people, shall not perish from the earth.

FOR DISCUSSION

1. Point out sentences in this speech that reveal Lincoln's humility and deep sense of responsibility.
2. What does Lincoln feel the purpose of the living should be at this time?
3. Why do you think the last lines of this speech are so moving?
4. Lincoln's *Gettysburg Address* is one of the great speeches of history, not because of its length but because of its depth of thought and beauty of expression. Give examples of these qualities from the speech.

Second Inaugural Address

March 4, 1865

FELLOW COUNTRYMEN: At this second appearing to take the oath of the presidential office, there is less occasion for an extended address than there was at the first. Then a statement somewhat in detail of a course to be pursued seemed fitting and proper. Now at the expiration of four years, during which public declarations have been constantly called forth on every point and phase of the great contest which still absorbs the attention and engrosses the energies of the nation, little that is new could be presented. The progress of our arms, upon which all else chiefly depends, is as well known to the public as to myself; and it is, I trust, reasonably satisfactory and encouraging to all. With high hope for the future, no prediction in regard to it is ventured.

On the occasion corresponding to this four years ago, all thoughts were anxiously directed to an impending civil war. All dreaded it, all sought to avert it. While the inaugural address was being delivered from this place, devoted altogether to saving the Union without war, insurgent agents were in the city seeking to destroy it without war—seeking to dissolve the Union and divide effects by negotiation. Both parties deprecated[1] war; but one of them would make war rather than let the nation survive, and the other would accept war rather than let it perish. And the war came.

One-eighth of the whole population were colored slaves, not distributed generally over the Union but localized in the southern part of it. These slaves constituted a peculiar and powerful interest. All knew that this interest was, somehow, the cause of the war. To strengthen, perpetuate,[2] and extend this interest was the object for which the insurgents[3] would rend the Union, even by war; while the government claimed no right to do more than to restrict the territorial enlargement of it.

Neither party expected for the war the magnitude or the duration which it has already attained. Neither anticipated that the cause of the conflict might cease with, or even before, the conflict itself should cease. Each looked for an easier triumph and a result less fundamental and astounding. Both read the same Bible and pray to the same God, and each invokes His aid against the other. It may seem strange that any men should dare to ask a just God's assistance in wringing their bread from the sweat of other men's faces; but let us judge not, that we be not judged. The prayers of both could not be answered—that of neither has been answered fully.

The Almighty has His own purposes. "Woe unto the world because of offenses! for it must needs be that offenses come; but woe to that man by whom the offense cometh." If we shall suppose that American slavery is one of those courses which in the providence of God must needs come, but which, having continued through His appointed time, He now wills to remove, and that He gives to both North and South this terrible war as the woe due to those by whom the offense came, shall we discern therein any departure from those divine attributes which the believers in a living God always ascribe to Him? Fondly do we hope—fervently do we pray—that this mighty scourge of war may speedily pass away. Yet if God wills that it

[1] *deprecated:* disapproved of
[2] *perpetuate:* continue
[3] *insurgents:* rebels

continue until all the wealth piled by the bondmen's two hundred and fifty years of unrequited[4] toil shall be sunk and until every drop of blood drawn with the lash shall be paid by another drawn with the sword, as was said three thousand years ago, so still it must be said, "The judgments of the Lord are true and righteous altogether."

With malice toward none; with charity for all; with firmness in the right, as God gives us to see the right, let us strive on to finish the work we are in; to bind up the nation's wounds; to care for him who shall have borne the battle, and for his widow and his orphan—to do all which may achieve and cherish a just and lasting peace among ourselves and with all nations.

[4]*unrequited:* unrepaid

FOR DISCUSSION

1. Point out sentences that reveal Lincoln's devoutness and sense of right and wrong.
2. What would you say Lincoln's essential purpose is in this speech?
3. How do you think Lincoln would have dealt with the South after the war? Use sentences from this speech to support your opinion.
4. Simplicity of style and depth of feeling are characteristic of Lincoln's writing. Find examples of these in the various selections you have read.

FOR COMPOSITION

Write a composition in which you describe how you think Lincoln would react to one current event if he were President today. Be specific.

SANDBURG, PYLE, AND WHITE

The Civil War was a disastrous blow to the United States. Almost half the nation tasted for the first time the bitterness of defeat. But the losses to the nation's resources, manpower, and talent fell equally on both sides of the Mason-Dixon Line. Thousands of the most promising young men in the nation were killed. The most crippling stroke of all, however, was not to the population as such, but to their view of their universe. For one side came the stunning realization that God would not necessarily intervene in their behalf, however righteous they believed their cause. For all, came the slowly dawning comprehension that squalor, injustice, and stupidity might triumph in a given situation. For the first time, thousands of men felt themselves helpless to control or direct their own destinies, and history no longer seemed manageable and familiar, but a terrifying and impersonal machine slowly rolling over the individual.

The blow was so numbing that many found it difficult to assimilate. Some attempted to relive the past by idealizing it in the most sentimental fashion. But for all, there was no more evading the obvious truth that the present did not constitute the best of all possible worlds. In tawdry peculation, the second half of the nineteenth century is unexcelled in American history.

One man who seemed above the petty squabbling of shortsighted men was Abraham Lincoln. His assassination evoked so unprecedented and intense an outpouring of grief that it took Americans several decades to realize fully all that Lincoln symbolized, and the real basis for their anguish. He was more than a leader. He stood for the best virtues of the raw, energetic, self-confident nation. With his death some of that confidence died. In his biography of Lincoln, Carl Sandburg captures well the spirit of the funeral and the grief of a nation which did not mourn so much for Lincoln as for itself.

After Lincoln's death and the increased awareness of national problems which followed, a critical examination of American values developed. With it came a need for new definitions and a distrust of old mottoes. In American prose, writers tried in various ways to strip back the cover of things. It was widely assumed that appearances were always deceptive, and that the "truth" of anything resided in a hidden core. To reach this truth, one had to probe and cut and tear away exteriors. The assumption grew that basic, honest, or real things were simple, but were reached only through torturous labor. Such assumptions were even translated into theories of prose. The simple, bare style of the "Hemingway school" of writers which developed in the 1920's and 1930's exemplifies this approach to the English language. Ernie Pyle, a newspaper reporter during World War II, is an excellent representative of that school; and the essay which follows illustrates the effect of the Hemingway approach on journalistic reportage of historic events.

One historic event which accelerated the search for, and the longing for, simple and basic truths was the creation of the atomic bomb. Suddenly, moral questions involved in the conduct of foreign affairs seemed enormously and overwhelmingly complex. More than ever, the individual realized his own helplessness to fend off worldwide disaster. The 1950's dawned with the fear of the bomb as a major force against which Americans must come to terms. The omnipresence and psychological consequences of this fear are expressed sensitively by E. B. White in "The Age of Dust."

The Funeral Train

CARL SANDBURG

There was a funeral.

It took long to pass its many given points.

Many millions of people saw it and personally moved in it and were part of its procession.

The line of march ran seventeen hundred miles.

As a dead march nothing like it had ever been attempted before.

Like the beginning and the end of the Lincoln Administration, it had no precedents to go by.

It was garish, vulgar, massive, bewildering, chaotic.

Also, it was simple, final, majestic, august.

In spite of some of its mawkish[1] excess of show and various maudlin[2] proceedings, it gave solemn unforgettable moments to millions of people who had counted him great, warm and lovable.

The people, the masses, nameless and anonymous numbers of persons not listed nor published among those present—these redeemed it.

[1] *mawkish:* disgusting sentimentality
[2] *maudlin:* tearful

They gave it the dignity and authority of a sun darkened by a vast bird migration.

They shaped it into a drama awful in the sense of having naïve awe and tears without shame.

They gave it the color and heave of the sea which is the mother of tears.

They lent to it the color of the land and the earth which is the bread-giver of life and the quiet tomb of the Family of Man.

Yes, there was a funeral.

From his White House in Washington—where it began—they carried his coffin and followed it nights and days for twelve days.

By night bonfires and torches lighted the right of way for a slow-going railroad train.

By day troops with reversed arms, muffled drums, multitudinous feet seeking the pivotal box with the silver handles.

By day the bells tolling, bells sobbing the requiem,[3] the salute guns, cannon rumbling their inarticulate thunder.

To Baltimore, Harrisburg, Philadelphia, New York, they journeyed with the draped casket to meet overly ornate catafalques.[4]

To Albany, Utica, Syracuse, moved the funeral cortege[5] always met by marchers and throngs.

To Cleveland, Columbus, Indianapolis, Chicago, they took the mute oblong box, met by a hearse for convoy to where tens of thousands should have their last look.

Then to Springfield, Illinois, the old home town, the Sangamon near by, the New Salem hilltop near by, for the final rest of cherished dust.

Thus the route and the ceremonial rites in epitome.[6]

The weather was April and May but the smoke and haze was October and the feeling of the hour silent snow on the January earth of a hard winter.

The ground lay white with apple blossoms this April week. The redbird whistled. Through black branches shone blue

[3] *requiem:* music for the dead
[4] *catafalques:* platforms on which the dead are placed for honoring
[5] *cortege:* procession
[6] *epitome:* condensed and representative form

sky. Ships put out from port with white sails catching the wind. Farmers spoke to their horses and turned furrows till sundown on the cornfield. Boys drew circles in cinder paths and played marbles. Lilac bushes took on surprises of sweet, light purple. In many a back-yard the potato-planting was over. In this house was a wedding, in that one a newborn baby, in another a girl with a new betrothal ring. Life went on. Everywhere life went on.

. . . .

Friday morning, April 21, just six days after the death in the Peterson house on Tenth Street, President Johnson, General Grant, Stanton and other Cabinet members, saw the coffin placed aboard a special burial car at the Washington depot—joined by another and smaller casket, that of the son Willie, which had been disinterred and was to have burial in Springfield, Illinois, near his father. Railroad-yard engine bells tolled and a far-stretching crowd stood with uncovered heads as the train of seven cars—with a scout pilot engine ahead to test the roadway—moved out of Washington for Baltimore.

This was the start of a funeral journey that was to take the lifeless body on a seventeen-hundred-mile route which practically included the same points and stops that the living form had made four years and two months before on the way to the first inauguration. Aboard the coaches were five men who had made that earlier journey: Colonel Ward Hill Lamon, Justice David Davis, General David Hunter, John G. Nicolay, and John Hay. . . .

Baltimore wore mourning everywhere and paid reverence. In the rotunda[7] of the Exchange Building tens of thousands came to the coffin. The civic procession, the human outpouring, was unmistakable. More than surface changes had come to Maryland in the four furnace years.

As the funeral train moved slowly over Pennsylvania soil those aboard saw they were sharing in no mere official function, no conventional affair that the common people looked at from afar. At lonely country crossroads were people and faces, horsemen, farmers with their wives and children, standing where they had stood for hours before, waiting, performing

[7] *rotunda:* domed center

the last little possible act of ceremony and attention and love —with solemn faces and uncovered heads standing and gazing as the burial car passed. In villages and small towns stood waiting crowds, sometimes with a little silver cornet band, often with flowers in hope the train might stop and they could leave camellias, roses, lilies-of-the-valley, wreaths of color and perfume, on a coffin. At York in a short stop six ladies came aboard and laid a three-foot wreath of red and white roses on the coffin.

Through heavy rains at Harrisburg came thirty thousand in the night and morning to see the coffin in circles of white flowering almond. At noon of Saturday, April 22, Philadelphia was reached via Lancaster, where at a railroad bridge, on a rock, stood an old man alone with his thoughts, perhaps the loneliest man in the United States. He lifted his hat. No one could read what he meant by lifting his hat. It was Thad Stevens. And on the edge of the vast crowd at Lancaster sat a quiet old man in a carriage; this was Lincoln's predecessor, James Buchanan.

In Philadelphia a half-million people were on hand for the funeral train. In Independence Hall, where the Declaration of Independence was signed, stood the coffin, at its head the Liberty Bell and near by the chair in which John Hancock once sat. Outside was devotion, curiosity, hysteria. The line of mourners ran three miles. . . .

At Newark, New Jersey, on the morning of April 24 the train moved slowly amid acres of people, a square mile of them. "The city turned out *en masse*," wrote reporters. At Jersey City was a like scene. There the depot at one end had the motto "A Nation's Heart Was Struck" and at the other end "Be Still and Know That I Am God." A German chorus of seventy male voices sang "*Integer Vitae.*" Chauncey M. Depew, secretary of state for New York, in behalf of the unavoidably absent Governor Reuben E. Fenton, for the Empire State formally received the body from Governor Parker of New Jersey. Ten stalwart sergeants carried the casket to a hearse which moved through street crowds to the ferry house. The paint was fresh on a legend here reading "George Washington, the Father: Abraham Lincoln, the Saviour of His Country." The ferryboat *Jersey City* moved across the Hudson River, her pilot-house and cabins in crape, flags at half-mast. As she neared the wharf at Desbrosses Street, the German choral society gave a funeral ode from the first book of Horace.

Beyond the wharf as far as the eye could see stood waiting masses of people. A large force of police kept a wide space cleared. The Seventh Regiment National Guard formed a hollow square into which moved the funeral cortege. The procession marched to the City Hall through streets packed to capacity. The crowd gaze centered on the plate-glass hearse, topped with eight tall plumes of black and white feathers, draped with the American flag, drawn by six gray horses each led by a groom in black....

From near noon of Monday, April 24, to noon of the next day the remains of Abraham Lincoln, the clay tabernacle horizontal amid white satin, lay in the City Hall. A vast outpouring of people hour by hour passed by to see this effigy and remembrance of his face and form. They came for many and varied reasons.

Hundreds who had helped wreck, burn, and loot this city, killing scores of policemen and Negroes in the draft and race riots of year before last—these came now with curiosity, secret triumph, hate and contempt, a story traveling Manhattan that one entered a saloon hangout of their breed, saying, "I went down to the City Hall to see with my own eyes and be sure he was dead."

Some could not have told precisely why they were drawn by a spell that held them to wait five and six hours till they had slowly moved on to where they had their look at the victim of a sudden appalling tragedy touched with the supernatural.

An overwhelming many came as an act of faith and attestation;[8] they had come to love him and follow him; his many plain words and ways and stories told about him had reached them; he had become terribly real and beautifully alive to them....

At noon on Tuesday, April 25, a procession moved from the City Hall. It followed a giant canopied hearse drawn by sixteen black horses. From Broad to Fourteenth Street and then to Fifth Avenue wound the route—and up Fifth Avenue to

[8] *attestation:* an action giving evidence of a conviction

Thirty-fourth Street and thence to Ninth Avenue and the Hudson River Railroad depot.

. . . .

At the Union Square exercises following the parade the Roman Catholic Archbishop McCloskey pronounced the benediction, Rabbi Isaacs of the Jewish Synagogue read from their scriptures, the Reverend Stephen H. Tyng of St. George's Church offered a prayer, the historian George Bancroft delivered an oration, the Reverend Dr. Osgood read an ode by William Cullen Bryant, the Reverend J. P. Thompson intoned Lincoln's second inaugural. Evening had come. New York, the metropolis, had spoken. The funeral train with a locomotive named *Union* was moving up the Hudson River on its westward journey. . . .

The accusation was insinuated, or rather directly spoken, in various quarters that the body of Lincoln was being hawked about and vulgarly displayed in the interest of the Republican party and its radical wing. The very response of the people carried a reply to this. In the tumult of politics and in the crush of crowds he had had so much of his life, what was there of these few days before his burial not in accord? They wanted to see him as silent dust. What was the harm? In life he had met just about everyone who had sent word they wished to see him. So why not now again when he was beyond any and all harm? Those men with hats off along the railroad tracks at midnight and dawn, tears down the faces of many of them—why not? He would have wanted it. It went with his living and actual face and voice.

The vast and tireless outpourings of humanity at Washington and on through New York, the long lines of people waiting many hours in a tensed silence for the privileged fraction of a second when they could pass by a coffin and take a hurried glance at one memorable face, the spectacle of the rich and the poor, capitalists, wage-earners, the able-bodied and the lame and the crippled, an immense human family participating—this impressed the country. Those who might have had doubts about participating decided to be at least onlookers. The event was for an hour. It could never happen again. A deep interest grew into excitement. Here and there it verged into hysteria and delirium.

An epidemic of verse seized thousands. They sent their rhymed lines to the *New York Herald,* which publicly notified them that if it were all printed there would be no space for news, wherefore none at all would be printed. The *Chicago Tribune* editorially notified them it "suffered" from "this severe attack of poetry," that three days brought one hundred and sixty pieces beginning either "Toll, toll, ye mourning bells" or "Mourn, mourn, ye tolling bells."

Up the Hudson River east bank on the night of April 25 chugged the locomotive named *Union,* with its train of seven cars. On every mile of the route to Albany those on the train could see bonfires and torches, could hear bells and cannon and guns, could see forms of people and white sorry faces....

Soldiers and firemen escorted the hearse across the river, moved through immense crowds holding many from Vermont and Massachusetts, marched up the steep hill to the Assembly chamber of the State capitol. As elsewhere, every public building, store front, factory, and shop had its flags and mourning signs, likewise nearly every home, whether mansion or shanty....

Past midnight of April 25 into the morning hours of April 26 the columns of mourners passed the coffin. It was a few days more than four years since Lincoln had spoken in this same room, a weary man facing chaos....

. . . .

And four thousand persons an hour passed by the open coffin of Lincoln in Albany, sixty thousand swarmed the streets where they moved in procession to the funeral train. And across the Empire State that day and night it was a mural monotone of mourning....

The human past and future participated. At Buffalo Millard Fillmore, one of the three living ex-Presidents of the United States, attended the funeral, which also was witnessed by a youth Grover Cleveland....

On several railroad divisions of the journey the same locomotive pulled the train and handling it were the same railroad men as four years before. From Erie to Cleveland it was the same engine, the *William Jones,* and the same train conductor, E. D. Page. The engineer of 1861, William Congden, was dead, but his fireman George Martin had the throttle. The division superintendent, Henry Nottingham, as before had complete management.

At Cleveland the Committee on Location of Remains had decided no available building would accommodate the crowds, wherefore the Committee on Arrangements had a pagoda put up in the city park through which two columns would pass the coffin. . . .

From Cleveland to Crestline the rain kept on in torrents. Nevertheless at all towns and crossroads were the mourners, with uncovered heads, with torches and flags crossed with black. . . .

Along the railroad track in the morning five miles out from Columbus stood an old woman alone as the slow train came by, her gray hairs disheveled, tears coursing down her furrowed cheeks. In her right hand she held out a black mourning scarf. With her left hand she stretched imploringly toward the rain-and-storm-bedraggled funeral car, reaching and waving toward it her handful of wild flowers, her bouquet and token.

In the rotunda of Ohio's capitol, on a mound of green moss with white flower dots, rested the coffin on April 28, while eight thousand persons passed by each hour from half-past nine in the morning till four o'clock in the afternoon. . . .

It was now two weeks since the evening hour that Abraham Lincoln cheery and alive had left the White House in Washington to attend a performance of *Our American Cousin* in Ford's Theatre.

The slow night run from Columbus to Indianapolis saw from the car windows a countryside of people thronging to the route of the coffin. . . .

Tolling bells and falling rain at Indianapolis saw the coffin borne into the State House for a Sabbath to be remembered. . . . One hundred and fifty persons a minute passed the coffin, an estimated total of one hundred thousand.

At ten o'clock the doors closed, the marshals, the guards of honor, and the eight sergeants who bore the coffin took charge. . . . Amid acres of people, the men with heads uncovered, the coffin was put aboard a train made ready by the Lafayette Railroad Company.

On the slow night run to Chicago it was as in Ohio, thousands in Lafayette standing mute and daybreak not yet, thousands more at Michigan City, where the train stopped under a succession of arches and evergreen and flowers. . . .

Now over flat lands ran the slow train, between it and the blue levels of Lake Michigan the long slopes of pine-crept dunes and here and there the transient, wind-shaped piles of sand that tomorrow would be something else again.

The day was Monday, May 1, but in effect the Chicago obsequies[9] had begun the day before when Speaker Colfax delivered in Bryant Hall a formal funeral oration and a panegyric.[10] . . .

. . . .

By railway train, by wagon or buggy and on horseback, something like a hundred thousand people had come into Chicago from all points of the Northwest. . . .

Over the south door of the Cook County courthouse an inscription outside read "Illinois Clasps to Her Bosom Her Slain, but Glorified Son" and inside "He Was Sustained by Our Prayers, and Returns Embalmed by Our Tears." Over the north door the inscription outside read "The Beauty of Israel is Slain upon Thy High Places" and inside "The Altar of Freedom Has Borne No Nobler Sacrifice." . . .

Slowly at Twelfth Street and Michigan Avenue the funeral train came to a stop. Under a huge reception arch of side arches, columns, and Gothic windows in the lake-shore park near by, the eight sergeants carried the coffin and laid it on a dais. The pallbearers and guard of honor made their formation around it. Throughout brasses and drums gave a march written for the occasion, "The Lincoln Requiem." Thirty-six high school girls moved forward, in snow-white gowns, crape sashes, black-velvet bands with a single star over the forehead, some with sunny ringlets dropping to their shoulders, others with neat braids down the back. Over the bier two by two they strewed immortelles[11] and garlands of red and white roses.

[9] *obsequies:* funeral rites
[10] *panegyric:* a eulogy praising a person
[11] *immortelles:* a long-living flower

Then a procession of fifty thousand people, witnessed by double as many, escorted the hearse to the courthouse. . . .

All night long Monday, through all the night hours and through the day hours of Tuesday, the columns moved in and out the courthouse. When the doors closed, it was estimated one hundred and twenty-five thousand people had taken their last glance at the Man from Illinois.

A German chorus of three hundred voices chanted and a thousand men with blazing torches escorted the coffin from the courthouse to the depot and the funeral car for the slow night run to Springfield on the Alton Railroad.

At Joliet were midnight torches, evergreen arches, twelve thousand people. Every town and village, many a crossroads and lonely farm, spoke its mournful salutation across the hours of night and early morning. Here and there an arch or a depot doorway had the short flash "Come Home." At the town of Lincoln was an arch and a portrait inscribed "With Malice toward None; with Charity for All."

Then at last to Springfield came the coffin that had traveled seventeen hundred miles, that had been seen by more than seven million people—and the rigid face on which more than one million five hundred thousand people had gazed a moment or longer. The estimated figures were given. They were curious, incidental, not important—though such a final pilgrimage had never before moved with such somber human outpourings on so vast a national landscape.

In the state capitol, in the hall of the lower house of which he had been a member and where he had spoken his prophet warnings of the House Divided, stood the casket. Now passed those who had known him long. They were part of the seventy-five thousand who passed. They were awed, subdued, shaken, stony, strange. They came from Salem, Petersburg, Clary's Grove, Alton, Charleston, Mattoon, the old Eighth Circuit towns and villages. There were clients for whom he had won or lost, lawyers who had tried cases with him and against, neighbors who had seen him milk a cow and curry his horse, friends who had heard his stories around a hot stove and listened to his surmises on politics and religion. "We," wrote Bill Herndon, "who had known the illustrious dead in other days, and before the nation lay [*sic*] its claim upon him, moved sadly through and looked for the last time on the silent, upturned face of our departed friend."

All day long and through the night the unbroken line moved, the home town having its farewell.

On May 4 of this year 1865 Anno Domini a procession moved with its hearse from the State capitol to Oak Ridge Cemetery. There on green banks and hillsides flowing away from a burial vault the crowded thousands of listeners and watchers heard prayers and hymns, heard Bishop Matthew Simpson in a rounded, moving oration, heard the second inaugural read aloud.

Evergreen carpeted the stone floor of the vault. On the coffin set in a receptacle of black walnut they arranged flowers carefully and precisely, they poured flowers as symbols, they lavished heaps of fresh flowers as though there could never be enough to tell either their hearts or his.

And the night came with great quiet.

And there was rest.

FOR DISCUSSION

1. What is the effect in the first section of Sandburg's isolating each sentence in a separate paragraph? Why would the writer deliberately flout rules of composition? Is this unconventional style effective? Do you see any reason for Sandburg's allowing his sentences to grow gradually longer, and for ending the first section with a standard-sized paragraph?
2. What figures of speech and turns of phrase in section one do you find particularly effective? Do you find any that seem distracting?
3. What effect does Sandburg achieve by stating the facts about the funeral procession so flatly and dryly? Do you find instances in which he subtly colors these facts? Where?

FOR COMPOSITION

Write a eulogy or a poem for a slain president which does *not* begin either "Toll, toll, ye mourning bells," or "Mourn, mourn, ye tolling bells."

Mountain Fighting

ERNIE PYLE

The war in Italy was tough. The land and the weather were both against us. It rained and it rained. Vehicles bogged down and temporary bridges washed out. The country was shockingly beautiful, and just as shockingly hard to capture from the enemy. The hills rose to high ridges of almost solid rock. We couldn't go around them through the flat peaceful valleys, because the Germans were up there looking down upon us, and they would have let us have it. So we had to go up and over. A mere platoon of Germans, well dug in on a high, rock-spined hill, could hold out for a long time against tremendous onslaughts.

I know the folks back home were disappointed and puzzled by the slow progress in Italy. They wondered why we moved northward so imperceptibly. They were impatient for us to get to Rome. Well, I can say this—our troops were just as impatient for Rome. But on all sides I heard: "It never was this bad in Tunisia." "We ran into a new brand of Krauts over here." "If it would only stop raining." "Every day we don't advance is one day longer before we get home."

Our troops were living in almost inconceivable misery. The fertile black valleys were knee-deep in mud. Thousands of the men had not been dry for weeks. Other thousands lay at night in the high mountains with the temperature below freezing and the thin snow sifting over them. They dug into the stones and slept in little chasms and behind rocks and in half-caves. They lived like men of prehistoric times, and a club would have become them more than a machine gun. How they survived the dreadful winter at all was beyond us who had the opportunity of drier beds in the warmer valleys.

That the northward path was a tedious one was not the fault of our troops, nor of the direction either. It was the weather and the terrain and the weather again. If there had been no German fighting troops in Italy, if there had been merely German engineers to blow the bridges in the passes, if never a shot had been fired at all, our northward march would still have been slow. The country was so difficult that we formed a great deal of cavalry for use in the mountains. Each division had hundreds of horses and mules to carry supplies beyond the point where vehicles could go no farther. On beyond the mules' ability, mere men—American men—took it on their backs.

On my way to Italy, I flew across the Mediterranean in a cargo plane weighted down with more than a thousand pounds beyond the normal load. The cabin was filled with big pasteboard boxes which had been given priority above all other freight. In the boxes were packboards, hundreds of them, with which husky men would pack 100, even 150, pounds of food and ammunition, on their backs, to comrades high in those miserable mountains.

But we could take consolation from many things. The air was almost wholly ours. All day long Spitfires patrolled above our fighting troops like a half dozen policemen running up and down the street watching for bandits.

What's more, our artillery prevailed—and how! We were prodigal with ammunition against those rocky crags, and well we might be, for a $50 shell could often save ten lives in country like that. Little by little, the fiendish rain of explosives upon the hillsides softened the Germans. They always were impressed by and afraid of our artillery, and we had concentrations of it there that were demoralizing.

And lastly, no matter how cold the mountains, or how wet the snow, or how sticky the mud, it was just as miserable for the German soldier as for the American.

Our men were going to get to Rome all right. There was no question about that. But the way was cruel. No one who had not seen that mud, those dark skies, those forbidding ridges and ghostlike clouds that unveiled and then quickly hid the enemy, had the right to be impatient with the progress along the road to Rome.

The mountain fighting went on week after dreary week. For a while I hung around with one of the mule-pack outfits. There was an average of one mule-packing outfit for every infantry battalion in the mountains. Some were run by Americans, some by Italian soldiers.

The pack outfit I was with supplied a battalion that was fighting on a bald, rocky ridge nearly four thousand feet high. That battalion fought constantly for ten days and nights, and when the men finally came down less than a third of them were left.

All through those terrible days every ounce of their supplies had to go up to them on the backs of mules and men. Mules took it the first third of the way. Men took it the last bitter two-thirds, because the trail was too steep even for mules.

The mule skinners of my outfit were Italian soldiers. The human packers were mostly American soldiers. The Italian mule skinners were from Sardinia. They belonged to a mountain artillery regiment, and thus were experienced in climbing and in handling mules. They were bivouacked[1] in an olive grove alongside a highway at the foot of the mountain. They made no trips in the daytime, except in emergencies, because most of the trail was exposed to artillery fire. Supplies were brought into the olive grove by truck during the day, and stacked under trees. Just before dusk they would start loading the stuff onto mules. The Americans who actually managed the supply chain liked to get the mules loaded by dark, because if there was any shelling the Italians instantly disappeared and could never be found.

[1] *bivouacked:* camped

There were 155 skinners in this outfit and usually about eighty mules were used each night. Every mule had a man to lead it. About ten extra men went along to help get mules up if they fell, to repack any loads that came loose, and to unpack at the top. They could be up and back in less than three hours. Usually a skinner made just one trip a night, but sometimes in an emergency he made two.

On an average night the supplies would run something like this—85 cans of water, 100 cases of K ration, 10 cases of D ration, 10 miles of telephone wire, 25 cases of grenades and rifle and machine-gun ammunition, about 100 rounds of heavy mortar shells, 1 radio, 2 telephones, and 4 cases of first-aid packets and sulfa drugs. In addition, the packers would cram their pockets with cigarettes for the boys on top; also cans of Sterno, so they could heat some coffee once in a while.

Also, during that period, they took up more than five hundred of the heavy combat suits we were issuing to the troops to help keep them warm. They carried up cellophane gas capes for some of the men to use as sleeping bags, and they took extra socks for them too.

Mail was their most tragic cargo. Every night they would take up sacks of mail, and every night they'd bring a large portion of it back down—the recipients would have been killed or wounded the day their letters came.

On the long man-killing climb above the end of the mule trail they used anywhere from twenty to three hundred men a night. They rang in cooks, truck drivers, clerks, and anybody else they could lay their hands on. A lot of stuff was packed up by the fighting soldiers themselves. On a big night, when they were building up supplies for an attack, another battalion which was in reserve sent three hundred first-line combat troops to do the packing. The mule packs would leave the olive grove in bunches of twenty, starting just after dark. American soldiers were posted within shouting distance of each other all along the trail, to keep the Italians from getting lost in the dark.

Those guides—everybody who thought he was having a tough time in this war should know about them. They were men who had fought all through a long and bitter battle at the top of the mountain. For more than a week they had been far up there, perched behind rocks in the rain and cold, eating cold K rations, sleeping without blankets, scourged constantly with artillery and mortar shells, fighting and ducking and growing more and more weary, seeing their comrades wounded one by one and taken down the mountain.

Finally sickness and exhaustion overtook many of those who were left, so they were sent back down the mountain under their own power to report to the medics there and then go to a rest camp. It took most of them the better part of a day to get two-thirds of the way down, so sore were their feet and so weary their muscles.

And then—when actually in sight of their haven of rest and peace—they were stopped and pressed into guide service, because there just wasn't anybody else to do it. So there they stayed on the mountainside, for at least three additional days and nights that I know of, just lying miserably alongside the trail, shouting in the darkness to guide the mules.

They had no blankets to keep them warm, no beds but the rocks. And they did it without complaining. The human spirit is an astounding thing.

In this war I have known a lot of officers who were loved and respected by the soldiers under them. But never have I crossed the trail of any man as beloved as Captain Henry T. Waskow, of Belton, Texas.

Captain Waskow was a company commander in the Thirty-sixth Division. He had led his company since long before it left the States. He was very young, only in his middle twenties, but he carried in him a sincerity and a gentleness that made people want to be guided by him.

"After my father, he came next," a sergeant told me.

"He always looked after us," a soldier said. "He'd go to bat for us every time."

"I've never known him to do anything unfair," another said.

I was at the foot of the mule trail the night they brought Captain Waskow down. The moon was nearly full, and you could see far up the trail, and even partway across the valley below.

Dead men had been coming down the mountain all evening, lashed onto the backs of mules. They came lying belly-down across the wooden packsaddles, their heads hanging down on one side, their stiffened legs sticking out awkwardly from the other, bobbing up and down as the mules walked.

The Italian mule skinners were afraid to walk beside dead men, so Americans had to lead the mules down that night. Even the Americans were reluctant to unlash and lift off the bodies when they got to the bottom, so an officer had to do it himself and ask others to help.

I don't know who that first one was. You feel small in the presence of dead men, and you don't ask silly questions.

They slid him down from the mule, and stood him on his feet for a moment. In the half-light he might have been merely a sick man standing there leaning on the others. Then they laid him on the ground in the shadow of the stone wall alongside the road. We left him there beside the road, that first one, and we all went back into the cowshed and sat on water cans or lay on the straw, waiting for the next batch of mules.

Somebody said the dead soldier had been dead for four days, and then nobody said anything more about it. We talked soldier talk for an hour or more; the dead man lay all alone, outside in the shadow of the wall.

Then a soldier came into the cowshed and said there were some more bodies outside. We went out into the road. Four mules stood there in the moonlight, in the road where the trail came down off the mountain. The soldiers who led them stood there waiting.

"This one is Captain Waskow," one of them said quietly.

Two men unlashed his body from the mule and lifted it off and laid it in the shadow beside the stone wall. Other men took the other bodies off. Finally, there were five lying end to end in a long row. You don't cover up dead men in the combat zones. They just lie there in the shadows until somebody comes after them.

The unburdened mules moved off to their olive grove. The men in the road seemed reluctant to leave. They stood around, and gradually I could sense them moving, one by one, close to Captain Waskow's body. Not so much to look, I think, as to say something in finality to him and to themselves. I stood close by and I could hear.

One soldier came and looked down, and he said out loud, "Damn it!"

That's all he said, and then he walked away.

Another one came, and he said, "Damn it to hell anyway!" He looked down for a few last moments and then turned and left.

Another man came. I think he was an officer. It was hard to tell officers from men in the dim light, for everybody was bearded and grimy. The man looked down into the dead captain's face and then spoke directly to him, as though he were alive, "I'm sorry, old man."

Then a soldier came and stood beside the officer and bent over, and he too spoke to his dead captain, not in a whisper but awfully tenderly, and he said, "I sure am sorry, sir."

Then the first man squatted down, and he reached down and took the captain's hand, and he sat there for a full five minutes holding the dead hand in his own and looking intently into the dead face. And he never uttered a sound all the time he sat there.

Finally he put the hand down. He reached over and gently straightened the points of the captain's shirt collar, and then he sort of rearranged the tattered edges of the uniform around the wound, and then he got up and walked away down the road in the moonlight, all alone.

The rest of us went back into the cowshed, leaving the five dead men lying in a line end to end in the shadow of the low stone wall. We lay down on the straw in the cowshed, and pretty soon we were all asleep.

FOR DISCUSSION

1. Look at the series of short, flat, choppy sentences with which this selection begins. What effect does Pyle gain by stringing such short sentences together? Do you notice any other unconventional touches in this paragraph?
2. What are the similarities and differences between the way Pyle uses details in this selection and the way Sandburg used them in the previous one?

3. Which details make the misery of war particularly vivid? Why is the description of Captain Waskow so effective? Would the selection be more, or less, memorable without a reference to the Captain? Why?
4. What impression of the American soldiers is conveyed through this selection? What purpose do you think Pyle may have had in mind when he wrote it?
5. What different statements about war does Pyle imply through his last sentence? Why do you think he ended the piece in this way?

FOR COMPOSITION

Describe an extremely hazardous or difficult undertaking, using the same kind of understatement Pyle uses here. Try to lead your reader to a particular conclusion without stating the generalization directly.

The Age of Dust

August 26, 1950

E. B. WHITE

On a sunny morning last week, we went out and put up a swing for a little girl, age three, under an apple tree—the tree being much older than the girl, the sky being blue, the clouds white. We pushed the little girl for a few minutes, then returned to the house and settled down to an article on death dust, or radiological[1] warfare, in the July *Bulletin of the Atomic Scientists,* Volume VI, No. 7.

The article ended on a note of disappointment. "The area that can be poisoned with the fission products available to us today is disappointingly small; it amounts to not more than two or three major cities per month." At first glance, the sentence sounded satirical, but a rereading convinced us that the scientist's disappointment was real enough—that it had the purity of detachment. The world of the child in the swing (the trip to the blue sky and back again) seemed, as we studied the ABC of death dust, more and more a dream world with no true relation to things as they are or to the real world of discouragement over the slow rate of the disappearance of cities.

[1] *radiological:* involving atomic radiation

Probably the scientist-author of the death-dust article, if he were revising his literary labors with a critical eye, would change the wording of that queer sentence. But the fact is, the sentence got written and published. The terror of the atom age is not the violence of the new power but the speed of man's adjustment to it—the speed of his acceptance. Already bomb-proofing is on approximately the same level as mothproofing. Two or three major cities per month isn't much of an area, but it is a start. To the purity of science (which hopes to enlarge the area) there seems to be no corresponding purity of political thought, never the same detachment. We sorely need, from a delegate in the Security Council,[2] a statement as detached in its way as the statement of the scientist on death dust. This delegate (and it makes no difference what nation he draws his pay from) must be a man who has not adjusted to the age of dust. He must be a person who still dwells in the mysterious dream world of swings, and little girls in swings. He must be more than a good chess player studying the future; he must be a memoirist remembering the past.

We couldn't seem to separate the little girl from radiological warfare—she seemed to belong with it, although inhabiting another sphere. The article kept getting back to her. "This is a novel type of warfare, in that it produces no destruction, except to life." The weapon, said the author, can be regarded as a horrid one, or, on the other hand, it "can be regarded as a remarkably humane one. In a sense, it gives each member of the target population [including each little girl] a choice of whether he will live or die." It turns out that the way to live—if that be your choice—is to leave the city as soon as the dust arrives, holding "a folded, dampened handkerchief" over your nose and mouth. We went outdoors again to push the swing some more for the little girl, who is always forgetting her handkerchief. At lunch we watched her try to fold her napkin. It seemed to take forever.

As we lay in bed that night, thinking of cities and target populations, we saw the child again. This time she was with

[2] *Security Council:* the committee of the United Nations charged with maintaining international peace

the other little girls in the subway. When the train got to 242nd Street, which is as far as it goes into unreality, the children got off. They started to walk slowly north. Each child had a handkerchief, and every handkerchief was properly moistened and folded neatly—the way it said in the story.

FOR DISCUSSION

1. What words make the outdoor scene which E. B. White describes in his first sentence seem so idyllic? What effect results from the contrast at the end of the paragraph?
2. Why did the word *disappointingly* (paragraph 2) seem at first to be satiric to White? What is his attitude toward the scientist who wrote the word?
3. What does White find most terrifying about the Atomic Age? Why is a characteristic of his ideal statesman that he understands the past? Why is understanding the past more important to White than studying the future?
4. Why is the last sentence ironic? What point does White imply through his irony?

FOR COMPOSITION

Write an essay discussing the differences between the outlooks of scientists such as the one who wrote of death dust and humanists such as E. B. White.

HERSEY AND SCHLESINGER

After the Second World War, the United States was no longer a "youthful giant" but a self-possessed power which could judge current events with an experienced and sometimes temperate eye. One major sign of this maturity was the end of the self-preoccupation that had characterized her nineteenth-century adolescence. Now the nation could see herself in relation to the rest of the world. Indeed, after the perfection of "The Bomb," she had no choice but to see herself in this way. She could, occasionally, even recognize in the struggles of other peoples her own trials and triumphs.

No abortive uprising ever captured the imagination of United States citizens more thoroughly than the uprising in Hungary in 1956. Hungarian boys and girls opposed Russian tanks with guns, and even sticks and stones for weapons—and almost won. Among many Americans, a great wave of sympathy swelled in response to the young people of Hungary. John Hersey's account of the fortunes of a family in the Hungarian uprising was one of the more influential of many which discussed, in human terms, both the politics and the history of another nation.

Then dramatically in the early 1960's came the rebirth of a belief in the dignity of public life. With John Fitzgerald Kennedy's inauguration, hope grew that once again thoughtful men might shape human affairs with intelligence and reason. Almost afraid to trust in or to articulate the new spirit, individuals nevertheless felt themselves caught up in a slowly growing delight over the creative possibilities in politics. It is this intangible spirit of the New Frontier which Arthur Schlesinger, Jr., analyzes in his study of the Kennedy administration entitled *A Thousand Days*. The New Frontier was not so much a political as a psychological event: the nation discovered to its surprise that it was still capable not only of hope for the future but also of enthusiasm for the present.

Journey Toward a Sense of Being Treated Well

JOHN HERSEY

At about eight o'clock in the evening of Monday, November 19, 1956, there appeared at the door of a small apartment on the rise of Buda, above the right bank of the Danube at Budapest, a man in a thin, faded blue raincoat, who had an extraordinarily haggard face—all bones, hair, and wires, it seemed. The face had no cheeks—only scoops on either side of a black mustache—and its sharp cheekbones shelved back to conical bumps of bone just in front of big ears, and the ears seemed to have been pulled forward by the wirelike steel bows of a pair of delicate, twisted spectacles. The wire bridge of these glasses had found a resting place a quarter of the way down the man's straight nose, so that the pupils of his sad brown sunken eyes looked out just under the wirelike upper rims; the lenses were tilted up and out at two different angles, making the glasses seem an apparatus for ventilation, or perhaps shelter, rather than for clear examination of the world. Above the eyes were black brows, taut over the bone, and now and then the man shot up these brows, as if to demonstrate that they were not, as they appeared, rooted in his skull, and when he did this, his enormous forehead was gathered up toward his thick black hair in terrible arching creases that told a lot about the years just past. The man was forty, but he looked ageless—simply out of connection with any time of life at all. At that moment, he also looked cold and tired, and, in fact, he was, for it had taken him two hours to walk home from the food-canning plant on the outskirts of Budapest where he worked as a lawyer. As soon as he had opened the door, he said to his wife, who had been waiting for him, "We can go tomorrow."

There were three rooms in the apartment, which the man, whose name was Vilmos Fekete, had rented for twelve years; now he shared them with his wife, his two daughters, his brother-in-law, and his father-in-law. His own father and mother, two brothers, and a sister lived elsewhere in the city. After the family had had some supper, Fekete and his wife, Elvira, prepared for the journey that they, together with their daughters—Klara, who was twelve, and Magdalena, who was nine—planned to take. They told the girls merely that they were all going to a city called Veszprém, near Lake Balaton, to visit some friends—the truth, though only part of the whole truth, for the Feketes intended to make Veszprém their first stop on a longer journey westward. Fekete did not know how dangerous the trip might be. He had learned caution at a high cost during the children's lifetime, and he felt sure that if the Avo, the Hungarian secret police, were to take him and his family into custody along the way, they would question the children separately, and in case that unthinkable thing should happen, he wanted the children to have the strength of truth-telling on their side. The girls were thrilled, because in the past they had had carefree vacations at Lake Balaton.

There was really almost nothing to be done to get ready for the trip. Packing anything was out of the question. Fekete knew that it would be impossible to take any baggage, because parts of the trip would have to be made on foot. Elvira baked some biscuits and wrapped them up, along with a crucifix on which she had given her wedding oath fourteen years before, and some toilet articles, into a small parcel. Fekete put in a box his most important documents, such as his school and university diplomas and his favorite photographs of his family. He next called on the superintendent of the apartment building, who kept the official register of tenants, and told him that because of the disorganization of life in Budapest since the October uprising, he and his family were going to live in Veszprém, and that a friend and his family, who had been shelled out of their home during the Russian counterattack, would move into the flat in the Feketes' places, if the authorities approved. Then Fekete took the box of papers to this same friend, for later delivery to Fekete's father.

Fekete borrowed some money from his friend. His salary from the factory had been a thousand forints a month. At the official rate of exchange, this was about ninety dollars; at the black-market rate, it was only twenty dollars. Fekete had no savings. On the previous day, he had drawn his salary for the second half of November, and he actually had about a hundred forints left over from the first half, because it had been impossible to buy anything during the worst of the fighting; his factory director had given him and the other employees four pounds of flour, two pounds of sugar, and a pound of salt to tide them over while the shops were closed. Altogether, counting his own money and some that he had been able to borrow from his father and what he now borrowed from his friend, he found himself with about two thousand forints for his journey. Fekete returned home and went to bed at about ten o'clock.

The family arose at five in the morning, drank some tea, and started out. As they left, Fekete turned on the landing and looked back into the apartment. This was the only home he and his wife had ever had, and in abandoning it he felt a sense of loss, not over the possessions he was leaving behind—the threadbare furniture his godfather had given him, a Telefunken radio with a short-wave band he had bought after saving for many months—but over the words said and the things done in these rooms in twelve years of the prime of his life. The one material thing he hated to leave was his stamp collection, which represented thousands of hours of deep absorption scattered over twenty-six years. Elvira, seeing tears behind the tilted spectacles, stood on the landing silently waiting, her close-set eyes hooded and dry. She had always been a more practical person than Vilmos; a question she often asked was "For what?" To her this small apartment had been a center of hard work and crowded living.

It was barely getting light as the Fekete family walked down the hill toward the railroad station. It was a ghostly hour in an exhausted city. Signs of bombardment were plentiful; the streets were cluttered with fallen bricks. The day was going to be gray, and it was cold. There was no traffic at all. A general strike was in progress, and few people were out. In Szena Place, the family walked past two railroad cars that the Freedom Fighters had rolled up from the station on streetcar tracks and overturned for barricades; in Moscow Place there was a similar barricade. Half an hour's walk took the Feketes to the station.

Trains had started running from Budapest the day before, for the first time in a month, but, as Fekete had explained to his wife, he had wanted to wait one day before leaving, to make sure that the tracks out in the countryside had not been mined by Freedom Fighters to inhibit deportations to the Soviet Union. The previous afternoon, he had sent a friend to scout the station for him, and this explorer had reported that the trains had gone through safely and that the Avo did not seem to be watching the station.

Fekete walked up to a window and bought four third-class tickets to Veszprém, for eighty-four forints. At a few minutes before seven, the family boarded their train. Nobody asked any questions. The Feketes made their way to a section of a third-class coach that was partly cut off from the rest of the car —a coupé, with wooden benches for about ten passengers. Shortly after they had entered, two young couples joined them in the coupé. The Feketes inspected the newcomers; the newcomers glanced at them. These people, Fekete observed, were warmly dressed, carried no luggage, and had small parcels under their arms. He said with his eyes to his wife, "Their destination is the same as ours."

That train went only about thirty miles, to a place called Szekesfehérvár, and there, in a station jammed with warmly clad people who had no baggage, the Feketes bought tea and bread. In the afternoon, a train was announced for Veszprém. The Feketes, on boarding it, found places on benches; the aisles were soon crowded with standees. The travelers were silent until a conductor, entering the car as the train started, said in a loud voice, "Nobody remains in Budapest? *Everyone* comes out?" This seemed to be a joke, and all the people laughed.

As the cars went through a cold countryside of low hills and eroded scarps of limestone, Fekete sat still and looked out, enjoying the swift motion of the train. He had long dreamed of this journey. He had lived the four decades of his life under a warring Emperor,[1] a Communist leader[2] who established his reforms by bathing the country in blood, a ruthless Fascist regent[3] who called himself an admiral in a landlocked country, a German dictator[4] who regarded Hungary as a pawn, and another Communist regime, this one sustained by Russian-controlled secret police. For a brief, dreamlike moment between the last two of these political numbings, he had experienced democratic parliamentary government—at first hand, for he himself had been elected a member of the Hungarian Parliament in 1947. He had quickly paid, and expensively, for this honor, and the payment was the nightmare memory of his life. Yes, he had long wished for the sensation of momentum this crowded train gave him.

Late in the afternoon, Fekete saw the forested mound of Mount Bakony off to the right, and at its foot a number of bauxite mines and factories; then the train arrived in Veszprém. Fekete led his wife and children to the home of an old friend, a lady schoolteacher, and because she had no spare food, she took the Feketes to a hotel to eat. There two other families, friends of the teacher, joined the group—among them a physician and a member of the local county council. At first, Fekete, who wanted to find out how best to go forward on his journey, felt impatient at having strangers at the table. For a long time, he made it a practice to speak not a word to people he did not know. But he trusted the teacher's judgment, and the waiter who came for their order took Fekete's breath away by saying

[1] *Emperor:* Charles I, ruler of Austria-Hungary, 1916-1918
[2] *Communist leader:* Béla Kun, head of a revolutionary government in 1919
[3] *Fascist regent:* Nicholas von Horthy, regent of Hungary, 1920-1944
[4] *German dictator:* Adolf Hitler

quite openly, "You can talk about anything you want. The people at the next table are all right."

At once, the guests began asking Fekete questions about the revolt in Budapest. Was it true, one asked, that though shop-windows had been broken in the fighting there had been no looting?

Fekete said that one day he passed a shop with a smashed window, and inside, on the broken fragments of glass, within easy reach of the sidewalk, he had seen a box heaped with coins and paper money, with a sign on it reading, "We are praying for money for the relatives of those dead in the revolution. In this revolution we can leave this box here, and tonight we will get it."

Another guest asked: What of the assertion by the Kádár regime that the revolution had been the work of Fascists?

Fekete, a Catholic, said he considered anti-Semitism the worst manifestation of the kind of Fascism that Hungary had had under Admiral Horthy before the war; for him anti-Semitism was the badge of Fascism. One day early in the revolt, he said, while walking home from his factory, he had heard a man on a street corner make a remark about the Jews. Two young men with rifles who were standing nearby had turned on the man, and one had slapped him in the face and said that the Freedom Fighters would not stand for that kind of talk.

A little later, Magdalena, the Feketes' nine-year-old, a restless child with a broad face and huge eyes, announced with satisfaction, "There is a big hole in our school."

The teacher asked Fekete what the schools in Budapest had been like during the last couple of years.

Not too bad, Fekete said. One day, a friend of his, the director of an elementary school, had said to him, "I'm very glad that among the teachers in my school are some members of the Party but no Communists." Such teachers, Fekete said, had joined the Party only for food cards. They had taught the children how to answer questions on dialectics[5] when the inspector came around, but they had made it clear that all those things were only for the inspector.

[5] *dialectics:* logical arguments

One of the men asked: Had Fekete seen any actual fighting?

Fekete was now experiencing for the first time in several years the pleasurable sensation of a loose tongue in his mouth. He had, he said. On the third day of the revolution, October 25th, in the afternoon, while he was dodging along the streets on his way home from the factory, he had seen a boy not more than fourteen years old jump on a tank and open the lid and drop in a bottle full of benzine. And very near his factory were situated the Kilian Barracks, where General Pál Maléter, the commander of the Freedom Fighters in the city, had held out for several days with nine hundred men. And on October 26th and the two days following, when there was fighting around his home and his wife wouldn't let him go to the factory, he had looked down on the square below their windows and had seen the young men hiding in doorways and shooting, and he had seen a barricade being made of two railway cars.

He had been only a witness, he said. This had been a young people's fight.

It had all started, he said, on October 23rd in the evening, when the man who was then Premier, Ernö Gerö, announced on the radio that the students' demonstration that afternoon, in favor of the Gomulka liberalization in Poland, had been staged by Fascists and criminals. Fekete said that he had heard the speech, and that it had made him angry. The students had been very angry, and they had marched to the radio station to demand time to answer Gerö, and the guards had become excited and at ten o'clock in the evening had fired shots into the crowd of young people. That was the first thing that had made it a real revolution, Fekete said. He had heard shots during that night. The next morning, the twenty-fourth, he had started out for his office and had found the streets practically deserted. He had walked all the way to the factory both that day and the next, in order that he might be where he could telephone his father and find out how he was.

In the very first days of the revolution, Fekete had begun to hear that Hungarians who lived near the Austrian border were going into exile, and he talked over with his wife the question of whether they should try to go, too. Maybe they could even get to the United States, he said.

On the twenty-ninth, the fighting had died down. Imre Nagy was Premier, and in his Cabinet was a member of the non-communist Smallholders' Party, Béla Kovács, whom Fekete had known since the time when he himself was a Smallholder. On the thirty-first—a day of great illusory[6] joy in Budapest, as Soviet tanks withdrew from the city and it seemed that a few boys with rifles and bottles of flammables had set back a great military power—Fekete had gone to see Kovács and had talked with him about a possible rejuvenation[7] of the Smallholders' Party.

Then, on the following days, there were ominous rumors of Russian reinforcements. Fekete heard on the radio that Nagy had taken Hungary out of the Warsaw Pact and had proclaimed the nation's neutrality, and that he had appealed to the United Nations for protection.

On the morning of Sunday, November 4th, at five o'clock, the Feketes awoke to sounds of heavy bombardment. Hundreds of Russian tanks were pouring into the city. Nagy took asylum in the Yugoslav Embassy, and the Feketes took refuge in the cellar of their apartment house. There the family stayed, off and on, for a full week, and there, for the first time, they made the acquaintance of the people who had been living in the same building with them for years. The rule of Fekete's life had been: Tranquillity lies in isolation, in saying nothing, in living like a wild beast in the love and protection of one's immediate family. At the factory, everyone had known who the tiny handful of hard-core Communists were, and everyone had kept them, as the expression went, "three steps of air away." No one had taken seriously the pathetic group of food-card Communists, who were pushed into all the front positions and given all the titles. But in the apartment building there had been no way of knowing who thought what; the Avo penetrated everywhere. Now, in the cellar, where someone had set up a radio, it was a staggering revelation to see tears in every eye when, on November 6th, the rebel radio said farewell to the world in defeat. All those in the building whom Fekete had feared had felt the same way as he!

[6]*illusory:* false or mistaken
[7]*rejuvenation:* rebirth

For an hour or so each day, during lulls in the fighting, the Feketes went up to their apartment, and had a meal. They carried a sofa down to the cellar for the girls; the parents slept on the basement floor. Twice that week, Fekete risked going out into the streets, in order to visit his father and make sure he was all right. The wreckage along the streets was appalling.

By Sunday, November 11, most of the fighting was over. The next day, Fekete walked to the factory. He felt obliged to do this, because he was running low on money and food for his family. He was given his emergency rations that day. He walked to the plant all that week. Everyone there was deeply depressed. The Kádár government was announcing repressive measures; the hopes of late October had proved false; there were reports of wholesale deportations of young men to the Soviet Union; the wreckage in the city was far greater than it had been during the entire war; people had no energy, no desire for work. The official radio and the papers were saying that Soviet troops were guarding the border with Austria, and that the people who had fled to that country were being held as prisoners in camps or made to work in mines, and were given but one piece of bread a day.

On Monday, November 18th, Fekete heard at the factory that trains were going to start running again the next day, and he decided that the time had come to try to escape.

Fekete's new acquaintances in the hotel in Veszprém were so open and warm, and they listened to him with such visible emotion, that he felt once again, as he had in the cellar at home, a poignant shock of emergence from isolation. These people had confidence in him! And he trusted them! One of the men said that he admired and envied Fekete for his courage in attempting to leave the country—that only the dangers of the frontier and fear of a Russian prison held him back—and others agreed.

Now Fekete felt safe in asking what these people had been hearing about the frontier.

The consensus of their opinion, based on reports that had drifted back from the border, was that the best region in which to try an escape was around a town called Kapuvár, about eighty miles northwest of Veszprém. Here the worst dangers were natural: It would be necessary to go through swampy land in cold weather.

The Feketes rested a full day in Veszprém. The schoolteacher suggested that they go to Celldömölk, the first large town on the way to the Kapuvár swamps, by automobile. She said she had in her class the son of a taxi-driver whom she knew to be an honest man; the Feketes could ride with him. Fekete asked her to arrange this, and she did. Early in the morning of November 22nd, the Feketes were picked up by the driver, a taciturn[8] man of about fifty, in a black Russian-built Pobeda. Fekete considered trying to arrange the fare in advance, but he decided that this might be embarrassing; after all, the schoolteacher had said the man was honest.

The black taxi set out across flat farm country on a broad paved highway, one of the main arteries of Hungary, which was bordered in places with rows of poplars and locusts. It was a lonely drive through an empty land, for there was hardly any traffic—not a single car, and only a few trucks—and the farmers were not in the fields. Fekete, who had traveled widely in the country as a lawyer and a politician, in war and peace, had never seen a crisis before that had caused the farmers to stop work. Nowhere had winter rye or wheat or cover crops been planted.

The drive to Celldömölk took two and a half hours, and when the driver set the Feketes down in the center of town, he asked for eight hundred and eighty-two forints. From his former trips, Fekete knew that this fare was quite normal for the distance, and he gave the driver nine hundred forints and told him to keep the change—a tip that Fekete would have thought twice about if money and budgets had meant anything to him any more.

Now Fekete had no idea what to do. He took his family to the railway station, simply for shelter; no trains were running in the direction of Kapuvár. Then he walked out in the town alone. Near a market place, he saw an open farm truck, an old

[8]*taciturn:* silent

three-ton Hungarian diesel with a cloth canopy over the back; the driver, a peasant, was standing by the cab. Fekete approached him and said, "Which direction do you take?"

"Your direction," the peasant said. "I know where you want to go. Hop in. Let's go."

Fekete said that the farmer was very kind but that his wife and children were at the station.

The man told Fekete to go and get them and any others who might be waiting to go toward Kapuvár.

Fekete ran off to the station, and there he found, besides his family, two coal miners who wanted to leave the country.

When the Feketes and the miners reached the truck, the driver was in the cab, and the motor was running, and in the back were a number of villagers who had been to market. Fekete's party got aboard, and the truck left Celldömölk. The villagers said they were from a collective farm about twelve miles north of Celldömölk, and were heading back there now. They estimated that it was twenty miles to Kapuvár from their farm. There is a perfectly good Hungarian word for collective farm, "*szövetkezet*," but to Fekete's surprise these peasants used the Russian term "*kolkhoz*," and used it with the same contemptuous force that Fekete's friends in the city gave it. In Budapest, the lawyers' groups set up by the Communists were also widely called "collective farms," with this same Russian word, for laughs.

At the farm, the truck dropped the Feketes and the miners. Fekete reached for his wallet, but the driver waved him off and said, "Good luck." He was about to drive away when he turned back and beckoned to Fekete, and said, "Don't let them forget us out where you're going."

The Feketes and the miners walked through a cold noon hour as far as the next village, which was called Kenyeri. As they walked, the miners told Fekete that this was their second try. They had been caught by Russian soldiers in their first attempt to cross the border, near Szombathely, farther south. The Russians had turned them over to Hungarian frontier guards, and these Hungarians had taken them a few miles back from the border and set them free, and one of the guards had said, "Be more careful next time."

As the group entered Kenyeri, a woman accosted them in the main street and said, "You must hurry. The milk truck from Répcelak is unloading. It can take you farther."

Fekete was disconcerted at the thought that his group could be so easily recognized for what it was. The truck was about three hundred yards up the street, and he and one of the miners started to run toward it. All at once, Fekete saw in the street, on the near side of the truck, a policeman holding a bicycle and talking with two armed civilians. At the sight of the uniform and the guns, he was suddenly afraid, and he pulled the miner with him into the front yard of a house that was surrounded by a high board fence. The two men were standing there, unsure of what to do, when a peasant woman came out of the house and asked what the matter was. Fekete said, "We saw a policeman. We don't want to be caught."

The woman went to her front gate and looked up the street, and then said, "Dear God! That's *our* policeman. He wouldn't hurt a flea. It's perfectly safe to go on. Ask him how to get to the border. You'll see."

Fekete and the miner went on up the street, at a walk. The policeman nodded benignly to them. They asked the driver of the milk truck if he would give the party a lift, and he said he would be glad to, but he was not quite ready to go, and he suggested that they wait for him on a street corner about a hundred yards ahead.

Fekete went back for the others and took them to the corner. It was cold. In a few minutes, a peasant woman came out of her house and invited them inside to get warm. In her house, she fed them all soup and bread, and when it came time to leave, Fekete wanted to pay her for the food, but she refused the money. Indeed, when they were in the street and about to board the truck, one of the miners told Fekete that the woman had drawn him aside and pushed a hundred-forint note into his pocket. He had fished it out and tried to make her take it back, but she had said that he and his friends would need it up the line.

The driver took the two little girls in the cab with him; the others climbed up into the back and sat on empty milk cans there. Suddenly, Fekete felt tears well up.

Elvira Fekete asked her husband reproachfully, as if he were a small boy, what his trouble was.

He leaned toward her and said, in a low voice, "Everybody wants to help us. I never thought the whole Hungarian people could be so equal. These miners are really our friends. Everybody is together. Why did that woman want to give us food and money? She never saw us before, and she'll never see us again! It's all amazing!"

In the summer of 1933, in his seventeenth year, having finished grammar school, Vilmos Fekete attended a Boy Scout World Jamboree in Budapest, and in talking with English and German Scouts he found that he had pretty well mastered the second and third languages he had studied in school. After the Jamboree, he sent his name around to the various hotels in the city with notice that he would be glad to serve as a tourist guide for English- and German-speaking visitors. That autumn, he began studying law at Peter Pazmany University, in Budapest, and from then on for several years, he earned spending money by working as a guide and, later, as a clerk in his father's law office. In 1938, when the International Eucharistic Congress was held in Budapest, Fekete had his last big fling as a guide, because after Hitler entered the Sudetenland few tourists ventured into Central Europe. Fekete received his law baccalaureate in 1939 and his doctorate in 1941. He entered private practice with his father, and because he served as counsel to an association of small leather-goods tradesmen who sold holsters, belts, and saddlery to the Hungarian Army, his military service was at first deferred, but on October 7, 1942—four days after his marriage to Elvira, whom he had met at a law-school party—he was drafted, and was assigned to desk work in Szeged, near the Yugoslav border. Army life disagreed with him, and he developed asthma, and in February, 1944, he was given a medical discharge. He resumed his law practice. The Soviet Army entered Pest in January, 1945, and Buda the next month, and at once rounded up, as prisoners of war, all the Hungarian men it could find who were or had been soldiers. Fekete was picked up on February 17, 1945. He was interned with five thousand men of various nationalities in a school on the Pest side of the river until mid-March, when he heard that a Czech mission had arrived in Hungary, and that everyone who claimed Czech nationality was being assigned to the mission, which promptly turned all pseudo-Czechs[9] loose. Upon being asked his nationality by a Russian in an interview on March 16th, Fekete knew what to say: He was a Czech. Where were his documents? Sorry, he said—taken from him by a Russian soldier. The Russian sent him to join a band of seventeen men for delivery to the Czech mission; five of them were real Czechs. Two days later, he was at home with his wife, who was seven months pregnant. Fekete, a liberal idealist who had always considered himself mild, gentle, and sickly, was surprised to find during this experience that his nerves were steady under stress.

Fekete entered politics as a member of the Smallholders' Party. This party, a holdover from before the war, had a long record of representing the peasants' interests against the landlords. In the first postwar election, in November, 1945, which was altogether open and free, it received fifty-seven per cent of the popular vote, while the Communists received only seventeen per cent. The Soviet Army and secret police were still in Hungary, however, and during the next two years, as Fekete gradually rose to membership in the central committee of the Smallholders' Party, he saw many of the men he regarded as the best in the Party pushed out, discredited, or arrested, while by infiltration and pressure the Communists drove the surviving Smallholders further and further to the Left. Fekete was one of a group that broke with the Smallholders' leadership in the summer of 1947, and just a month before the second postwar election, he and his friends set up a new party, the Independents, and Fekete was elected to Parliament with forty-seven of his colleagues—a large number, considering the shortness of their campaign. The Communists, who by then had an efficient machine, seated a hundred members of Parliament, the Smallholders about seventy.

So wildly and quickly had the Independents' fire spread that it was clear to the Communists that the new party would have to be suppressed, and the job of liquidating it was given

[9]*pseudo-Czechs:* false Czechoslovakians

to the secret police. This was when Fekete fell into his nightmare time; somehow he survived it sane. For five years afterward, he tried to resume private law practice, but nothing came of that. In 1953, discriminatory taxes were levied against private businessmen and professional men, and Fekete, who was earning about twelve hundred forints a month, found himself obliged to pay six hundred and fifty forints of his earnings in taxes. He dropped his practice and took what he could get—a job at a cannery in the Ferencváros section of Budapest, where he was mostly engaged in arranging contracts with shopping centers and restaurants. He worked surrounded by food and got thinner and thinner.

There was no cover over the back of the milk truck, and it was bitterly cold. Along the way, the driver stopped to pick up three men and three women who were also headed for the border. Two of the men were in filthy, sooty clothes, and wore a kind of harness over their shoulders; as soon as they were settled on the cans, the miners and Fekete congratulated each other and touched them, for they were chimney sweeps, symbols of good luck. Each New Year's Eve in Budapest before the war, chimney sweeps used to go from restaurant to restaurant, often carrying suckling pigs under their arms, and people would rush to touch them for luck. Now the miners laughed and said the trip across the border would be easy.

The truck arrived at a milk-and-cheese plant in Répcelak at a little after four in the afternoon. The village was about twenty-five miles from the border, the driver said, and it was obvious that the Feketes and their friends would not be able to cross the frontier that night; they would have to find a place to sleep. Fekete, who still had a fair amount of money, asked a passerby in the street whether there was an inn in Répcelak. The stranger was friendly; like everyone else along the way, he knew, without being told, where these people were going, and he said that they had better not stay in Répcelak overnight, because there were quite a few hard-core Communists in the village, who might make trouble for them.

Fekete remembered seeing along the highway, not far back, a sign-post pointing to a village called Vamoscsalad, and he also remembered that in Budapest the father of a schoolmate of one of his daughters had once spoken of having relatives in that village. This was a rather tenuous connection, but on the strength of it the Feketes and their friends the miners walked four miles through the twilight to Vamoscsalad. They found a village of farmers' houses, round about which were ranged, in scattered strips, the lands the people worked. Fekete knocked at the door of the first house the party came to, and asked the farmer who answered if he knew such a name as that of his daughter's classmate's father.

"Do I know it?" the farmer said. "Three-quarters of the village has that name."

Fekete then asked if the farmer knew of a family, among the three-quarters, that owned a young man who was now working in Budapest and had a little daughter.

Why, the farmer said, directly across the street!

The Feketes and the miners received cordial shelter that night from the mother and father of a man who was a virtual stranger to Fekete. The farmer and his wife gave their guests a hot supper—and, better than that, they gave them advice. They said there had been numerous reports in recent days of a strongly reinforced Russian border guard on this side of the swampland around Kapuvár. There were said to have been some shootings. It would be best, the hosts thought, to take a local train that paralleled the border, and attempt their crossing farther along, where the frontier was said to be much less carefully guarded.

At one point during the evening, Fekete said that as far as he could observe, few farmers seemed to be leaving the country. "Almost none," the old farmer said. Fekete asked why that was. "Because they cannot leave the land," the old man said. "They used to say we peasants were slaves of landowners. No, it's deeper. We are slaves of the land."

There were three beds in the farmhouse, and the Fekete family was given two of them. The miners slept out in a barn.

The next morning, when it came time to leave, Fekete offered the farmer money for the family's and the miners' food and lodging. The farmer refused it, and, gripping Fekete's slender hand with his hard one, he said with great earnestness, "No, I owe you a debt. You will risk your life to get out. You are of the intelligentsia. You must explain to them in the other countries everything that has happened. Tell them not to forget us!"

At seven o'clock, the Feketes and the miners caught a local train, consisting of only four cars, from Vamoscsalad. There was nobody else aboard who seemed to be border-bound. The passengers were workers and peasants. The train went for only about half an hour, as far as a place called Hegyfalu. There the group had a three-hour wait for the next train. More and more people gathered in the station to take it, and among them were about forty who appeared to be headed for the border. Peasants and railway officials talked freely with them about the frontier, and confirmed what the old farmer had said the night before. At the moment, the best place to cross seemed to be near a village named Repcevis, some distance up the line. In that sector, the border patrols were Russian and Hungarian troops working together. Every few hundred yards, one Russian walked with one Hungarian. In the last few nights, there had been wholesale crossings near Repcevis, with no loss of life.

Somebody warned Fekete not to let himself be cheated at the frontier. He told a story about a border guide who had accepted two thousands forints in advance to take a party into Austria and who, on hearing shooting, had run away, abandoning even women and children. Hungarian soldiers had found the group. Things had turned out well, however. The soldiers had finished the guide's work—led the people to the border and sent them across with good wishes.

Was there any danger of secret police along the way? Yes. The Avo had been setting up check points at various railway stations—a different one each day—but the stationmasters were in constant communication with each other by telegraph, and the conductors would warn the passengers ahead of time if there was any danger.

At last, the train came. It was five cars long and was already packed. There seemed to be many travelers to foreign lands. The Feketes and the miners had to stand in an aisle. At each station, conductors and trainmen went along the platform, stopping at the doors of the cars and quietly speaking to the passengers inside: "The next station is clear. Go forward." The railway officials did this, that is, until the train reached a place called Bö, five stations before Repcevis. There, as they went from door to door, they said, "Avo at the next station. You will need documents at the next station."

Three hundred passengers got off the train, and it went lightly on. Vilmos Fekete was among the most eager to get off, for he never wanted to see the Avo again.

On the evening of September 16, 1947, two weeks after Fekete had been elected a member of Parliament, he and his wife paid a visit to his father. While they were talking, there came a knock on the door. As a kind of reflex, the Feketes went into a bedroom and shut themselves in. Fekete's father, opening the door, found two plainclothes policemen on the landing, and Fekete could hear one of them ask the father whether his son was with him. Quite calmly, the older man said that his son lived on Logodi Street, as doubtless the gentlemen already knew; perhaps the gentlemen would find his son there. The Avo men left without making a search. Fekete and his wife spent the night in the apartment of a friend.

Fekete knew why the Avo wanted him. About two months before, on July 22nd, two hundred members of the central committee of the Smallholders' Party had convened in Budapest to discuss the national election that was to be held at the end of August. Many of the delegates were worried because the Party's incumbent leaders had been going further to the Left than the membership wanted, or even knew about. The committee sent a delegation of twenty men to call on Zoltan Tildy, the President of Hungary, who was the titular head of the Smallholders' Party. The single representative from Budapest in that delegation, and its spokesman, was Vilmos Fekete, who told the President that the central committee felt that the Party's leaders had drifted from its rank and file, and that the committee was afraid the Smallholders had lost the confidence of the public and would lose the election. Tildy said he did not see things so dark; he believed the Party leaders were taking the proper course. The delegation returned to the committee, and Fekete, after reporting Tildy's words, proposed a resolution censuring the Party leaders. Some of those leaders, including several Cabinet ministers, appealed to the central committee not to take this action, and it adjourned without voting on the resolution. But the next day more than half the central committee resigned, and the dissidents formed the Hungarian Independence Party.

With only a month to go before the election, the Independents set up a slate of candidates, all of whom had the official approval of the elections board, dominated by the four principal parties—the Communists, the Smallholders, the Social Democrats, and the Peasants. Fekete and his friends began to campaign in the countryside; because Fekete had exercised his English and German during his days as a tourist guide, he was given charge of the Party's relations with the foreign press. On Election Day, the Independents discovered that the Communists were making wholesale fraudulent use of blue forms that had been issued for absentee voting—driving in cars from town to town and voting over and over. In the days after the election, the Independence Party gathered proof of these frauds, and Fekete had the evidence in his apartment.

The morning after the visit from the two Avo men, Fekete sent his wife home, instructing her to take the vote-fraud material to a friend's house. He himself went to the headquarters of the Independents. On the way, he bought a newspaper and read the surprising news that he had been arrested the night before, along with seventy others, all designated as Fascists. At the Independents' headquarters, he learned that most of the seventy had only been held overnight. One of the Party leaders telephoned the Avo on Fekete's behalf and asked what the police wanted of him. The chief of the Avo himself got on the phone, and said he simply wanted a brief interview with Fekete; he gave his personal word of honor that the man would be free within an hour.

On the strength of that promise, Fekete voluntarily went to the headquarters of the secret police, at 60 Stalin Street. The interview lasted six weeks, and Fekete was set free a little less than a year later.

That morning, the chief of the Avo told Fekete that he wanted only two things of him—admission that the Independence Party had perpetrated vote frauds during the election and that through his contacts with the foreign press Fekete and the Independence Party had received funds and instructions from outside the country. Upon hearing this, and realizing that he was in for something far more serious than an hour's chat, Fekete made three important decisions: to speak only the truth as he understood it, and never to make anything up; to shut his lips firmly rather than say anything that might be dangerous to his friends or his family; and never to speak another person's name.

As for the first question, Fekete replied to the Avo chief, it was not true that the Independents had been guilty of vote frauds; it was, in fact, the Communist Party that had perpetrated such frauds, and the Independents had proof of them. As for the second, he had been merely a press-relations officer for the Independents. He could speak a little English and German, so he had been given the job of interpreting to the foreign correspondents what the leaders of the Party said. That was all.

The chief pressed his questions, and elaborated them, and when he grew tired he turned the interview over to three subordinates, and when they grew tired they were replaced by three others, and they by three others, and this went on for three days and three nights, with an hour off now and then. Fekete clung to his three rules. Finally, this first question period ended, and Fekete was taken to a small, damp room in the cellar, which contained nothing but a bed and a bare two-hundred-watt bulb hanging from the ceiling directly above the bed. There was no window. There was a peephole in the strong door.

Fekete, who had heard about such things, understood that he was to be honored with the breakdown treatment. This form of slow torture, which was based on the empirical observation that nervous breakdowns often follow periods of severe insomnia, consisted simply of keeping the victim awake until, on the verge of a breakdown, he would be ready for even the most bizarre variants of that well-known form of therapy, confession. The brilliant bulb in Fekete's cell was kept on all the time, day and night. Whenever a passing guard, peeping through the hole in the door, saw Fekete asleep, he woke him up. From time to time, Fekete was taken upstairs for relays of questioning.

Fekete kept his sanity during the following weeks by concentrating on his three rules as if they were all that a human mind was supposed to contain. He did not let his thoughts ramble in daydreams and memories. He learned to sleep deeply for five or ten minutes at a time. He dozed standing up. As the days passed, he began to derive more and more courage from his interviews. Telling only the truth as he saw it meant that his answers never changed, and that he never gave his inquisitors openings to force inconsistencies from him. They grew angry with him now and then, and he took this as a sign that they were breaking down, not he. He grew thinner than ever, and physically weak, but his nerves and mind remained sound.

One day toward the end of his sixth week in prison, during questioning by the chief himself, who had often threatened Fekete with a thrashing if he didn't coöperate, Fekete was amazed to hear himself say, in his quiet voice, "If it would make you feel better to beat me, why don't you?" It was perfectly clear to Fekete that the moment the chief began to beat his body, Fekete would have got the better of the chief's mind. The chief did, in fact, fly into a rage, and he beat Fekete into a bloody, unconscious heap.

The next two sessions, which followed periods of recuperation, were also beatings.

The day after the third beating, the chief summoned Fekete to his office and said, "You are no longer important to us. Your party has no more influence. You understand, of course, that a powerful organ of the state cannot now simply release you and say it has made a mistake. But we are willing to change your charge from a political crime to a civil crime. You will sign a document saying you falsified a document for a friend."

Fekete said he would sign the statement and then would say in court that he had been forced to sign it—that he had been beaten just before signing it.

The chief said he wouldn't dare.

Fekete signed the statement, and in the civil tribunal on Marko Street, a few days later, he told exactly what had happened in the secret-police building. The court acquitted him.

But Fekete was in for a new shock. He was told that prisoners who had been acquitted in civil trials initiated by the secret police had to be remanded to the Avo building for their release. Fekete was taken back to 60 Stalin Street. He was not released; he was returned to his dazzling cell. Three weeks later, in December, the chief instructed him to sign a paper reiterating his previous admission and repudiating his repudiation of it. Fekete said he could not sign such lies. The chief said he would find ways to make him sign. Fekete said, "What would be the use of that when you know I would say in court all over again that you made me sign it?"

The chief then asked Fekete how he would feel about starting afresh—signing a statement to the effect that he had not actually falsified the document but that he knew it was false?

Fekete signed this statement. He was transferred to the civil prison and was held for eight months awaiting his second trial.

During this time, Elvira Fekete, who had been notified that her husband was alive but who did not know whether he would ever be freed, went to work as a bookkeeper to support her children. She was obliged to sell many of the family's belongings, including some of her husband's most precious stamps.

At Fekete's second trial, in August, he told the court that he had been forced to sign the new Avo paper. By that time, the court knew its duty better than it had back in November, and it found Fekete guilty and sentenced him to ten months in prison. Since he had already spent more time than that in jail, he was to be set free—and he finally was, after one more night in the bright room in the cellar of 60 Stalin Street.

Fekete immediately appealed his case. The appellate judges heard his appeal in 1950; they summoned and questioned a number of witnesses. It was by then all too evident that the case of this one man was unimportant to the government. The Independence Party had been wiped out. What was more, the Smallholders' Party, the Social Democratic Party, and the Peasants' Party were practically defunct. Zoltan Tildy, the former President and leader of the Smallholders, who had been so sanguine[10] before the 1947 elections, had been ousted in disgrace. There was no longer any problem about vote frauds, for Hungary had long since had its last multiple-choice election. At any rate, the appellate court—a Communist court—reversed the judgment of the civil tribunal and declared Vilmos Fekete innocent of all he had been charged with.

Such a crowd of people bound for the border had detrained at Bö that for a long time there was the utmost confusion. It was about noon. No one seemed to know what to do. Soon the crowd began to sway and stretch, and small groups split away from it, and after a while Fekete and his family and the faithful miners found themselves on a side street of the town, in a cluster of about thirty people surrounding a farm boy of seventeen or eighteen, a native of Bö. The boy told the travelers that the border was something like fourteen miles from the town, and that there was no natural frontier here; the border simply ran through open fields. It was best to cross at night; very many people were crossing the border every night. Someone asked the boy if he could lead this group of thirty to the border, and he said he could, but he thought they should wait until the early afternoon to leave Bö, since there was to be a funeral that afternoon at two and the whole village would be at it; while the funeral was in progress, it would be easy to go off unnoticed through the fields behind the houses. In the meanwhile, he said, the people—all thirty of them—were welcome to come and wait in his family's home, and he took them there. They quite filled the small farmhouse. The boy's family gave the people bread and tea and milk; they said they had been doing this every day for two weeks. When Fekete and one or two others offered money for the food, the peasants, with stoic generosity, refused to accept it, saying that the escapees might have to give money to the border guards or be turned back. The peasants changed into their best clothes for the funeral and left.

Then the boy took his charges out the back door of his house and led them across fields on which could be seen the dead stubble of autumn grains. The country was unremittingly flat.

[10] *sanguine:* hopeful

Near the villages that the party passed, and along the road, stood bare locusts and poplars. The land looked grim under a gray sky. There were occasional flurries of delicate snow. In one way, the extreme cold was a blessing: the ground was firm and not muddy.

More than half the group of which the Feketes and the miners were a part consisted of young men in their late teens and early twenties—Freedom Fighters and youths who were fleeing because they had heard that the Russians were indiscriminately deporting able-bodied men to the Soviet Union. There were six children in the group, the oldest of whom was Klara Fekete and the youngest a baby about three months old that two men carried in a blanket slung from a pole. Mostly, the people were of the laboring class; a few were white-collar workers. Nobody spoke to anyone else. The party moved in a long file, and every head was down as the walkers watched their footing on the furrowed ground.

As dusk fell, the young guide's course seemed to grow erratic, and Fekete had a feeling that the boy was lost. During the last of the light, the party approached a road that lay across their way, and saw the headlights of an automobile coming from the left. Someone in the group shouted in alarm that it might be a carful of soldiers, and everybody threw himself on the ground. Almost at that moment, the car stopped and turned off its lights. Fekete and the others lay silent on the frozen ground for what seemed a very long time—probably about a quarter of an hour, in fact—during which it became entirely dark. Finally, the people heard the car's motor start up, and it moved slowly along the road without turning on its lights. When it was certainly gone, the party moved on.

Now that it was dark, the guide passed word back along the line that there should be no smoking. He also informed his followers that some lights they could see not far away were those of a village called Szakon; he was not lost, after all. In the darkness, the walking was hard over the rough fields. Two by two, the young men began to help the women and children.

At about seven o'clock, the group approached another village, Gyaloka, which the guide said was the last big settlement before the border and was about three and a half miles from it. He led the party straight to the village, and at one of the first houses they reached he said he would go in and arrange for everybody to have a rest. Someone asked if he knew the people who lived in the house. He said that he didn't, but that there was nothing to worry about, because in the villages along the frontier every Hungarian, without exception, helped his fellow-Hungarians on their way.

The house belonged to a tradesman, who, with unemotional hospitality, led the whole party into the capacious kitchen of his home. His guests had been walking for five hours in freezing weather. The tradesman's wife prepared hot tea. The children took off their shoes and hung their socks by the kitchen stove. The guide went out in the village to get information, and in a few minutes he came back with three men and a story.

The story was that some people had driven into Gyaloka in a car about an hour before, and had told of seeing a troop of soldiers in the dusk in a field near Szakon. They had stopped their car and turned out their lights; the soldiers had deployed by the road. After dark, the driver of the car had started it up and got away safely without turning on his lights. The guide had put the villagers' minds at rest about the troop of soldiers.

The three men were peasants, about thirty years old, wearing waterproof coats and cloth caps. They said they lived in a cluster of houses right on the border and knew the countryside well; in fact, they had already taken three parties across to Austria during broad daylight that very day, and they would take this group across, too. The young man who had led the party from Bö whispered to Fekete that he would start out with the three to see that they were going in the right direction, and Fekete, remembering the story of the runaway guide, was glad to hear this. He took up a collection of about two thousand forints from the party in the kitchen and offered it to the boy, who refused it, saying he was not a professional guide; he had only been doing what he felt was right. But Fekete said that refugees would have no use for forints in Austria, and finally the boy took the money.

One of the three men now gave the party a briefing. Between here and the border was the zone of danger. Nobody was to speak from this point on, or smoke, and if anyone had to sneeze or cough, he should do it into cupped gloves, as quietly as possible. The party would walk very fast—almost run. No one should lag behind, because it would be easy to get lost.

During this speech, the Feketes' nine-year-old, Magdalena, began to weep, and afterward, when her mother tried to get her to put on her shoes and socks, the child said she didn't want to go out in the night. Couldn't they wait until the next morning? Magdalena grew increasingly frightened, and finally Fekete gave her a sedative called Legatin; a doctor whom the Feketes had met in the basement of their apartment during the fighting had given him some for the children, to tide them over the bombardments. Magdalena soon became calm.

At eight-thirty, the party started out on the final leg. The three men led the group at very nearly a dogtrot. The young man from Bö went with them for about a mile, and then, quite satisfied that the guides were trustworthy, he turned back for home. For Elvira Fekete, who was wearing heavy overshoes, the pace was trying, and before long she began to have palpitations of the heart, but she could not stop to rest. Two strong young men gripped her arms and at times almost carried her.

It took better than an hour to reach the constellation of houses at the border where the three men lived. The party halted while one of the three ran into the hamlet to find out where, at the moment, the Hungarian soldier and his Russian sidekick were who had been assigned to the few hundred yards along the frontier at this point. He discovered them supping at a tavern that stood among the houses. He ran back to the group and said that if someone would give him a hundred forints, he thought he might be able to make good use of the money. A collection was taken. The guide returned to the tavern, managed to get the Hungarian soldier aside just before the pair set out to renew their patrol, and, in return for the money, got an assurance from the soldier that he would take his Russian colleague westward for their first sweep, leaving the area to the east of the houses free for the guides and their party. The Hungarian told the guide, furthermore, that his party should not be alarmed at the sound of shooting; he had to demonstrate to his officer that he was being vigilant, and he would do a little shooting at nothing—certainly not in the direction of the party.

The guide returned and whispered the good news, and the group set out on their last dash. Soon there was indeed some shooting off to the left. The people came to a dry ditch in a flat field, and one of the guides said, in what seemed a startlingly loud voice, that the ditch marked the line between Hungary and Austria.

Upon crossing the ditch, Fekete felt empty of emotion. He consciously told himself that he ought to have grand feelings, but all he felt was weariness and cold.

The guides took the refugees a hundred yards farther and then told them they could stop to rest in perfect safety. They could smoke now. There were some lights about five hundred yards ahead, and a church tower with an illuminated clock, and Fekete, who had not owned a watch since 1945, read and announced to his wife the time of their arrival at that place: twenty minutes past ten on the evening of November 23, 1956.

One of the guides told the refugees to go straight to the lights, where they would find people waiting to help them. Again Fekete took up a collection, and the thirty people gave the three guides a thousand forints apiece. When it was all over, Fekete had about eight hundred forints left, and he was sorry he had them.

As the party approached the Austrian village of Lutzmannsburg, Fekete could see many people on the roads that converged on the place—some with children, a few carrying small suitcases. All these walking people, and Fekete's group, too, made their way to a school near the church. The school building was already crowded with something like three hundred refugees, and still more were pouring in.

In the school, the Feketes were fed a hot meal of stew, bread, and tea, and then they were taken to a classroom on the second floor, which contained a teacher's table and several straight wooden benches for scholars. On the walls were pictures of animals, a relief map of Austria, and a map of Burgenland, the province of Austria that adjoins Hungary. Within a few minutes of the Feketes' arrival, there were more than fifty refugees in the room. A party of Austrians brought in some straw-filled mattresses for the children to sleep on.

The director of the school, a brisk, short man in a black hat and coat, entered the room and made a stiff but affecting speech of welcome. The Red Cross, he said, had offered to send a harvest of food and a regiment of staff to this negligible village, to receive the refugees from Hungary, but the people of Lutzmannsburg had not wanted to accept help from the outside world; they had wanted to give their guests from Hungary food from their own cupboards and greetings with their own hands, and this they had been doing day and night for two weeks now, and they were glad that they could do it but sorry that what they did was so crude and so poor.

After the schoolmaster left the room, the exhausted refugees settled down to sleep. The room was so crowded that Fekete had to sit up on the floor with his back against a wall. Suddenly, as the room grew quiet, one of the refugees, a young man, began to sing the Hungarian national anthem, and at the sound Fekete felt all the emotions surge up in him that he had expected to feel at the moment he crossed the border. He struggled to his feet and saw men and women and children getting up all over the room, and they all stood and sang and wept together.

FOR DISCUSSION

1. This account of Vilmos Fekete is true. Therefore, John Hersey could not alter the facts to make the account more dramatic. He could, however, present the facts in whatever order he considered best suited to his purpose. What advantage can you see in his beginning his story with a description of Fekete and with Fekete's announcement, "We can go tomorrow"? What was its dramatic impact? What tone did it set for the entire article?
2. Although this is Fekete's story, what do you learn about his wife and daughters? Compare the reactions of Vilmos and Elvira Fekete as they left their apartment in Budapest for the last time. What one material thing did he hate to leave?
3. During the family's walk to the railroad station, Hersey describes the city as it appeared to them. What purpose does this description serve when Fekete retells his experiences at dinner with his

school-teacher friend at Veszprém? What touched off the revolution on October 23, 1956? Why had the brief hope of peace been an illusion? How had the people's revolt been brought to an end?

4. What, for many years, had been Fekete's rule of life? What were the personal and social consequences of this pattern of behavior? How was the rule broken when the family took refuge in the cellar of the apartment with the other tenants?
5. Describe Fekete's feelings on being able to tell his new acquaintances at Veszprém about the events in Budapest.
6. All along their journey to the border, the Feketes have unexpected experiences with strangers. What do they discover about people from these experiences; for example, about the taxi driver, truck driver, policeman, the villagers, farmers and miners?
7. The next chronological break in the story is an extended flashback in which the author tells more about Fekete's personal and political life up to 1947. What liberalizing influences had there been in his life as a youth? What was his political affiliation? How had this affiliation affected his professional career as a lawyer?
8. From the time the Feketes get off on the milk truck until they leave the train, they have uncommonly good luck. According to superstition, what brought them this luck? In reality, why are they able to get so far without being picked up by the police?
9. Fekete is no stranger to the Avo, the dreaded secret police, or to the Soviet police, as the account of his arrest shows. Why had he been arrested? How did he maintain his sanity despite the "breakdown treatment"? What personal qualities did he show in appealing his case even after he had been freed?
10. In what ways are the Feketes aided in making good their escape, even during the last dash across the border? Under what circumstances does the first outbreak of emotion among the refugees occur?

FOR COMPOSITION

1. Hersey's report touched on several points of recent history you could delve into more closely. Choose for further research one aspect of Hungary's history since 1914, especially the 1956 uprising. Write a report based on your findings.
2. Fekete says of the 1956 uprising, "This had been a young people's fight." Write an essay discussing the political opportunities and responsibilities of young people today.

The Spirit of the New Frontier

ARTHUR M. SCHLESINGER, JR.

The excitement in the White House infected the whole executive branch. A new breed had come to town, and the New Frontiersmen carried a thrust of action and purpose wherever they went. It is hard to generalize about so varied and exuberant a group; but it can be said that many shared a number of characteristics.

For one thing, like the New Dealers a quarter century earlier, they brought with them the ideas of national reconstruction and reform which had been germinating under the surface of a decade of inaction. They had stood by too long while a complaisant government had ignored the needs and potentialities of the nation—a nation whose economy was slowing down and whose population was overrunning its public facilities and services; a nation where the victims of racism and poverty lived on in sullen misery and the ideals held out by the leaders to the people were parochial and mediocre. Now the New Frontiersmen swarmed in from state governments, the universities, the foundations, the newspapers, determined to complete the unfinished business of American society. Like

Rexford G. Tugwell[1] in another age, they proposed to roll up their sleeves and make America over.

For another, they aspired, like their President, to the world of ideas as well as to the world of power. They had mostly gone to college during the intellectual ferment of the thirties. Not all by any means (despite the newspapers and the jokes) had gone to Harvard, but a good many had, though Sir Denis Brogan,[2] after a tour of inspection, remarked that the New Frontier seemed to him to bear even more the imprint of Oxford. Certainly there were Rhodes Scholars on every side—Rostow[3] and Kermit Gordon[4] in the Executive Office, Rusk,[5] Harlan Cleveland,[6] George McGhee,[7] Richard Gardner,[8] Philip Kaiser[9] and Lane Timmons[10] in State, Byron White[11] and Nicholas Katzenbach[12] in justice, Elvis Stahr[13] and Charles Hitch[14] in Defense, as well as such congressional leaders as William Fulbright[15] and Carl Albert.[16] Many of the New Frontiersmen had been college professors. (Seymour Harris has pointed out that of Kennedy's first 200 top appointments, nearly half came from backgrounds in government,

[1] *Rexford G. Tugwell:* prominent official in Franklin D. Roosevelt's first administration who advocated restoring the depression-hit economy through a reorganization of the nation's social structure

[2] *Sir Denis Brogan:* British political scientist who is an authority on American law and politics

[3] *Rostow:* Walt Rostow, Deputy Special Assistant for National Security Affairs, on the White House Staff

[4] *Kermit Gordon:* an economist and member of the Council of Economic Advisers

[5] *Rusk:* Dean Rusk, Secretary of State

[6] *Harlan Cleveland:* Assistant Secretary for International Affairs in the State Department

[7] *George McGhee:* Chairman of the Policy Planning Council and Counselor of the State Department

[8] *Richard Gardner:* Assistant Secretary of State for International Organizations

[9] *Philip Kaiser:* Ambassador to Senegal

[10] *Lane Timmons:* member of the delegation to the North Atlantic Treaty Organization and the South-East Asia Treaty Organization

[11] *Byron White:* Deputy Attorney General, and later Supreme Court Justice

[12] *Nicholas Katzenbach:* Deputy Attorney General, and later Assistant Secretary of State

[13] *Elvis Stahr:* Secretary of the Army

[14] *Charles Hitch:* Assistant Secretary of Defense

[15] *William Fulbright:* Senator from Arkansas and Chairman of the Foreign Relations Committee

[16] *Carl Albert:* Congressman from Oklahoma and Majority Whip

whether politics or public service, 18 per cent from universities and foundations and 6 per cent from the business world; the figures for Eisenhower were 42 per cent from business and 6 percent from universities and foundations.[17]) A surprisingly large number had written books. Even the Postmaster General had published a novel. They had no fear of ideas nor, though they liked to be sprightly in manner, of serious talk. One day in March, Robert Triffin, the economist, and I paid a call on Jean Monnet.[18] We asked him what he thought of the New Frontier. He said, "The thing I note most is that the conversation is recommencing. You cannot have serious government without collective discussion. I have missed that in Washington in recent years."

Another thing that defined the New Frontiersmen was the fact that many had fought in the war. Kennedy and McGovern[19] were not the only heroes in the new Washington. Lieutenant Orville Freeman[20] had had half his jaw shot off by the Japanese in the swamps of Bougainville in 1943. Lieutenant Kenneth O'Donnell[21] had flown thirty missions over Germany as a bombardier for the 8th Air Force; his plane had been shot up, and twice he had made emergency landings. Lieutenants McGeorge Bundy[22] and Mortimer Caplin[23] had been on the Normandy beaches on D-day plus 1, while a few miles away William Walton[24] was parachuted in as a correspondent, accompanying Colonel James Gavin[25] in the fighting for Ste. Mère-Église. Lieutenant Nicholas Katzenbach, a B-25 navigator, had been shot down in the Mediterranean and

[17]*Seymour E. Harris, The Economics of the Political Parties* (New York, The Macmillan Co., 1962) p. 25. Mr. Harris was Economic Adviser to the Treasury Department.

[18]*Jean Monnet:* a directing force in the formation of the European Coal and Steel community, who advocates a United States of Europe

[19]*McGovern:* George McGovern, later Senator from South Dakota, who served as head of the Food for Peace Program

[20]*Orville Freeman:* Secretary of Agriculture

[21]*Kenneth O'Donnell:* Special Assistant to the President

[22]*McGeorge Bundy:* Special Assistant for National Security Affairs on the White House Staff

[23]*Mortimer Caplin:* Commissioner of Internal Revenue

[24]*William Walton:* painter and personal friend of the Kennedys

[25]*James Gavin:* Army Deputy Chief of Staff for Plans and Research

spent two years in Italian and German prison camps; he twice escaped and was twice recaptured. Lieutenant Commander Douglas Dillon[26] had been under Kamikaze attack in Lingayen Gulf and had flown a dozen combat patrol missions. Captain Roger Hilsman[27] had led a band of native guerrillas behind Japanese lines in Burma. Lieutenant Edward Day[28] had served on a submarine chaser in the Solomons and a destroyer escort in the Atlantic. Lieutenant Byron White had fought in the Solomons. Ensign Pierre Salinger[29] had been decorated for a dangerous rescue in the middle of a typhoon from his subchaser off Okinawa. Major Dean Rusk had been a staff officer in the China-Burma-India theater. Major Arthur Goldberg[30] had organized labor espionage for the OSS in Europe. Lieutenant Stewart Udall[31] had served in the Air Force. Lieutenants Paul Fay[32] and James Reed[33] were veterans of the PT-boat war in the Pacific.

The war experience helped give the New Frontier generation its casual and laconic[34] tone, its grim, puncturing humor and its mistrust of evangelism. It accounted in particular, I think, for the differences in style between the New Frontiersmen and the New Dealers. The New Dealers were incorrigible philosophizers—"chain talkers," someone had sourly called them thirty years before—and the New Deal had a distinctive and rather moralistic rhetoric. The men of the thirties used to invoke 'the people,' their ultimate wisdom and the importance of doing things for them in a way quite alien to the New Frontier. The mood of the new Washington was more to do things because they were rational and necessary than because they were just and right, though this should not be exag-

[26]*Douglas Dillon:* Secretary of the Treasury

[27]*Roger Hilsman:* the State Department's Director of Intelligence and Research

[28]*Edward Day:* Postmaster General

[29]*Pierre Salinger:* Presidential Press Secretary

[30]*Arthur Goldberg:* Secretary of Labor; later Supreme Court Justice and Ambassador to the United Nations

[31]*Stewart Udall:* Secretary of the Interior

[32]*Paul Fay:* Under Secretary of the Navy

[33]*James Reed:* Assistant Secretary for Law Enforcement in the Treasury Department

[34]*laconic:* using few words

gerated. In the thirties idealism was sometimes declared, even when it did not exist; in the sixties, it was sometimes deprecated, even when it was the dominant motive.

The New Frontiersmen had another common characteristic: versatility. They would try anything. Most had some profession or skill to which they could always return; but ordinarily they used it as a springboard for general meddling. Kenneth Galbraith was an economist who, as ambassador to India, reviewed novels for *The New Yorker* and wrote a series of pseudonymous[35] satiric skits for *Esquire*. Bill Walton was a newspaperman turned abstract painter. This was especially true in the White House itself. Where Eisenhower had wanted a staff with clearly defined functions, Kennedy resisted pressures toward specialization; he wanted a group of all-purpose men to whom he could toss anything. It seemed to me that in many ways Dick Goodwin,[36] though younger than the average, was the archetypal[37] New Frontiersman. His two years in the Army had been too late for the war, even too late for Korea. But he was the supreme generalist who could turn from Latin America to saving the Nile monuments at Abu Simbel, from civil rights to planning the White House dinner for the Nobel Prize winners, from composing a parody of Norman Mailer[38] to drafting a piece of legislation, from lunching with a Supreme Court Justice to dining with Jean Seberg[39]—and at the same time retain an unquenchable spirit of sardonic liberalism and an unceasing drive to get things done.

Not everyone liked the new people. Washington never had. "A plague of young lawyers settled on Washington," one observer had said of the New Dealers. ". . . They floated airily into offices, took desks, asked for papers and found no end of things to be busy about. I never found out why they came, what they did or why they left." Even Learned Hand[40] complained in

[35]*pseudonymous:* bearing an invented name
[36]*Dick Goodwin:* speech writer and Special Assistant to the President
[37]*archetypal:* original model
[38]*Norman Mailer:* American novelist who wrote several articles on the Kennedys for popular magazines
[39]*Jean Seberg:* movie actress
[40]*Learned Hand:* American judge who was acclaimed as the greatest American jurist of the mid-twentieth century

1934 that they were "so conceited, so insensitive, so arrogant." Old-timers felt the same resentments in March 1961. One could not deny a sense of New Frontier autointoxication; one felt it oneself. The pleasures of power, so long untasted, were now being happily devoured – the chauffeur-driven limousines, the special telephones, the top secret documents, the personal aides, the meetings in the Cabinet Room, the calls from the President. Merriman Smith,[41] who had seen many administrations come and go, wrote about what he called the New People: "hot-eyed, curious but unconcerned with protocol, and yeasty with shocking ideas . . . they also have their moments of shortsightedness, bias, prejudice and needlessly argumentative verbosity." The verbosity,[42] I have suggested, was marked only in comparison with the muteness of the Eisenhower days; but the rest was true enough, especially in these first heady weeks.

The currents of vitality radiated out of the White House, flowed through the government and created a sense of vast possibility. The very idea of the new President taking command as tranquilly and naturally as if his whole life had prepared him for it could not but stimulate a flood of buoyant optimism. The Presidency was suddenly the center of action: in the first three months, thirty-nine messages and letters to Congress calling for legislation, ten prominent foreign visitors (including Macmillan,[43] Adenauer[44] and Nkrumah[45]), nine press conferences, new leadership in the regulatory agencies and such dramatic beginnings as the Alliance for Progress and the Peace Corps. Above all, Kennedy held out such promise of hope. Intelligence at last was being applied to public affairs. Euphoria reigned; we thought for a moment that the world was plastic and the future unlimited.

Yet I don't suppose we really thought this. At bottom we knew how intractable the world was – the poverty and disorder of Latin America, the insoluble conflict in Laos, the bitter

[41]*Merriman Smith:* UPI White House correspondent since 1941
[42]*verbosity:* excessive wordiness
[43]*Macmillan:* Harold Macmillan, Prime Minister of England
[44]*Adenauer:* Konrad Adenauer, Chancellor of Germany
[45]*Nkrumah:* Kwame Nkrumah, Prime Minister and later President of Ghana

war in Vietnam, the murky turbulence of Africa, the problems of discrimination and unemployment in our own country, the continuing hostility of Russia and China. The President knew better than anyone how hard his life was to be. Though he incited the euphoria, he did so involuntarily, for he did not share it himself. I never heard him now use the phrase 'New Frontier'; I think he regarded it with some embarrassment as a temporary capitulation to rhetoric. Still even Kennedy, the ironist and skeptic, had an embarrassed confidence in his luck and in these weeks may have permitted himself moments of optimism. In any case, he knew the supreme importance of a first impression and was determined to create a picture of drive, purpose and hope.

I had gone to the White House for dinner a few nights before leaving for South America. It was a small party for Sam Rayburn[46] and his sister. The Vice-President and his wife were there, the Fulbrights, the Arthur Krocks,[47] Mrs. Nicholas Longworth[48] and myself. The historian looking around the table could not but be impressed by the continuities of our national life—Alice Roosevelt Longworth, who had lived in this house sixty years before; Rayburn, who had come to Congress fifty years ago; Krock, who had covered Washington for forty years; Johnson, who had drawn his inspiration from the second Roosevelt; Fulbright, who had served the country so well since the Second World War; and then Kennedy, younger than any of them, courteously enjoying their stories, soliciting their counsel, and all the while preserving his easy domination of the evening and seeming almost to pull the threads of history together in his hands.

[46] *Sam Rayburn:* Congressman from Texas and Speaker of the House
[47] *Arthur Krock:* newspaper columnist
[48] *Mrs. Nicholas Longworth:* daughter of Theodore Roosevelt

FOR DISCUSSION

1. Why would war experiences produce a "casual and laconic tone," a "grim, puncturing humor," and a "mistrust of evangelism"?

Would the kind of war Ernie Pyle describes in a preceding selection have produced these reactions? What kind of experience might produce opposite effects?

2. Summarize or describe the typical New Frontiersman. What are his dominant traits? What are his virtues and flaws?
3. This selection begins by emphasizing the newness and difference of the New Frontier in the first weeks of the Kennedy administration. What does Schlesinger emphasize at the end of his selection? Do you think he accidentally contradicts himself, or is this apparent contradiction deliberately inserted? What could he have hoped to gain from such a contradiction?
4. Schlesinger has been particularly praised for his prose style. What are the major characteristics of the Schlesinger style? How are the sentences constructed? What kind of structure do you find in the whole passage? What keeps the selection from reading like dull, dry history?

FOR COMPOSITION

Describe the attitudes, mood, and spirit of a group of people you know (or knew) well. You might choose a group of campers, a club, a church or school group at some particular time, or the neighbors you live near. Follow Schlesinger's excellent example and alternate your broad generalizations with a variety of specific examples and proofs.

THE INDIVIDUAL EXPERIENCE

KNIGHT AND EDWARDS

From the beginning, American literature has been filled with personal writings of exceptional merit. The category of the personal essay is broad, and includes reflections, recollections, observations, and autobiography. Perhaps it is easiest to think of the personal essay as a work which primarily describes the writer himself, or some aspect of his thought and individual experience. Thus, the category can include a statement of philosophy or belief, such as Jonathan Edwards' sermons or Ralph Waldo Emerson's orations; an account of travels or of life in unusual circumstances, such as Sarah Kemble Knight's entries in her *Journal*, describing a trip from Boston to New York in 1704, or Henry David Thoreau's *Walden*; reflections and observations as one finds them in the letters and notations of Benjamin Franklin and Thomas Jefferson; and autobiography, as exemplified in writings of Mark Twain, Henry Adams, Ernest Hemingway, and James Baldwin.

The category of the personal essay is important to Americans; for the roots of the American personal essay are in the sermon—the first polished American art form—and in the "educational" travel literature which was popular before the American Revolution and continued to be in great demand throughout the nineteenth century. These two particular types of personal statement reveal much about American history and culture. Early and excellent examples of each form are to be found in Jonathan Edwards' fiery sermons and in Sarah Kemble Knight's delightful *Journal*. For contrast, it is difficult to imagine two personalities more different than Edwards and Mrs. Knight.

The brilliant theologian and orator, Jonathan Edwards, has come to represent the typical Calvinist minister, particularly because of his famous sermon, "Sinners in the Hands of an Angry God," part of which follows. With its fierce and accusing tone, this sermon spares no listener, warning all impartially of the Hell-flames licking at their heels. Edwards assumes the total depravity of man and his complete worthlessness in the sight of God. This viewpoint is evident in his famous spider image, in which man, like a spider, appears abhorrent and repulsive. Edwards assures his audience that neither prudence nor good works can keep man from Hell, because no virtue is enough to balance his corrupt soul.

Perhaps the most interesting thing about Edwards' sermon is the series of violent images he uses to describe God. God is compared to black clouds, a dreadful storm, thunder, rough winds, a whirlwind, a flood or torrential river, a bow and an arrow. Particularly arresting is the last image, for the arrow thirsts actively for human blood. The most psychologically devastating image, however, is the one with which Edwards ends this part of his sermon: here God is pictured as a hand, holding above the flames the fragile thread to which the man-spider desperately clings. This view of human life was intended to leave the listener crushed and submissive, overwhelmed by his own vulnerability.

Mrs. Knight is Edwards' antithesis. Though she lived and wrote half a century before Edwards, she seems more modern because she is thoroughly, contentedly of this world. She is rather pleased with her own superior social position, and complains, in the journal she kept of her travels during 1704-

1705, that she finds Connecticut Yankees "a little too much Independent in their principalls. . . ." Her condescension to all whom she saw as country bumpkins, her stereotyping of the farm folk, is unmistakable but entertaining; for Mrs. Knight has a sharp eye, a lively style, and an irrepressible sense of humor.

She enjoys her comforts. A remarkable proportion of her diary describes the meals she eats and the facilities she shares. Trade interests her because the goods one buys interest her.

But above all, Mrs. Knight is a Bostonian and proud of it. She views all other communities from Boston to New York with tolerance, secure in the knowledge that none of them—not even New York itself—will fully measure up to her home. And as befits a woman of her stature, force of character, and accomplishments, she finds on returning to Boston that she is still well-loved and warmly greeted by her family and friends, once again secure in a secure universe which is untroubled by passionate excesses of feeling. At the end of her journey, she offers God the polite thanks for her safe return which one would expect of a woman with good manners.

Mrs. Knight is the other side of that New England Yankee, soon to appear as the prototype of the American. She is confident of herself and troubled only when her inferiors refuse to give her proper due. She chafes at social mores which are too rigid to allow a little pleasant amusement among the young people. She loathes provinciality, especially the kind that assumes strangers will know where "uncle Sams Lott" is. She is happy.

A Journey from Boston to New York

SARAH KEMBLE KNIGHT

Saturday, Oct. 7th, wee sett out early in the Morning, and being something unaquainted with the way, having ask't it of some wee mett, they told us wee must Ride a mile or two and turne down a Lane on the Right hand; and by their Direction wee Rode on but not Yet comeing to the turning, we mett a Young fellow and ask't him how farr it was to the Lane which turn'd down toward Guilford. Hee said wee must Ride a little further, and turn down by the Corner of uncle Sams Lott. My Guide vented his Spleen at the Lubber; and we soon after came into the Rhode, and keeping still on, without any thing further Remarkabell, about two a clock afternoon we arrived at New Haven, where I was received with all Posible Respects and civility. Here I discharged Mr. Wheeler with a reward to his satisfaction, and took some time to rest after so long and toilsome a Journey; And Inform'd myselfe of the manners and customs of the place, and at the same time employed myselfe in the afair I went there upon.

They are Govern'd by the same Laws as wee in Boston, (or little differing,) thr'out this whole Colony of Connecticot, And much the same way of Church Government, and many of them good, Sociable people, and I hope Religious too: but a little too much Independant in their principalls, and, as I have been told, were formerly in their Zeal very Riggid in their Administrations towards such as their Lawes made Offenders, even to a harmless Kiss or Innocent merriment among Young people. Whipping being a frequent and counted an easy Punishment, about which, as other Crimes, the Judges were absolute in their Sentances....

They give the title of merchant to every trader; who Rate their Goods according to the time and spetia[1] they pay in: viz. Pay, mony, Pay as mony, and trusting. *Pay* is Grain, Pork, Beef, &c. at the prices sett by the General Court that Year; *mony* is pieces of Eight, Ryalls, or Boston or Bay shillings (as they call them,) or Good hard money, as sometimes silver coin is termed by them; also Wampom, vizt. Indian beads which serves for change. *Pay as mony* is provisions, as aforesaid one Third cheaper then as the Assembly or General Court sets it; and *Trust* as they and the merchant agree for time.

Now, when the buyer comes to ask for a comodity, sometimes before the merchant answers that he has it, he sais, *is Your pay redy?* Perhaps the Chap Reply's Yes: what do You pay in? say's the merchant. The buyer having answered, then the price is set; as suppose he wants a sixpenny knife, in pay it is 12d—in pay as money eight pence, and hard money its own price, viz. 6d. It seems a very Intricate way of trade and what Lex Mercatoria[2] had not thought of.

Being at a merchants house, in come a tall country fellow, with his alfogeos[3] full of Tobacco; for they seldom Loose their Cudd, but keep Chewing and Spitting as long as they'r eyes are open,—he advanc't to the midle of the Room, makes an Awkward Nodd, and spitting a Large deal of Aromatick Tincture, he gave a scrape with his shovel like shoo, leaving a small shovel full of dirt on the floor, made a full stop, Hugging his own pretty Body with his hands under his arms, Stood staring rown'd him, like a Catt let out of a Baskett. At last, like the creature Balaam Rode on,[4] he opened his mouth and said:

[1] *spetia:* paper money

[2] *Lex Mercatoria:* the law of merchants

[3] *alfogeos:* cheeks

[4] *creature . . . on:* Numbers XXII: 21-33. Balaam's ass saw an angel of the Lord and refused to carry Balaam any further. Balaam struck the ass and the ass asked why.

have You any Ribinen for Hatbands to sell I pray? The Questions and Answers about the pay being past, the Ribin is bro't and opened. Bumpkin Simpers, cryes its confounded Gay I vow; and beckning to the door, in comes Jone Tawdry dropping about 50 curtsees, and stands by him: hee shows her the Ribin. *Law, You,* sais shee, *its right Gent,*[5] do You, take it, *tis dreadfull pretty.* Then she enquires, *have you any hood silk I pray?* which being brought and bought, *Have You any thred silk to sew it with* says shee, which being accommodated with they Departed. They Generaly stand after they come in a great while speachless, and sometimes dont say a word till they are askt what they want, which I impute to the Awe they stand in of the merchants, who they are constantly almost Indebted too; and must take what they bring without Liberty to choose for themselves; but they serve them as well, making the merchants stay long enough for their pay.

We may Observe here the great necessity and bennifitt both of Education and Conversation; for these people have as Large a portion of mother witt, and sometimes a Larger, than those who have bin brought up in Citties; But for want of emprovements, Render themselves almost Ridiculos, as above. I should be glad if they would leave such follies, and am sure all that Love Clean Houses (at least) would be glad on't too.

They are generaly very plain in their dress, throuout all the Colony, as I saw, and follow one another in their modes; that You may know where they belong, especially the women, meet them where you will.

Their Chief Red Letter day is St. Election, which is annually Observed according to Charter, to choose their Govenr: a blessing they can never be thankfull enough for, as they will find, if ever it be their hard fortune to loose it.[6] The present Govenor in Conecticott is the Honorable John Winthrop Esq. A Gentleman of an Ancient and Honourable Family, whose Father was Govenor here sometime before, and his Grand father had bin Govr of the Massachusetts. This gentleman is a very curteous and afable person, much Given to Hospitality,

[5] *Gent:* elegant

[6] *to choose . . . to loose it:* The people of Massachusetts were discontented at this time because their governor was appointed by the English King.

and has by his Good services Gain'd the affections of the people as much as any who had bin before him in that post.

Decr. 6th. Being by this time well Recruited and rested after my Journy, my business lying unfinished by some concerns at New York depending thereupon, my Kinsman, Mr. Thomas Trowbridge of New Haven, must needs take a Journy there before it could be accomplished, I resolved to go there in company with him, and a man of the town which I engaged to wait on[7] me there. Accordingly, Dec. 6th we set out from New Haven, and about 11 same morning came to Stratford ferry; which crossing, about two miles on the other side Baited our horses and would have eat a morsell ourselves, But the Pumpkin and Indian mixt Bred had such an Aspect, and the Bare-legg'd Punch[8] so awkerd or rather Awfull a sound, that we left both, and proceeded forward, and about seven at night come to Fairfield, where we met with good entertainment and Lodg'd; and early next morning set forward to Norowalk, from its halfe Indian name *Northwalk*, when about 12 at noon we arrived, and Had a Dinner of Fryed Venison, very savoury. Landlady wanting some pepper in the seasoning, bid the Girl hand her the spice in the little *Gay* cupp on the shelfe. From hence we Hasted towards Rye, walking and Leading our Horses neer a mile together, up a prodigios high Hill; and so Riding till about nine at night, and there arrived and took up our Lodgings at an ordinary, which a French family kept. Here being very hungry, I desired a fricasee, which the Frenchman undertakeing, mannaged so contrary to my notion of Cookery, that I hastned to Bed superless; And being shewd the way up a pair of stairs which had such a narrow passage that I had almost stopt by the Bulk of my Body; But arriving at my apartment found it to be a little Lento[9] Chamber furnisht amongst other Rubbish with a High Bedd and a Low one, a Long Table, a Bench and a Bottomless chair,—Little Miss went to scratch up my Kennell[10] which Russelled as if shee'd bin in the Barn amongst the Husks, and supose such was the con-

[7] *wait on:* accompany
[8] *Bare-legg'd Punch:* apparently a local name for some kind of drink
[9] *Lento:* lean-to
[10] *scratch up my Kennell:* make up my bed

tents of the tickin—nevertheless being exceeding weary, down I laid my poor Carkes (never more tired) and found my Covering as scanty as my Bed was hard. Annon I heard another Russelling noise in The Room—called to know the matter—Little miss said shee was making a bed for the men; who, when they were in Bed, complained their leggs lay out of it by reason of its shortness—my poor bones complained bitterly not being used to such Lodgings, and so did the man who was with us; and poor I made but one Grone, which was from the time I went to bed to the time I Riss, which was about three in the morning, Setting up by the Fire till Light, and having discharged our ordinary which was as dear as if we had had far Better fare—wee took our leave of Monsier and about seven in the morn come to New Rochell a french town, where we had a good Breakfast. And in the strength of that about an how'r before sunsett got to York. Here I applyd myself to Mr. Burroughs, a merchant to whom I was recommended by my Kinsman Capt. Prout, and received great Civilities from him and his spouse, who were now both Deaf but very agreeable in their Conversation, Diverting me with pleasant stories of their knowledge in Brittan from whence they both come. . . .

The Cittie of New York is a pleasant, well compacted place, situated on a Commodius River which is a fine harbour for shipping. The Buildings Brick Generaly, very stately and high, though not altogether like ours in Boston. The Bricks in some of the Houses are of divers Coullers and laid in Checkers, being glazed look very agreeable. The inside of them are neat to admiration, the wooden work, for only the walls are plasterd, and the Sumers and Gist[11] are plained and kept very white scowr'd as so is all the partitions if made of Bords. The fire places have no Jambs (as ours have) But the Backs run flush with the walls, and the Hearth is of Tyles and is as farr out into the Room at the Ends as before the fire, which is Generally Five foot in the Low'r rooms, and the peice over where the mantle tree should be is made as ours with Joyners work, and as I supose is fasten'd to iron rodds inside. The House where the Vendue[12] was, had Chimney Corners like ours, and

[11] *Sumers and Gist:* supporting beams and joists
[12] *Vendue:* auction

they and the hearths were laid with the finest tile that I ever see, and the stair cases laid all with white tile which is ever clean, and so are the walls of the Kitchen which had a Brick floor. They were making Great preparations to Receive their Govenor, Lord Cornbury from the Jerseys, and for that end raised the militia to Gard him on shore to the fort. . . .

January 6th. Being now well Recruited and fitt for business I discoursed the persons I was concerned with, that we might finnish in order to my return to Boston. They delayd as they had hitherto done hoping to tire my Patience. But I was resolute to stay and see an End of the matter let it be never so much to my disadvantage—So January 9th they come again and promise the Wednesday following to go through with the distribution of the Estate which they delayed till Thursday and then come with new amusements. But at length by the mediation of that holy good Gentleman, the Rev. Mr. James Pierpont, the minister of New Haven, and with the advice and assistance of other our Good friends we come to an accommodation and distribution, which having finished though not till February, the man that waited on me to York taking charge of me I sit out for Boston. We went from New Haven upon the ice (the ferry being not passable thereby) and the Rev. Mr. Pierpont with Madam Prout Cuzin Trowbridge and divers others were taking leave wee went onward without anything Remarkabl till wee come to New London and Lodged again at Mr. Saltonstalls—and here I dismist my Guide, and my Generos entertainer provided me Mr. Samuel Rogers of that place to go home with me—I stayed a day here Longer than I intended by the Commands of the Honorable Governor Winthrop to stay and take a supper with him whose wonderful civility I may not omitt. The next morning I Crossed the Ferry to Groton, having had the Honor of the Company, of Madam Livingston (who is the Govenors Daughter) and Mary Christophers and divers others to the boat—And that night Lodged at Stonington and had Rost Beef and pumpkin sause for supper. The next night at Haven's and had Rost fowle, and the next day wee come to a river which by Reason of The Freshetts coming down was swell'd so high wee feard it impassable and the rapid stream was very terryfying—However we must over and that in a small Cannoo. Mr. Rogers assuring me of his good Conduct,[13] I after a stay of near an how'r on the shore for consultation went into the Cannoo, and Mr. Rogers paddled about 100 yards up the Creek by the shore side, turned into the swift stream and dexterously steering her in a moment wee come to the other side as swiftly passing as an arrow shott out of the Bow by a strong arm. I staid on the shore till Hee returned to fetch our horses, which he caused to swim over himself bringing the furniture in the Cannoo. But it is past my skill to express the Exceeding fright all their transactions formed in me. Wee were now in the colony of the Massachusetts and taking Lodgings at the first Inn we come too had a pretty difficult passage the next day which was the second of March by reason of the sloughy ways then thawed by the Sunn. Here I mett Capt. John Richards of Boston who was going home, So being very glad of his Company we Rode something harder than hitherto, and missing my way in going up a very steep Hill, my horse dropt down under me as Dead; this new surprize no little hurt me meeting it Just at the Entrance into Dedham from whence we intended to reach home that night. But was now obliged to gett another Hors there and leave my own, resolving for Boston that night if possible. But in going over the Causeway at Dedham the Bridge being overflowed by the high waters comming down I very narrowly escaped falling over into the river Hors and all which twas almost a miracle I did not—now it grew late in the afternoon and the people having very much discouraged us about the sloughy way which they said wee should find very difficult and hazardous it so wrought on mee being tired and dispirited and disapointed of my desires of going home that I agreed to Lodg there that night which wee did at the house of one Draper, and the next day being March 3d wee got safe home to Boston, where I found my aged and tender mother and my Dear and only Child in good health with open arms redy to receive me, and my kind relations and friends flocking in to welcome mee and hear the story of my transactions and travails I having this day bin five months from home and now I

[13]*Conduct:* ability

cannot fully express my Joy and Satisfaction. But desire sincearly to adore my Great Benefactor for thus graciously carying forth and returning in safety his unworthy handmaid.

FOR DISCUSSION

1. When Mrs. Knight made her journey, New England was developing rapidly, but much of it was still backwoods and farm country. What evidence does she give of the problems of the traveler and the differences between country and city living? What is her attitude towards the "tall country fellow" who enters the merchant's shop?
2. Diaries, which are usually not intended for publication, must be approached as personal rather than public literature. Which parts of this diary tell us more about Mrs. Knight herself than about the places she describes? What kind of person was she?

FOR COMPOSITION

Rewrite the first paragraph from the diary as Mrs. Knight would probably have written it today. In addition to changing the spelling and punctuation, you will need to change the order of some of the words—even the words themselves when they are archaic (no longer in common use). When in doubt about the meaning of a word or phrase, consult a dictionary. As you discuss your "modern versions" in class, point out the ways in which Mrs. Knight's is different.

Sinners in the Hands of an Angry God

JONATHAN EDWARDS

Your wickedness makes you as it were heavy as lead, and to tend downwards with great weight and pressure towards hell; and if God should let you go, you would immediately sink and swiftly descend and plunge into the bottomless gulf, and your healthy constitution, and your own care and prudence, and best contrivance, and all your righteousness, would have no more influence to uphold you and keep you out of hell, than a spider's web would have to stop a fallen rock. Were it not for the sovereign pleasure of God, the earth would not bear you one moment; for you are a burden to it; the creation groans with you; the creature is made subject to the bondage of your corruption, not willingly; the sun does not willingly shine upon you to give you light to serve sin and Satan; the earth does not willingly yield her increase to satisfy your lusts; nor is it willingly a stage for your wickedness to be acted upon; the air does not willingly serve you for breath to maintain the flame of life in your vitals, while you spend your life in the service of God's enemies. God's creatures are good, and were made for men to serve God with, and do not willingly subserve to any other purpose, and groan when they are abused to purposes so directly contrary to their nature and end. And the world would spew[1] you out, were it not for the sovereign hand of him who hath subjected it in hope. There are black clouds of God's wrath now hanging directly over your heads, full of the dreadful storm, and big with thunder; and were it not for the restraining hand of God, it would immediately burst forth upon you. The sovereign pleasure of God, for the present, stays his rough wind; otherwise it would come with fury, and your destruction would come like a whirlwind, and you would be like the chaff of the summer threshing floor.

The wrath of God is like great waters that are dammed for the present; they increase more and more, and rise higher and higher, till an outlet is given; and the longer the stream is stopped, the more rapid and mighty is its course, when once it is let loose. It is true, that judgment against your evil works has not been executed hitherto; the floods of God's vengeance have been withheld; but your guilt in the mean time is constantly increasing, and you are every day treasuring up more wrath; the waters are constantly rising, and waxing more and more mighty; and there is nothing but the mere pleasure of God, that holds the waters back, that are unwilling to be stopped, and press hard to go forward. If God should only withdraw his hand from the flood-gate, it would immediately fly open, and the fiery floods of the fierceness and wrath of God, would rush forth with inconceivable fury, and would come upon you with omnipotent power; and if your strength were ten thousand times greater than it is, yea, ten thousand times greater than the strength of the stoutest, sturdiest devil in hell, it would be nothing to withstand or endure it.

The bow of God's wrath is bent, and the arrow made ready on the string, and justice bends the arrow at your heart, and strains the bow, and it is nothing but the mere pleasure of God, and that of an angry God, without any promise or obligation at all, that keeps the arrow one moment from being made drunk with your blood. Thus all you that never passed under a great change of heart, by the mighty power of the Spirit of God upon your souls; all you that were never born again, and made new creatures, and raised from being dead in sin, to a state of

[1] *spew:* spit

new, and before altogether unexperienced light and life, are in the hands of an angry God. However you may have reformed your life in many things, and may have had religious affections, and may keep up a form of religion in your families and closets, and in the house of God, it is nothing but his mere pleasure that keeps you from being this moment swallowed up in everlasting destruction. However unconvinced you may now be of the truth of what you hear, by and by you will be fully convinced of it. Those that are gone from being in the like circumstances with you, see that it was so with them; for destruction came suddenly upon most of them; when they expected nothing of it, and while they were saying, Peace and safety: now they see, that those things on which they depended for peace and safety, were nothing but thin air and empty shadows.

The God that holds you over the pit of hell, much as one holds a spider, or some loathsome insect over the fire, abhors you, and is dreadfully provoked: his wrath towards you burns like fire; he looks upon you as worthy of nothing else, but to be cast into the fire; he is of purer eyes than to bear to have you in his sight; you are ten thousand times more abominable in his eyes, than the most hateful venomous serpent is in ours. You have offended him infinitely more than ever a stubborn rebel did his prince; and yet it is nothing but his hand that holds you from falling into the fire every moment. It is to be ascribed to nothing else, that you did not go to hell the last night; that you was suffered to awake again in this world, after you closed your eyes to sleep. And there is no other reason to be given, why you have not dropped into hell since you arose in the morning, but that God's hand has held you up. There is no other reason to be given why you have not gone to hell, since you have sat here in the house of God, provoking his pure eyes by your sinful wicked manner of attending his solemn worship. Yea, there is nothing else that is to be given as a reason why you do not this very moment drop down into hell.

O sinner! Consider the fearful danger you are in: it is a great furnace of wrath, a wide and bottomless pit, full of the fire of wrath, that you are held over in the hand of that God, whose wrath is provoked and incensed as much against you, as against many of the damned in hell. You hang by a slender thread, with the flames of divine wrath flashing about it, and ready every moment to singe it, and burn it asunder; and you have no interest in any Mediator, and nothing to lay hold of to save yourself, nothing to keep off the flames of wrath, nothing of your own, nothing that you ever have done, nothing that you can do, to induce God to spare you one moment. . . .

FOR DISCUSSION

1. What is Jonathan Edwards' concept of the relationship between man and God? What does Edwards mean by being "born again, and made new creatures"?
2. In order to appeal to his listeners' emotions, Edwards uses several traditional literary devices. Note, for example, the simile in the first line. What idea does it convey? Point out other similes and metaphors.
3. Another literary device is the image—a word or phrase that creates a picture in the mind of the reader; for example, "the floods of God's vengeance." Make a list of the major images in the order in which they appear in the sermon. In your opinion, do they build to a dramatic climax? Explain.

FRANKLIN AND JEFFERSON

In eighteenth-century America, as well as in England, cultured men assumed that their personal letters might be preserved. They therefore took great pains to insure their literary merit. Many writers seem to have spent as much time polishing the prose of their correspondence as they did their writing for immediate publication. Thus, the personal letter became a form of the personal essay. In formal letter writing, as in other creative fields, the personality of the writer influences what is written. Thus the letters of Thomas Jefferson and Benjamin Franklin stand in pleasant contrast, each in its way a tribute to the individual experience of the writer.

In the selections which follow, Jefferson seems the more formal of the two. His letter bears witness to his belief in balance, discipline, and order. His whole discussion of education is testimony to the fact that he finds human life an eminently reasonable thing. He assumes that the best preparation for life is to develop reason and absorb knowledge; for by *knowing* enough, the human can always reason his way to a proper solution of problems he is likely to encounter. Jefferson is quite conscious of his role as gentleman: and a gentleman obviously knows a little about all things and can discourse on them with intelligence.

Franklin appears quite the gallant in two of the letters reprinted here. He loves the ladies and enjoys their company—as they obviously enjoy his. His letters to them suggest a playful and comfortable relationship, and also convey the gently ironic humor of his observations about human foibles. In the letter to Lord Howe, however, we see Benjamin Franklin the statesman. He is warm and mannerly, but ruthlessly firm about the principles in which he believes. Perhaps Franklin is at his best in such a letter: the document shows beautifully how a man can be high-principled without being self-righteous, and patriotic without being impolite.

Franklin's prose in *Poor Richard's Almanac,* from which the Preface and Proverbs are taken, is somewhat different. Here he voices the homely observations full of common sense which the farmers and townsmen of his time would most appreciate. Neither the audience nor the speaker needs much formal education, for Richard is the true democratic hero—poor in possessions, but rich in native intelligence. His humble station in no way impedes his worth. And the aptness of his observations demonstrates that he need consider himself inferior to no man. Poor Richard was just the kind of spokesman which the colonies needed to increase their self-respect. He represented all the good traits they desired and hoped were present in American citizens.

From Poor Richard's Almanac

A Preface and Selected Proverbs

BENJAMIN FRANKLIN

Courteous Readers,

Your kind and charitable Assistance last Year, in purchasing so large an Impression[1] of my Almanacks, has made my Circumstances much more easy in the World, and requiries my grateful Acknowledgment. My Wife has been enabled to get a Pot of her own, and is no longer oblig'd to borrow one from a Neighbour; nor have we ever since been without something of our own to put in it. She has also got a pair of Shoes, two new Shifts,[2] and a new warm Petticoat; and for my part, I have bought a second-hand Coat, so good that I am now not asham'd to go to Town or be seen there. These Things have render'd her Temper so much more pacific than it us'd to be, that I may say, I have slept more, and more quietly within this last Year, than in the three foregoing Years put together. Accept my hearty Thanks therefor, and my sincere Wishes for your Health and Prosperity.

[1] *Impression:* printing
[2] *Shifts:* chemises or undergarments

"Fish and visitors smell in three days."
"There'll be sleeping enough in the grave."
"If you would have your business done, go; if not, send."
"Be ashamed to catch yourself idle."
"The eye of the master will do more work than both his hands."
"He does not possess wealth; it possesses him."
"Want of care does us more damage than want of knowledge."
"A fat kitchen makes a lean will."
"Glass, china, and reputation are easily cracked and never well mended."
"Many have been ruined by buying good pennyworths."
"The worst wheel of the cart makes the most noise."
"If you would know the value of money, go and try to borrow some."
"Pride is as loud a beggar as want and a great deal more saucy."
" 'Tis hard for an empty bag to stand upright."
"If you will not hear Reason she'll surely rap your knuckles."
"Experience keeps a dear school, but fools will learn in no other."
"Necessity never made a good bargain."
"Three may keep a secret if two of them are dead."
"At twenty years the will reigns; at thirty, the wit; at forty, the judgment."

FOR DISCUSSION

1. From 1732 to 1757, Franklin published annually his *Poor Richard's Almanac*, which contained not only maxims devoted to encouraging the virtues of diligence, thrift, and independence, but also comments on subjects as widely different as "New Fashions" and "Signs of a Tempest." The supposed author, Poor Richard, was a fictional character—the first in America to win recognition in the colonies and abroad. From the Preface addressed to "Courteous Readers," what impression do you gain of Poor Richard? Why would the subscribers to the *Almanac* find this Preface amusing?

2. As you discuss the proverbs, point out what virtues each encourages, and why the way each proverb is expressed is so effective. How would you know they had not been written by one of the early colonists?

FOR COMPOSITION

1. Select one of the proverbs as the subject for a short informal essay. As you express what you think and feel about the idea stated in the proverb, also reveal *why* you think and feel that way. You can, of course, list several reasons, but a more interesting method would be to use some incident as an example – something that happened to you or that you heard about or read in a book.
2. Bring to class five other proverbs, including some you have written yourself.

Three Letters

BENJAMIN FRANKLIN

The Ephemera

An Emblem of Human Life

You may remember, my dear friend, that when we lately spent that happy day in the delightful garden and sweet society of the Moulin Joly,[1] I stopt a little in one of our walks, and staid some time behind the company. We had been shown numberless skeletons of a kind of little fly, called an ephemera, whose successive generations, we were told, were bred and expired within the day. I happened to see a living company of them on a leaf, who appeared to be engaged in conversation. You know I understand all the inferior animal tongues: my too great application to the study of them is the best excuse I can give for the little progress I have made in your charming language. I listened through curiosity to the discourse of these little creatures; but as they, in their national vivacity, spoke three or four together, I could make but little of their conversation. I found, however, by some broken expressions that I heard now and then, they were disputing warmly on the merit

[1] *Moulin Joly:* a small island in the River Seine, where Franklin enjoyed the company of a group of distinguished French men and women, including that of Madame Brillon de Jouy, the "ever amiable *Brillante*" referred to at the end of this essay

of two foreign musicians, one a *cousin*,[2] the other a *moscheto*,[3] in which dispute they spent their time, seemingly as regardless of the shortness of life as if they had been sure of living a month. Happy people! thought I, you live certainly under a wise, just, and mild government, since you have no public grievances to complain of, nor any subject of contention but the perfections and imperfections of foreign music. I turned my head from them to an old grey-headed one, who was single on another leaf, and talking to himself. Being amused with his soliloquy, I put it down in writing, in hopes it will likewise amuse her to whom I am so much indebted for the most pleasing of all amusements, her delicious company and heavenly harmony.

"It was," said he, "the opinion of learned philosophers of our race, who lived and flourished long before my time, that this vast world, the Moulin Joly, could not itself subsist more than eighteen hours; and I think there was some foundation for that opinion, since, by the apparent motion of the great luminary that gives life to all nature, and which in my time has evidently declined considerably towards the ocean at the end of our earth, it must then finish its course, be extinguished in the waters that surround us, and leave the world in cold and darkness, necessarily producing universal death and destruction. I have lived seven of those hours, a great age, being no less than four hundred and twenty minutes of time. How very few of us continue so long! I have seen generations born, flourish, and expire. My present friends are the children and grandchildren of the friends of my youth, who are now, alas, no more! And I must soon follow them; for, by the course of nature, though still in health, I cannot expect to live above seven or eight minutes longer. What now avails all my toil and labor, in amassing honey-dew on this leaf, which I cannot live to enjoy! What the political struggles I have been engaged in, for the good of my compatriot inhabitants of this bush, or my philosophical studies for the benefit of our race in general! for, in politics, what can laws do without morals? Our present race of ephemeræ will in a course of minutes become corrupt, like those of other and older bushes, and consequently as

[2] *cousin:* gnat
[3] *moscheto:* mosquito

wretched. And in philosophy how small our progress! Alas! art is long, and life is short. My friends would comfort me with the idea of a name, they say, I shall leave behind me; and they tell me I have lived long enough to nature and to glory. But what will fame be to an ephemera who no longer exists? And what will become of all history in the eighteenth hour, when the world itself, even the whole Moulin Joly, shall come to its end, and be buried in universal ruin?"

To me, after all my eager pursuits, no solid pleasures now remain, but the reflection of a long life spent in meaning well, the sensible conversation of a few good lady ephemeræ, and now and then a kind smile and a tune from the ever amiable *Brillante*.

FOR DISCUSSION

1. Why does Franklin describe the ephemeræ as "happy people"? How does he make this incident seem convincing, even though impossible? In his "best excuse" for making little progress in French, is he poking fun at himself or at the language?
2. What convinces the "old grey-headed one" that the learned philosophers of his race were right in their opinion? How does he feel about the way he has spent his life and the world he is soon to leave behind? In your opinion is Franklin poking fun at people who share the same feelings? Or is he using the ephemera to express his own opinions? Cite evidence from the essay to support your opinion.
3. In an informal essay, the author is free to use whatever method is best suited to his purpose; namely, to reveal himself through what he says and the way he says it. What method does Franklin use in this essay? Why is it suited to his purpose? What kind of person does he reveal himself to be? What idea, stated or implied, provides the central focus for this essay?
4. The tone of an informal essay reflects the author's attitude and mood. What word best describes the tone of this essay—whimsical, amusing, philosophical, or ironical? Point out phrases and sentences which help to set the tone.
5. You have probably heard the expression, "Style is the man." Style is the distinctive manner in which a writer uses language—his choice and arrangement of words. What impressed you as "distinctive" about the language Franklin uses in this essay?

To Polly

At the time Franklin wrote this letter to his young English friend Polly Stevenson, he was already recognized as the leader of the restless colonies in North America. Whether he was aware of it or not, the attention he received in France, and the politeness shown him by French officials, was at the order of Louis XV, the king mentioned in this letter. France favored a separation of the colonies from the mother country since this would weaken the too-powerful British Empire.

Paris, September 14, 1767

Dear Polly: I am always pleased with a letter from you, and I flatter myself you may be sometimes pleased in receiving one from me, though it should be of little importance, such as this, which is to consist of a few occasional remarks made here, and in my journey hither.

Soon after I left you in that agreeable society at Bromley,[1] I took the resolution of making a trip with Sir John Pringle into France. We set out the 28th past. All the way to Dover we were furnished with post-chaises,[2] hung so as to lean forward, the top coming down over one's eyes, like a hood, as if to prevent one's seeing the country; which being one of my great pleasures, I was engaged in perpetual disputes with the innkeepers, ostlers, and postilions,[3] about getting the straps taken up a hole or two before, and let down as much behind, they insisting that the chaise leaning forward was an ease to the horses, and that the contrary would kill them. I suppose the chaise leaning forward looks to them like a willingness to go

[1] *Bromley:* England
[2] *post-chaises:* closed carriage
[3] *postilions:* coachboys

forward, and that its hanging back shows reluctance. They added other reasons, that were no reasons at all, and made me, as upon a hundred other occasions, almost wish that mankind had never been endowed with a reasoning faculty, since they know so little how to make use of it, and so often mislead themselves by it, and that they had been furnished with a good sensible instinct instead of it.

At Dover[4] the next morning we embarked for Calais[5] with a number of passengers who had never before been at sea. They would previously make a hearty breakfast, because if the wind should fail we might not get over till supper time. Doubtless they thought that when they had paid for their breakfast they had a right to it, and that when they had swallowed it they were sure of it. But they had scarce been out half an hour before the sea laid claim to it, and they were obliged to deliver it up. So that it seems there are uncertainties, even beyond those between the cup and the lip. If ever you go to sea, take my advice and live sparingly a day or two beforehand. The sickness, if any, will be lighter and sooner over. We got to Calais that evening.

Various impositions we suffered from boatmen, porters, and the like on both sides of the water. I know not which are most rapacious,[6] the English or French; but the latter have, with their knavery, most politeness.

The roads we found equally good with ours in England, in some places paved with smooth stones, like our new streets, for many miles together, and rows of trees on each side, and yet there are no turnpikes. But then the poor peasants complained to us grievously that they were obliged to work upon the roads full two months in the year without being paid for their labor. Whether this is truth, or whether like Englishmen they grumble cause or no cause, I have not yet been able fully to inform myself.

The women we saw at Calais, on the road, at Boulogne, and in the inns and villages, were generally of dark complexions;

[4]*Dover:* English seaport on the English Channel
[5]*Calais:* French seaport on the English Channel
[6]*rapacious:* greedy

but arriving at Abbeville we found a sudden change, a multitude of both women and men in that place appearing remarkably fair. Whether this is owing to a small colony of spinners, wool-combers, and weavers brought hither from Holland with the woollen manufactory about sixty years ago, or to their being less exposed to the sun than in other places, their business keeping them much within doors, I know not. Perhaps, as in some cases, different causes may club[7] in producing the effect; but the effect itself is certain. Never was I in a place of greater industry, wheels and looms going in every house.

As soon as we left Abbeville the swarthiness returned. I speak generally; for here are some fair women at Paris, who I think are not whitened by art. As to rouge, they don't pretend to imitate nature in laying it on. There is no gradual diminution of the color from the full bloom in the middle of the cheek to the faint tint near the sides; nor does it show itself differently in different faces. I have not had the honor of being at any lady's toilette[8] to see how it is laid on; but I fancy I can tell you how it is or may be done. Cut a hole of three inches diameter in a piece of paper; place it on the side of your face in such a manner that the top of the hole may be just under the eye, then, with a brush dipped in the color, paint face and paper together; so when the paper is taken off there will remain a round patch of red exactly the form of the hole. This is the mode, from the actresses on the stage upwards through all ranks of ladies to the princesses of the blood; but it stops there, the Queen not using it, having in the serenity, complacence, and benignity that shine so eminently in, or rather through, her countenance, sufficient beauty, though now an old woman, to do extremely well without it.

You see I speak of the Queen as if I had seen her; and so I have for you must know I have been at Court. We went to Versailles[9] last Sunday, and had the honor of being presented to the King. He spoke to both of us very graciously and cheer-

[7] *club:* combine
[8] *toilette:* process of dressing, applying make-up, and arranging the hair
[9] *Versailles:* town near Paris, site of the royal palace

fully, is a handsome man, has a very lively look, and appears younger than he is. In the evening we were at the *Grand Couvert,* where the family sup in public. The form of their sitting at the table was this:

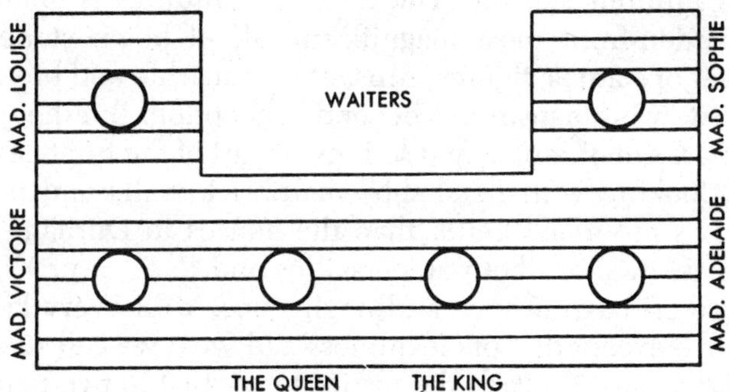

The table was, as you see, a hollow square, the service gold. When either made a sign for drink, the word was given by one of the waiters: *A boire pour le Roi,* or *A boire pour la Reine.*[10] Then two persons within the square approached, one with wine the other with water in carafes. Each drank a little glass of what he brought,[11] and then put both the carafes with a glass on a salver and presented it. Their distance from each other was such that two chairs might have been placed between any two of them. An officer of the Court brought us up through the crowd of spectators, and placed Sir John so as to stand between the King and Madame Adelaide, and me between the Queen and Madame Victoire. The King talked a good deal to Sir John, asking many questions about our Royal family;[12] and did me too the honor of taking some notice of me. That's saying enough, for I would not have you think me

[10]*A boire . . . Reine:* A drink for the King, a drink for the Queen

[11]*Each . . . brought:* The servants tasted the drinks before serving them to make sure that the wine and water were not poisoned

[12]*our Royal family:* the King and Queen of England. America was still an English colony at this time.

so much pleased with this King and Queen as to have a whit less regard than I used to have for ours. No Frenchman shall go beyond me in thinking my own King and Queen the very best in the world, and the most amiable.

Versailles has had infinite sums laid out in building it and supplying it with water. Some say the expenses exceeded eighty millions sterling. The range of buildings is immense; the garden-front most magnificent, all of hewn stone; the number of statues, figures, urns, etc., in marble and bronze of exquisite workmanship, is beyond conception. But the water-works are out of repair, and so is great part of the front next the town, looking with its shabby, half-brick walls and broken windows not much better than the houses in Durham Yard. There is, in short, both at Versailles and Paris, a prodigious mixture of magnificence and negligence, with every kind of elegance except that of cleanliness and what we call *tidiness*. Though I must do Paris the justice to say that in two points of cleanliness they exceed us. The water they drink, though from the river, they render as pure as that of the best spring, by filtering it through cisterns filled with sand; and the streets with constant sweeping are fit to walk in, though there is no paved foot-path. Accordingly, many well dressed people are constantly seen walking in them. The crowd of coaches and chairs for this reason is not so great. Men, as well as women, carry umbrellas in their hands, which they extend in case of rain or too much sun; and, a man with an umbrella not taking up more than three foot square, or nine square feet of the street, when, if in a coach, he would take up two hundred and forty square feet, you can easily conceive that, though the streets here are narrow, they may be much less encumbered. They are extremely well paved, and the stones, being generally cubes, when worn on one side, may be turned and become new.

The civilities[13] we everywhere receive give us the strongest impressions of the French politeness. It seems to be a point settled here universally that strangers are to be treated with respect; and one has just the same deference shown one here by being a stranger, as in England by being a lady. The custom-house officers at Port St. Denis, as we entered Paris, were about to seize two dozen of excellent Bordeaux wine given us

[13]*civilities:* courtesies

at Boulogne, and which we brought with us; but soon as they found we were strangers, it was immediately remitted on that account. At the Church of Notre Dame, where we went to see a magnificent illumination, with figures, etc., for the deceased Dauphiness,[14] we found an immense crowd who were kept out by guards; but the officer being told that we were strangers from England, he immediately admitted us, accompanied and showed us everything. Why don't we practice this urbanity[15] to Frenchmen? Why should they be allowed to outdo us in any thing?

Here is an exhibition of paintings, like ours in London, to which multitudes flock daily. I am not connoisseur enough to judge which has most merit. Every night, Sundays not excepted, here are plays or operas; and though the weather has been hot, and the houses full, one is not incommoded by the heat so much as with us in winter. They must have some way of changing the air that we are not acquainted with. I shall inquire into it.

Traveling is one way of lengthening life, at least in appearance. It is but about a fortnight since we left London, but the variety of scenes we have gone through makes it seem equal to six months living in one place. Perhaps I have suffered a greater change, too, in my own person than I could have done in six years at home. I had not been here six days before my tailor and perruquier[16] had transformed me into a Frenchman. Only think what a figure I make in a little bag-wig and with naked ears! They told me I was become twenty years younger, and looked very gallant.

So, being in Paris where the mode is to be sacredly followed, I was once very near making love to my friend's wife.

This letter shall cost you a shilling, and you may consider it cheap, when you reflect that it has cost me at least fifty guineas to get into the situation that enables me to write it. Besides, I might, if I had stayed at home, have won perhaps two shillings of you at cribbage. By the way, now I mention cards, let me tell you that quadrille is quite out of fashion here and English whisk all the mode at Paris and the Court.

[14]*Dauphiness:* wife of the heir to the French throne
[15]*urbanity:* graceful custom
[16]*perruquier:* wig-maker

And pray look upon it as no small matter, that, surrounded as I am by the glories of the world, and amusements of all sorts, I remember you, and Dolly, and all the dear good folks at Bromley. 'Tis true, I can't help it, but must and ever shall remember you all with pleasure.

Need I add that I am particularly, my dear good friend, yours most affectionately. . . .

FOR DISCUSSION

1. What advantages did Franklin find in traveling? In what ways was he like many travelers, and in what ways was he different? What does he reveal about himself by what he describes to Polly and the comments he makes about what he saw?
2. Why does Franklin "almost wish that mankind had never been endowed with a reasoning faculty"? What leads him to give Polly advice about sea travel? Point out and discuss other observations he makes, including those about the English and the French.
3. Franklin is both amazed and shocked at what he sees when visiting Versailles. Why? In what ways was Paris superior to the large cities in England? What conclusion does he draw about Frenchmen from the way he is treated?
4. Why would the receiver of this letter have enjoyed it so much that she kept it all her life? Is it still interesting to modern readers mainly because of what Franklin describes or because of the way he describes it? Is it a combination of both? Find evidence in the letter to support your answer.
5. In everything Franklin wrote, he revealed aspects of his personality. What impressions do you gain of him from this letter?

FOR COMPOSITION

1. If you had accompanied Franklin on this trip, which of the many things he described would have impressed you most? In a short composition, state what these are and why they impressed you.
2. Franklin apparently enjoyed being a "man-about-town." In a paragraph show how his feelings are brought out through what he describes and the comments he makes.

To Lord Howe

A week after the Declaration of Independence was adopted, Lord Howe, commander of the British fleet, arrived off Sandy Hook with instructions to make peace with the rebels if possible. Since Britain did not recognize the American Congress, Howe wrote to Franklin, with whom he had previously negotiated in London. Franklin turned Howe's letter over to Congress which, on July 20, authorized Franklin to state, in his reply, the attitude of the colonies. Thus his letter was semi-official as well as personal.

Philadelphia, July 20, 1776

My Lord: I received safe the letters your Lordship so kindly forwarded to me, and beg you to accept my thanks.

The official despatches to which you refer me contain nothing more than what we had seen in the act of Parliament, viz.. offers of pardon upon submission, which I am sorry to find, as it must give your Lordship pain to be sent so far on so hopeless a business.

Directing pardons to be offered the colonies, who are the very parties injured, expresses indeed that opinion of our ignorance, baseness, and insensibility which your uninformed and proud nation has long been pleased to entertain of us; but it can have no other effect than that of increasing our resentments. It is impossible we should think of submission to a government that has with the most wanton barbarity and cruelty burnt our defenseless towns in the midst of winter, excited the savages to massacre our farmers and our slaves to murder their masters and is even now bringing foreign mercenaries to deluge our settlements with blood. These atrocious injuries have extinguished every remaining spark of affection for that parent country we once held so dear; but were it possible for *us* to forget and forgive them, it is not possible for *you* (I mean the British nation) to forgive the people you have so heavily injured. You can never confide again in those as fellow-subjects and permit them to enjoy equal freedom, to whom you know you have given such just cause of lasting enmity. And this must impel you, were we again under your government, to endeavor the breaking our spirit by the severest tyranny, and obstructing by every means in your power our growing strength and prosperity.

But your Lordship mentions "the King's paternal solicitude for promoting the establishment of lasting *peace* and union with the colonies." If by peace is here meant a peace to be entered into between Britain and America, as distinct states now at war and his Majesty has given your Lordship powers to treat with us of such a peace, I may venture to say, though without authority, that I think a treaty for that purpose not yet quite impracticable, before we enter into foreign alliances. But I am persuaded you have no such powers. Your nation, though, by punishing those American governors who have created and fomented the discord, rebuilding our burnt towns and repairing as far as possible the mischiefs done us, might yet recover a great share of our regard and the greatest part of our growing commerce, with all the advantage of that additional strength to be derived from a friendship with us; but I know too well her abounding pride and deficient wisdom to believe she will ever take such salutary[1] measures. Her fondness for conquest, as a warlike nation, her lust of dominion as an ambitious one, and her thirst for a gainful monopoly as a commercial one (none of them legitimate causes of war) will all join to hide from her eyes every view of her true interests and continually goad her on in those ruinous distant expeditions, so destructive both of lives and treasure, that must prove as pernicious to her in the end as the crusades formerly were to most of the nations of Europe.

[1] *salutary:* beneficial

I have not the vanity, my Lord, to think of intimidating by thus predicting the effects of this war; for I know it will in England have the fate of all my former predictions, not to be believed till the event shall verify it.

Long did I endeavor, with unfeigned and unwearied zeal, to preserve from breaking that fine and noble china vase, the British Empire, for I knew that, being once broken, the separate parts could not retain even their shares of the strength or value that existed in the whole, and that a perfect reunion of those parts could scarce ever be hoped for. Your Lordship may possibly remember the tears of joy that wet my cheek when, at your good sister's in London, you once gave me expectations that a reconciliation might soon take place. I had the misfortune to find those expectations disappointed, and to be treated as the cause of the mischief I was laboring to prevent. My consolation under that groundless and malevolent treatment was that I retained the friendship of many wise and good men in that country, and, among the rest, some share in the regard of Lord Howe.

The well-founded esteem and, permit me to say, affection which I shall always have for your Lordship, makes it painful to me to see you engaged in conducting a war the great ground of which, as expressed in your letter, is "the necessity of preventing the American trade from passing into foreign channels." To me it seems that neither the obtaining or retaining of any trade, how valuable soever, is an object for which men may justly spill each other's blood; that the true and sure means of extending and securing commerce is the goodness and cheapness of commodities; and that the profit of no trade can ever be equal to the expense of compelling it, and of holding it, by fleets and armies.

I consider this war against us, therefore, as both unjust and unwise; and I am persuaded that cool, dispassionate posterity will condemn to infamy those who advised it, and that even success will not save from some degree of dishonor those who voluntarily engaged to conduct it. I know your great motive in coming hither was the hope of being instrumental in a reconciliation; and I believe, when you find *that* to be impossible on any terms given you to propose, you will relinquish so odious a command and return to a more honorable private station.

With the greatest and most sincere respect, I have the honor to be, my Lord, your Lordship's most obedient humble servant. . . .

FOR DISCUSSION

1. What had been the purpose of Lord Howe's letter to Franklin? What lack of hope does Franklin see in England's offers of pardon? Why is submission by the colonists impossible? Why would forgiveness by England be equally impossible and, in addition, the cause of future trouble?
2. How might England recover a great share of the colonies' regard and commerce? What would keep her from taking such "salutary measures"?
3. What reasons does Franklin give for England's present and ruinous expeditions? Why does he consider none of them legitimate causes of war? Did the colonies have a legitimate cause? Find evidence in this letter to support your answer.
4. What mischief is Franklin blamed for causing? Why does he attack as evil and foolish the reason Lord Howe has given for England's waging war against the colonies?
5. In this letter does Franklin reveal himself as the economist, the humanitarian, or both? How applicable are his comments to the struggle going on today between certain colonies and the countries attempting to maintain authority over them? How important is trade as a cause of the struggle? Name other causes.
6. Describe the tone of this letter. What would you say was Franklin's mood when he wrote it, and his attitude toward the man to whom it was addressed? What words, phrases, and sentences convey these things?

FOR COMPOSITION

1. This letter was selected because it so clearly reveals the kind of person Franklin was and the ideals and values he championed throughout his life. In a paragraph, state what impresses you most about the man *and* his beliefs. Base your comments on this letter and the class discussion of it.
2. General Howe did *not* relinquish his command as Franklin had hoped he would. Point out in a paragraph the means which Franklin used to persuade Howe, and why, in your opinion, he failed.

On Education: A Letter

To Thomas Mann Randolph, Jr.

THOMAS JEFFERSON

Paris, Aug. 27, 1786

Dear Sir,—I am honoured with your favour of the 16th instant, and desirous, without delay, of manifesting my wishes to be useful to you, I shall venture to you some thoughts on the course of your studies, which must be submitted to the better choice with which you are surrounded. A longer race through life may have entitled me to seize some truths which have not yet been presented to your observation. And more intimate knowledge of the country in which you are to live and of the circumstances in which you will be placed, may enable me to point your attention to the branches of science which will administer the most to your happiness there. The foundations which you have laid in languages and mathematics are proper for every superstructure. The former exercises our memory while that and no other faculty is yet matured and prevents our acquiring habits of idleness. The latter gives exercise to our reason,.as soon as that has acquired a certain degree of strength, and stores the mind with truths which are useful in other branches of science.

At this moment then a second order of preparation is to commence. I shall propose to you that it be extensive, comprehending Astronomy, Natural Philosophy (or Physics), Natural History, Anatomy, Botany and Chemistry. No inquisitive mind will be content to be ignorant of any of these branches. But I would advise you to be contented with a course of lectures in most of them, without attempting to make yourself master of the whole. This is more than any genius joined to any length of life is equal to. You will find among them some one study to which your mind will more particularly attach itself. This then I would pursue and propose to attain eminence in. Your own country furnishes the most aliment[1] for Natural History, Botany and Physics, and as you express a fondness for the former you might make it your principal object, endeavoring however to make yourself more acquainted with the two latter than with other branches likely to be less useful. In fact you will find botany offering its charms to you at every step—during summer and Physics in every season. All these branches of science will be better attained by attending courses of lectures in them.

You are now in a place where the best courses upon earth are within your reach and being delivered in your native language—you lose no part of their benefit. Such an opportunity you will never again have. I would therefore strongly press on you to fix no other limit to your stay in Edinborough than your having got thro this whole course. The omission of any one part of it will be an affliction and loss to you as long as you live. Beside the comfort of knowledge, every science is auxiliary to every other.

While you are attending these courses you can proceed by yourself in a regular series of historical reading. It would be a waste of time to attend a professor of this. It is to be acquired from books and if you pursue it by yourself you can accommodate it to your other reading so as to fill up those chasms of time not otherwise appropriated. There are portions of the day too when the mind should be eased, particularly after dinner it should be applied to lighter occupation: history is of this kind. It exercises principally the memory. Reflection also indeed is

[1] *aliment:* sustaining food

necessary but not generally in a laborious degree. To conduct yourself in this branch of science you have only to consider what æras of it merit a grasp and what a particular attention, and in each æra also to distinguish between the countries the knowledge of whose history will be useful and those where it suffices only to be not altogether ignorant. Having laid down your plan as to the branches of history you would pursue, the order of time will be your sufficient guide. After what you have read in antient[2] history I should suppose Millot's digest would be useful and sufficient. The histories of Greece and Rome are worthy a good degree of attention, they should be read in the original authors. The transition from antient to modern history will be best effected by reading Gibbon's. Then a general history of the principal states of Europe, but particular ones of England. Here too the original writers are to be preferred. Kennet published a considerable collection of these in 3 vols. folio, but there are some others not in his collection well worth being read. After the history of England that of America will claim your attention. Here too original authors and not compilers are best. An author who writes of his own times or of times near his own presents in his own ideas and manner the best picture of the moment of which he writes. History need not be hurried but may give way to the other sciences because history can be pursued after you shall have left your present situation as well as while you remain in it.

When you shall have got thro this second order of preparation the study of the law is to be begun. This like history is to be acquired from books. All the aid you will want will be a catalogue of the books to be read and the order in which they are to be read. It being absolutely indifferent in what place you carry on this reading, I should propose your doing it in France. The advantages of this will be that you will at the same time acquire the habit of speaking French which is the object of a year or two. You may be giving attention to such of the fine arts as your turn may lead you to and you will be forming an acquaintance with the individuals and characters of a nation with whom we must long remain in the closest inti-

[2] *antient:* ancient

macy and to whom we are bound by the strong ties of gratitude and policy. A nation in short of the most amiable dispositions on earth, the whole mass of which is penetrated with an affection for us. You might before you return to your own country make a visit to Italy also.

I should have performed the office of but half a friend were I to confine myself to the improvement of the mind only. Knowledge indeed is a desirable, a lovely possession, but I do not scruple to say that health is more so. It is of little consequence to store the mind with science if the body be permitted to become debilitated.[3] If the body be feeble, the mind will not be strong—the sovereign invigorator of the body is exercise, and of all exercises walking is best. A horse gives but a kind of half exercise, and a carriage is no better than a cradle. No one knows, till he tries, how easily a habit of walking is acquired. A person who never walked three miles will in the course of a month become able to walk 15 or 20 without fatigue. I have known some great walkers and had particular accounts of many more: and I never knew or heard of one who was not healthy and long lived. This species of exercise therefore is much to be advised. Should you be disposed to try it, as your health has been feeble, it will be necessary for you to begin with a little, and to increase it by degrees. For the same reason you must probably at first ascribe to it the hours most precious for study, I mean those about the middle of the day. But when you shall find yourself strong you may venture to take your walks in the evening after the digestion of the dinner is pretty well over. This is making a compromise between health and study. The latter would be too much interrupted were you to take from it the early hours of the day and habit will soon render the evening's exercise as salutary as that of the morning.

I speak this from my own experience having, from an attachment to study, very early in life, made this arrangement of my time, having ever observed it, and still observing it, and always with perfect success. Not less than two hours a day should be devoted to exercise, and the weather should be little regarded. A person not sick will not be injured by getting

[3] *debilitated:* weakened

wet. It is but taking a cold bath which never gives a cold to any one. Brute animals are the most healthy, and they are exposed to all weather and, of men, those are healthiest who are the most exposed. The recipe of those two descriptions of beings is simple diet, exercise and the open air, be it's state what it will; and we may venture to say that this recipe will give health and vigor to every other description.

By this time I am sure you will think I have sermonized enough. I have given you indeed a lengthy lecture. I have been led through it by my zeal to serve you; if in the whole you find one useful counsel, that will be my reward, and a sufficient one. Few persons in your own country have started from as advantageous ground as that whereon you will be placed. Nature and fortune have been liberal to you. Every thing honourable or profitable there is placed within your own reach, and will depend on your own efforts. If these are exerted with assiduity,[4] and guided by unswerving honesty, your success is infallible:[5] and that it may be as great as you wish is the sincere desire of Dear Sir, your most affectionate humble servant.

P.S. Be so good as to present me affectionately to your brother and cousin.

[4] *assiduity:* unceasing effort
[5] *infallible:* completely sure

FOR DISCUSSION

1. Which disciplines does Jefferson consider the proper bases for all knowledge? Which one prevents idleness? How? Which develops reason?
2. According to Jefferson, what disciplines should be included in the second stage of learning? Is the primary goal of this stage depth or breadth of knowledge? Do the sciences seem exclusive areas or are they dependent on each other?
3. How does Jefferson view history and historical readings? Is history hard or easy to study? How challenging is it?
4. Why does Jefferson advise reading law in France? What historical facts explain Jefferson's attitude toward France? What are the countries worth visiting, according to this letter?

5. What is Jefferson's attitude toward education? Is education more a duty, a chore, or a pleasure to acquire?
6. What do you think of Jefferson's advice about walking? What would *he* think about the amount of walking you do each day? What would he think about the way you spend your day?
7. What do you think about the advice Jefferson gives in this letter? Do you think it is applicable to studies today? Has anything changed which his letter could not take into account?

FOR COMPOSITION

Write a letter advising a friend, or a younger member of your family, about his education and daily routine. Try to write in a tone he would respect and respond to.

EMERSON AND THOREAU

In the first half of the nineteenth century, the new nation was beginning to flex its muscles, to enjoy its independence, and to react angrily when Europeans charged that America was largely a nation of barbarians (a charge the East coast would later hurl at the Western frontier). The new nation, having won its independence from one of the great powers, was content, for the moment, with its own possibilities. The spirit of America was much like that of an adolescent boy who has won a big fight, who has been miraculously spared public defeat, and who exuberantly envisions the future as a field for further conquest and glory.

The spokesman for this surging confidence and sense of well-being was Ralph Waldo Emerson. Though his personal life was marked by tragedy, Emerson voiced in his essays a fervent praise of the individual and his potential goodness and wisdom. According to Emerson's philosophy, a man needs only to trust fully in himself; if he follows his own honest instincts, he will act rightly. Though he was not so naive as to state that most men were honest, just, and kind, Emerson still insisted that such qualities were well within human reach, if the individual was properly self-reliant. His essay on self-reliance follows.

If Emerson was the spokesman for reliance on one's personal instincts, Henry David Thoreau was the man with the courage to put Emerson's advice into action. For years, therefore, Thoreau was considered a mere disciple, a shadow of the master. Recently, however, public esteem for these two has changed proportions. Now Thoreau is the more honored, not only for his courageous spirit but also for his mastery of literary style. Although Thoreau's journals seem to be his day-by-day jottings, there is ample evidence that he polished and pruned what he wrote there, always seeking a higher level of literary excellence. As a shaper of beautifully wrought sentences, Thoreau is one of the best American writers. He is nowhere better than in "Where I Lived and What I Lived For," from his famous work, *Walden*.

Self-Reliance

RALPH WALDO EMERSON

. . . To believe your own thought, to believe that what is true for you in your private heart is true for all men, — that is genius. Speak your latent conviction, and it shall be the universal sense; for the inmost in due time becomes the outmost, and our first thought is rendered back to us by the trumpets of the Last Judgment. Familiar as the voice of the mind is to each, the highest merit we ascribe to Moses, Plato and Milton is that they set at naught books and traditions, and spoke not what men, but what *they* thought. A man should learn to detect and watch that gleam of light which flashes across his mind from within, more than the lustre of the firmament of bards and sages. Yet he dismisses without notice his thought, because it is his. In every work of genius we recognize our own rejected thoughts; they come back to us with a certain alienated majesty. Great works of art have no more affecting lesson for us than this. They teach us to abide by our spontaneous impression with good-humored inflexibility then most when the whole cry of voices is on the other side. Else to-morrow a stranger will say with masterly good sense precisely what we have thought and felt all the time, and we shall be forced to take with shame our own opinion from another.

There is a time in every man's education when he arrives at the conviction that envy is ignorance; that imitation is suicide; that he must take himself for better for worse as his portion; that though the wide universe is full of good, no kernel of nourishing corn can come to him but through his toil bestowed on that plot of ground which is given to him to till. The power which resides in him is new in nature, and none but he knows what that is which he can do, nor does he know until he has tried. . . .

Trust thyself: every heart vibrates to that iron string. Accept the place the divine providence has found for you, the society of your contemporaries, the connection of events. Great men have always done so, and confided themselves childlike to the genius[1] of their age, betraying their perception that the absolutely trustworthy was seated at their heart, working through their hands, predominating in all their being. And we are now men, and must accept in the highest mind the same transcendent destiny; and not minors and invalids in a protected corner, not cowards fleeing before a revolution, but guides, redeemers and benefactors, obeying the Almighty effort and advancing on Chaos and the Dark.[2]

What pretty oracles[3] nature yields us on this text in the face and behavior of children, babes, and even brutes! That divided and rebel mind, that distrust of a sentiment because our arithmetic has computed the strength and means opposed to our purpose, these have not. Their mind being whole, their eye is as yet unconquered, and when we look in their faces we are disconcerted. Infancy conforms to nobody; all conform to it; so that one babe commonly makes four or five out of the adults who prattle and play to it. So God has armed youth and puberty and manhood no less with its own piquancy and charm, and made it enviable and gracious and its claims not to be put by, if it will stand by itself. Do not think the youth has no force, because he cannot speak to you and me. Hark! in the

[1] *genius:* spirit
[2] *Chaos and the Dark:* evil (See Milton's *Paradise Lost*, I, 543)
[3] *oracles:* revelations

next room his voice is sufficiently clear and emphatic. It seems he knows how to speak to his contemporaries. Bashful or bold then, he will know how to make us seniors very unnecessary.

The nonchalance of boys who are sure of a dinner, and would disdain as much as a lord to do or say aught to conciliate[4] one, is the healthy attitude of human nature. A boy is in the parlor what the pit[5] is in the playhouse; independent, irresponsible, looking out from his corner on such people and facts as pass by, he tries and sentences them on their merits, in the swift, summary way of boys, as good, bad, interesting, silly, eloquent, troublesome. He cumbers himself never about consequences, about interests; he gives an independent, genuine verdict....

Society everywhere is in conspiracy against the manhood of every one of its members. Society is a joint-stock company, in which the members agree, for the better securing of his bread to each shareholder, to surrender the liberty and culture of the eater. The virtue in most request[6] is conformity. Self-reliance is its aversion. It loves not realities and creators, but names and customs.

Who so would be a man, must be a nonconformist. He who would gather immortal palms[7] must not be hindered by the name of goodness, but must explore if it be goodness. Nothing is at last sacred but the integrity of your own mind. Absolve you to yourself, and you shall have the suffrage[8] of the world. ... No law can be sacred to me but that of my nature. Good and bad are but names very readily transferrable to that or this; the only right is what is after my constitution; the only wrong what is against it. A man is to carry himself in the presence of all opposition as if every thing were titular[9] and ephemeral[10] but he. I am ashamed to think how easily we capitulate to badges and names, to large societies and dead institutions. Every

[4] *conciliate:* win over
[5] *pit:* orchestra or ground floor of a theater. In Elizabethan days this was the cheapest location and was occupied by the "groundlings."
[6] *request:* demand
[7] *palms:* symbol of triumph or success
[8] *suffrage:* favorable vote
[9] *titular:* existing in name only
[10] *ephemeral:* short-lived

decent and well-spoken individual affects and sways me more than is right. I ought to go upright and vital, and speak the rude truth in all ways. . . .

What I must do is all that concerns me, not what the people think. This rule, equally arduous in actual and in intellectual life, may serve for the whole distinction between greatness and meanness. It is the harder because you will always find those who think they know what is your duty better than you know it. It is easy in the world to live after the world's opinion; it is easy in solitude to live after your own; but the great man is he who in the midst of the crowd keeps with perfect sweetness the independence of solitude. . . .

Most men have bound their eyes with one or another handkerchief, and attached themselves to some one of these communities of opinion. This conformity makes them not false in a few particulars, authors of a few lies, but false in all particulars. Their every truth is not quite true. Their two is not the real two, their four not the real four: so that every word they say chagrins us and we know not where to begin to set them right. Meantime nature is not slow to equip us in the prison-uniform of the party to which we adhere. We come to wear one cut of face and figure, and acquire by degrees the gentlest asinine expression. There is a mortifying experience in particular, which does not fail to wreck itself also in the general history; I mean "foolish face of praise," the forced smile which we put on in company where we do not feel at ease, in answer to conversation which does not interest us. The muscles, not spontaneously moved but moved by a low usurping wilfulness, grow tight about the outline of the face, with the most disagreeable sensation.

For nonconformity the world whips you with its displeasure. And therefore a man must know how to estimate a sour face. The by-standers look askance on him in the public street or in the friend's parlor. If this aversion had its origin in contempt and resistance like his own he might well go home with a sad countenance; but the sour faces of the multitude, like their sweet faces, have no deep cause, but are put on and off as the wind blows and a newspaper directs. Yet is the discontent of the multitude more formidable than that of the senate and the college. It is easy enough for a firm man who knows the world to brook the rage of the cultivated classes....

The other terror that scares us from self-trust is our consistency; a reverence for our past act or word because the eyes of other have no other data for computing our orbit than our past acts, and we are loth to disappoint them.

But why should you keep your head over your shoulder? Why drag about this corpse of your memory, lest you contradict somewhat you have stated in this or that public place? Suppose you should contradict yourself; what then? It seems to be a rule of wisdom never to rely on your memory alone, scarcely even in acts of pure memory, but to bring the past for judgment into the thousand-eyed present, and live ever in a new day....

A foolish consistency is the hobgoblin of little minds, adored by little statesmen and philosophers and divines. With consistency a great soul has simply nothing to do. He may as well concern himself with his shadow on the wall. Speak what you think now in hard words and to-morrow speak what to-morrow thinks in hard words again, though it contradict every thing you said to-day.—"Ah, so you shall be sure to be misunderstood."—Is it so bad then to be misunderstood? Pythagoras[11] was misunderstood, and Socrates, and Jesus, and Luther, and Copernicus, and Galileo, and Newton, and every pure and wise spirit that ever took flesh. To be great is to be misunderstood....

I hope in these days we have heard the last of conformity and consistency. Let the words be gazetted[12] and ridiculous henceforward. Instead of the gong for dinner, let us hear a whistle from the Spartan fife.[13] Let us never bow and apologize more.... Let us affront and reprimand the smooth mediocrity and squalid contentment of the times, and hurl in the face of custom and trade and office, the fact which is the upshot of all history, that there is a great responsible Thinker and Actor working wherever a man works; that a true man belongs

[11] *Pythagoras:* 6th century B.C. Greek philosopher and mathematician. When Pythagoras tried to establish a school on his native island of Samos, he was disowned by his own people, and his followers were persecuted.

[12] *gazetted:* abolished

[13] *fife:* the only music allowed in ancient Sparta

to no other time or place, but is the center of things. . . . Every true man is a cause, a country, and an age; requires infinite spaces and numbers and time fully to accomplish his design; —and posterity seem to follow his steps as a train of clients. A man Caeser is born, and for ages after we have a Roman Empire. Christ is born, and millions of minds so grow and cleave to his genius that he is confounded with virtue and the possible of man. An institution is the lengthened shadow of one man . . . and all history resolves itself very easily into the biography of a few stout and earnest persons. . . .

Man is timid and apologetic; he is no longer upright; he dares not say "I think," "I am," but quotes some saint or sage. He is ashamed before the blade of grass or the blowing rose. These roses under my window make no reference to former roses or to better ones; they are for what they are; they exist with God today. There is no time to them. There is simply the rose; it is perfect in every moment of its existence. Before a leaf-bud has burst, its whole life acts; in the full-blown flower there is no more; in the leafless root there is no less. Its nature is satisfied and it satisfies nature in all moments alike. But man postpones or remembers; he does not live in the present, but with reverted eye laments the past, or, heedless of the riches that surround him, stands on tiptoe to foresee the future. He cannot be happy and strong until he too lives with nature in the present, above time.

This should be plain enough. Yet see what strong intellects dare not yet hear God himself unless he speak the phraseology of I know not what David, or Jeremiah, or Paul. We shall not always set so great a price on a few texts, on a few lives. We are like children who repeat by rote the sentences of grandames and tutors, and, as they grow older, of the men of talents and character they chance to see,—painfully recollecting the exact words they spoke; afterwards, when they come into the point of view which those had who uttered these sayings, they understand them and are willing to let the words go; for at any time they can use words as good when occasion comes. If we live truly, we shall see truly. It is as easy for the strong man to be strong, as it is for the weak to be weak. When we have new perception, we shall gladly disburden the memory of its hoarded treasures as old rubbish. When a man lives with God, his voice shall be as sweet as the murmur of the brook and the rustle of the corn. . . .

And truly it demands something godlike in him who has cast off the common motives of humanity and has ventured to trust himself for a taskmaster. High be his heart, faithful his will, clear his sight, that he may in good earnest be doctrine, society, law, to himself, that a simple purpose may be to him as strong as iron necessity is to others!

If any man consider the present aspects of what is called by distinction *society*, he will see the need of these ethics. The sinew and heart of man seem to be drawn out, and we are become timorous, desponding whimperers. We are afraid of truth, afraid of fortune, afraid of death, and afraid of each other. Our age yields no great and perfect persons. We want men and women who shall renovate[14] life and our social state, but we see that most natures are insolvent,[15] cannot satisfy their own wants, have an ambition out of all proportion to their practical force and do lean and beg day and night continually. Our housekeeping is mendicant,[16] our arts, our occupations, our marriages, our religion we have not chosen, but society has chosen for us. We are parlor soldiers. We shun the rugged battle of fate, where strength is born.

If our young men miscarry[17] in their first enterprises they lose all heart. If the young merchant fails, men say he is *ruined*. If the finest genius studies at one of our colleges and is not installed in an office within one year afterwards in the cities or suburbs of Boston or New York, it seems to his friends and to himself that he is right in being disheartened and in complaining the rest of his life. A sturdy lad from New Hampshire or Vermont, who in turn tries all the professions, who *teams it, farms it, peddles*, keeps a school, preaches, edits a newspaper, goes to Congress, buys a township, and so forth, in successive years, and always like a cat falls on his feet, is worth a hundred of these city dolls. He walks abreast with his

[14] *renovate:* remodel
[15] *insolvent:* poor
[16] *mendicant:* begging
[17] *miscarry:* fail

days and feels no shame in not "studying a profession," for he does not postpone his life, but lives already. He has not one chance, but a hundred chances. Let a Stoic[18] open the resources of man and tell men they are not leaning willows, but can and must detach themselves; that with the exercise of self-trust, new powers shall appear; that a man is the word made flesh, born to shed healing to the nations; that he should be ashamed of our compassion, and that the moment he acts from himself, tossing the laws, the books, idolatries and customs out of the window, we pity him no more but thank and revere him;—and that teacher shall restore the life of man to splendor and make his name dear to all history.

It is easy to see that a greater self-reliance must work a revolution in all the offices and relations of men; in their religion; in their education; in their pursuits; their modes of living; their association; in their property; in their speculative views.

1. In what prayers do men allow themselves! That which they call a holy office is not so much as brave and manly. Prayer looks abroad and asks for some foreign addition to come through some foreign virtue, and loses itself in endless mazes of natural and supernatural, and mediatorial[19] and miraculous. Prayer that craves a particular commodity, anything less than all good, is vicious. Prayer is the contemplation of the facts of life from the highest point of view. It is the soliloquy of a beholding and jubilant soul. It is the spirit of God pronouncing his works good. But prayer as a means to effect a private end is meanness and theft. It supposes dualism and not unity in nature and consciousness. As soon as the man is at one with God, he will not beg. He will then see prayer in all action. The prayer of the farmer kneeling in his field to weed it, the prayer of the rower kneeling with the stroke of his oar, are true prayers heard throughout nature, though for cheap ends. . . .

Another sort of false prayers are our regrets. Discontent is the want of self-reliance: it is infirmity of will. Regret calamities if you can thereby help the sufferer; if not, attend your

[18] *Stoic:* a member of a school of philosophy founded by Zeno about 308 B.C., who taught that since all events were the result of a divine will, men should accept these events calmly and should be free from passions and indifferent to pleasure and pain

[19] *mediatorial:* intervening

own work and already the evil begins to be repaired. Our sympathy is just as base. We come to them who weep foolishly and sit down and cry for company, instead of imparting to them truth and health in rough electric shocks, putting them once more in communication with their own reason. The secret of fortune is joy in our hands. Welcome evermore to gods and men is the self-helping man. For him all doors are flung wide; him all tongues greet, all honors crown, all eyes follow with desire. Our love goes out to him and embraces him because he did not need it. We solicitously and apologetically caress and celebrate him because he held on his way and scorned our disapprobation.[20] The gods love him because men hated him. . . .

2. It is for want of self-culture that the superstition of Traveling, whose idols are Italy, England, Egypt, retains its fascination for all educated Americans. They who made England, Italy, or Greece venerable in the imagination, did so by sticking fast where they were, like an axis of the earth. In manly hours we feel that duty is our place. The soul is no traveler; the wise man stays at home, and when his necessities, his duties, on any occasion call him from his house, or into foreign lands, he is at home still and shall make men sensible by the expression of his countenance that he goes, the missionary of wisdom and virtue, and visits cities and men like a sovereign and not like an interloper or a valet.

I have no churlish objection to the circumnavigation[21] of the globe for the purposes of art, of study, and benevolence, so that the man is first domesticated, or does not go abroad with the hope of finding somewhat greater than he knows. He who travels to be amused, or to get somewhat which he does not carry, travels away from himself, and grows old even in youth among old things. In Thebes, in Palmyra, his will and mind have become old and dilapidated as they. He carries ruins to ruins.

Traveling is a fool's paradise. Our first journeys discover to us the indifference of places. At home I dream that at Naples, at Rome, I can be intoxicated with beauty and lose my sadness. I pack my trunk, embrace my friends, embark on the sea

[20] *disapprobation:* disapproval
[21] *circumnavigation:* sailing around

and at last wake up in Naples, and there beside me is the stern fact, the sad self, unrelenting, identical, that I fled from. I seek the Vatican and the palaces. I affect to be intoxicated with sights and suggestions, but I am not intoxicated. My giant goes with me wherever I go.

3. But the rage of traveling is a symptom of a deeper unsounding affecting the whole intellectual action. The intellect is vagabond, and our system of education fosters restlessness. Our minds travel when our bodies are forced to stay at home. We imitate; and what is imitation but the traveling of the mind? Our houses are built with foreign taste; our shelves are garnished with foreign ornaments; our opinions, our tastes, our faculties lean, and follow the Past and the Distant. The soul created the arts wherever they have flourished. It was in his own mind that the artist sought his model. It was an application of his own thought to the thing to be done and the conditions to be observed. And why need we copy the Doric or the Gothic model? Beauty, convenience, grandeur of thought and quaint expression are as near to us as to any, and if the American artist will study with hope and love the precise thing to be done by him, considering the climate, the soil, the length of the day, the wants of the people, the habit and form of the government, he will create a house in which all these will find themselves fitted, and taste and sentiment will be satisfied also.

Insist on yourself; never imitate. Your own gift you can present every moment with the cumulative force of a whole life's cultivation; but of the adopted talent of another you have only an extemporaneous half possession. That which each can do best, none but his Maker can teach him. No man yet knows what it is, nor can, till that person has exhibited it. Where is the master who could have taught Shakespeare? Where is the master who could have instructed Franklin, or Washington, or Bacon, or Newton? Every great man is a unique. . . . Shakespeare will never be made by the study of Shakespeare. Do that which is assigned you, and you cannot hope too much or dare too much. There is at this moment for you an utterance brave and grand as that of the colossal chisel of Phidias,[22] or

[22] *Phidias:* (498-432 B.C.), Greek sculptor

trowel[23] of the Egyptians, or the pen of Moses or Dante, but different from all these. Not possibly will the soul, all rich, all eloquent, with thousand-cloven tongue, deign to repeat itself; but if you can hear what these patriarchs say, surely you can reply to them in the same pitch of voice; for the ear and the tongue are two organs of one nature. Abide in the simple and noble regions of thy life, obey thy heart, and thou shalt reproduce the Foreworld again. . . . Nothing can bring you peace but yourself. Nothing can bring you peace but the triumph of principles.

[23]*trowel:* the symbol of the mason. The Egyptians used stone for many of their buildings.

FOR DISCUSSION

1. When this essay was published in 1841, it aroused considerable controversy because its readers did not know how to interpret Emerson's thought. Three years later he considered this essay the "highest note" in his philosophy, since one inevitably comes to learn "that self-reliance, the height and perfection of man, is reliance on God." From your reading of this essay, do you think he presents that principle convincingly and with sufficient evidence? What ideas impress you most? Which can you accept fully or in part? Which do you reject? Discuss.
2. What conviction does every man arrive at in the course of his education? Why is self-reliance essential to knowing what one can do and to accepting one's destiny?
3. In what ways is society "in conspiracy against the manhood of every one of its members"? Why is self-reliance its aversion? What reasons does Emerson give for insisting, "Nothing is at last sacred but the integrity of your own mind"? How should a person "carry himself in the face of all opposition"?
4. What reasons does Emerson give to justify the statement, "What I must do is all that concerns me, not what people think"?
5. According to Emerson, we are scared from self-trust by two terrors: conformity and consistency. How do they affect both what we are like and the society in which we live and work? What gives our actions unity and harmony although they appear so varied? Do you agree that "To be great is to be misunderstood"? Explain.

6. Emerson makes very clear the distinction between prayer that is "true" and prayer that is "false." What is this distinction?
7. Travel is now considered an education, not "a fool's paradise." What explanation does Emerson give for America's fascination with distant countries? Why does the wise man stay at home? Why is nothing to be gained by imitation?
8. As you discuss his concluding sentences, review what he means by "peace" and what "principles" he feels must triumph if we find that peace. In your opinion, if self-reliance were practiced today, would many of the world's problems be solved? Or is this outlook on life too idealistic and impractical? Give reasons to support your answer.

FOR COMPOSITION

1. Select any one of Emerson's stimulating sentences which make a strong impression on you. In a paragraph or two state the meaning you think it expresses and your reaction to it. Perhaps it confirms something you already believe; perhaps it raises a question in your mind about some of the values of present-day life and society. In your writing, keep in mind Emerson's advice to express what you think honestly and with self-trust.
2. In a short essay, present your own philosophy of self-reliance. Use examples from your own experiences, or the experiences of others, to make your meaning clear.
3. Many young people anticipate the time when they can be their own masters. State in writing what useful advice they could gain from reading this essay.

From Walden

HENRY DAVID THOREAU

WHERE I LIVED, AND WHAT I LIVED FOR

At a certain season of our life we are accustomed to consider every spot as the possible site of a house. I have thus surveyed the country on every side within a dozen miles of where I live. In imagination I have bought all the farms in succession, for all were to be bought, and I knew their price. I walked over each farmer's premises, tasted his wild apples, discoursed on husbandry with him, took his farm at his price, at any price, mortgaging it to him in my mind; even put a higher price on it, —took every thing but a deed of it,—took his word for his deed, for I dearly love to talk,—cultivated it, and him too to some extent, I trust, and withdrew when I had enjoyed it long enough, leaving him to carry it on. This experience entitled me to be regarded as a sort of real-estate broker by my friends. Wherever I sat, there I might live, and the landscape radiated from me accordingly. What is a house but a *sedes*, a seat?—better if a country seat. I discovered many a site for a house not likely to be soon improved, which some might have thought too far from the village, but to my eyes the village was too far from it. Well, there I might live, I said; and there I did live, for an hour, a summer and winter life; saw how I could let the years run off, buffet the winter through, and see the spring come in. The future inhabitants of this region, wherever they may place their houses, may be sure that they have been anticipated. An afternoon sufficed to lay out the land into orchard, woodlot, and pasture, and to decide what fine oaks or pines should be left to stand before the door, and whence each blasted tree could be seen to the best advantage; and then I let it lie, fallow perchance, for a man is rich in proportion to the number of things which he can afford to let alone.

My imagination carried me so far that I even had the refusal of several farms,—the refusal was all I wanted,—but I never got my fingers burned by actual possession. The nearest that I came to actual possession was when I bought the Hollowell place, and had begun to sort my seeds, and collected materials with which to make a wheelbarrow to carry it on or off with; but before the owner gave me a deed of it, his wife—every man has such a wife—changed her mind and wished to keep it, and he offered me ten dollars to release him. Now, to speak the truth, I had but ten cents in the world, and it surpassed my arithmetic to tell, if I was that man who had ten cents, or who had a farm, or ten dollars, or all together. However, I let him keep the ten dollars and the farm too, for I had carried it far enough; or rather, to be generous, I sold him the farm for just what I gave for it, and, as he was not a rich man, made him a present of ten dollars, and still had my ten cents, and seeds, and materials for a wheelbarrow left. I found thus that I had been a rich man without any damage to my property. But I retained the landscape, and I have since annually carried off what it yielded without a wheelbarrow. With respect to landscapes,—

> I am monarch of all I *survey*,
> My right there is none to dispute.

I have frequently seen a poet withdraw, having enjoyed the most valuable part of a farm, while the crusty farmer supposed that he had got a few wild apples only. Why, the owner does not know it for many years when a poet has put his farm in rhyme, the most admirable kind of invisible fence, has fairly impounded it, milked it, skimmed it, and got all the cream, and left the farmer only the skimmed milk.

The real attractions of the Hollowell farm, to me, were: its complete retirement, being about two miles from the village, half a mile from the nearest neighbor, and separated from the highway by a broad field; its bounding on the river, which the owner said protected it by its fogs from frosts in the spring, though that was nothing to me; the gray color and ruinous state of the house and barn, and the dilapidated fences, which put such an interval between me and that last occupant; the hollow and lichen-covered apple trees, gnawed by rabbits, showing what kind of neighbors I should have; but above all, the recollection I had of it from my earliest voyages[1] up the river, when the house was concealed behind a dense grove of red maples, through which I heard the house-dog bark. I was in haste to buy it, before the proprietor finished getting out some rocks, cutting down the hollow apple trees, and grubbing up some young birches which had sprung up in the pasture, or, in short, had made any more of his improvements. To enjoy these advantages I was ready to carry it on; like Atlas, to take the world on my shoulders,—I never heard what compensation he received for that,—and do all those things which had no other motive or excuse but that I might pay for it and be unmolested in my possession of it; for I knew all the while that it would yield the most abundant crop of the kind I wanted if I could only afford to let it alone. But it turned out as I have said.

All that I could say, then, with respect to farming on a large scale (I have always cultivated a garden), was, that I had had my seeds ready. Many think that seeds improve with age. I have no doubt that time discriminates between the good and the bad; and when at last I shall plant, I shall be less likely to be disappointed. But I would say to my fellows, once for all, As long as possible live free and uncommitted. It makes but little difference whether you are committed to a farm or the county jail.

Old Cato, whose *De Re Rusticâ*[2] is my "Cultivator," says, and the only translation I have seen makes sheer nonsense of the passage, "When you think of getting a farm, turn it thus in your mind, not to buy greedily; nor spare your pains to look at

[1]*earliest voyages:* a reference to Thoreau's trip up the Concord and Merrimack Rivers in 1839

[2]*De Re Rusticâ:* a Roman treatise on farm management

it, and do not think it enough to go round it once. The oftener you go there the more it will please you, if it is good." I think I shall not buy greedily, but go round and round it as long as I live, and be buried in it first, that it may please me the more at last.

The present was my next experiment of this kind, which I purpose to describe more at length; for convenience, putting the experience of two years into one. As I have said, I do not propose to write an ode to dejection, but to brag as lustily as chanticleer[3] in the morning, standing on his roost, if only to wake my neighbors up.

When first I took up my abode in the woods, that is, began to spend my nights as well as days there, which, by accident, was on Independence day, or the fourth of July, 1845, my house was not finished for winter, but was merely a defense against the rain, without plastering or chimney, the walls being of rough weather-stained boards, with wide chinks, which made it cool at night. The upright white hewn studs and freshly planed door and window casings gave it a clean and airy look, especially in the morning, when its timbers were saturated with dew, so that I fancied that by noon some sweet gum would exude from them. To my imagination it retained throughout the day more or less of this auroral[4] character, reminding me of a certain house on a mountain which I had visited the year before. This was an airy and unplastered cabin, fit to entertain a traveling god, and where a goddess might trail her garments. The winds which passed over my dwelling were such as sweep over the ridges of mountains, bearing the broken strains, or celestial parts only, of terrestrial music. The morning wind forever blows, the poem of creation is uninterrupted; but few are the ears that hear it. Olympus is but the outside of the earth every where.

The only house I had been the owner of before, if I except a boat, was a tent, which I used occasionally when making excursions in the summer, and this is still rolled up in my garret; but the boat, after passing from hand to hand, has gone down the stream of time. With this more substantial shelter about

[3]*chanticleer:* a rooster
[4]*auroral:* dawn-like

me, I had made some progress toward settling in the world. This frame, so slightly clad, was a sort of crystallization around me, and reacted on the builder. It was suggestive somewhat as a picture in outlines. I did not need to go out doors to take the air, for the atmosphere within had lost none of its freshness. It was not so much within doors as behind a door where I sat, even in the rainiest weather. The Harivansa[5] says, "An abode without birds is like a meat without seasoning." Such was not my abode, for I found myself suddenly neighbor to the birds; not by having imprisoned one, but having caged myself near them. I was not only nearer to some of those which commonly frequent the garden and the orchard, but to those wilder and more thrilling songsters of this forest which never, or rarely, serenade a villager,—the wood-thrush, the veery, the scarlet tanager, the field-sparrow, the whippoorwill, and many others.

I was seated by the shore of a small pond, about a mile and a half south of the village of Concord and somewhat higher than it, in the midst of an extensive wood between that town and Lincoln; and about two miles south of that our only field known to fame, Concord Battle Ground; but I was so low in the woods that the opposite shore, half a mile off, like the rest, covered with wood, was my most distant horizon. For the first week, whenever I looked out on the pond it impressed me like a tarn[6] high up on the side of a mountain, its bottom far above the surface of other lakes, and, as the sun arose, I saw it throwing off its nightly clothing of mist, and here and there, by degrees, its soft ripples or its smooth reflecting surface was revealed, while the mists, like ghosts, were stealthily withdrawing in every direction into the woods, as at the breaking up of some nocturnal conventicle.[7] The very dew seemed to hang upon the trees later into the day than usual, as on the sides of mountains.

This small lake was of most value as a neighbor in the intervals of a gentle rain storm in August, when, both air and water being perfectly still, but the sky overcast, mid-afternoon had all the serenity of evening, and the wood-thrush sang around, and was heard from shore to shore. A lake like this is never

[5]*Harivansa:* a part of the great Indian epic
[6]*tarn:* small mountain lake
[7]*conventicle:* secret meeting

smoother than at such a time; and the clear portion of the air above it being shallow and darkened by clouds, the water, full of light and reflections, becomes a lower heaven itself so much the more important. From a hill top near by, where the wood had been recently cut off, there was a pleasing vista southward across the pond, through a wide indentation in the hills which form the shore there, where their opposite sides sloping toward each other suggested a stream flowing out in that direction through a wooded valley, but stream there was none. That way I looked between and over the near green hills to some distant and higher ones in the horizon, tinged with blue. Indeed, by standing on tiptoe I could catch a glimpse of some of the peaks of the still bluer and more distant mountain ranges in the northwest, those true-blue coins from heaven's own mint, and also of some portion of the village. But in other directions, even from this point, I could not see over or beyond the woods which surrounded me. It is well to have some water in your neighborhood, to give buoyancy to and float the earth. One value even of the smallest well is, that when you look into it you see that earth is not continent but insular. This is as important as that it keeps butter cool. When I looked across the pond from this peak toward the Sudbury meadows, which in time of flood I distinguished elevated perhaps by a mirage in their seething valley, like a coin in a basin, all the earth beyond the pond appeared like a thin crust insulated and floated even by this small sheet of intervening water, and I was reminded that this on which I dwelt was but *dry land.*

Though the view from my door was still more contracted, I did not feel crowded or confined in the least. There was pasture enough for my imagination. The low shrub-oak plateau to which the opposite shore arose, stretched away toward the prairies of the West and the steppes of Tartary, affording ample room for all the roving families of men. "There are none happy in the world but beings who enjoy freely a vast horizon,"—said Damodara, when his herds required new and larger pastures.

Both place and time were changed, and I dwelt nearer to those parts of the universe and to those eras in history which had most attracted me. Where I lived was as far off as many a region viewed nightly by astronomers. We are wont to imagine rare and delectable places in some remote and more celestial corner of the system, behind the constellation of Cassiopeia's Chair, far from noise and disturbance. I discovered that my house actually had its site in such a withdrawn, but forever new and unprofaned, part of the universe. If it were worth the while to settle in those parts near to the Pleiades or the Hyades,[8] to Aldebaran[9] or Altair,[10] then I was really there, or at an equal remoteness from the life which I had left behind, dwindled and twinkling with as fine a ray to my nearest neighbor, and to be seen only in moonless nights by him. Such was that part of creation where I had squatted;—

> There was a shepherd that did live,
> And held his thoughts as high
> As were the mounts whereon his flocks
> Did hourly feed him by.

What should we think of the shepherd's life if his flocks always wandered to higher pastures than his thoughts?

Every morning was a cheerful invitation to make my life of equal simplicity, and I may say innocence, with Nature herself. I have been as sincere a worshipper of Aurora[11] as the Greeks. I got up early and bathed in the pond; that was a religious exercise, and one of the best things which I did. They say that characters were engraven on the bathing tub of king Tching-thang to this effect: "Renew thyself completely each day; do it again, and again, and forever again." I can understand that. Morning brings back the heroic ages. I was as much affected by the faint hum of a mosquito making its invisible and unimaginable tour through my apartment at earliest dawn, when I was sitting with door and windows open, as I could be by any trumpet that ever sang of fame. It was Homer's requiem; itself an Iliad and Odyssey in the air, singing its own wrath and wanderings. There was something cosmical about it; a standing advertisement, till forbidden, of the everlasting vigor and fertility of the world. The morning, which is the

[8] *Pleiades; Hyades:* groups of small stars in the constellation Taurus
[9] *Aldebaran:* a star in the constellation Taurus
[10] *Altair:* a star in the constellation Aquila
[11] *Aurora:* Greek goddess of the dawn

most memorable season of the day, is the awakening hour. Then there is least somnolence in us; and for an hour, at least, some part of us awakes which slumbers all the rest of the day and night. Little is to be expected of that day, if it can be called a day, to which we are not awakened by our Genius,[12] but by the mechanical nudgings of some servitor, are not awakened by our own newly-acquired force and aspirations from within, accompanied by the undulations of celestial music, instead of factory bells, and a fragrance filling the air—to a higher life than we fell asleep from; and thus the darkness bear its fruit, and prove itself to be good, no less than the light. That man who does not believe that each day contains an earlier, more sacred, and auroral hour than he has yet profaned, has despaired of life, and is pursuing a descending and darkening way. After a partial cessation of his sensuous life, the soul of man, or its organs rather, are reinvigorated each day, and his Genius tries again what noble life it can make. All memorable events, I should say, transpire in morning time and in a morning atmosphere. The Vedas[13] say, "All intelligences awake with the morning." Poetry and art, and the fairest and most memorable of the actions of men, date from such an hour. All poets and heroes, like Memnon,[14] are the children of Aurora, and emit their music at sunrise. To him whose elastic and vigorous thought keeps pace with the sun, the day is a perpetual morning. It matters not what the clocks say or the attitudes and labors of men. Morning is when I am awake and there is a dawn in me. Moral reform is the effort to throw off sleep. Why is it that men give so poor an account of their day if they have not been slumbering? They are not such poor calculators. If they had not been overcome with drowsiness they would have performed something. The millions are awake enough for physical labor; but only one in a million is awake enough for effective intellectual exertion, only one in a hundred millions to a poetic or divine life. To be awake is to be alive. I have never yet met a man who was quite awake. How could I have looked him in the face.

[12]*Genius:* guardian spirit, the guide of the individual
[13]*Vedas:* devotional literature of the Hindus
[14]*Memnon:* The statue in the temple at Memnon (Thebes) was said to emit harp-like sounds when it was struck by the rays of the sun.

We must learn to reawaken and keep ourselves awake, not by mechanical aids, but by an infinite expectation of the dawn, which does not forsake us in our soundest sleep. I know of no more encouraging fact than the unquestionable ability of man to elevate his life by a conscious endeavor. It is something to be able to paint a particular picture, or to carve a statue, or so to make a few objects beautiful; but it is far more glorious to carve and paint the very atmosphere and medium through which we look, which morally we can do. To affect the quality of the day, that is the highest of arts. Every man is tasked to make his life, even in its details, worthy of contemplation of his most elevated and critical hour. If we refused, or rather used up, such paltry information as we get, the oracles would distinctly inform us how this might be done.

I went to the woods because I wished to live deliberately, to front only the essential facts of life, and see if I could not learn what it had to teach, and not, when I came to die, discover that I had not lived. I did not wish to live what was not life, living is so dear;[15] nor did I wish to practise resignation, unless it was quite necessary. I wanted to live deep and suck out all the marrow of life, to live so sturdily and Spartan-like[16] as to put to rout all that was not life, to cut a broad swath and shave close, to drive life into a corner, and reduce it to its lowest terms, and, if it proved to be mean, why then to get the whole and genuine meanness of it, and publish its meanness to the world; or if it were sublime, to know it by experience, and be able to give a true account of it in my next excursion. For most men, it appears to me, are in a strange uncertainty about it, whether it is of the devil or of God, and have *somewhat hastily* concluded that it is the chief end of man here to "glorify God and enjoy him forever."[17]

Still we live meanly, like ants; though the fable tells us that we were long ago changed into men; like pygmies we fight with cranes; it is error upon error, and clout upon clout, and our best virtue has for its occasion a superfluous and evitable wretchedness. Our life is frittered away by detail. An honest

[15] *dear:* precious

[16] *Spartan-like:* The ancient Spartans lived a rigorous physical life.

[17] *"glorify . . . forever.":* from the Westminster Catechism, written for the Presbyterian faith

man has hardly need to count more than his ten fingers, or in extreme cases he may add his ten toes, and lump the rest. Simplicity, simplicity, simplicity! I say, let your affairs be as two or three, and not a hundred or a thousand; instead of a million count half a dozen, and keep your accounts on your thumb nail. In the midst of this chopping sea of civilized life, such are the clouds and storms and quicksands and thousand-and-one items to be allowed for, that a man has to live, if he would not founder and go to the bottom and not make his port at all, by dead reckoning, and he must be a great calculator indeed who succeeds. Simplify, simplify. Instead of three meals a day, if it be necessary eat but one; instead of a hundred dishes, five; and reduce other things in proportion. Our life is like a German Confederacy, made up of petty states, with its boundary forever fluctuating, so that even a German cannot tell you how it is bounded at any moment. The nation itself, with all its so called internal improvements, which, by the way, are all external and superficial, is just such an unwieldy and overgrown establishment, cluttered with furniture and tripped up by its own traps, ruined by luxury and heedless expense, by want of calculation and a worthy aim, as the million households in the land; and the only cure for it as for them is in a rigid economy, a stern and more than Spartan simplicity of life and elevation of purpose. It lives too fast. Men think that it is essential that the *Nation* have commerce, and export ice, and talk through a telegraph, and ride thirty miles an hour, without a doubt, whether *they* do or not; but whether we should live like baboons or like men, is a little uncertain. If we do not get our sleepers,[18] and forge rails, and devote days and nights to the work, but go to tinkering upon our *lives* to improve *them*, who will build railroads? And if railroads are not built, how shall we get to heaven in season?[19] But if we stay at home and mind our business, who will want railroads? We do not ride on the railroad; it rides upon us. Did you ever think what those sleepers are that underlie the railroad? Each one is a man, an Irishman, or a Yankee man. The rails are laid on them, and they are covered with sand, and the cars run smoothly over them.

[18] *sleepers:* railway ties

[19] *And . . . season:* apparently a reference to Hawthorne's story, "The Celestial Railroad"

They are sound sleepers, I assure you. And every few years a new lot is laid down and run over; so that, if some have the pleasure of riding on a rail, others have the misfortune to be ridden upon. And when they run over a man that is walking in his sleep, a supernumerary[20] sleeper in the wrong position, and wake him up, they suddenly stop the cars, and make a hue and cry about it, as if this were an exception. I am glad to know that it takes a gang of men for every five miles to keep the sleepers down and level in their beds as it is, for this is a sign that they may sometimes get up again.

Why should we live with such hurry and waste of life? We are determined to be starved before we are hungry. Men say that a stitch in time saves nine, and so they take a thousand stitches to-day to save nine to-morrow. As for *work*, we haven't any of any consequence. We have the Saint Vitus' dance,[21] and cannot possibly keep our heads still. If I should only give a few pulls at the parish bell-rope, as for a fire, that is, without setting the bell, there is hardly a man on his farm in the outskirts of Concord, notwithstanding that press of engagements which was his excuse so many times this morning, nor a boy, nor a woman, I might almost say, but would forsake all and follow that sound, not mainly to save property from the flames, but, if we will confess the truth, much more to see it burn, since burn it must, and we, be it known, did not set it on fire,—or to see it put out, and have a hand in it, if that is done as handsomely; yes, even if it were the parish church itself. Hardly a man takes a half hour's nap after dinner, but when he wakes he holds up his head and asks, "What's the news?" as if the rest of mankind had stood his sentinels. Some give directions to be waked every half hour, doubtless for no other purpose; and then, to pay for it, they tell what they have dreamed. After a night's sleep the news is as indispensable as the breakfast. "Pray tell me any thing new that has happened to a man any where on this globe,"—and he reads it over his coffee and rolls, that a man has had his eyes gouged out this morning on the Wachita River;[22] never dreaming the while that he lives in

[20] *supernumerary:* extra

[21] *Saint Vitus' dance:* a disease of the nerves in which there are muscular contractions and twitching

[22] *Wachita River:* the Ouachita River on the Arkansas frontier

the dark unfathomed mammoth cave[23] of this world, and has but the rudiment of an eye himself.

For my part, I could easily do without the post-office. I think that there are very few important communications made through it. To speak critically, I never received more than one or two letters in my life—I wrote this some years ago—that were worth the postage. The penny-post is, commonly, an institution through which you seriously offer a man that penny for his thoughts which is so often safely offered in jest. And I am sure that I never read any memorable news in a newspaper. If we read of one man robbed, or murdered, or killed by accident, or one house burned, or one vessel wrecked, or one steamboat blown up, or one cow run over on the Western Railroad, or one mad dog killed, or one lot of grasshoppers in the winter,—we never need read of another. One is enough. If you are acquainted with the principle, what do you care for a myriad instances and applications? To a philosopher all *news*, as it is called, is gossip, and they who edit and read it are old women over their tea. Yet not a few are greedy after this gossip. There was such a rush, as I hear, the other day at one of the offices to learn the foreign news by the last arrival, that several large squares of plate glass belonging to the establishment were broken by the pressure,—news which I seriously think a ready wit might write a twelvemonth or twelve years beforehand with sufficient accuracy. As for Spain, for instance, if you know how to throw in Don Carlos and the Infanta, and Don Pedro and Seville and Granada,[24] from time to time in the right proportions,—they may have changed the names a little since I saw the papers,—and serve up a bull-fight when other entertainments fail, it will be true to the letter, and give us as good an idea of the exact state or ruin of things in Spain as the most succinct and lucid reports under this head in the newspapers: and as for England, almost the last significant scrap of news from that quarter was the revolution of 1649; and if you have learned the history of her crops for an average year, you never need attend to that thing again, unless your speculations

[23] *mammoth cave:* the Mammoth Cave in Kentucky. Also, figuratively, Thoreau seems to be speaking of man's blindness to reality; see the myth of the cave in Plato's *Republic*.

[24] *Don Carlos . . . Granada:* the principal figures and places of the Civil War in Spain during the 1830's and 1840's

are of a merely pecuniary character. If one may judge who rarely looks into the newspapers, nothing new does ever happen in foreign parts, a French revolution not excepted.

What news! how much more important to know what that is which was never old! "Kieou-he-yu (great dignitary of the State of Wei) sent a man to Khoung-tseu to know his news. Khoung-tseu caused the messenger to be seated near him, and questioned him in these terms: What is your master doing? The messenger answered with respect: My master desires to diminish the number of his faults, but he cannot come to the end of them. The messenger being gone, the philosopher remarked: What a worthy messenger! What a worthy messenger!" The preacher, instead of vexing the ears of drowsy farmers on their day of rest at the end of the week,—for Sunday is the fit conclusion of an ill-spent week, and not the fresh and brave beginning of a new one,—with this one other draggletail of a sermon, should shout with thundering voice,—"Pause! Avast! Why so seemingly fast, but deadly slow?"

Shams and delusions are esteemed for soundest truths, while reality is fabulous. If men would steadily observe realities only, and not allow themselves to be deluded, life, to compare it with such things as we know, would be like a fairy tale and the Arabian Nights' Entertainments. If we respected only what is inevitable and has a right to be, music and poetry would resound along the streets. When we are unhurried and wise, we perceive that only great and worthy things have any permanent and absolute existence,—that petty fears and petty pleasures are but the shadow of the reality. This is always exhilarating and sublime. By closing the eyes and slumbering, and consenting to be deceived by shows, men establish and confirm their daily life of routine and habit every where, which still is built on purely illusory foundations. Children, who play life, discern its true law and relations more clearly than men, who fail to live it worthily, but who think that they are wiser by experience, that is, by failure. I have read in a Hindoo book, that "there was a king's son, who, being expelled in infancy from his native city, was brought up by a forester, and, growing up to maturity in that state, imagined himself to belong to the barbarous race with which he lived. One of his father's ministers having discovered him, revealed to him what he was, and the misconception of his character was removed, and he knew himself to be a prince. So soul," continues the Hindoo philosopher, "from the circumstances in which it is placed, mistakes its own character, until the truth is revealed to it by some holy teacher, and then it knows itself to be *Brahme.*"[25] I perceive that we inhabitants of New England live this mean life that we do because our vision does not penetrate the surface of things. We think that that *is* which *appears* to be. If a man should walk through this town and see only the reality, where, think you, would the "Mill-dam" go to? If he should give us an account of the realities he beheld there, we should not recognize the place in his description. Look at a meeting-house, or a court-house, or a jail, or a shop, or a dwelling-house, and say what that thing really is before a true gaze, and they would all go to pieces in your account of them. Men esteem truth remote, in the outskirts of the system, behind the farthest star, before Adam and after the last man. In eternity there is indeed something true and sublime. But all these times and places and occasions are now and here. God himself culminates in the present moment, and will never be more divine in the lapse of all the ages. And we are enabled to apprehend at all what is sublime and noble only by the perpetual instilling and drenching of the reality that surrounds us. The universe constantly and obediently answers to our conceptions; whether we travel fast or slow, the track is laid for us. Let us spend our lives in conceiving then. The poet or the artist never yet had so fair and noble a design but some of his posterity at least could accomplish it.

Let us spend one day as deliberately as Nature, and not be thrown off the track by every nutshell and mosquito's wing that falls on the rails. Let us rise early and fast, or break fast, gently and without perturbation; let company come and let company go, let the bells ring and the children cry,—determined to make a day of it. Why should we knock under and go with the stream? Let us not be upset and overwhelmed in that terrible rapid and whirlpool called a dinner, situated in the meridian shallows. Weather this danger and you are safe, for

[25] *Brahme* (or Brahma): to the Transcendentalists, the supreme spirit who saw things as they were rather than as they appear to be

the rest of the way is down hill. With unrelaxed nerves, with morning vigor, sail by it, looking another way, tied to the mast like Ulysses.[26] If the engine whistles, let it whistle till it is hoarse for its pains. If the bell rings, why should we run? We will consider what kind of music they are like. Let us settle ourselves, and work and wedge our feet downward through the mud and slush of opinion, and prejudice, and tradition, and delusion, and appearance, that alluvion which covers the globe, through Paris and London, through New York and Boston and Concord, through church and state, through poetry and philosophy and religion, till we come to a hard bottom and rocks in place, which we can call *reality*, and say, This is, and no mistake; and then begin, having a *point d'appui*,[27] below freshet and frost and fire, a place where you might found a wall or a state, or set a lamp-post safely, or perhaps a gauge, not a Nilometer,[28] but a Realometer,[29] that future ages might know how deep a freshet of shams and appearances had gathered from time to time. If you stand right fronting and face to face to a fact, you will see the sun glimmer on both its surfaces, as if it were a cimeter,[30] and feel its sweet edge dividing you through the heart and marrow, and so you will happily conclude your mortal career. Be it life or death, we crave only reality. If we are really dying, let us hear the rattle in our throats and feel cold in the extremities; if we are alive, let us go about our business.

Time is but the stream I go a-fishing in. I drink at it; but while I drink I see the sandy bottom and detect how shallow it is. Its thin current slides away, but eternity remains. I would drink deeper; fish in the sky, whose bottom is pebbly with stars. I cannot count one. I know not the first letter of the alphabet. I have always been regretting that I was not as wise as the day I was born. The intellect is a cleaver; it discerns and rifts its way into the secret of things. I do not wish to be any more busy with my hands than is necessary. My head is hands

[26] *Ulysses:* In the *Odyssey*, Book 12, Ulysses was tied to protect him from the seductive songs of the Sirens.

[27] *point d'appui:* support

[28] *Nilometer:* an instrument for measuring the height of water in the Nile River

[29] *Realometer:* Thoreau's imaginary instrument for measuring reality

[30] *cimeter:* curved sword

and feet. I feel all my best faculties concentrated in it. My instinct tells me that my head is an organ for burrowing, as some creatures use their snout and fore-paws, and with it I would mine and burrow my way through these hills. I think that the richest vein is somewhere hereabouts; so by the divining rod[31] and thin rising vapors I judge; and here I will begin to mine.

[31] *divining rod:* a forked wooden rod used to find underground metals or water

FOR DISCUSSION

1. In this selection from *Walden*, what does Thoreau hope to learn by going to the woods "to live deliberately"? How would this act determine the way he conducts his life thereafter? To discover the truth about life, why does he feel he must "drive life into a corner"?
2. Does Thoreau actually want to *own* a farm? What attracts him to the Hollowell farm? Why is he in a haste to buy it,yet willing to give it back to its owner? What advice does he give to his "fellows"? What conclusions does he draw from Old Cato's advice?
3. Why is Thoreau's abode *not* "like meat without seasoning"? What are the advantages of being "seated" in this particular part of the country? Point out those sights and views which delight him most and the images he uses in describing them.
4. For most people, morning is a time of day. What is it for Thoreau? For what kind of person is the day "a perpetual morning"? What proof does Thoreau give in support of his statement, "I have never yet met a man who was quite awake"? How would such a man differ from "the millions"?
5. What paradox (contradiction) does Thoreau see between what most men consider their chief end in life and the way they live; namely, like ants? How would "simplicity" solve many individual and national problems? In your opinion, would it interfere with what is called "progress"? Why is Thoreau opposed to this kind of progress?
6. Thoreau passes judgment not only on the way his countrymen behaved but also on what they considered important. As you discuss these judgments, tell why you think they are, or are not, justified by the evidence he gives. Also tell why you do, or do not, agree with his judgments.

7. Why do children, "who play life, discern its true law and relations more clearly than men"? Do you agree with this observation? Where should man search for the truth? How can he recognize what is sublime and noble? What must he do if he is to reach that "hard bottom" which can be called "*reality*"?
8. Like a true poet, Thoreau expresses profound thoughts and observations through simple images and comparisons. Note, for example, the metaphor in the next to the last paragraph, in which a fact is compared to a curved sword—a cimeter. Show the relationship between this comparison and the two statements that follow.
9. The ideas in the last paragraph are expressed almost entirely through such implied comparisons as, time is a stream, and the intellect is a cleaver. Find others. What thought does each make clear?
10. Note that the last line brings the reader back to the central idea of this chapter from *Walden:* why Thoreau chooses to live in the woods and what he lives for. From your reading of this chapter, what would you say is the "vein" he is going to mine? What reasons does he have for believing that it is "richest" in that part of New England he has chosen as his "seat"?

FOR COMPOSITION

1. Write a short essay based on any one of the following quotations. You may, if you like, tell why you do, or do not, agree with the thought or opinion expressed. Or you may show why this thought or opinion is applicable to life and people today—even to yourself.
   a. ". . . a man is rich in proportion to the number of things he can afford to let alone."
   b. "Our life is frittered away by detail."
   c. ". . . [we] live this mean life that we do because our vision does not penetrate the surface of things. We think that that *is* which *appears* to be."
   d. "We do not ride on the railroad; it rides on us."
2. In a short composition make clear the ideas stated in one of the following quotations. Base your interpretation on what is expressed in this chapter from *Walden*.
   a. "To be awake is to be alive."
   b. "Moral reform is the effort to throw off sleep."
   c. "We are determined to be starved before we are hungry."

From Thoreau's Journal

A BROKEN FRIENDSHIP

And now another friendship is ended. I do not know what has made my friend doubt me, but I know that in love there is no mistake, and that every estrangement is well founded. But my destiny is not narrowed, but if possible the broader for it. The heavens withdraw and arch themselves higher. I am sensible not only of a moral, but even a grand physical pain, such as gods may feel, about my head and breast, a certain ache and fullness. This rending of a tie, it is not my work nor thine. It is no accident that we mind; it is only the awards of fate that are affecting.[1] I know of no æons, or periods, no life and death, but these meetings and separations. My life is like a stream that is suddenly dammed and has no outlet; but it rises the higher up the hills that shut it in, and will become a deep and silent lake. Certainly there is no event comparable for grandeur with the eternal separation—if we may conceive it so—from a being that we have known. I become in a degree sensible of the

[1] *affecting:* acting upon (the mind or feelings)

meaning of finite and infinite. What a grand significance the word "never" acquires! With one with whom we have walked on high ground we cannot deal on any lower ground ever after. We have tried for so many years to put each other to this immortal use, and have failed. Undoubtedly our good genii have mutually found the material unsuitable. We have hitherto paid each other the highest possible compliment; we have recognized each other constantly as divine, have afforded each other that opportunity to live that no other wealth or kindness can afford. And now, for some reason inappreciable by us, it has become necessary for us to withhold this mutual aid. Perchance there is none beside who knows us for a god, and none whom we know for such. Each man and woman is a veritable god or goddess, but to the mass of their fellows disguised. There is only one in each case who sees through the disguise. That one who does not stand so near to any man as to see the divinity in him is truly alone. I am perfectly sad at parting from you. I could better have the earth taken away from under my feet, than the thought of you from my mind. One while I think that some great injury has been done, with which you are implicated, again that you are no party to it. I fear that there may be incessant tragedies, that one may treat his fellow as a god but receive somewhat less regard from him. I now almost for the first time *fear* this. Yet I believe that in the long run there is no such inequality.

(February 8, 1857)

FOR DISCUSSION

1. From his entry in the *Journal* what evidence do you find that Thoreau feels the need of friends? What quality of close friendship does he value? What effect does this "eternal separation" have on him? Why does he say, "My life is like a stream"?
2. Who is "truly alone"? Explain.
3. Whom or what does he blame for the separation? What doubt (in the final three sentences) seems to disturb him?

CONCORD VS. PARIS

When it was proposed to me to go abroad, rub off some rust, and *better my condition* in a worldly sense, I feared lest my life would lose some of its homeliness. If these fields and streams and woods, the phenomena of nature here, and the simple occupations of the inhabitants should cease to interest and inspire me, no culture or wealth would atone for the loss. I fear the dissipation that traveling, going into society, even the best, the enjoyment of intellectual luxuries, imply. If Paris is much in your mind, if it is more and more to you, Concord is less and less, and yet it would be a wretched bargain to accept the proudest Paris in exchange for my native village. At best, Paris could only be a school in which to learn to live here, a stepping-stone to Concord, a school in which to fit for this university. I wish so to live ever as to derive my satisfactions and inspirations from the commonest events, every-day phenomena, so that what my senses hourly perceive, my daily walk, the conversation of my neighbors, may inspire me, and I may dream of no heaven but that which lies about me. A man may acquire a taste for wine or brandy, and so lose his love for water, but should we not pity him?

(March 11, 1856)

FOR DISCUSSION

1. What are Thoreau's reasons for preferring Concord to Paris? What is the value of "everyday phenomena"?
2. What is the meaning of the last sentence? How does it sum up his attitude toward experience?

NOVEMBER TWILIGHT

As the afternoons grow shorter, and the early evening drives us home to complete our chores, we are reminded of the shortness of life, and become more pensive, at least in this twilight of the year. We are prompted to make haste and finish our work before the night comes. I leaned over a rail in the twilight on the Walden road, waiting for the evening mail to be distributed, when such thoughts visited me. I seemed to recognize the November evening as a familiar thing come round again, and yet I could hardly tell whether I had ever known it or only divined it. The November twilights just begun! It appeared like a part of a panorama at which I sat spectator, a part with which I was perfectly familiar just coming into view, and I foresaw how it would look and roll along, and prepared to be pleased. Just such a piece of art merely, though infinitely sweet and grand, did it appear to me, and just as little were any active duties required of me. We are independent on all that we see. The hangman whom I have *seen* cannot hang me. The earth which I have *seen* cannot bury me. Such doubleness and distance does sight prove. Only the rich and such as are troubled with ennui[1] are implicated in the maze of phenomena. You cannot see anything until you are clear of it. The long railroad causeway through the meadows west of me, the still twilight in which hardly a cricket was heard, the dark bank of clouds in the horizon long after sunset, the villagers crowding to the post-office, and the hastening home to supper by candlelight, had I not seen all this before! What new sweet was I to extract from it? Truly they mean that we shall learn our lesson well. Nature gets thumbed like an old spelling book. The alms-house and Frederick were still as last November. I was no nearer, methinks, nor further off from my friends. Yet I sat the bench with perfect contentment, unwilling to exchange the familiar vision that was to be unrolled for any treasure or heaven that could be imagined. Sure to keep just so far apart in our orbits still, in obedience to the laws of attraction and repulsion, affording each other only steady but indispensable starlight. It was as if I was promised the greatest novelty the world has ever seen or shall see, though the utmost possible novelty would be the difference between me and myself a year ago. This alone encouraged me, and was my fuel for the approaching winter. That we may behold the panorama with this slight improvement or change, this is what we sustain life for with so much effort from year to year.

[1] *ennui:* boredom

And yet there is no more tempting novelty than this new November. No going to Europe or another world is to be named with it. Give me the old familiar walk, post-office and all, with this ever new self, with this infinite expectation and faith, which does not know when it is beaten. We'll go nutting once more. We'll pluck the nut of the world, and crack it in the winter evenings. Theatres and all other sightseeing are puppet-shows in comparison. I will take another walk to the Cliff, another row on the river, another skate on the meadow, be out in the first snow, and associate with the winter birds. Here I am at home. In the bare and bleached crust of the earth I recognize my friend.

(November 1, 1858)

FOR DISCUSSION

1. What effect does twilight have on Thoreau? What likeness does he see between life and the "twilight of the year"? What feeling does this selection convey? What passages do you consider particularly moving? What familiar details add a sense of reality to the writer's meditation?
2. How do you interpret Thoreau's comment, "You cannot see anything until you are clear of it"? Why is the panorama so familiar? To what does he prefer it?
3. What is the great novelty which the coming season offered? What is the "utmost possible novelty"? How is it related to man's will to live?
4. Despite his distress at the folly of men and nations, Thoreau loved life. How is this fact revealed in the last paragraph? What view of life and death is expressed in the last two lines of this entry, written only four years before his death at forty-five?

TWAIN AND ADAMS

The most personal of all kinds of writing is the autobiographical reminiscence. Since the American experience is as varied as the citizens of the nation, the four selections which follow were chosen to reveal some of the diversity in American autobiography.

As Mark Twain describes his youthful days on his uncle's farm in his *Autobiography,* he conjures up a picture of childhood innocence and delight. Here are children growing up among rural scenes which leave them untainted by the greater wickedness of cities. Here are affectionate and wise adults who make such carefree pleasures possible. All the ingredients idealized for two centuries are present: plenty of playmates, moonlight escapades, the one-room schoolhouse, the delicious treats and stories available around the nightly fire. And however much Twain's biographers may doubt that things were really so delightful as he said they were, Twain still performed a great service by describing this idyllic scene in words future readers might enjoy.

Henry Adams was a different kind of man altogether, and his reminiscences are likewise different. Shy, introspective, full of doubts and regrets, Henry Adams left a far more critical commentary on American life in his great classic, *The Education of Henry Adams;* but his memories are no less real than Twain's. It is ironic to notice that at the ends of their lives, Adams's view of the future of humanity, though wistful and sad, is far less bitter than Twain's. Twain ended his days suggesting that the most wholesome prospect for the future would be the total obliteration of the "damned human race."

My Uncle's Farm

MARK TWAIN

I

My uncle, John A. Quarles, was a farmer and his place was in the country four miles from Florida.[1] He had eight children and fifteen or twenty Negroes and was also fortunate in other ways, particularly in his character. I have not come across a better man than he was. I was his guest for two or three months every year, from the fourth year after we removed to Hannibal[2] till I was eleven or twelve years old. I have never consciously used him or his wife in a book, but his farm has come very handy to me in literature once or twice. In *Huck Finn* and in *Tom Sawyer, Detective* I moved it down to Arkansas. It was all of six hundred miles but it was no trouble; it was not a very large farm, five hundred acres perhaps, but I could have done it if it had been twice as large. And as for the morality of it, I cared nothing for that; I would move a state if the exigencies[3] of literature required it.

[1] *Florida:* the town in Missouri which was Mark Twain's birthplace
[2] *Hannibal:* town in Missouri
[3] *exigencies:* requirements

It was a heavenly place for a boy, that farm of my uncle John's. The house was a double log one with a spacious floor (roofed in) connecting it with the kitchen. In the summer the table was set in the middle of that shady and breezy floor, and the sumptuous meals—well, it makes me cry to think of them. Fried chicken, roast pig, wild and tame turkeys, ducks and geese, venison just killed, squirrels, rabbits, pheasants, partridges, prairie-chickens, biscuits, hot battercakes, hot buckwheat cakes, hot "wheat bread," hot rolls, hot corn pone; fresh corn boiled on the ear, succotash, butter-beans, string-beans, tomatoes, peas, Irish potatoes, sweet potatoes; buttermilk, sweet milk; "clabber";[4] watermelons, muskmelons, cantaloupes—all fresh from the garden—apple pie, peach pie, pumpkin pie, apple dumplings, peach cobbler—I can't remember the rest. The way that the things were cooked was perhaps the main splendor, particularly a certain few of the dishes. For instance the corn bread, the hot biscuits and wheat bread, and the fried chicken. These things have never been properly cooked in the North—in fact no one there is able to learn the art, so far as my experience goes. The North thinks it knows how to make corn bread but this is mere superstition. Perhaps no bread in the world is quite so good as Southern corn bread, and perhaps no bread in the world is quite so bad as the Northern imitation of it. The North seldom tries to fry chicken and this is well; the art cannot be learned north of the line of Mason and Dixon, nor anywhere in Europe. This is not hearsay; it is experience that is speaking. In Europe it is imagined that the custom of serving various kinds of bread blazing hot is "American" but that is too broad a spread; it is custom in the South but is much less than that in the North. In the North and in Europe hot bread is considered unhealthy. This is probably another fussy superstition, like the European superstition that ice-water is unhealthy. Europe does not need ice-water and does not drink it; and yet notwithstanding this its word for it is better than ours, because it describes it, whereas ours doesn't. Europe calls it "iced" water. Our word describes water made from melted ice—a drink which has a characterless taste and which we have but little acquaintance with.

[4]*clabber:* thick, sour milk

It seems a pity that the world should throw away so many good things merely because they are unwholesome. I doubt if God has given us any refreshment which, taken in moderation, is unwholesome, except microbes. Yet there are people who strictly deprive themselves of each and every eatable, drinkable, and smokable which has in anyway acquired a shady reputation. They pay this price for health. And health is all they get for it. How strange it is. It is like paying out your whole fortune for a cow that has gone dry.

The farm-house stood in the middle of a very large yard and the yard was fenced on three sides with rails and on the rear side with high palings; against these stood the smoke-house; beyond the palings was the orchard; beyond the orchard were the Negro quarter and the tobacco fields. The front yard was entered over a stile made of sawed-off logs of graduated heights; I do not remember any gate. In a corner of the front yard were a dozen lofty hickory trees and a dozen black walnuts, and in the nutting season riches were to be gathered there.

Down a piece, abreast the house, stood a little log cabin against the rail fence; and there the woody hill fell sharply away, past the barns, the corn-crib, the stables, and the tobacco-curing house, to a limpid brook which sang along over its gravelly bed and curved and frisked in and out and here and there and yonder in the deep shade of overhanging foliage and vines—a divine place for wading, and it had swimming-pools too, which were forbidden to us and therefore much frequented by us. For we were little Christian children and had early been taught the value of forbidden fruit.

In the little log cabin lived a bedridden white-headed slave woman whom we visited daily and looked upon with awe, for we believed she was upward of a thousand years old and had talked with Moses. The younger Negroes credited these statistics and had furnished them to us in good faith. We accommodated all the details which came to us about her, and so we believed that she had lost her health in the long desert trip coming out of Egypt and had never been able to get it back again. She had a round bald place on the crown of her head, and we used to creep around and gaze at it in reverent silence and reflect that it was caused by fright through seeing Pharaoh drowned. We called her "Aunt" Hannah, Southern fashion. She was superstitious, like the other Negroes; also, like them, she was deeply religious. Like them, she had great faith in prayer and employed it in all ordinary exigencies, but not in cases where a dead certainty of result was urgent. Whenever witches were around she tied up the remnant of her wool in little tufts with white thread, and this promptly made the witches impotent.

All the Negroes were friends of ours and with those of our own age we were in effect comrades. I say in effect, using the phrase as a modification. We were comrades and yet not comrades; color and condition interposed a subtle line which both parties were conscious of and which rendered complete fusion impossible. We had a faithful and affectionate good friend, ally, and adviser in "Uncle Dan'l," a middle-aged slave whose head was the best one in the Negro quarter, whose sympathies were wide and warm, and whose heart was honest and simple and knew no guile. He has served me well these many, many years. I have not seen him for more than half a century, and yet spiritually I have had his welcome company a good part of that time and have staged him in books under his own name and as Jim and carted him all around, to Hannibal, down the Mississippi on a raft, and even across the Desert of Sahara in a balloon—and he has endured it all with the patience and friendliness and loyalty which were his birthright. It was on the farm that I got my strong liking for his race and my appreciation of certain of its fine qualities. This feeling and this estimate have stood the test of sixty years and more, and have suffered no impairment. The black face is as welcome to me now as it was then.

In my school-boy days I had no aversion to slavery. I was not aware that there was anything wrong about it. No one arraigned it in my hearing; the local papers said nothing against it; the local pulpit taught us that God approved it, that it was a holy thing, and that the doubter need only look in the Bible if he wished to settle his mind—and then the texts were read aloud to us to make the matter sure; if the slaves themselves had an aversion to slavery, they were wise and said nothing.

In Hannibal we seldom saw a slave misused; on the farm, never.

There was, however, one small incident of my boyhood days which touched this matter and it must have meant a good deal to me or it would not have stayed in my memory, clear and sharp, vivid and shadowless, all these slow-drifting years. We had a little slave boy whom we had hired from someone, there in Hannibal. He was from the Eastern Shore of Maryland and had been brought away from his family and his friends, halfway across the American continent, and sold. He was a cheery spirit, innocent and gentle, and the noisiest creature that ever was perhaps. All day long he was singing, whistling, yelling, whooping, laughing—it was maddening, devastating, unendurable. At last, one day, I lost all my temper and went raging to my mother and said Sandy had been singing for an hour without a single break, and I couldn't stand it, and *wouldn't* she please shut him up. The tears came into her eyes and her lip trembled, and she said something like this:

"Poor thing, when he sings it shows that he is not remembering, and that comforts me but when he is still I am afraid he is thinking and I cannot bear it. He will never see his mother again; if he can sing, I must not hinder it but be thankful for it. If you were older, you would understand me; then that friendless child's noise would make you glad."

It was a simple speech and made up of small words but it went home, and Sandy's noise was not a trouble to me any more. She never used large words but she had a natural gift for making small ones do effective work. She lived to reach the neighborhood of ninety years and was capable with her tongue to the last, especially when a meanness or an injustice roused her spirit. She has come handy to me several times in my books, where she figures as Tom Sawyer's Aunt Polly. I fitted her out with a dialect and tried to think up other improvements for her, but did not find any. I used Sandy once, also; it was in *Tom Sawyer*. I tried to get him to whitewash the fence but it did not work. I do not remember what name I called him by in the book.

I can see the farm yet with perfect clearness. I can see all its belongings, all its details: the family room of the house with a "trundle" bed in one corner and a spinning-wheel in another, a wheel whose rising and falling wail, heard from a distance, was the mournfulest of all sounds to me and made me homesick and low-spirited and filled my atmosphere with the wandering spirits of the dead; the vast fireplace, piled high on winter nights with flaming hickory logs from whose ends a sugary sap bubbled out but did not go to waste, for we scraped it off and ate it; the lazy cat spread out on the rough hearthstones; the drowsy dogs braced against the jambs and blinking; my aunt in one chimney corner, knitting; my uncle in the other, smoking his corn-cob pipe; the slick and carpetless oak floor faintly mirroring the dancing flame-tongues and freckled with black indentations where fire-coals had popped out and died a leisurely death; half a dozen children romping in the background twilight; split-bottomed chairs here and there, some with rockers; a cradle, out of service but waiting with confidence; in the early cold mornings a snuggle of children in shirts and chemises occupying the hearth-stone and procrastinating—they could not bear to leave that comfortable place and go out on the wind-swept floor-space between the house and kitchen where the general tin basin stood, and wash.

Along outside of the front fence ran the country road, dusty in the summertime and a good place for snakes—they liked to lie in it and sun themselves; when they were rattlesnakes or puff adders, we killed them; when they were black snakes or racers or belonged to the fabled "hoop" breed, we fled, without shame; when they were "house-snakes" or "garters" we carried them home and put them in Aunt Patsy's work-basket for a surprise; for she was prejudiced against snakes and always when she took the basket in her lap and they began to climb out of it, it disordered her mind. She never could seem to get used to them, her opportunities went for nothing. And she was always cold toward bats, too, and could not bear them; and yet I think a bat is as friendly a bird as there is. My mother was Aunt Patsy's sister and had the same wild superstitions. A bat is beautifully soft and silky; I do not know any creature that is pleasanter to the touch or is more grateful for caressings, if offered in the right spirit. I know all about these coleoptera because our great cave, three miles below Hannibal, was multitudinously stocked with them and often I brought them home to amuse my mother with. It was easy to manage if it was a school-day, because then I had ostensibly been to school and hadn't any bats. She was not a suspicious person but full of trust and confidence, and when I said, "There's something in my coat-pocket for you," she would put her hand in. But she always took it out again, herself; I didn't have to tell her. It was remarkable, the way she couldn't learn to like private bats. The more experience she had, the more she could not change her views.

I think she was never in the cave in her life; but everybody else went there. Many excursion parties came from considerable distances up and down the river to visit the cave. It was miles in extent and was a tangled wilderness of narrow and lofty clefts and passages. It was an easy place to get lost in; anybody could do it, including the bats. I got lost in it myself, along with a lady, and our last candle burned down to almost nothing before we glimpsed the search-party's lights winding about in the distance.

"Injun Joe," the half-breed, got lost in there once and would have starved to death if the bats had run short. But there was no chance of that, there were myriads of them. He told me all his story. In the book called *Tom Sawyer* I starved him entirely to death in the cave but that was in the interest of art: it never happened. "General" Gaines, who was our first town drunkard before Jimmy Finn got the place, was lost in there for the space of a week and finally pushed his handkerchief out of a hole in a hilltop near Saverton, several miles down the river from the cave's mouth, and somebody saw it and dug him out. There is nothing the matter with his statistics except the handkerchief. I knew him for years and he hadn't any. But it could have been his nose. That would attract attention.

The cave was an uncanny place for it contained a corpse, the corpse of a young girl of fourteen. It was in a glass cylinder inclosed in a copper one which was suspended from a rail which bridged a narrow passage. The body was preserved in alcohol, and it was said that loafers and rowdies used to drag it up by the hair and look at the dead face. The girl was the daughter of a St. Louis surgeon of extraordinary ability and wide celebrity. He was an eccentric man and did many strange things. He put the poor thing in that forlorn place himself.

II

Beyond the road where the snakes sunned themselves was a dense young thicket, and through it a dim-lighted path led a quarter of a mile; then out of the dimness one emerged abruptly upon a level great prairie which was covered with wild strawberry plants, vividly starred with prairie pinks, and walled in on all sides by forests. The strawberries were fragrant and fine and in the season we were generally there in the crisp freshness of the early morning, while the dew-beads still sparkled upon the grass and the woods were ringing with the first songs of the birds.

Down the forest-slopes to the left were the swings. They were made of bark stripped from hickory saplings. When they became dry they were dangerous. They usually broke when a child was forty feet in the air, and this was why so many bones had to be mended every year. I had no ill luck myself, but none of my cousins escaped. There were eight of them and at one time and another they broke fourteen arms among them. But it cost next to nothing, for the doctor worked by the year—twenty-five dollars for the whole family. I remember two of the Florida doctors, Chowning and Meredith. They not only tended an entire family for twenty-five dollars a year but furnished the medicines themselves. Good measure, too. Only the largest persons could hold a whole dose. Castor oil was the principal beverage. The dose was half a dipperful, with half a dipperful of New Orleans molasses added to help it down and make it taste good, which it never did. The next standby was calomel, the next rhubarb, and the next jalap. Then they bled the patient and put mustard plasters on him. It was a dreadful system and yet the death-rate was not heavy. The calomel was nearly sure to salivate the patient and cost him some of his teeth. There were no dentists. When teeth became touched with decay or were otherwise ailing, the doctor knew of but one thing to do: he fetched his tongs and dragged them out. If the jaw remained, it was not his fault. Doctors were not called in cases of ordinary illness; the family grandmother attended to those. Every old woman was a doctor and gathered her own medicines in the woods, and knew how to compound doses that would stir the vitals of a cast-iron dog. And then there was the "Indian doctor," a grave savage, remnant of his tribe, deeply read in the mysteries of nature and the secret properties of herbs; and most backwoodsmen had high faith in his powers and could tell of wonderful cures achieved by him. In Mauritius, away off yonder in the solitudes of the Indian Ocean, there is a person who answers to our Indian doctor of the old times. He is a Negro and has had no teaching as a doctor, yet there is one disease which he is master of and can cure and the doctors can't. They send for him when they have a case. It is a child's disease of a strange and deadly sort, and the Negro cures it with an herb-medicine which he makes himself, from a prescription which has come down to him from his father and grandfather. He will not let anyone see it. He keeps the secret of its components to himself, and it is feared that he will die without divulging it; then there will be consternation in Mauritius. I was told these things by the people there, in 1896.

We had the "faith doctor" too, in those early days, a woman. Her specialty was toothache. She was a farmer's old wife and lived five miles from Hannibal. She would lay her hand on the patient's jaw and say, "Believe!" and the cure was prompt. Mrs. Utterback. I remember her very well. Twice I rode out there behind my mother, horseback, and saw the cure performed. My mother was the patient.

Dr. Meredith removed to Hannibal by and by, and was our family physician there, and saved my life several times. Still, he was a good man and meant well. Let it go.

I was always told that I was a sickly and precarious and tiresome and uncertain child, and lived mainly on allopathic medicines during the first seven years of my life. I asked my mother about this in her old age—she was in her eighty-eighth year—and said:

"I suppose that during all that time you were uneasy about me?"

"Yes, the whole time."

"Afraid I wouldn't live?"

After a reflective pause, ostensibly to think out the facts, "No—afraid you would."

The country school-house was three miles from my uncle's farm. It stood in a clearing in the woods and would hold about twenty-five boys and girls. We attended the school with more or less regularity once or twice a week in summer, walking to it in the cool of the morning by the forest paths and back in the gloaming at the end of the day. All the pupils brought their dinners in baskets—corn dodger, buttermilk, and other good things—and sat in the shade of the trees at noon and ate them. It is the part of my education which I look back upon with the most satisfaction. My first visit to the school was when I was seven. A strapping girl of fifteen, in the customary sunbonnet and calico dress, asked me if I "used tobacco," meaning did I chew it. I said no. It roused her scorn. She reported me to all the crowd and said:

"Here is a boy seven years old who can't chew tobacco."

By the looks and comments which this produced I realized that I was a degraded object, and was cruelly ashamed of myself. I determined to reform. But I only made myself sick; I was not able to learn to chew tobacco. I learned to smoke fairly well but that did not conciliate anybody and I remained a poor thing, and characterless. I longed to be respected but I never was able to rise. Children have but little charity for each other's defects.

As I have said, I spent some part of every year at the farm until I was twelve or thirteen years old. The life which I led there with my cousins was full of charm and so is the memory of it yet. I can call back the solemn twilight and mystery of the deep woods, the earthy smells, the faint odors of the wild flowers, the sheen of rainwashed foliage, the rattling clatter of drops when the wind shook the trees, the far-off hammering of woodpeckers and the muffled drumming of wood-pheasants in the remoteness of the forest, the snapshot glimpses of disturbed wild creatures scurrying through the grass—I can call it all back and make it as real as it ever was, and as blessed. I can call back the prairie, and its loneliness and peace, and a vast hawk hanging motionless in the sky with his wings spread wide and the blue of the vault showing through the fringe of their end-feathers. I can see the woods in their autumn dress, the oaks purple, the hickories washed with gold, the maples and the sumachs luminous with crimson fires, and I can hear the rustle made by the fallen leaves as we plowed through them. I can see the blue clusters of wild grapes hanging amongst the foliage of the saplings, and I remember the taste of them and the smell. I know how the wild blackberries looked and how they tasted; and the same with the pawpaws, the hazelnuts, and the persimmons; and I can feel the thumping rain upon my head of hickory-nuts and walnuts when we were out in the frosty dawn to scramble for them with the pigs, and the gusts of wind loosed them and sent them down. I know the stain of blackberries and how pretty it is, and I know the stain of walnut hulls and how little it minds soap and water, also what grudged experience it had of either of them. I know the taste of maple sap and when to gather it, and how to arrange the troughs and the delivery tubes, and how to boil down the juice, and how to hook[5] the sugar after it is made; also how much better hooked sugar tastes than any that is honestly come by, let bigots[6] say what they will.

I know how a prize watermelon looks when it is sunning its fat rotundity among pumpkin vines and "simblins"; I know how to tell when it is ripe without "plugging"[7] it. I know how inviting it looks when it is cooling itself in a tub of water under the bed, waiting; I know how it looks when it lies on the table in the sheltered great floor-space between house and kitchen, and the children gathered for the sacrifice and their mouths watering. I know the crackling sound it makes when the carving knife enters its end and I can see the split fly along in front of the blade as the knife cleaves its way to the other end; I can see its halves fall apart and display the rich red meat and the black seeds, and the heart standing up, a luxury fit for the elect. I know how a boy looks behind a yard-long slice of that melon and I know how he feels, for I have been there. I know the taste of the watermelon which has been honestly come by and I know the taste of the watermelon which has been acquired by art. Both taste good but the experienced know which tastes best.

[5] *hook:* steal
[6] *bigots:* fanatics or very prejudiced persons
[7] *plugging:* cutting out a small piece

I know the look of green apples and peaches and pears on the trees, and I know how entertaining they are when they are inside of a person. I know how ripe ones look when they are piled in pyramids under the trees, and how pretty they are and how vivid their colors. I know how a frozen apple looks in a barrel down cellar in the wintertime, and how hard it is to bite and how the frost makes the teeth ache, and yet how good it is notwithstanding. I know the disposition of elderly people to select the specked apples for the children and I once knew ways to beat the game. I know the look of an apple that is roasting and sizzling on a hearth on a winter's evening, and I know the comfort that comes of eating it hot, along with some sugar and a drench of cream. I know the delicate art and mystery of so cracking hickory-nuts and walnuts on a flatiron with a hammer that the kernels will be delivered whole, and I know how the nuts, taken in conjunction with winter apples, cider, and doughnuts, make old people's old tales and old jokes sound fresh and crisp and enchanting, and juggle an evening away before you know what went with the time. I know the look of Uncle Dan'l's kitchen as it was on privileged nights when I was a child, and I can see the white and black children grouped on the hearth, with firelight playing on their faces and the shadows flickering upon the walls clear back toward the cavernous gloom of the rear, and I can hear Uncle Dan'l telling the immortal tales which Uncle Remus Harris was to gather into his book and charm the world with, by and by. And I can feel again the creepy joy which quivered through me when the time for the ghost story was reached—and the sense of regret too which came over me, for it was always the last story of the evening and there was nothing between it and the unwelcome bed.

I can remember the bare wooden stairway in my uncle's house and the turn to the left above the landing, and the rafters and the slanting roof over my bed, and the squares of moonlight on the floor and the white cold world of snow outside, seen through the curtainless window. I can remember the howling of the wind and the quaking of the house on stormy nights, and how snug and cozy one felt under the blankets, listening; and how the powdery snow used to sift in around the sashes and lie in little ridges on the floor, and make the place look chilly in the morning and curb the wild desire to get up—in case there was any. I can remember how very dark that room was in the dark of the moon, and how packed it was with ghostly stillness when one woke up by accident away in the night, and forgotten sins came flocking out of the secret chambers of the memory and wanted a hearing; and how ill-chosen the time seemed for this kind of business and how dismal was the hoo-hooing of the owl and the wailing of the wolf, sent mourning by on the night wind.

I remember the raging of the rain on that roof, summer nights, and how pleasant it was to lie and listen to it and enjoy the white splendor of the lightning and the majestic booming and crashing of the thunder. It was a very satisfactory room, and there was a lightning rod which was reachable from the window, an adorable and skittish thing to climb up and down, summer nights when there were duties on hand of a sort to make privacy desirable.

I remember the 'coon and 'possum hunts, nights, with the Negroes, and the long marches through the black gloom of the woods and the excitement which fired everybody when the distant bay of an experienced dog announced that the game was treed; then the wild scramblings and stumblings through briers and bushes and over roots to get to the spot; then the lighting of a fire and the felling of the tree, the joyful frenzy of the dogs and the Negroes, and the weird picture it all made in the red glare—I remember it all well, and the delight that everyone got out of it, except the 'coon.

I remember the pigeon seasons, when the birds would come in millions and cover the trees and by their weight break down the branches. They were clubbed to death with sticks; guns were not necessary and were not used. I remember the squirrel hunts and prairie-chicken hunts and wild-turkey hunts, and all that; and how we turned out, mornings, while it was still dark to go on these expeditions, and how chilly and dismal it was and how often I regretted that I was well enough to go. A toot on a tin horn brought twice as many dogs as were needed, and in their happiness they raced and scampered about and knocked small people down and made no end of unnecessary noise. At the word, they vanished away toward the woods and we drifted silently after them in the melancholy gloom. But presently the gray dawn stole over the world, the birds piped up, then the sun rose and poured light and comfort all around, everything was fresh and dewy and fragrant, and life was a boon again. After three hours of tramping we arrived back wholesomely tired, overladen with game, very hungry, and just in time for breakfast.

FOR DISCUSSION

1. From these first chapters, what kind of person does Twain reveal himself to be? What contributes more to your understanding of his character: what he tells you about his boyhood experiences and impressions or the way he tells you about them? Cite evidence from these chapters to support your answer.
2. Even as a boy, Twain felt a strong bond between himself and the people whose lives were a part of his own: Aunt Hannah, Uncle Dan'l, the little slave boy Sandy, his mother, and his playmates and schoolmates. Discuss his feelings toward each of these and the examples he chooses in order to make clear what these feelings were and the reasons for them.
3. More than any other regional writer, Twain succeeds in painting for his readers the scenery, manners, and people of his own picturesque part of America—the towns and farmlands that bordered the Mississippi, and even the river itself. What do you learn from the incidents, descriptions, and comments that Twain includes in his "painting"? Why would the time, place, and way of life seem picturesque to readers of his day as well as to modern readers? Is Twain's way of presenting these romantic, realistic, or a combination of the two? Cite evidence from the selection to support your answers.
4. Few people can recall *in detail* a simple experience or impression of the previous day or hour. Twain could "call it all back and make it as clear as it ever was, and as blessed." Point out the many different kinds of experiences he "called back" in these two chapters. Also point out the images he uses to picture the woods and prairies and to create impressions of sight, sound, smell, taste, touch, and movement—even of mood.
5. After recalling his mother's comments about Sandy's singing, Twain remarks, "She never used large words but she had a natural

gift for making small ones do effective work." Cite examples from this work demonstrating that Twain had the same gift. Which examples impress you the most? Tell why. Discuss the qualities which you feel are not only characteristic of his style but which have also led critics to consider him one of America's great writers.

6. Like Bret Harte, Twain uses exaggeration to add humor to his stories and novels, particularly when he is poking fun at the foolishness or stupidity of men, or at certain customs and governments. What touches of humor do you find in this work? Discuss whether they are due to exaggeration, to sharp common sense, or to the element of surprise. In what instances does he combine sentiment and humor?

FOR COMPOSITION

1. Like a true storyteller, Twain does more than describe his experiences; he makes them come to life. Select the experience which you found most interesting, amusing, or dramatic. In a short composition, tell why this experience impresses you, both because of what happens and because of the way Twain presents it.
2. Twain remembers his uncle John's farm as a "heavenly place." Of all the pleasures he mentions in these chapters, select the ones that would have appealed most to you at the age of eleven. In two or three paragraphs tell why you would have enjoyed them too, though perhaps not in the same way.

Harvard College

HENRY ADAMS

The next regular step was Harvard College. He was more than glad to go. For generation after generation, Adamses and Brookses and Boylstons and Gorhams[1] had gone to Harvard College, and although none of them, as far as known, had ever done any good there, or thought himself the better for it, custom, social ties, convenience, and, above all, economy, kept each generation in the track. Any other education would have required a serious effort, but no one took Harvard College seriously. All went there because their friends went there, and the College was their ideal of social self-respect.

Harvard College, as far as it educated at all, was a mild and liberal school, which sent young men into the world with all they needed to make respectable citizens, and something of what they wanted to make useful ones. Leaders of men it never tried to make. Its ideals were altogether different. The Unitarian clergy had given to the College a character of moderation, balance, judgment, restraint, what the French called *mesure;* excellent traits, which the College attained with sin-

[1]*Adamses and Brookses and Boylstons and Gorhams:* names of Henry Adams's ancestors

gular success, so that its graduates could commonly be recognized by the stamp, but such a type of character rarely lent itself to autobiography. In effect, the school created a type but not a will. Four years of Harvard College, if successful, resulted in an autobiographical blank, a mind on which only a water-mark had been stamped.

The stamp, as such things went, was a good one. The chief wonder of education is that it does not ruin everybody concerned in it, teachers and taught. Sometimes in after life, Adams debated whether in fact it had not ruined him and most of his companions, but, disappointment apart, Harvard College was probably less hurtful than any other university then in existence. It taught little, and that little ill, but it left the mind open, free from bias, ignorant of facts, but docile. The graduate had few strong prejudices. He knew little, but his mind remained supple, ready to receive knowledge.

What caused the boy most disappointment was the little he got from his mates. Speaking exactly, he got less than nothing, a result common enough in education. Yet the College Catalogue for the years 1854 to 1861 shows a list of names rather distinguished in their time. Alexander Agassiz[2] and Phillips Brooks[3] led it; H. H. Richardson[4] and O. W. Holmes[5] helped to close it. As a rule the most promising of all die early, and never get their names into a Dictionary of Contemporaries, which seems to be the only popular standard of success. Many died in the war. Adams knew them all, more or less; he felt as much regard, and quite as much respect for them then, as he did after they won great names and were objects of a vastly wider respect; but, as help towards education, he got nothing whatever from them or they from him until long after they had left college. Possibly the fault was his, but one would like to know how many others shared it. Accident counts for much in

[2]*Alexander Agassiz:* son of Jean Louis Agassiz, one of America's most famous naturalists and teachers of science

[3]*Phillips Brooks:* Episcopal bishop known for his piety, oratory, and support of the Union cause during the Civil War

[4]*H. H. Richardson:* famous American architect who set architectural styles between 1880 and the turn of the century

[5]*O. W. Holmes:* poet, essayist, teacher, and physician, whose best works include the novel *Elsie Venner* and the informal essays in *The Autocrat of the Breakfast Table*

companionship as in marriage. Life offers perhaps only a score of possible companions, and it is mere chance whether they meet as early as school or college, but it is more than a chance that boys brought up together under like conditions have nothing to give each other. The Class of 1858, to which Henry Adams belonged, was a typical collection of young New Englanders, quietly penetrating and aggressively commonplace; free from meannesses, jealousies, intrigues, enthusiasms, and passions; not exceptionally quick; not consciously sceptical; singularly indifferent to display, artifice, florid expression, but not hostile to it when it amused them; distrustful of themselves, but little disposed to trust any one else; with not much humor of their own, but full of readiness to enjoy the humor of others; negative to a degree that in the long run became positive and triumphant. Not harsh in manners or judgment, rather liberal and open-minded, they were still as a body the most formidable critics one would care to meet, in a long life exposed to criticism. They never flattered, seldom praised; free from vanity, they were not intolerant of it; but they were objectiveness itself; their attitude was a law of nature; their judgment beyond appeal, not an act either of intellect or emotion or of will, but a sort of gravitation.

This was Harvard College incarnate, but even for Harvard College, the Class of 1858 was somewhat extreme. Of unity this band of nearly one hundred young men had no keen sense, but they had equally little energy of repulsion. They were pleasant to live with, and above the average of students —German, French, English, or what not—but chiefly because each individual appeared satisfied to stand alone. It seemed a sign of force; yet to stand alone is quite natural when one has no passions; still easier when one has no pains.

The Harvard graduate was neither American nor European, nor even wholly Yankee; his admirers were few, and his critics many; perhaps his worst weakness was his self-criticism and self-consciousness; but his ambitions, social or intellectual were not necessarily cheap even though they might be negative. Afraid of serious risks, and still more afraid of personal ridicule he seldom made a great failure of life, and nearly always led a life more or less worth living. So Henry

Adams, well aware that he could not succeed as a scholar, and finding his social position beyond improvement or need of effort, betook himself to the single ambition which otherwise would scarcely have seemed a true outcome of the college, though it was the last remnant of the old Unitarian supremacy. He took to the pen. He wrote.

The College Magazine printed his work, and the College Societies listened to his addresses. Lavish of praise the readers were not; the audiences, too, listened in silence; but this was all the encouragement any Harvard collegian had a reasonable hope to receive; grave silence was a form of patience that meant possible future acceptance; and Henry Adams went on writing. No one cared enough to criticise, except himself who soon began to suffer from reaching his own limits. He found that he could not be this—or that—or the other; always precisely the things he wanted to be. He had not wit or scope or force. Judges always ranked him beneath a rival, if he had any; and he believed the judges were right. His work seemed to him thin, commonplace, feeble. At times he felt his own weakness so fatally that he could not go on; when he had nothing to say, he could not say it, and he found that he had very little to say at best. Much that he then wrote must be still in existence in print or manuscript, though he never cared to see it again, for he felt no doubt that it was in reality just what he thought it. At best it showed only a feeling for form; an instinct of exclusion. Nothing shocked—not even its weakness.

Inevitably an effort leads to an ambition—creates it—and at that time the ambition of the literary student, which almost took place of the regular prizes of scholarship, was that of being chosen as the representative of his class—the Class Orator—at the close of their course. This was political as well as literary success, and precisely the sort of eighteenth-century combination that fascinated an eighteenth-century boy. The idea lurked in his mind, at first as a dream, in no way serious or even possible for he stood outside the number of what were known as popular men. Year by year, his position seemed to improve, or perhaps his rivals disappeared, until at last, to his own great astonishment, he found himself a candidate. The habits of the college permitted no active candidacy; he and his rivals had not a word to say for or against themselves, and he was never even consulted on the subject; he was not present at any of the proceedings, and how it happened he never could quite divine, but it did happen, that one evening on returning from Boston he received notice of his election, after a very close contest, as Class Orator over the head of the first scholar, who was undoubtedly a better orator and a more popular man. In politics the success of the poorer candidate is common enough, and Henry Adams was a fairly trained politician, but he never understood how he managed to defeat not only a more capable but a more popular rival.

To him the election seemed a miracle. This was no mock-modesty; his head was as clear as ever it was in an indifferent canvass, and he knew his rivals and their following as well as he knew himself. What he did not know, even after four years of education, was Harvard College. What he could never measure was the bewildering impersonality of the men, who, at twenty years old, seemed to set no value either on official or personal standards. Here were nearly a hundred young men who had lived together intimately during four of the most impressionable years of life, and who, not only once but again and again, in different ways, deliberately, seriously, dispassionately, chose as their representatives precisely those of their companions who seemed least to represent them. As far as these Orators and Marshals had any position at all in a collegiate sense, it was that of indifference to the college. Henry Adams never professed the smallest faith in universities of any kind, either as boy or man, nor had he the faintest admiration for the university graduate, either in Europe or in America; as a collegian he was only known apart from his fellows by his habit of standing outside the college; and yet the singular fact remained that this commonplace body of young men chose him repeatedly to express his and their commonplaces. Secretly, of course, the successful candidate flattered himself—and them—with the hope that they might perhaps not be so commonplace as they thought themselves; but this was only another proof that all were identical. They saw in him a representative—the kind of representative they wanted—and he saw in them the most formidable array of judges he could ever meet, like so many mirrors of himself, an infinite reflection of his own shortcomings.

All the same, the choice was flattering; so flattering that it actually shocked his vanity; and would have shocked it more, if possible, had he known that it was to be the only flattery of the sort he was ever to receive. The function of Class Day was, in the eyes of nine-tenths of the students, altogether the most important of the college, and the figure of the Orator was the most conspicuous in the function. Unlike the Orators at regular Commencements, the Class Day Orator stood alone, or had only the Poet for rival. Crowded into the large church, the students, their families, friends, aunts, uncles and chaperones, attended all the girls of sixteen or twenty who wanted to show their summer dresses or fresh complexions, and there, for an hour or two, in a heat that might have melted bronze, they listened to an Orator and a Poet in clergyman's gowns, reciting such platitudes as their own experience and their mild censors permitted them to utter. What Henry Adams said in his Class Oration of 1858 he soon forgot to the last word, nor had it the least value for education; but he naturally remembered what was said of it. He remembered especially one of his eminent uncles or relations remarking that, as the work of so young a man, the oration was singularly wanting in enthusiasm. The young man—always in search of education—asked himself whether, setting rhetoric aside, this absence of enthusiasm was a defect or a merit, since, in either case, it was all that Harvard College taught, and all that the hundred young men, whom he was trying to represent, expressed. Another comment threw more light on the effect of the college education. One of the elderly gentlemen noticed the orator's "perfect self-possession." Self-possession indeed! If Harvard College gave nothing else, it gave calm. For four years each student had been obliged to figure daily before dozens of young men who knew each other to the last fibre. One had done little but read papers to Societies, or act comedy in the Hasty Pudding, not to speak of all sorts of regular exercises, and no audience in future life would ever be so intimately and terribly intelligent as these. Three-fourths of the graduates would rather have addressed the Council of Trent or the British Parliament than have acted Sir Anthony Absolute or Dr. Ollapod before a gala audience of the Hasty Pudding. Self-possession was the strongest part of Harvard College, which certainly taught men to stand alone, so that nothing seemed stranger to its graduates than the paroxysms of terror before the public which often overcame the graduates of European universities. Whether this was, or was not, education, Henry Adams never knew. He was ready to stand up before any audience in America or Europe, with nerves rather steadier for the excitement, but whether he should ever have anything to say, remained to be proved. As yet he knew nothing. Education had not begun.

FOR DISCUSSION

1. Does the "image" of Harvard College which Adams describes seem different from Harvard's image today? According to Adams, why did the men of the nineteenth century go to Harvard? Do people ever go to college for these same reasons today?
2. Adams appears rather critical of Harvard in this selection. What do you think his ideal college might be like? What kind of people would go there? What would they be like when they graduated? What does Adams mean by *education*, and why does he say that at the time of his college graduation, "education had not begun"?
3. Adams complains that he got less than nothing from his classmates, though many distinguished themselves later. What can one justifiably expect to get from his classmates? If Harvard had not changed at all since 1858, would you like to go there?
4. Adams says that Harvard men often unaccountably chose as their representatives the ones who least represented them. Why would they have behaved this way? Why do people sometimes vote for those *unlike* themselves?
5. Do you think Adams's "lack of enthusiasm" in his oration is a defect or a merit? Why?
6. Henry Adams always thought of himself as an eighteenth-century gentleman born accidentally in the nineteenth century. In the letter of advice to Thomas Randolph, Jr. (page 162), Thomas Jefferson implies a great deal about what the eighteenth-century gentleman was like, how he viewed the world, and how he saw himself. Do you think Adams would seem a familiar type to such an eighteenth century gentleman as Thomas Jefferson?

FOR COMPOSITION

Describe what you see as the primary purpose of higher education and of a university. Include in your essay a description of the graduates whom such a university would hope to produce.

HEMINGWAY AND ANGELOU

As America moved into the twentieth century, another kind of experience became common for young people just launching their literary careers: expatriation. A great many of the American writers who were young in the 1920's, and who were to make their mark in the years ahead, were living abroad—usually in "Bohemian" sections of Paris. What drove a generation of sensitive young Americans to Europe was partially rebellion against the social structure and values of their home towns. Hemingway, however, suggests another reason in "A Good Café on the Place St. Michel" (a chapter from his book of reminiscences *A Moveable Feast*).

The good writer must first of all know who he is; and American writers were forced to define what it meant for them to be American. But America seemed too vast and too diverse to be "taken in" when one was in the midst of it. For some expatriates at least, it was necessary to go away to find out how American they really were.

A generation later, we find another American with a background vastly different from Hemingway's—a woman, a black, a child of the rural South—seeking to understand her roots. Maya Angelou too has been an expatriate, in the sense that she has had a brilliant career working in many parts of the world (see her biography on page 442). But she is essentially an American. What this has meant to her, and to innumerable others in similar circumstances, is revealed with wit, passion, and unsparing realism in her autobiography, *I Know Why the Caged Bird Sings*. You will read here two excerpts from this book, deeply expressive of the black experience in America in a bygone but recent era.

A Good Café on the Place St. Michel

ERNEST HEMINGWAY

All of the sadness of the city came suddenly with the first cold rains of winter, and there were no more tops to the high white houses as you walked but only the wet blackness of the street and the closed doors of the small shops, the herb sellers, the stationery and the newspaper shops, the midwife—second class—and the hotel where Verlaine[1] had died where I had a room on the top floor where I worked.

It was either six or eight flights up to the top floor and it was very cold and I knew how much it would cost for a bundle of small twigs, three wire-wrapped packets of short, half-pencil length pieces of split pine to catch fire from the twigs, and then the bundle of half-dried lengths of hard wood that I must buy to make a fire that would warm the room. So I went to the far side of the street to look up at the roof in the rain and see if any chimneys were going, and how the smoke blew. There was no smoke and I thought about how the chimney would be cold and might not draw and of the room possibly filling with smoke, and the fuel wasted, and the money gone with it, and I walked on in the rain. I walked down past the Lycée[2] Henri

[1] *Verlaine:* Paul Verlaine (1844-1896), French symbolist poet
[2] *Lycée:* school

Quatre and the ancient church of St.-Étienne-du-Mont and the windswept Place du Panthéon and cut in for shelter to the right and finally came out on the lee side of the Boulevard St.-Michel and worked on down it past the Cluny and the Boulevard St.-Germain until I came to a good café that I knew on the Place St.-Michel.

It was a pleasant café, warm and clean and friendly, and I hung up my old waterproof on the coat rack to dry and put my worn and weathered felt hat on the rack above the bench and ordered a *café au lait.* The waiter brought it and I took out a notebook from the pocket of the coat and a pencil and started to write. I was writing about up in Michigan and since it was a wild, cold, blowing day it was that sort of day in the story. I had already seen the end of fall come through boyhood, youth and young manhood, and in one place you could write about it better than in another. That was called transplanting yourself, I thought, and it could be as necessary with people as with other sorts of growing things. But in the story the boys were drinking and this made me thirsty and I ordered a rum St. James. This tasted wonderful on the cold day and I kept on writing, feeling very well and feeling the good Martinique rum warm me all through my body and my spirit.

A girl came in the café and sat by herself at a table near the window. She was very pretty with a face fresh as a newly minted coin if they minted coins in smooth flesh with rain-freshened skin, and her hair was black as a crow's wing and cut sharply and diagonally across her cheek.

I looked at her and she disturbed me and made me very excited. I wished I could put her in the story, or anywhere, but she had placed herself so she could watch the street and the entry and I knew she was waiting for someone. So I went on writing.

The story was writing itself and I was having a hard time keeping up with it. I ordered another rum St. James and I watched the girl whenever I looked up, or when I sharpened the pencil with a pencil sharpener with the shavings curling into the saucer under my drink.

I've seen you, beauty, and you belong to me now, whoever you are waiting for and if I never see you again, I thought. You belong to me and all Paris belongs to me and I belong to this notebook and this pencil.

Then I went back to writing and I entered far into the story and was lost in it. I was writing it now and it was not writing itself and I did not look up nor know anything about the time nor think where I was nor order any more rum St. James. I was tired of rum St. James without thinking about it. Then the story was finished and I was very tired. I read the last paragraph and then I looked up and looked for the girl and she had gone. I hope she's gone with a good man, I thought. But I felt sad.

I closed up the story in the notebook and put it in my inside pocket and I asked the waiter for a dozen *portugaises* and a half-carafe of the dry white wine they had there. After writing a story I was always empty and both sad and happy, as though I had made love, and I was sure this was a very good story although I would not know truly how good until I read it over the next day.

As I ate the oysters with their strong taste of the sea and their faint metallic taste that the cold white wine washed away, leaving only the sea taste and the succulent texture, and as I drank their cold liquid from each shell and washed it down with the crisp taste of the wine, I lost the empty feeling and began to be happy and to make plans.

Now that the bad weather had come, we could leave Paris for a while for a place where this rain would be snow coming down through the pines and covering the road and the high hillsides and at an altitude where we would hear it creak as we walked home at night. Below Les Avants there was a chalet where the pension was wonderful and where we would be together and have our books and at night be warm in bed together with the windows open and the stars bright. That was where we could go. Traveling third class on the train was not expensive. The pension cost very little more than we spent in Paris.

I would give up the room in the hotel where I wrote and there was only the rent of 74 rue Cardinal Lemoine which was nominal. I had written journalism for Toronto and the checks for that were due. I could write that anywhere under any circumstances and we had money to make the trip.

Maybe away from Paris I could write about Paris as in Paris I could write about Michigan. I did not know it was too early for that because I did not know Paris well enough. But that was how it worked out eventually. Anyway we would go if my wife wanted to, and I finished the oysters and the wine and paid my score in the café and made it the shortest way back up the Montagne Ste. Geneviève through the rain, that was now only local weather and not something that changed your life, to the flat at the top of the hill.

"I think it would be wonderful, Tatie," my wife said. She had a gently modeled face and her eyes and her smile lighted up at decisions as though they were rich presents. "When should we leave?"

"Whenever you want."

"Oh, I want to right away. Didn't you know?"

"Maybe it will be fine and clear when we come back. It can be very fine when it is clear and cold."

"I'm sure it will be," she said. "Weren't you good to think of going, too."

FOR DISCUSSION

1. Hemingway was especially talented in his writing in creating a mood. Actually the mood in this selection changes at least twice. Where do you feel that the shifts occur? How, and with what details, does Hemingway manage the shifts?
2. What do you think Hemingway means by the story's "writing itself" as opposed to his writing the story? Which do you think he prefers? Why?
3. Why do you think Hemingway found it so much easier to write about places in which he had been, rather than one he was in when writing? What does this fact tell you about the way writers select their material?
4. Why does he mention the girl who appeared in the café? What does the description of her tell you about Paris, the café, Hemingway, and the period? Why is he so careful to mention what he ate and drank? What would the selection be like without these references?

5. The portrait of Hemingway's wife which emerges from this selection is exceptionally well done. With a minimum of words, Hemingway tells us a great deal about her appearance, her character and attitudes, and about their relationship. What is she like and what statements convey this information?

FOR COMPOSITION

Describe what it was like to write a recent composition, poem, or story. Try creating a particular mood by mentioning small details, seemingly insignificant observations and interruptions, and your sensations while writing. You may take liberties with facts in order to achieve the effects you want.

I Know Why the Caged Bird Sings

MAYA ANGELOU

When Maya Angelou was three years old, her parents, living in Long Beach, California, broke up their marriage. The child, then named Marguerite Johnson, was sent with her brother Bailey, one year older, to live with her grandmother (her father's mother) in the rural town of Stamps, Arkansas.

I Know Why the Caged Bird Sings is the story of "growing up black" in this "musty little town" in the 1930's. By the close of the book, the author, now fifteen years old, has moved to San Francisco and is opening a new chapter in her life.

Two selections from this autobiography of childhood are given below. The indomitable grandmother is called "Momma" by the children. (She is also referred to as "Grandmother Henderson" and "Sister Henderson.") "Uncle Willie" is the crippled grown son of Momma, and thus the actual uncle of the children. As of the time of writing, Momma had for some twenty-five years been running a general store for the local black community. "We lived with our grandmother and uncle in the rear of the Store (it was always spoken of with a capital *s*)." The first selection begins with Marguerite ("Ritie") working in the Store.

Weighing the half-pounds of flour, excluding the scoop, and depositing them dust-free into the thin paper sacks held a simple kind of adventure for me. I developed an eye for measuring how full a silver-looking ladle of flour, mash, meal, sugar or corn had to be to push the scale indicator over to eight ounces or one pound. When I was absolutely accurate our appreciative customers used to admire: "Sister Henderson sure got some smart grandchildrens." If I was off in the Store's favor, the eagle-eyed women would say, "Put some more in that sack, child. Don't you try to make your profit offa me."

Then I would quietly but persistently punish myself. For every bad judgment, the fine was no silver-wrapped Kisses, the sweet chocolate drops that I loved more than anything in the world, except Bailey. And maybe canned pineapples. My obsession with pineapples nearly drove me mad. I dreamt of the days when I would be grown and able to buy a whole carton for myself alone.

Although the syrupy golden rings sat in their exotic cans on our shelves year round, we only tasted them during Christmas. Momma used the juice to make almost-black fruit cakes. Then she lined heavy soot-encrusted iron skillets with the pineapple rings for rich upside-down cakes. Bailey and I received one slice each, and I carried mine around for hours, shredding off the fruit until nothing was left except the perfume on my fingers. I'd like to think that my desire for pineapples was so sacred that I wouldn't allow myself to steal a can (which was possible) and eat it alone out in the garden, but I'm certain that I must have weighed the possibility of the scent exposing me and didn't have the nerve to attempt it.

Until I was thirteen and left Arkansas for good, the Store was my favorite place to be. Alone and empty in the mornings, it looked like an unopened present from a stranger. Opening the front doors was pulling the ribbon off the unexpected gift. The light would come in softly (we faced north), easing itself over the shelves of mackerel, salmon, tobacco, thread. It fell flat on the big vat of lard and by noontime during the summer the grease had softened to a thick soup. Whenever I walked into the Store in the afternoon, I sensed that it was tired. I alone could hear the slow pulse of its job half done. But just before bedtime, after numerous people had walked in and out, had argued over their bills, or joked about their neighbors, or just dropped in "to give Sister Henderson a 'Hi y'all,'" the promise of magic mornings returned to the Store and spread itself over the family in washed life waves.

Momma opened boxes of crispy crackers and we sat around the meat block at the rear of the Store. I sliced onions, and Bailey opened two or even three cans of sardines and allowed their juice of oil and fishing boats to ooze down and around the sides. That was supper. In the evening, when we were alone like that, Uncle Willie didn't stutter or shake or give any indication that he had an "affliction." It seemed that the peace of a day's ending was an assurance that the covenant[1] God made with children, Negroes and the crippled was still in effect.

Throwing scoops of corn to the chickens and mixing sour dry mash with leftover food and oily dish water for the hogs were among our evening chores. Bailey and I sloshed down twilight trails to the pig pens, and standing on the first fence rungs we poured down the unappealing concoctions to our grateful hogs. They mashed their tender pink snouts down into the slop, and rooted and grunted their satisfaction. We always grunted a reply only half in jest. We were also grateful that we had concluded the dirtiest of chores and had only gotten the evil-smelling swill on our shoes, stockings, feet and hands.

Late one day, as we were attending to the pigs, I heard a horse in the front yard (it really should have been called a driveway, except that there was nothing to drive into it), and ran to find out who had come riding up on a Thursday evening when even Mr. Steward, the quiet, bitter man who owned a riding horse, would be resting by his warm fire until the morning called him out to turn over his field.

The used-to-be sheriff sat rakishly astraddle his horse. His nonchalance was meant to convey his authority and power

[1] *covenant:* solemn agreement or understanding

over even dumb animals. How much more capable he would be with Negroes. It went without saying.

His twang jogged in the brittle air. From the side of the Store, Bailey and I heard him say to Momma, "Annie, tell Willie he better lay low tonight. A crazy nigger messed with a white lady today. Some of the boys'll be coming over here later." Even after the slow drag of years, I remember the sense of fear which filled my mouth with hot, dry air, and made my body light.

The "boys"? Those cement faces and eyes of hate that burned the clothes off you if they happened to see you lounging on the main street downtown on Saturday. Boys? It seemed that youth had never happened to them. Boys? No, rather men who were covered with graves' dust and age without beauty or learning. The ugliness and rottenness of old abominations.

If on Judgment Day I were summoned by St. Peter to give testimony to the used-to-be sheriff's act of kindness, I would be unable to say anything in his behalf. His confidence that my uncle and every other Black man who heard of the Klan's coming ride would scurry under their houses to hide in chicken droppings was too humiliating to bear. Without waiting for Momma's thanks, he rode out of the yard, sure that things were as they should be and that he was a gentle squire, saving those deserving serfs from the laws of the land, which he condoned.

Immediately, while his horse's hoofs were still loudly thudding the ground, Momma blew out the coal-oil lamps. She had a quiet, hard talk with Uncle Willie and called Bailey and me into the Store.

We were told to take the potatoes and onions out of their bins and knock out the dividing walls that kept them apart. Then with a tedious and fearful slowness Uncle Willie gave me his rubber-tipped cane and bent down to get into the now-enlarged empty bin. It took forever before he lay down flat, and then we covered him with potatoes and onions, layer upon layer, like a casserole. Grandmother knelt praying in the darkened Store.

It was fortunate that the "boys" didn't ride into our yard that evening and insist that Momma open the Store. They would have surely found Uncle Willie and just as surely lynched him. He moaned the whole night through as if he had, in fact, been guilty of some heinous crime. The heavy sounds pushed their way up out of the blanket of vegetables and I pictured his mouth pulling down on the right side and his saliva flowing into the eyes of new potatoes and waiting there like dew drops for the warmth of morning.

* * *

Weekdays revolved on a sameness wheel. They turned into themselves so steadily and inevitably that each seemed to be the original of yesterday's rough draft. Saturdays, however, always broke the mold and dared to be different.

Farmers trekked into town with their children and wives streaming around them. Their board-stiff khaki pants and shirts revealed the painstaking care of a dutiful daughter or wife. They often stopped at the Store to get change for bills so they could give out jangling coins to their children, who shook with their eagerness to get to town. The young kids openly resented their parents' dawdling in the Store and Uncle Willie would call them in and spread among them bits of sweet peanut patties that had been broken in shipping. They gobbled down the candies and were out again, kicking up the powdery dust in the road and worrying if there was going to be time to get to town after all.

Bailey played mumbledypeg[2] with the older boys around the chinaberry tree, and Momma and Uncle Willie listened to the farmers' latest news of the country. I thought of myself as hanging in the Store, a mote imprisoned on a shaft of sunlight. Pushed and pulled by the slightest shift of air, but never falling free into the tempting darkness.

In the warm months, morning began with a quick wash in unheated well water. The suds were dashed on a plot of ground beside the kitchen door. It was called the bait garden (Bailey raised worms). After prayers, breakfast in summer

2 *mumbledypeg:* a game in which the players try to throw a knife from various positions so that the blade will stick in the ground

was usually dry cereal and fresh milk. Then to our chores (which on Saturday included weekday jobs)—scrubbing the floors, raking the yards, polishing our shoes for Sunday (Uncle Willie's had to be shined with a biscuit) and attending to the customers who came breathlessly, also in their Saturday hurry.

Looking through the years, I marvel that Saturday was my favorite day in the week. What pleasures could have been squeezed between the fan folds of unending tasks? Children's talent to endure stems from their ignorance of alternatives.

After our retreat from St. Louis,[3] Momma gave us a weekly allowance. Since she seldom dealt with money, other than to take it in and to tithe[4] to the church, I supposed that the weekly ten cents was to tell us that even she realized that a change had come over us, and that our new unfamiliarity caused her to treat us with a strangeness.

I usually gave my money to Bailey, who went to the movies nearly every Saturday. He brought back Street and Smith cowboy books for me.

One Saturday Bailey was late coming back from the Rye-al-toh.[5] Momma had begun heating water for the Saturday-night baths, and all the evening chores were done. Uncle Willie sat in the twilight on the front porch mumbling or maybe singing, and smoking a ready-made.[6] It was quite late. Mothers had called in their children from the group games, and fading sounds of "Yah . . . Yah . . . you didn't catch me" still hung and floated into the Store.

Uncle Willie said, "Sister, better light the light." On Saturdays we used the electric lights so that last-minute Sunday shoppers could look down the hill and see if the Store was open. Momma hadn't told me to turn them on because she didn't want to believe that night had fallen hard and Bailey was still out in the ungodly dark.

Her apprehension was evident in the hurried movements around the kitchen and in her lonely fearing eyes. The Black

[3] *After our retreat from St. Louis . . . :* Some time before, the children had paid a visit to St. Louis, where they lived with their mother's parents.

[4] *tithe:* a regular contribution made to a church or other religious organization (literally, a tenth)

[5] *Rye-al-toh:* a phonetic spelling of the way the children pronounced *Rialto* (the name of the movie theater)

[6] *ready-made:* in this sense, a regular, factory-made cigarette

woman in the South who raises sons, grandsons and nephews had her heartstrings tied to a hanging noose. Any break from routine may herald for them unbearable news. For this reason, Southern Blacks until the present generation could be counted among America's arch conservatives.

Like most self-pitying people, I had very little pity for my relatives' anxiety. If something indeed had happened to Bailey, Uncle Willie would always have Momma, and Momma had the Store. Then, after all, we weren't their children. But I would be the major loser if Bailey turned up dead. For he was all I claimed, if not all I had.

The bath water was steaming on the cooking stove, but Momma was scrubbing the kitchen table for the umpteenth time.

"Momma," Uncle Willie called and she jumped. "Momma." I waited in the bright lights of the Store, jealous that someone had come along and told these strangers something about my brother and I would be the last to know.

"Momma, why don't you and Sister walk down to meet him?"

To my knowledge Bailey's name hadn't been mentioned for hours, but we all knew whom he meant.

Of course. Why didn't that occur to me? I wanted to be gone. Momma said, "Wait a minute, little lady. Go get your sweater, and bring me my shawl."

It was darker in the road than I'd thought it would be. Momma swung the flashlight's arc over the path and weeds and scary tree trunks. The night suddenly became enemy territory, and I knew that if my brother was lost in this land he was forever lost. He was eleven and very smart, that I granted, but after all he was so small. The Bluebeards and tigers and Rippers[7] could eat him up before he could scream for help.

Momma told me to take the light and she reached for my hand. Her voice came from a high hill above me and in the dark my hand was enclosed in hers. I loved her with a rush. She said nothing—no "Don't worry" or "Don't get tender-

[7] *The Bluebeards and tigers and Rippers:* creatures of fantasy who might attack little boys lost at night

hearted." Just the gentle pressure of her rough hand conveyed her own concern and assurance to me.

We passed houses which I knew well by daylight but couldn't recollect in the swarthy gloom.

"Evening, Miz Jenkins." Walking and pulling me along.

"Sister Henderson? Anything wrong?" That was from an outline blacker than the night.

"No, ma'am. Not a thing. Bless the Lord." By the time she finished speaking we had left the worried neighbors far behind.

Mr. Willie Williams' Do Drop Inn was bright with furry red lights in the distance and the pond's fishy smell enveloped us. Momma's hand tightened and let go, and I saw the small figure plodding along, tired and old-mannish. Hands in his pockets and head bent, he walked like a man trudging up the hill behind a coffin.

"Bailey." It jumped out as Momma said, "Ju,"[8] and I started to run, but her hand caught mine again and became a vise. I pulled, but she yanked me back to her side. "We'll walk, just like we been walking, young lady." There was no chance to warn Bailey that he was dangerously late, that everybody had been worried and that he should create a good lie or, better, a great one.

Momma said, "Bailey, Junior," and he looked up without surprise. "You know it's night and you just now getting home?"

"Yes, ma'am." He was empty. Where was his alibi?

"What you been doing?"

"Nothing."

"That's all you got to say?"

"Yes, ma'am."

"All right, young man. We'll see when you get home."

She had turned me loose, so I made a grab for Bailey's hand, but he snatched it away. I said, "Hey, Bail," hoping to remind him that I was his sister and his only friend, but he grumbled something like "Leave me alone."

Momma didn't turn on the flashlight on the way back, nor did she answer the questioning Good evenings that floated around us as we passed the darkened houses.

[8] *Ju:* short for *junior*

I was confused and frightened. He was going to get a whipping and maybe he had done something terrible. If he couldn't talk to me it must have been serious. But there was no air of spent revelry about him. He just seemed sad. I didn't know what to think.

Uncle Willie said, "Getting too big for your britches, huh? You can't come home. You want to worry your grandmother to death?" Bailey was so far away he was beyond fear. Uncle Willie had a leather belt in his good hand but Bailey didn't notice or didn't care. "I'm going to whip you this time." Our uncle had only whipped us once before and then only with a peach-tree switch, so maybe now he was going to kill my brother. I screamed and grabbed for the belt, but Momma caught me. "Now, don't get uppity, miss, 'less you want some of the same thing. He got a lesson coming to him. You come on and get your bath."

From the kitchen I heard the belt fall down, dry and raspy on naked skin. Uncle Willie was gasping for breath, but Bailey made no sound. I was too afraid to splash water or even to cry and take a chance of drowning out Bailey's pleas for help, but the pleas never came and the whipping was finally over.

I lay awake an eternity, waiting for a sign, a whimper or a whisper, from the next room that he was still alive. Just before I fell exhausted into sleep, I heard Bailey: "Now I lay me down to sleep, I pray the Lord my soul to keep, if I should die before I wake, I pray the Lord my soul to take."

My last memory of that night was the question, Why is he saying the baby prayer? We had been saying the "Our Father, which art in heaven" for years.

For days the Store was a strange country, and we were all newly arrived immigrants. Bailey didn't talk, smile or apologize. His eyes were so vacant, it seemed his soul had flown away, and at meals I tried to give him the best pieces of meat and the largest portion of dessert, but he turned them down.

Then one evening at the pig pen he said without warning, "I saw Mother Dear."

If he said it, it was bound to be the truth. He wouldn't lie to me. I don't think I asked him where or when.

"In the movies." He laid his head on the wooden railing. "It wasn't really her. It was a woman named Kay Francis. She's a white movie star who looks just like Mother Dear."

There was no difficulty believing that a white movie star looked like our mother and that Bailey had seen her. He told me that the movies were changed each week, but when another picture came to Stamps starring Kay Francis he would tell me and we'd go together. He even promised to sit with me.

He had stayed late on the previous Saturday to see the film over again. I understood, and understood too why he couldn't tell Momma or Uncle Willie. She was our mother and belonged to us. She was never mentioned to anyone because we simply didn't have enough of her to share.

We had to wait nearly two months before Kay Francis returned to Stamps. Bailey's mood had lightened considerably, but he lived in a state of expectation and it made him more nervous than he was usually. When he told me that the movie would be shown, we went into our best behavior and were the exemplary children that Grandmother deserved and wished to think us.

It was a gay light comedy, and Kay Francis wore long-sleeved white silk shirts with big cuff links. Her bedroom was all satin and flowers in vases, and her maid, who was Black, went around saying "Lawsy, missy" all the time. There was a Negro chauffeur too, who rolled his eyes and scratched his head, and I wondered how on earth an idiot like that could be trusted with her beautiful cars.

The whitefolks downstairs laughed every few minutes, throwing the discarded snicker up to the Negroes in the buzzards' roost. The sound would jag around in our air for an indecisive second before the balcony's occupants accepted it and sent their own guffaws to riot with it against the walls of the theater.

I laughed, too, but not at the hateful jokes made on my people. I laughed because, except that she was white, the big movie star looked just like my mother. Except that she lived in a big mansion with a thousand servants, she lived just like my mother. And it was funny to think of the whitefolks' not knowing that the woman they were adoring could be my mother's twin, except that she was white and my mother was prettier. Much prettier.

FOR DISCUSSION

1. The author is trying to help you "see" this little rural store and to "feel" something of the lives of the family group that ran it and the poor black people who traded in it. Has she succeeded? Point to some of the details and phrases that help to convey the very special atmosphere of the Store.
2. Uncle Willie's "affliction" seemed to disappear at the peaceful close of the long day's work. How does the author explain this? What is meant by the "covenant God made with children, Negroes and the crippled . . ."?
3. Although Uncle Willie had not the remotest connection with the reported molesting of the "white lady," he decided to "lay low" by hiding in the vegetable bin. Why? How did Marguerite (the author) feel about this? Describe three different emotions she felt. Which of these emotions would be likely to predominate today?
4. In the monotonous routine of the impoverished black community, Saturday was the day that "always broke the mold and dared to be different." What was "different" about it? Yet, the author, looking back through the years, marvels that "Saturday was my favorite day in the week." She asks: "What pleasures could have been squeezed between the fan folds of unending tasks?" How does she answer this seeming paradox?
5. When Bailey was late in returning home from the movies, his grandmother was alarmed. This in itself is not surprising, but the *degree* of her apprehension may seem to some of us to be exaggerated and unrealistic. However, the author explains vividly, in terms of the life experience of these Southern black people, why Momma was so terrified. Quote the sentences in which Ms. Angelou gives us this background. Rephrase them in your own words.
6. The title, *I Know Why the Caged Bird Sings,* comes from a poem by Paul Laurence Dunbar. What are the implications of this phrase? Knowing what you do of Ms. Angelou's theme and spirit, do you think this is a good title for her book?

FOR COMPOSITION

1. If you have seen many movies of the era which Ms. Angelou is describing, you will know that her description of how black people were presented in these films is not exaggerated. Research the topic, and write an essay on "Racial Stereotypes in the Mass Communication Media." You should aim to show what conditions were like a generation or two ago, and how and why they have changed in recent years.
2. Ms. Angelou writes of how many thousands of times the United States has been crossed "by frightened Black children traveling alone to their newly affluent parents in Northern cities or back to grandmothers in Southern towns when the urban North reneged on its economic promises." The story of black migrations within America (it has been called *in*-migration) is fascinating and important. Prepare a report on this process, explaining where, when, and why it has occurred, and what it has meant to the black people and to the nation as a whole.

THE LITERARY LIFE

IRVING, WEBSTER, AND POE

Since Plato's day, men have argued about the merits of poetry and of all literature which does not serve a utilitarian purpose. One of Plato's arguments against poetry was that it encouraged idleness and those emotions of which one should be wary. Further, it offered no concrete service to the state. But, notwithstanding the unquestioned respect in which Plato's opinions continue to be held, poetry and other seemingly non-utilitarian forms of literature have always found their champions, many of whom, like Aristotle, simply *assume* that sensible men will understand their value.

In America, too, sensitive men began to demand, soon after they had attained their political freedom, a corresponding cultural independence. In order for cultural and literary independence from England to develop, of course, America had to produce her own writers and cultural leaders.

And what, after all, is so important about having a national literature? Don't other concerns, like economic stability or political strength, take precedence over poetry? Such were the questions asked in the first half of the nineteenth century. But always some men insisted that the literature of the nation was as important as the national income. Their insistence came partly from a desire to show that America was as good as England and could produce as good a body of literature. But the demand for a national literature also came from the implicit recognition that a people never thoroughly know who they are until a perceptive writer has described them. The greatest dignity and sense of identity comes not from economic power but from tradition, and tradition is often created by literature. Thus, an important division of the American essay deals with literature and literary matters.

Washington Irving, Noah Webster, and Edgar Allan Poe represent three important and very different kinds of beginnings in American literature. Though several spinners of tales had appeared before Irving, still he was the first American to show decided talent at writing fiction. His style, imitated from English periodicals such as the *Spectator*, was witty, informal, conversational, and graceful. In the selection included here, Irving discusses not only himself, but his literary interests and his reasons for finding European spots more satisfactory to visit than American ones. He also satirizes, in a gentle but effective manner, the pompous pretensions of Europeans who assume their own moral superiority because their cultures are older than America's. Irving's voice is the first which was heard widely and which raised questions publicly about the lack of culture in the United States.

Noah Webster was the first to take important steps toward American literary independence. It would be difficult to overestimate the importance of his first American dictionary. Once it had appeared, the principle was established that the American language was not a substandard dialect of English, and that the American idiom was a perfectly appropriate vehicle for literature of quality. Interestingly enough, Webster encountered some violent criticism. He was accused of encouraging the use of "substandard" or slang words and of corrupting the language of Shakespeare and Milton. But Webster argued that people in different environments will automatically develop different vocabularies. No word is innately superior to any other word. Different words are simply more useful in different situations.

A fast-developing national pride is also evident in the fact that Webster no longer wished to appeal to English authorities for examples of proper usage. His decision to use American documents as examples of proper literary style was another blow he struck for American literary independence.

Although he is the writer of the greatest importance, Edgar Allan Poe remains a somewhat inexplicable figure on the American literary scene. He was a man clearly born out of his time: his theories would have been revolutionary had they appeared fifty years later. In a period when most people believed that great literature should either serve the national interest or teach a moral, Poe argued that the poem or short story should exist for itself alone. The sole goal of the writer was to entertain by stimulating the emotions. The question of truth or the lack of it, he said, is totally irrelevant to art.

Poe was the first American to write literary criticism of great sophistication and long-lasting interest. The occasion for his "Theory of the Short Story" was a review he wrote of Hawthorne's *Twice-Told Tales.* Not content with exploring the nature of the short story, however, he also probed the requirements for good poetry. Part of his long essay on "The Poetic Principle" is reprinted here.

The craftsmanship of Poe's stories is just beginning to be fully appreciated. His literary theories—though their limitations are easily recognized—continue to influence American letters in this century. Perhaps Poe's influence partially explains the fact that the short story is so thoroughly an American form. England had to learn the principles of a major literary *genre* from her country cousin across the Atlantic.

The Author's Account of Himself

WASHINGTON IRVING

I was always fond of visiting new scenes, and observing strange characters and manners. Even when a mere child I began my travels, and made many tours of discovery into foreign parts and unknown regions of my native city, to the frequent alarm of my parents, and the emolument[1] of the town-crier. As I grew into boyhood, I extended the range of my observations. My holiday afternoons were spent in rambles about the surrounding country. I made myself familiar with all its places famous in history or fable. I knew every spot where a murder or robbery had been committed, or a ghost seen. I visited the neighboring villages, and added greatly to my stock of knowledge, by noting their habits and customs, and conversing with their sages and great men. I even journeyed one long summer's day to the summit of the most distant hill, whence I stretched my eye over many a mile of terra incognita, and was astonished to find how vast a globe I inhabited.

This rambling propensity strengthened with my years. Books of voyages and travels became my passion, and in de-

[1] *emolument:* financial reward

vouring their contents, I neglected the regular exercises of the school. How wistfully would I wander about the pier-heads in fine weather, and watch the parting ships, bound to distant climes—with what longing eyes would I gaze after their lessening sails, and waft myself in imagination to the ends of the earth!

Further reading and thinking, though they brought this vague inclination into more reasonable bounds, only served to make it more decided. I visited various parts of my own country; and had I been merely a lover of fine scenery, I should have felt little desire to seek elsewhere its gratification, for on no country have the charms of nature been more prodigally lavished. Her mighty lakes, like oceans of liquid silver; her mountains, with their bright aerial tints; her valleys, teeming with wild fertility; her tremendous cataracts, thundering in their solitudes; her boundless plains, waving with spontaneous verdure; her broad deep rivers, rolling in solemn silence to the ocean; her trackless forests, where vegetation puts forth all its magnificence; her skies, kindling with the magic of summer clouds and glorious sunshine;—no, never need an American look beyond his own country for the sublime and beautiful of natural scenery.

But Europe held forth the charms of storied and poetical association. There were to be seen the masterpieces of art, the refinements of highly-cultivated society, the quaint peculiarities of ancient and local custom. My native country was full of youthful promise: Europe was rich in the accumulated treasures of age. Her very ruins told the history of times gone by, and every moldering stone was a chronicle. I longed to wander over the scenes of renowned achievement—to tread, as it were, in the footsteps of antiquity—to loiter about the ruined castle—to meditate on the falling tower—to escape, in short, from the commonplace realities of the present, and lose myself among the shadowy grandeurs of the past.

I had, beside all this, an earnest desire to see the great men of the earth. We have, it is true, our great men in America: not a city but has an ample share of them. I have mingled among them in my time, and been almost withered by the shade into which they cast me; for there is nothing so baleful to a small man as the shade of a great one, particularly the great man of a city. But I was anxious to see the great men of Europe; for I had read in the works of various philosophers, that all animals degenerated in America, and man among the number. A great man of Europe, thought I, must therefore be as superior to a great man of America, as a peak of the Alps to a high land of the Hudson; and in this idea I was confirmed, by observing the comparative importance and swelling magnitude of many English travelers among us, who, I was assured, were very little people in their own country. I will visit this land of wonders, thought I, and see the gigantic race from which I am degenerated.[2]

It has been either my good or evil lot to have my roving passion gratified. I have wandered through different countries, and witnessed many of the shifting scenes of life. I cannot say that I have studied them with the eye of a philosopher; but rather with the sauntering gaze with which humble lovers of the picturesque stroll from the window of one print-shop to another; caught sometimes by the delineations of beauty, sometimes by the distortions of caricature, and sometimes by the loveliness of landscape. As it is the fashion for modern tourists to travel pencil in hand, and bring home their portfolios filled with sketches, I am disposed to get up a few for the entertainment of my friends. When, however, I look over the hints and memorandums I have taken down for the purpose, my heart almost fails me at finding how my idle humor has led me aside from the great objects studied by every regular traveler who would make a book. I fear I shall give equal disappointment with an unlucky landscape painter, who had traveled on the continent, but, following the bent of his vagrant[3] inclination, had sketched in nooks, and corners, and by-places. His sketchbook was accordingly crowded with cottages, and landscapes, and obscure ruins; but he had neglected to paint St. Peter's, or the Coliseum; the cascade of Terni, or the bay of Naples; and had not a single glacier or volcano in his whole collection.

[2] *degenerated:* descended
[3] *vagrant:* wandering

FOR DISCUSSION

1. Which qualities of mind and character evident in this account would make Irving an effective "cultural ambassador" from the New World to the Old?
2. Throughout this account Irving reveals how much he was influenced by the spirit of romanticism which motivated this country's "first men of letters." (See paragraphs 4 and 5 of the introductory essay.) Even in the first line he mentions two characteristics of this spirit: an interest in the unfamiliar and a fascination with the strange. Point out other examples of the romantic spirit in what Irving enjoyed most and in his attitude toward America and Europe.
3. In his comparison of America with Europe, what conclusions does he draw and on what does he base them? Where, in this account, is there evidence of Irving's "half concealed vein of humor"? Is he being satirical? Explain.
4. What impression do you gain of Irving as a boy and as a man?

FOR COMPOSITION

Write an account of a trip you took to a new city or a new vacation spot. Describe your impressions of the landscape, the people, the qualities you liked or disliked about the place.

The Need for an American Dictionary

NOAH WEBSTER

It is not only important, but, in a degree necessary, that the people of this country, should have an *American Dictionary* of the English Language; for, although the body of the language is the same as in England, and it is desirable to perpetuate that sameness, yet some differences must exist. Language is the expression of ideas; and if the people of one country cannot preserve an identity of ideas, they cannot retain an identity of language. Now an identity of ideas depends materially upon a sameness of things or objects with which the people of the two countries are conversant. But in no two portions of the earth, remote from each other, can such identity be found. Even physical objects must be different. But the principal differences between the people of this country and of all others, arise from different forms of government, different laws, institutions and customs. Thus the practice of hawking and hunting, the institution of heraldry, and the feudal system of England originated terms which formed, and some of which now form, a necessary part of the language of that country; but, in the United States, many of these terms are no part of our present language,—and they cannot be, for the things which they express do not exist in this country. They can be known to us only as obsolete or as foreign words. On the other hand, the institutions in this country which are new and peculiar, give rise to new terms or to new applications of old terms, unknown to the people of England; which cannot be explained by them and which will not be inserted in their dictionaries, unless copied from ours. Thus the terms, *land-office; land-warrant; location of land; consociation* of churches; *regent* of a university; *intendant* of a city; *plantation, selectmen, senate, congress, court, assembly, escheat,* &c. are either words not belonging to the language of England, or they are applied to things in this country which do not exist in that. No person in this country will be satisfied with the English definitions of the words *congress, senate* and *assembly, court,* &c. for although these are words used in England, yet they are applied in this country to express ideas which they do not express in that country. With our present constitutions of government, *escheat* can never have its feudal sense in the United States.

But this is not all. In many cases, the nature of our governments, and of our civil institutions, requires an appropriate language in the definition of words, even when the words express the same thing, as in England. Thus the English Dictionaries inform us that a *Justice* is one deputed by the *King* to do right by way of judgment—he is a *Lord* by his office—Justices of the peace are appointed by the *King's commission*—language which is inaccurate in respect to this officer in the United States. So *constitutionally* is defined by Todd or Chalmers, *legally,* but in this country the distinction between *constitution* and *law* requires a different definition. In the United States, a *plantation* is a very different thing from what it is in England. The word *marshal,* in this country, has one important application unknown in England or in Europe.

A great number of words in our language require to be defined in a phraseology accommodated to the condition and institutions of the people in these states, and the people of England must look to an American Dictionary for a correct understanding of such terms.

The necessity therefore of a Dictionary suited to the people of the United States is obvious; and I should suppose that this fact being admitted, there could be no difference of opinion as to the *time,* when such a work ought to be substituted for English Dictionaries.

There are many other considerations of a public nature, which serve to justify this attempt to furnish an American Work which shall be a guide to the youth of the United States. Most of these are too obvious to require illustration.

One consideration however which is dictated by my own feelings, but which I trust will meet with approbation[1] in correspondent feelings in my fellow citizens, ought not to be passed in silence. It is this. "The chief glory of a nation," says Dr. Johnson, "arises from its authors." With this opinion deeply impressed on my mind, I have the same ambition which actuated that great man when he expressed a wish to give celebrity to Bacon, to Hooker, to Milton and Boyle.

I do not indeed expect to add celebrity to the names of *Franklin, Washington, Adams, Jay, Madison, Marshall, Ramsay, Dwight, Smith, Trumbull, Hamilton, Belknap, Ames, Mason, Kent, Hare, Silliman, Cleaveland, Walsh, Irving,* and many other Americans distinguished by their writings or by their science; but it is with pride and satisfaction, that I can place them, as authorities, on the same page with those of *Boyle, Hooker, Milton, Dryden, Addison, Ray, Milner, Cowper, Davy, Thomson* and *Jameson.*

A life devoted to reading and to an investigation of the origin and principles of our vernacular[2] language, and especially a particular examination of the best English writers, with a view to a comparison of their style and phraseology, with those of the best American writers, and our colloquial[3] usage, enables me to affirm with confidence, that the genuine English idiom is as well preserved by the unmixed English of this country, as it is by the best *English* writers. Examples to prove this fact will be found in the Introduction to this

[1] *approbation:* approval
[2] *vernacular:* language which originates and is used in a particular place
[3] *colloquial:* idioms and usage developed by a group to be used in informal conversation

work. It is true, that many of our writers have neglected to cultivate taste, and the embellishments of style; but even these have written the language in its genuine *idiom.*[4] In this respect, Franklin and Washington, whose language is their hereditary mother tongue, unsophisticated by modern grammar, present as pure models of genuine English, as Addison or Swift. But I may go farther, and affirm, with truth, that our country has produced some of the best models of composition. The style of President Smith; of the authors of the Federalist; of Mr. Ames; of Dr. Mason; of Mr. Harper; of Chancellor Kent; [the prose] of Mr. Barlow; of the legal decisions of the Supreme Court of the United States; of the reports of legal decisions in some of the particular states; and many other writings; in purity, in elegance and in technical precision, is equaled only by that of the best British authors, and surpassed by that of no English compositions of a similar kind.

The United States commenced their existence under circumstances wholly novel and unexampled in the history of nations. They commenced with civilization, with learning, with science, with constitutions of free government, and with that best gift of God to man, the christian religion. Their population is now equal to that of England; in arts and sciences, our citizens are very little behind the most enlightened people on earth; in some respects, they have no superiors; and our language, within two centuries, will be spoken by more people in this country, than any other language on earth, except the Chinese, in Asia, and even that may not be an exception.

It has been my aim in this work, now offered to my fellow citizens, to ascertain the true principles of the language, in its orthography[5] and structure; to purify it from some palpable errors, and reduce the number of its anomalies,[6] thus giving it more regularity and consistency in its forms, both of words and sentences; and in this manner, to furnish a standard of our vernacular tongue, which we shall not be ashamed to

[4] *idiom:* unique phrasings which convey more than their literal meaning, such as, "so long" for "goodbye"
[5] *orthography:* the art of writing with correct letters and spellings
[6] *anomalies:* discrepancies or illogical combinations

bequeath to *three hundred millions of people*, who are destined to occupy, and I hope, to adorn the vast territory within our jurisdiction.

If the language can be improved in regularity, so as to be more easily acquired by our own citizens, and by foreigners, and thus be rendered a more useful instrument for the propagation of science, arts, civilization and christianity; if it can be rescued from the mischievous influence of sciolists and that dabbling spirit of innovation which is perpetually disturbing its settled usages and filling it with anomalies; if, in short, our vernacular language can be redeemed from corruptions, and our philology and literature from degradation; it would be a source of great satisfaction to me to be one among the instruments of promoting these valuable objects. If this object cannot be effected, and my wishes and hopes are to be frustrated, my labor will be lost, and this work must sink into oblivion.

This Dictionary, like all others of the kind, must be left, in some degree, imperfect; for what individual is competent to trace to their source, and define in all their various applications, popular, scientific and technical, *sixty* or *seventy thousand* words! It satisfies my mind that I have done all that my health, my talents and my pecuniary[7] means would enable me to accomplish. I present it to my fellow citizens, not with frigid indifference, but with my ardent wishes for their improvement and their happiness; and for the continued increase of the wealth, the learning, the moral and religious elevation of character, and the glory of my country.

To that great and benevolent Being, who, during the preparation of this work, has sustained a feeble consituation, amidst obstacles and toils, disappointments, infirmities and depression; who has twice borne me and my manuscripts in safety across the Atlantic, and given me strength and resolution to bring the work to a close, I would present the tribute of my most grateful acknowledgments. And if the talent which he entrusted to my care, has not been put to the most profitable use in his service, I hope it has not been "kept laid up in a napkin," and that any misapplication of it may be graciously forgiven.

[7] *pecuniary:* relating to money

FOR DISCUSSION

1. In this essay, published in 1828, why does Webster argue that the "genuine English idiom is as well preserved by the unmixed English of this country, as it is by the best *English* writers"? What assumptions about dialects and speech deviations lie behind this assertion? Does Webster unknowingly contradict his major argument in this statement? Do you think Webster is really ready to accept a genuine *American* literature, which isn't to be judged by English models?
2. Webster's argument is closely and logically ordered. What is the basic premise or assumption of the argument? What are the steps in the argument? What connection can you find between each step in the argument and the one that precedes it?
3. Did you know the meaning of all the words Webster lists as uniquely *American*? Have any of these words become obsolete, as did English hawking and hunting terms? Look up the "American" words you cannot define.

FOR COMPOSITION

Write a biographical sketch of one of the following men Webster refers to in his essay as men of distinction. Be *sure*, if you choose a common name, that you write on the man Webster would most likely have had in mind; that is, the man most prominent in 1828. You'll want to consult encyclopedias, *The Dictionary of American Biography, Who Was Who in America,* or Van Wyck Brooks's *The Flowering of New England.* Names to choose from are: Jay, Marshall, Ramsay, Dwight, Trumbull, Belknap, Ames, Mason, Kent, Hare, Silliman, Cleaveland, Walsh.

Theory of the Short Story

EDGAR ALLAN POE

The tale proper, in our opinion, affords unquestionably the fairest field for the exercise of the loftiest talent, which can be afforded by the wide domains of mere prose. Were we bidden to say how the highest genius could be most advantageously employed for the best display of its own powers, we should answer, without hesitation—in the composition of a rhymed poem, not to exceed in length what might be perused in an hour. Within this limit alone can the highest order of true poetry exist. We need only here say, upon this topic, that, in almost all classes of composition, the unity of effect or impression is a point of the greatest importance. It is clear, moreover, that this unity cannot be thoroughly preserved in productions whose perusal cannot be completed at one sitting. We may continue the reading of a prose composition, from the very nature of prose itself, much longer than we can persevere, to any good purpose, in the perusal of a poem. This latter, if truly fulfilling the demands of the poetic sentiment, induces an exaltation of the soul which cannot be long sustained. All high excitements are necessarily transient. Thus a long poem is a paradox. And, without unity of impression, the deepest effects cannot be brought about. . . .

The ordinary novel is objectionable, from its length, for reasons already stated in substance. As it cannot be read at one sitting, it deprives itself, of course, of the immense force derivable from *totality*. Worldly interests intervening during the pauses of perusal, modify, annul, or counteract, in a greater or less degree, the impressions of the book. But simple cessation in reading, would, of itself, be sufficient to destroy the true unity. In the brief tale, however, the author is enabled to carry out the fullness of his intention, be it what it may. During the hour of perusal the soul of the reader is at the writer's control. There are no external or extrinsic influences —resulting from weariness or interruption.

A skilful literary artist has constructed a tale. If wise, he has not fashioned his thoughts to accommodate his incidents; but having conceived, with deliberate care, a certain unique or single *effect* to be wrought out, he then invents such incidents —he then combines such events as may best aid him in establishing this preconceived effect. If his very initial sentence tend not to the outbringing of this effect, then he has failed in his first step. In the whole composition there should be no word written, of which the tendency, direct or indirect, is not to the one pre-established design. And by such means, with such care and skill, a picture is at length painted which leaves in the mind of him who contemplates it with a kindred art, a sense of the fullest satisfaction. The idea of the tale has been presented unblemished, because undisturbed; and this is an end unattainable by the novel. Undue brevity is just as exceptionable here as in the poem; but undue length is yet more to be avoided.

We have said that the tale has a point of superiority even over the poem. In fact, while the *rhythm* of this latter is an essential aid in the development of the poet's highest idea—the idea of the Beautiful—the artificialities of this rhythm are an inseparable bar to the development of all points of thought or expression which have their basis in *Truth*. But Truth is often, and in very great degree, the aim of the tale. Some of the finest tales are tales of ratiocination.[1] Thus the field of this species of composition, if not in so elevated a region on

[1] *ratiocination:* reasoning or deduction

the mountain of Mind, is a table-land of far vaster extent than the domain of the mere poem. Its products are never so rich, but infinitely more numerous, and more appreciable by the mass of mankind. The writer of the prose tale, in short, may bring to his theme a vast variety of modes or inflections of thought and expression—(the ratiocinative, for example, the sarcastic, or the humorous) which are not only antagonistical[2] to the nature of the poem, but absolutely forbidden by one of its most peculiar and indispensable adjuncts; we allude, of course, to rhythm. It may be added here, *par parenthèse*[3] that the author who aims at the purely beautiful in a prose tale is laboring at great disadvantage. For Beauty can be better treated in the poem. Not so with terror, or passion, or horror, or a multitude of such other points. And here it will be seen how full of prejudice are the usual animadversions[4] against those *tales of effect*, many fine examples of which were found in the earlier numbers of Blackwood.[5] The impressions produced were wrought in a legitimate sphere of action, and constituted a legitimate although sometimes an exaggerated interest. They were relished by every man of genius: although there were found many men of genius who condemned them without just ground. The true critic will but demand that the design intended be accomplished, to the fullest extent, by the means most advantageously applicable. . . .

[2] *antagonistical:* detrimental or opposed
[3] *par parenthèse:* parenthetically
[4] *animadversions:* adverse criticisms
[5] *Blackwood:* an English periodical

FOR DISCUSSION

1. What is of "greatest importance" in almost all classes of composition? Why does Poe say that "a long poem is a paradox"?
2. What advantage has the tale over the novel? Why can "Truth" be better expressed in a tale, and "Beauty" better in a poem?
3. What procedure will a skillful artist follow in constructing a tale?
4. Why does Poe consider the prejudice against "tales of effect' unjustified? What will the "true critic" demand of them?

The Poetic Principle

EDGAR ALLAN POE

In speaking of the Poetic Principle, I have no design to be either thorough or profound. . . .

By "minor poems" I mean, of course, poems of little length. And here, in the beginning, permit me to say a few words in regard to a somewhat peculiar principle, which, whether rightfully or wrongfully, has always had its influence in my own critical estimate of the poem. I hold that a long poem does not exist. I maintain that the phrase, "a long poem," is simply a flat contradiction in terms.

I need scarcely observe that a poem deserves its title only inasmuch as it excites, by elevating the soul. The value of the poem is in the ratio of this elevating excitement. But all excitements are, through a psychal[1] necessity, transient.[2] That degree of excitement which would entitle a poem to be so called at all, cannot be sustained throughout a composition of any great length. After the lapse of half an hour, at the very utmost, it flags—fails—a revulsion ensues—and then the poem is, in effect, and in fact, no longer such.

[1] *psychal:* mental
[2] *transient:* passing

There are, no doubt, many who have found difficulty in reconciling the critical dictum that the "Paradise Lost" is to be devoutly admired throughout, with the absolute impossibility of maintaining for it, during perusal, the amount of enthusiasm which that critical dictum would demand. This great work, in fact, is to be regarded as poetical, only when, losing sight of that vital requisite in all works of Art, Unity, we view it merely as a series of minor poems. If, to preserve its Unity—its totality of effect or impression—we read it (as would be necessary) at a single sitting, the result is but a constant alternation of excitement and depression. After a passage of what we feel to be true poetry, there follows, inevitably, a passage of platitude which no critical prejudgment can force us to admire; but if, upon completing the work we read it again, omitting the first book—that is to say, commencing with the second—we shall be surprised at now finding that admirable which we before condemned—that damnable which we had previously so much admired. It follows from all this that the ultimate, aggregate,[3] or absolute effect of even the best epic under the sun, is a nullity:[4]—and this is precisely the fact.

In regard to the Iliad, we have, if not positive proof, at least very good reason for believing it intended as a series of lyrics; but, granting the epic intention, I can say only that the work is based in an imperfect sense of art. The modern epic is, of the supposititious ancient model, but an inconsiderate and blindfold imitation. But the day of these artistic anomalies is over. If, at any time, any very long poem *were* popular in reality—which I doubt—it is at least clear that no very long poem will ever be popular again. . . .

On the other hand, it is clear that a poem may be improperly brief. Undue brevity degenerates into mere epigrammatism.[5] A *very* short poem, while now and then producing a brilliant or vivid, never produces a profound or enduring effect. There must be the steady pressing down of the stamp upon the wax. De Béranger has wrought innumerable things, pungent and

[3] *aggregate:* cumulative
[4] *nullify:* void
[5] *epigrammatism:* cleverly turned phrases

spirit-stirring; but in general they have been too imponderous to stamp themselves deeply into the public attention, and thus, as so many feathers of fancy, have been blown aloft only to be whistled down the wind. . . .

While the epic mania—while the idea that, to merit in poetry, prolixity[6] is indispensable—has for some years past been gradually dying out of the public mind, by mere dint of its own absurdity—we find it succeeded by a heresy too palpably false to be long tolerated, but one which, in the brief period it has already endured, may be said to have accomplished more in the corruption of our Poetical Literature than all its other enemies combined. I allude to the heresy of *The Didactic.* It has been assumed, tacitly and avowedly, directly and indirectly, that the ultimate object of all Poetry is Truth. Every poem, it is said, should inculcate[7] a moral; and by this moral is the poetical merit of the work to be adjudged. We Americans, especially, have patronized this happy idea; and we Bostonians, very especially, have developed it in full. We have taken it into our heads that to write a poem simply for the poem's sake, and to acknowledge such to have been our design, would be to confess ourselves radically wanting in the true Poetic dignity and force:—but the simple fact is, that, would we but permit ourselves to look into our own souls, we should immediately there discover that under the sun there neither exists nor *can* exist any work more thoroughly dignified—more supremely noble than this very poem—this poem *per se*—this poem which is a poem and nothing more—this poem written solely for the poem's sake.

With as deep a reverence for the True as ever inspired the bosom of man, I would, nevertheless, limit, in some measure, its modes of inculcation. I would limit to enforce them. I would not enfeeble them by dissipation. The demands of Truth are severe. She has no sympathy with the myrtles. All *that* which is so indispensable in Song, is precisely all *that* with which *she* has nothing whatever to do. It is but making her a flaunting paradox, to wreathe her in gems and flowers. In enforcing a truth, we need severity rather than efflores-

[6] *prolixity:* tediously long
[7] *inculcate:* teach

cence[8] of language. We must be simple, precise, terse. We must be cool, calm, unimpassioned. In a word, we must be in that mood which, as nearly as possible, is the exact converse of the poetical. *He* must be blind, indeed, who does not perceive the radical and chasmal[9] differences between the truthful and the poetical modes of inculcation.[10] He must be theory-mad beyond redemption who, in spite of these differences, shall still persist in attempting to reconcile the obstinate oils and waters of Poetry and Truth.

Dividing the world of mind into its three most immediately obvious distinctions, we have the Pure Intellect, Taste, and the Moral Sense. I place Taste in the middle, because it is just this position which, in the mind, it occupies. . . . Just as the Intellect concerns itself with Truth, so Taste informs us of the Beautiful, while the Moral Sense is regardful of Duty. . . .

An immortal instinct, deep within the spirit of man, is thus, plainly, a sense of the Beautiful. This it is which administers to his delight in the manifold forms, and sounds, and odours, and sentiments, amid which he exists. And just as the lily is repeated in the lake, or the eyes of Amaryllis in the mirror, so is the mere oral or written repetition of these forms, and sounds, and colours, and odours, and sentiments, a duplicate source of delight. But this mere repetition is not poetry. He who shall simply sing, with however glowing enthusiasm, or with however vivid a truth of description, of the sights, and sounds, and odours, and colours, and sentiments, which greet *him* in common with all mankind—he, I say, has yet failed to prove his divine title. There is still a something in the distance which he has been unable to attain. We have still a thirst unquenchable, to allay which he has not shown us the crystal springs. This thirst belongs to the immortality of Man. It is at once a consequence and an indication of his perennial existence. It is the desire of the moth for the star. It is no mere appreciation of the Beauty before us—but a wild effort to reach the Beauty above. Inspired by an ecstatic prescience[11]

[8] *efflorescence:* flowery quality
[9] *chasmal:* enormous
[10] *inculcation:* teaching
[11] *prescience:* knowledge

of the glories beyond the grave, we struggle, by multiform combinations among the things and thoughts of Time, to attain a portion of that Loveliness whose very elements, perhaps, appertain to eternity alone. And thus when by Poetry—or when by Music, the most entrancing of the Poetic moods—we find ourselves melted into tears, we weep then—not as the Abbaté Gravina[12] supposes—through excess of pleasure, but through a certain, petulant, impatient sorrow at our inability to grasp *now*, wholly, here on earth, at once and for ever, those divine and rapturous joys, of which *through* the poem, or *through* the music, we attain to but brief and indeterminate glimpses. . . .

To recapitulate, then:—I would define, in brief, the Poetry of words as *The Rhythmical Creation of Beauty*. Its sole arbiter is Taste. With the Intellect or with the Conscience, it has only collateral[13] relations. Unless incidentally, it has no concern whatever either with Duty or with Truth. . . .

We shall reach, however, more immediately a distinct conception of what the true Poetry is, by mere reference to a few of the simple elements which induce in the Poet himself the true poetical effect. He recognizes the ambrosia which nourishes his soul, in the bright orbs that shine in Heaven, in the volutes[14] of the flower, in the clustering of low shrubberies, in the waving of the grain-fields, in the slanting of tall Eastern trees, in the blue distance of mountains—in the grouping of clouds, in the twinkling of half-hidden brooks, in the gleaming of silver rivers, in the repose of sequestered[15] lakes, in the star-mirroring depths of lonely wells. He perceives it in the songs of birds, in the harp of Æolus, in the sighing of the night-wind, in the repining voice of the forest, in the surf that complains to the shore, in the fresh breath of the woods, in the scent of the violet, in the voluptuous perfume of the hyacinth, in the suggestive odor that comes to him at eventide from far-distant, undiscovered islands, over

[12] *Abbaté Gravina:* an Italian scholar whose book, *Della Ragion Poetica* (1708) provided a general discussion of poetry

[13] *collateral:* side or auxiliary

[14] *volutes:* spiral or twisted formations

[15] *sequestered:* isolated

dim oceans, illimitable and unexplored. He owns it in all noble thoughts, in all unworldly motives, in all holy impulses, in all chivalrous, generous, and self-sacrificing deeds. He feels it in the beauty of woman, in the grace of her step, in the lustre of her eye, in the melody of her voice, in her soft laughter, in her sigh, in the harmony of the rustling of her robes. He deeply feels it in her winning endearments, in her burning enthusiasms, in her gentle charities, in her meek and devotional endurances, but above all—ah, far above all—he kneels to it, he worships it in the faith, in the purity, in the strength, in the altogether divine majesty, of her *love*.

Let me conclude by the recitation of yet another brief poem. . . . It is by Motherwell, and is called 'The Song of the Cavalier.' With our modern and altogether rational ideas of the absurdity and impiety of warfare, we are not precisely in that frame of mind best adapted to sympathize with the sentiments, and thus to appreciate the real excellence of the poem. To do this fully we must identify ourselves in fancy with the soul of the old cavalier.

'Then mounte! then mounte, brave gallants, all,
  And don your helmes amaine:
Deathe's couriers, Fame and Honor, call
  Us to the field againe.
No shrewish teares shall fill our eye
  When the sword-hilt's in our hand,—
Heart-whole we'll part, and no whit sighe
  For the fayrest of the land;
Let piping swaine, and craven wight,
  Thus weepe and puling crye,
Our business is like men to fight,
  And hero-like to die!'

FOR DISCUSSION

1. What does Poe say about very long poems? About very short ones? What is the proper length for a good poem? If "minor poems" are short poems, what would he consider "major poems"? How does a poem convey unity?

2. What is Poe's definition of a poem? How does one know when he has read a real poem?
3. What does Poe think of the epic form? How does he rate *Paradise Lost?*
4. How does Poe assess poems which teach a lesson? Can you remember any poems you'll have to dismiss if you feel Poe is right? Why would didactic or moralistic poetry appeal to Americans in particular?
5. How would Poe describe the poetic mood? How does it differ from a truth-seeking mood?
6. Why does Poe say a sense of the Beautiful is an *immortal* instinct? What does he mean by *immortal?* Where does he find Beauty most startlingly present?
7. Do you agree with Poe's divisions of the mind? Why or why not? What categories might he have included which he omits?

FOR COMPOSITION

Test your favorite poem by Poe's standards. Write an essay explaining how the poem would be rated if Poe were analyzing it.

MELVILLE, WHITMAN, AND HOWELLS

Although American aesthetic theorizing began auspiciously with the work of Webster and Poe, there was still work to be done and ground to be won. For one thing, American writers faced great difficulties in getting their work published. Partial blame for this neglect of American writers must be shared by American publishers. Publishers found it much more profitable to pirate the books of established English writers than to gamble on the uncertain reception of a countryman's works. Not until the International Copyright Act of 1891, in fact, did this situation change significantly.

Obviously, many outstanding American authors were writing before 1891. Yet to their difficult task of finding a publisher was added the problem of an active prejudice against them on the part of the reading public. Men and women who would have scorned to follow the dictates of English political leaders were content to spend their leisure reading European writers. Consequently, the cries for a native American literature, and a public which would support it, sometimes appear in retrospect surprisingly shrill. Among the shrillest was Herman Melville's 1850 essay on Nathaniel Hawthorne.

Melville begins his review by comparing Hawthorne to Shakespeare—not because the comparison is particularly appropriate, but because he wishes to pay the highest compliment to a fellow American. He goes on to make many startling statements, among them that men "not very much inferior to Shakespeare are this day being born on the banks of the Ohio." Of course, by confusing human worth with literary worth, Melville compromised his literary judgment in this essay. His goal, however, was not to judge American literature objectively, but simply to arouse some interest in American writing which would make possible the production of American literature. It is a tribute to Melville's inherent good taste that he chose so excellent a writer as Hawthorne to praise. Interestingly, one of the greatest of American novelists of the twentieth century, William Faulkner, later echoed Melville's paradoxical pronouncement that "failure is the true test of greatness."

One of Melville's main points was that "no American should write like an Englishman or a Frenchman," but rather in his own native idiom, form, and style. Walt Whitman filled such requirements with distinction. Though some thought Whitman's verse less beautiful poetry than a "barbaric yawp," still it was clearly new, native, and American. It was in a new form, rhythm, and style, the first authentic response to Melville's plea for a distinctive genius to express the distinctive American experience.

Because he chose to ignore old forms and patterns, Whitman was accused of despising the revered and comfortably familiar New England school of poets. He cleverly side-steps this charge in the selection that follows from *Specimen Days*, his rather formal journal. He praises the New Englanders for furnishing the best of all possible *beginnings* which any literature could hope for. In this graceful tribute, however, is the implicit statement that Whitman was aware of his own important role in American letters. With *Leaves of Grass,* first published in 1855 but significantly expanded in later editions, American poetry began a period of growth, a period in which the poet not only was aware of himself as an American, but also felt comfortable with the designation.

In the battle American critics fought for American literary recognition, an important document is an essay written by William Dean Howells, the honorary "dean of American letters." The eagerness with which Howells accepts in this essay a highly suspect description of American literature—simply because the description states that American and English literature are different—suggests the anxiety critics continued to feel throughout the nineteenth century about their independence.

Howells' essay shows perhaps better than any other the desperation of literary leaders to make American literature respectable. But since gaining respectability is his major concern, Howells leaves himself little time to examine critically the requirements of respectability. He simply accepts middle class standards for what is proper and then states categorically that of all literatures, American literature fits such standards best. Nevertheless, Howells was one of the most enlightened critics of his time; in this essay, he suggests a number of very important things. He reveals what goals the literary establishment had in mind in the closing decades of the nineteenth century, what pressures writers who wished to be recognized by the public were under, and what demands that public placed on the material they read. Perhaps Howells' most important critical function, however, was as a fighter of the last battles for American literature. After the arrival on the scene of his contemporaries—Mark Twain, Stephen Crane, Emily Dickinson, and Henry James—such battles were no longer necessary. American literature had, unmistakably, arrived.

Hawthorne and His Mosses

HERMAN MELVILLE

It is the least part of genius that attracts admiration. Where Hawthorne is known, he seems to be deemed a pleasant writer, with a pleasant style,—a sequestered, harmless man from whom any deep and weighty thing would hardly be anticipated—a man who means no meanings. But there is no man, in whom humor and love, like mountain peaks, soar to such a rapt height as to receive the irradiations of the upper skies;—there is no man in whom humor and love are developed in that high form called genius; no such man can exist without also possessing, as the indispensable complement of these, a great, deep intellect, which drops down into the universe like a plummet. Or, love and humor are only the eyes through which such an intellect views this world. The great beauty in such a mind is but the product of its strength. . . .

Spite of all the Indian-summer sunlight on the hither side of Hawthorne's soul, the other side—like the dark half of the physical sphere—is shrouded in a blackness, ten times black. But this darkness but gives more effect to the ever-moving dawn, that for ever advances through it, and circumnavigates his world. Whether Hawthorne has simply availed himself of this mystical blackness as a means to the wondrous effects he makes it to produce in his lights and shades; or whether there really lurks in him, perhaps unknown to himself, a touch of Puritanic gloom,—this, I cannot altogether tell. Certain it is, however, that this great power of blackness in him derives its force from its appeals to that Calvinistic sense of Innate Depravity[1] and Original Sin,[2] from whose visitations, in some shape or other, no deeply thinking mind is always and wholly free. For, in certain moods, no man can weigh this world without throwing in something, somehow like Original Sin, to strike the uneven balance. At all events, perhaps no writer has ever wielded this terrific thought with greater terror than this same harmless Hawthorne. Still more: this black conceit pervades him through and through. You may be witched by his sunlight,—transported by the bright gildings in the skies he builds over you; but there is the blackness of darkness beyond; and even his bright gildings but fringe and play upon the edges of thunderclouds. In one word, the world is mistaken in this Nathaniel Hawthorne. He himself must often have smiled at its absurd misconception of him. He is immeasurably deeper than the plummet of the mere critic. For it is not the brain that can test such a man; it is only the heart. You cannot come to know greatness by inspecting it; there is no glimpse to be caught of it, except by intuition; you need not ring it, you but touch it, and you find it is gold.

Now, it is that blackness in Hawthorne, of which I have spoken, that so fixes and fascinates me. It may be, nevertheless, that it is too largely developed in him. Perhaps he does not give us a ray of his light for every shade of his dark. But however this may be, this blackness it is that furnishes the infinite obscure of his back-ground,—that back-ground, against which Shakspeare plays his grandest conceits, the things that have made for Shakspeare his loftiest but most circumscribed renown, as the profoundest of thinkers. For by philosophers Shakspeare is not adored as the great man of

[1]*Innate Depravity:* the doctrine that evil is a basic part of man's nature, and that he is already evil at birth

[2]*Original Sin:* the doctrine that Adam's sin condemned all of mankind

tragedy and comedy.—"Off with his head; so much for Buckingham!" This sort of rant, interlined by another hand, brings down the house,—those mistaken souls, who dream of Shakspeare as a mere man of Richard-the-Third humps and Macbeth daggers. But it is those deep faraway things in him; those occasional flashings-forth of the intuitive Truth in him; those short, quick probings at the very axis of reality;—these are the things that makes Shakspeare, Shakspeare. Through the mouths of the dark characters of Hamlet, Timon, Lear, and Iago, he craftily says, or sometimes insinuates the things which we feel to be so terrifically true, that it were all but madness for any good man, in his own proper character, to utter, or even hint of them. Tormented into desperation, Lear, the frantic king, tears off the mask, and speaks the same madness of vital truth. But, as I before said, it is the least part of genius that attracts admiration. And so, much of the blind, unbridled admiration that has been heaped upon Shakspeare, has been lavished upon the least part of him. And few of his endless commentators and critics seem to have remembered, or even perceived, that the immediate products of a great mind are not so great as that undeveloped and sometimes undevelopable yet dimly-discernible greatness, to which those immediate products are but the infallible indices. In Shakspeare's tomb lies infinitely more than Shakspeare ever wrote. And if I magnify Shakspeare, it is not so much for what he did do as for what he did not do, or refrained from doing. For in this world of lies, Truth is forced to fly like a scared white doe in the woodlands; and only by cunning glimpses will she reveal herself, as in Shakspeare and other masters of the great Art of Telling the Truth,—even though it be covertly and by snatches.

But if this view of the all-popular Shakspeare be seldom taken by his readers, and if very few who extol him have ever read him deeply, or perhaps, only have seen him on the tricky stage (which alone made, and is still making him his mere mob renown)—if few men have time, or patience, or palate, for the spiritual truth as it is in that great genius;—it is then no matter of surprise, that in a contemporaneous age, Nathaniel Hawthorne is a man as yet almost utterly mistaken among men. Here and there, in some quiet arm-chair in the noisy town, or some deep nook among the noiseless mountains, he may be appreciated for something of what he is. But unlike Shakspeare, who was forced to the contrary course by circumstances, Hawthorne (either from simple disinclination, or else from inaptitude) refrains from all the popularizing noise and show of broad farce and blood-besmeared tragedy; content with the still, rich utterance of a great intellect in repose, and which sends few thoughts into circulation, except they be arterialized[3] at his large warm lungs, and expanded in his honest heart.

Nor need you fix upon that blackness in him, if it suit you not. Nor, indeed, will all readers discern it; for it is, mostly, insinuated to those who may best understand it, and account for it; it is not obtruded upon every one alike.

Some may start to read of Shakspeare and Hawthorne on the same page. They may say, that if an illustration were needed, a lesser light might have sufficed to elucidate this Hawthorne, this small man of yesterday. But I am not willingly one of those who, as touching Shakspeare at least, exemplify the maxim of Rochefoucauld,[4] that "we exalt the reputation of some, in order to depress that of others";—who, to teach all noble-souled aspirants that there is no hope for them, pronounce Shakspeare absolutely unapproachable. But Shakspeare has been approached. There are minds that have gone as far as Shakspeare into the universe. And hardly a mortal man, who, at some time or other, has not felt as great thoughts in him as any you will find in Hamlet. We must not inferentially malign mankind for the sake of any one man, whoever he may be. This is too cheap a purchase of contentment for conscious mediocrity to make. Besides, this absolute and unconditional adoration of Shakspeare has grown to be a part of our Anglo-Saxon superstitions. The Thirty-Nine Articles are now Forty. Intolerance has come to exist in this matter. You must believe in Shakspeare's unapproachability, or quit the country. But what sort of a belief is this for an American,

[3]*arterialized:* converted into arterial blood by the action of the lungs

[4]*Rochefoucauld:* François de la Rochefoucauld (1613-1680), French man-of-letters noted for his epigrammatic style

a man who is bound to carry republican progressiveness into Literature as well as into Life? Believe me, my friends, that men, not very much inferior to Shakspeare, are this day being born on the banks of the Ohio. And the day will come when you shall say, Who reads a book by an Englishman that is a modern? The great mistake seems to be, that even with those Americans who look forward to the coming of a great literary genius among us, they somehow fancy he will come in the costume of Queen Elizabeth's day; be a writer of dramas founded upon old English history or the tales of Boccaccio. Whereas, great geniuses are parts of the times, they themselves are the times, and possess a correspondent coloring. It is of a piece with the Jews, who, while their Shiloh was meekly walking in their streets, were still praying for his magnificent coming; looking for him in a chariot, who was already among them on an ass. Nor must we forget that, in his own lifetime, Shakspeare was not Shakspeare, but only Master William Shakspeare of the shrewd, thriving business firm of Condell, Shakspeare & Co., proprietors of the Globe Theatre in London; and by a courtly author, of the name of Chettle, was looked at as an "upstart crow," beautified "with other birds' feathers." For, mark it well, imitation is often the first charge brought against real originality. Why this is so, there is not space to set forth here. You must have plenty of sea-room to tell the Truth in; especially when it seems to have an aspect of newness, as America did in 1492, though it was then just as old, and perhaps older than Asia, only those sagacious philosophers, the common sailors, had never seen it before, swearing it was all water and moonshine there.

Now I do not say that Nathaniel of Salem is a greater than William of Avon, or as great. But the difference between the two men is by no means immeasurable. Not a very great deal more, and Nathaniel were verily William.

This, too, I mean, that if Shakspeare has not been equalled, give the world time, and he is sure to be surpassed, in one hemisphere or the other. Nor will it at all do to say, that the world is getting grey and grizzled now, and has lost that fresh charm which she wore of old, and by virtue of which the great poets of past times made themselves what we esteem them to be. Not so. The world is as young to-day as when it was created; and this Vermont morning dew is as wet to my feet, as Eden's dew to Adam's. Nor has nature been all over ransacked by our progenitors,[5] so that no new charms and mysteries remain for this latter generation to find. Far from it. The trillionth part has not yet been said; and all that has been said, but multiplies the avenues to what remains to be said. It is not so much paucity as superabundance of material that seems to incapacitate modern authors.

Let America, then, prize and cherish her writers; yea, let her glorify them. They are not so many in number as to exhaust her good-will. And while she has good kith and kin of her own, to take to her bosom, let her not lavish her embraces upon the household of an alien. For believe it or not, England, after all, is in many things an alien to us. China has more bonds of real love for us than she. But even were there no strong literary individualities among us, as there are some dozens at least, nevertheless, let America first praise mediocrity even, in her own children, before she praises (for everywhere, merit demands acknowledgment from every one) the best excellence in the children of any other land. Let her own authors, I say, have the priority of appreciation. I was much pleased with a hot-headed Carolina cousin of mine, who once said,—"If there were no other American to stand by, in literature, why, then, I would stand by Pop Emmons and his 'Fredoniad,' and till a better epic came along, swear it was not very far behind the Iliad." Take away the words, and in spirit he was sound.

Not that American genius needs patronage in order to expand. For that explosive sort of stuff will expand though screwed up in a vice, and burst it, though it were triple steel. It is for the nation's sake, and not for her authors' sake, that I would have America be heedful of the increasing greatness among her writers. For how great the shame, if other nations should be before her, in crowning her heroes of the pen! But this is almost the case now. American authors have received more just and discriminating praise (however loftily and ridiculously given, in certain cases) even from some

[5] *progenitors:* first ancestors

Englishmen, than from their own countrymen. There are hardly five critics in America; and several of them are asleep. As for patronage, it is the American author who now patronizes his country, and not his country him. And if at times some among them appeal to the people for more recognition, it is not always with selfish motives, but patriotic ones.

It is true, that but few of them as yet have evinced that decided originality which merits great praise. But that graceful writer, who perhaps of all Americans has received the most plaudits[6] from his own country for his productions,—that very popular and amiable writer, however good and self-reliant in many things, perhaps owes his chief reputation to the self-acknowledged imitation of a foreign model, and to the studied avoidance of all topics but smooth ones. But it is better to fail in originality than to succeed in imitation. He who has never failed somewhere, that man cannot be great. Failure is the true test of greatness. And if it be said, that continual success is a proof that a man wisely knows his powers,—it is only to be added, that, in that case, he knows them to be small. Let us believe it, then, once for all, that there is no hope for us in these smooth, pleasing writers that know their powers. Without malice, but to speak the plain fact, they but furnish an appendix to Goldsmith, and other English authors. And we want no American Goldsmiths: nay, we want no American Miltons. It were the vilest thing you could say of a true American author, that he were an American Tompkins. Call him an American and have done, for you cannot say a nobler thing of him. But it is not meant that all American writers should studiously cleave to nationality in their writings; only this, no American writer should write like an Englishman or a Frenchman; let him write like a man, for then he will be sure to write like an American. Let us away with this leaven of literary flunkeyism towards England. If either must play the flunkey in this thing, let England do it, not us. While we are rapidly preparing for that political supremacy among the nations which prophetically awaits us at the close of the present century, in a literary point of view, we are deplorably unprepared for it; and we seem stu-

[6]*plaudits:* praises

dious to remain so. Hitherto, reasons might have existed why this should be; but no good reason exists now. And all that is requisite to amendment in this matter, is simply this: that while freely acknowledging all excellence everywhere, we should refrain from unduly lauding foreign writers, and, at the same time, duly recognize meritorious writers that are our own;—those writers who breathe that unshackled, democratic spirit of Christianity in all things, which now takes the practical lead in this world, though at the same time led by ourselves—us Americans. Let us boldly contemn all imitation, though it comes to us graceful and fragrant as the morning; and foster all originality, though at first it be crabbed and ugly as our own pine knots. And if any of our authors fail, or seem to fail, then, in the words of my enthusiastic Carolina cousin, let us clap him on the shoulder, and back him against all Europe for his second round. The truth is, that in one point of view, this matter of a national literature has come to such a pass with us, that in some sense we must turn bullies, else the day is lost, or superiority so far beyond us, that we can hardly say it will ever be ours.

And now, my countrymen, as an excellent author of your own flesh and blood,—an unimitating, and, perhaps, in his way, an inimitable man—whom better can I commend to you, in the first place, than Nathaniel Hawthorne. He is one of the new, and far better generation of your writers. The smell of your beeches and hemlocks is upon him; your own broad prairies are in his soul; and if you travel away inland into his deep and noble nature, you will hear the far roar of his Niagara. Give not over to future generations the glad duty of acknowledging him for what he is. Take that joy to yourself, in your own generation; and so shall he feel those grateful impulses on him, that may possibly prompt him to the full flower of some still greater achievement in your eyes. And by confessing him you thereby confess others; you brace the whole brotherhood. For genius, all over the world, stands hand in hand, and one shock of recognition runs the whole circle round.

In treating of Hawthorne, or rather of Hawthorne in his writings (for I never saw the man; and in the chances of a quiet plantation life, remote from his haunts, perhaps never shall); in treating of his works, I say, I have thus far omitted all mention of his *Twice-Told Tales*, and *Scarlet Letter*. Both are excellent, but full of such manifold, strange, and diffusive beauties, that time would all but fail me to point the half of them out. But there are things in those two books, which, had they been written in England a century ago, Nathaniel Hawthorne had utterly displaced many of the bright names we now revere on authority. But I am content to leave Hawthorne to himself, and to the infallible finding of posterity; and however great may be the praise I have bestowed upon him, I feel that in so doing I have more served and honored myself, than him. For, at bottom, great excellence is praise enough to itself; but the feeling of a sincere and appreciative love and admiration towards it, this is relieved by utterance; and warm, honest praise, ever leaves a pleasant flavor in the mouth; and it is an honorable thing to confess to what is honorable in others.

FOR DISCUSSION

1. In the last Hawthorne story you read, what indicates the "other side" of his soul—the one which is "shrouded in a blackness, ten times black." What does Melville's fascination with Hawthorne's "blackness" tell you about Melville?
2. Review the comparison of Hawthorne to Shakespeare. How does Hawthorne appear in this comparison? Did you think the comparison is effective?
3. Do you feel that America today obeys Melville's injunction to "cherish her writers"? Why or why not? Do you detect an excessive patriotism in Melville's advice to praise mediocrity in one's own before praising excellence in another's? Why would a nineteenth-century writer say such a thing? What effect would such actions have on one's literary judgment?
4. Test Melville's doctrine that "Failure is the true test of greatness." According to this rule, who are the greatest American writers?
5. Why does Melville feel it is so important to have a national literature? What depends on such literature?

6. Using Melville's description of a genius and his relationship to the times, what is today's genius probably like? What are his concerns? What form does his work take?

FOR COMPOSITION

Using the essays of Webster, Poe, and Melville, write an essay on the struggle for American literary independence from England which took place over a half-century after the political struggle.

My Tribute to Four Poets

WALT WHITMAN

April 16.—A short but pleasant visit to Longfellow. I am not one of the calling kind, but as the author of "Evangeline" kindly took the trouble to come and see me three years ago in Camden, where I was ill, I felt not only the impulse of my own pleasure on that occasion, but a duty. He was the only particular eminence I called on in Boston, and I shall not soon forget his lit-up face and glowing warmth and courtesy, in the modes of what is called the old school.

And now just here I feel the impulse to interpolate something about the mighty four who stamp this first American century with its birth-marks of poetic literature. In a late magazine one of my reviewers, who ought to know better, speaks of my "attitude of contempt and scorn and intolerance" toward the leading poets—of my "deriding" them, and preaching their "uselessness." If anybody cares to know what I think—and have long thought and avow'd—about them, I am entirely willing to propound. I can't imagine any better luck befalling these States for a poetical beginning and initiation than has come from Emerson, Longfellow, Bryant, and Whittier. Emerson, to me, stands unmistakably at the head, but for the others I am at a loss where to give any precedence. Each illustrious, each rounded, each distinctive. Emerson for his sweet, vital-tasting melody, rhym'd philosophy, and poems as amber-clear as the honey of the wild bee he loves to sing. Longfellow for rich color, graceful forms and incidents—all that makes life beautiful and love refined—competing with the singers of Europe on their own ground, and, with one exception, better and finer work than that of any of them. Bryant pulsing the first interior verse-throbs of a mighty world—bard of the river and the wood, ever conveying a taste of open air, with scents as from hayfields, grapes, birch-borders—always lurkingly fond of threnodies[1]—beginning and ending his long career with chants of death, with here and there through all, poems, or passages of poems, touching the highest universal truths, enthusiasms, duties—morals as grim and eternal, if not as stormy and fateful, as anything in Aeschylus.[2] While in Whittier, with his special themes—(his outcropping love of heroism and war, for all his Quakerdom, his verses at times like the measur'd step of Cromwell's[3] old veterans)—in Whittier lives the zeal, the moral energy, that founded New England—the splendid rectitude and ardor of Luther, Milton, George Fox[4]—I must not, dare not, say the wilfulness and narrowness—though doubtless the world needs now, and always will need, almost above all, just such narrowness and wilfulness.

[1]*threnodies:* tributes to the dead
[2]*Aeschylus:* ancient Greek writer of tragedies
[3]*Cromwell:* Puritan commander during the seventeenth-century civil war in England and ruler for five years until his death
[4]*George Fox:* (1624-1691) British clergyman who founded the Society of Friends (the Quakers)

FOR DISCUSSION

1. What led Whitman to write this tribute? What impression do you gain of both Longfellow and Whitman from the opening paragraph?

2. Whitman uses the word "mighty" in referring to these four poets, yet he speaks of their contribution to American literature as "a poetical beginning and initiation." What does he mean? Do you think that critics and readers today share his opinion? Explain.
3. Emerson was not primarily a poet, yet Whitman placed him "unmistakably at the head" of all four. Why? Neither Thoreau nor Poe was mentioned. In your opinion, what qualities of their poetry might Whitman have praised?
4. Which qualities of Longfellow's poems most impressed Whitman? Which were largely responsible for Longfellow's popularity during his lifetime?
5. Whitman was as responsive to nature as Bryant, and as ardent in his beliefs as Whittier. What did he admire in each of these poets? Are all of his comments compliments? Support your answers with evidence drawn from Whitman's own words.
6. From your study of these four poets, do you think that Whitman does or does not , make an accurate evaluation of each poet and his work? Explain.

Criticism and Fiction

WILLIAM DEAN HOWELLS

It is no doubt such work as Mr. James's[1] that an English essayist (Mr. E. Hughes) has chiefly in mind, in a study of the differences of the English and American novel. He defines the English novel as working from within outwardly, and the American novel as working from without inwardly. The definition is very surprisingly accurate; and the critic's discovery of this fundamental difference is carried into particulars with a distinctness which is as unfailing as the courtesy he has in recognizing the present superiority of American work. He seems to think, however, that the English principle is the better, though why he should think so he does not make so clear. It appears a belated and rather voluntary effect of patriotism, disappointing in a philosopher of his degree; but it does not keep him from very explicit justice to the best characteristics of our fiction. "The American novelist is distinguished for the intellectual grip which he has of his characters. . . . He penetrates below the crust, and he recognizes no necessity of the crust to anticipate what is

[1] *Henry James:* famous American novelist and friend of Howells.

beneath. . . . He utterly discards heroics; he often even discards anything like a plot. . . . His story proper is often no more than a natural predicament. . . . It is no stage view we have of his characters, but one behind the scenes. . . . We are brought into contact with no strained virtues, illumined by strained lights upon strained heights of situation. . . . Whenever he appeals to the emotions it would seem to be with an appeal to the intellect too . . . because he weaves his story of the finer, less self-evident though common threads of human nature, seldom calling into play the grosser and more powerful strain. . . . Everywhere in his pages we come across acquaintances undisguised. . . . The characters in an American novel are never unapproachable to the reader. . . . The naturalness, with the every-day atmosphere which surrounds it, is one great charm of the American novel. . . . It is throughout examinative, discursory, even more—quizzical. Its characters are undergoing, at the hands of the author, calm, interested observation. . . . He is never caught identifying himself with them; he must preserve impartiality at all costs . . . but . . . the touch of nature is always felt, the feeling of kinship always follows. . . . The strength of the American novel is its optimistic faith. . . . If out of this persistent hopefulness it can evolve for men a new order of trustfulness, a tenet that between man and man there should be less suspicion, more confidence, since human nature sanctions it, its mission will have been more than an æsthetic, it will have been a moral one."

Not all of this will be found true of Mr. James, but all that relates to artistic methods and characteristics will, and the rest is true of American novels generally. For the most part in their range and tendency they are admirable. I will not say they are all good, or that any of them is wholly good; but I find in nearly every one of them a disposition to regard our life without the literary glasses so long thought desirable, and to see character, not as it is in other fiction, but as it abounds outside of all fiction. This disposition sometimes goes with poor enough performance, but in some of our novels it goes with performance that is excellent; and at any rate it is for the present more valuable then evenness of performance. It is what relates American fiction to the only living movement in imaginative literature, and distinguishes by a superior freshness and authenticity any group of American novels from a similarly accidental group of English novels, giving them the same good right to be as the like number of recent Russian novels, French novels, Spanish novels, Italian novels, Norwegian novels.

It is the difference of the American novelist's ideals from those of the English novelist that gives him his advantage, and seems to promise him the future. The love of the passionate and the heroic, as the Englishman has it, is such a crude and unwholesome thing, so deaf and blind to all the most delicate and important facts of art and life, so insensible to the subtle values in either that its presence or absence makes the whole difference, and enables one who is not obsessed by it to thank Heaven that he is not as that other man is.

There can be little question that many refinements of thought and spirit which every American is sensible of in the fiction of this continent, are necessarily lost upon our good kin beyond seas, whose thumb-fingered apprehension requires something gross and palpable for its assurance of reality. This is not their fault, and I am not sure that is wholly their misfortune: they are made so as not to miss what they do not find, and they are simply content without those subleties of life and character which it gives us so keen a pleasure to have noted in literature. If they perceive them at all it is as something vague and diaphanous,[2] something that filmily wavers before their sense and teases them, much as the beings of an invisible world might mock one of our material frame by intimations of their presence. It is with reason, therefore, on the part of an Englishman, that Mr. Henley complains of our fiction as a shadow-land, though we find more and more in it the faithful report of our life, its motives and emotions, and all the comparatively etherealized[3] passions and ideals that influence it.

[2]*diaphanous:* misty or translucent
[3]*etherealized:* made heavenly or spiritualized

In fact, the American who chooses to enjoy his birthright to the full, lives in a world wholly different from the Englishman's, and speaks (too often through his nose) another language: be breathes a rarefied and nimble air full of shining possibilities and radiant promises which the fog-and-soot-clogged lungs of those less-favored islanders struggle in vain to fill themselves with. But he ought to be modest in his advantage, and patient with the coughing and sputtering of his cousin who complains of finding himself in an exhausted receiver on plunging into one of our novels. To be quite just to the poor fellow, I have had some such experience as that myself in the atmosphere of some of our more attenuated[4] romances.

Yet every now and then I read a book with perfect comfort and much exhilaration, whose scenes the average Englishman would gasp in. Nothing happens; that is, nobody murders or debauches[5] anybody else; there is no arson or pillage of any sort; there is not a ghost, or a ravening beast, or a hair-breadth escape, or a shipwreck, or a monster of self-sacrifice, or a lady five thousand years old in the whole course of the story; "no promenade, no band of music, nossing!" as Mr. Du Maurier's Frenchman said of the meet for a fox-hunt. Yet it is alive with the keenest interest for those who enjoy the study of individual traits and general conditions as they make themselves known to American experience.

These conditions have been so favorable hitherto (though they are becoming always less so) that they easily account for the optimistic faith of our novel which Mr. Hughes notices. It used to be one of the disadvantages of the practice of romance in America, which Hawthorne more or less whimsically lamented, that there were so few shadows and inequalities in our broad level of prosperity; and it is one of the reflections suggested by Dostoïevsky's novel, The Crime and the Punishment, that whoever struck a note so profoundly tragic in American fiction would do a false and mistaken thing—as false and as mistaken in its way as dealing in American fiction with certain nudities which the Latin

[4]*attenuated:* drawn out or thin
[5]*debauches:* corrupts

peoples seem to find edifying. Whatever their deserts, very few American novelists have been led out to be shot, or finally exiled to the rigors of a winter at Duluth; and in a land where journeymen carpenters and plumbers strike for four dollars a day the sum of hunger and cold is comparatively small, and the wrong from class to class has been almost inappreciable, though all this is changing for the worse. Our novelists, therefore, concern themselves with the more smiling aspects of life, which are the more American, and seek the universal in the individual rather than the social interests. It is worth while, even at the risk of being called commonplace, to be true to our well-to-do actualities; the very passions themselves seem to be softened and modified by conditions which formerly at least could not be said to wrong any one, to cramp endeavor, or to cross lawful desire. Sin and suffering and shame there must always be in the world, I suppose, but I believe that in this new world of ours it is still mainly from one to another one, and oftener still from one to one's self. We have death too in America, and a great deal of disagreeable and painful disease, which the multiplicity of our patent medicines does not seem to cure; but this is tragedy that comes in the very nature of things, and is not peculiarly American, as the large, cheerful average of health and success and happy life is. It will not do to boast, but it is well to be true to the facts, and to see that, apart from these purely mortal troubles, the race here has enjoyed conditions in which most of the ills that have darkened its annals might be averted by honest work and unselfish behavior.

Fine artists we have among us, and right-minded as far as they go; and we must not forget this at evil moments when it seems as if all the women had taken to writing hysterical improprieties, and some of the men were trying to be at least as hysterical in despair of being as improper. If we kept to the complexion of a certain school—which sadly needs a school-master—we might very well be despondent; but, after all, that school is not representative of our conditions or our intentions. Other traits are much more characteristic of our life and our fiction. In most American novels, vivid and graphic as the best of them are, the people are segregated if not sequestered, and the scene is sparsely populated. The effect may be in instinctive response to the vacancy of our social life, and I shall not make haste to blame it. There are few places, few occasions among us, in which a novelist can get a large number of polite people together, or at least keep them together. Unless he carries a snap-camera his picture of them has no probability; they affect one like the figures perfunctorily associated in such deadly old engravings as that of "Washington Irving and his Friends." Perhaps it is for this reason that we excel in small pieces with three or four figures, or in studies of rustic communities, where there is propinquity[6] if not society. Our grasp of more urbane life is feeble; most attempts to assemble it in our pictures are failures, possibly because it is too transitory, too intangible in its nature with us, to be truthfully represented as really existent.

I am not sure that the Americans have not brought the short story nearer perfection in the all-round sense than almost any other people, and for reasons very simple and near at hand. It might be argued from the national hurry and impatience that it was a literary form peculiarly adapted to the American temperament, but I suspect that its extraordinary development among us is owing much more to more tangible facts. The success of American magazines, which is nothing less than prodigious, is only commensurate with their excellence. Their sort of success is not only from the courage to decide what ought to please, but from the knowledge of what does please; and it is probable that, aside from the pictures, it is the short stories which please the readers of our best magazines. The serial novels they must have, of course; but rather more of course they must have short stories, and by operation of the law of supply and demand, the short stories, abundant in quantity and excellent in quality, are forthcoming because they are wanted. By another operation of the same law, which political economists have more recently taken account of, the demand follows the supply, and short stories are sought for because there is a proven ability to

[6]*propinquity:* closeness or nearness

furnish them, and people read them willingly because they are usually very good. The art of writing them is now so disciplined and diffused with us that there is no lack either for the magazines or for the newspaper "syndicates" which deal in them almost to the exclusion of the serials. In other countries the feuilleton[7] of the journals is a novel continued from day to day, but with us the papers, whether daily or weekly, now more rarely print novels, whether they get them at first hand from the writers, as a great many do, or through the syndicates, which purvey a vast variety of literary wares, chiefly for the Sunday editions of the city journals. In the country papers the short story takes the place of the chapters of a serial which used to be given.

[7]*feuilleton:* the part of a newspaper devoted to light reading

FOR DISCUSSION

1. Do you think that the English essayist's definition of the differences between English and American novels is really accurate? Which novels have you read which fit this pattern? Which novels do not fit it? Does your experience suggest anything to you about simple definitions and categories?
2. This essay of Howells has become well-known, especially for the statement that American novelists should concern themselves with "the more smiling aspects of life which are the more American." How true is this definition of American life today? How true was the definition when Howells wrote it?
3. What does Howells' essay tell you about "the American dream"? What is that dream? Where and how did the dream originate? Who popularized it?
4. What does the statement that American literature is characterized by rural settings or small casts of characters suggest about Howells' views? What other statements in this essay tell you more about Howells than about America?
5. How does Howells reveal his patriotic pride in American literature?

FOR COMPOSITION

1. Analyze the last novel you read, applying Howells' standards in order to assess its merits. If you have read no novels outside of school, use *Moby Dick* or *The Scarlet Letter.*
2. Describe two characteristics of recent American literature, using examples to prove your generalizations.

FROST AND COWLEY

After the turn of the twentieth century, one does not find any important discussion of the need for an American literature, or plea for a distinctive American style. Both already existed. Having accepted the fact, critics and writers moved on to a discussion of literary excellence. Finally, the standards they aimed to develop were not *American* standards or particularly *Western* standards. Critics began searching for criteria by which to recognize great art, wherever and in whatever form they found it.

Robert Frost became, after the publication of his first two volumes of poetry in 1913 and 1914, one of the most honored and widely read twentieth-century poets. Those with tastes or styles leading in radically different directions still recognized the excellence of Frost's verse. Those who care about good poetry are interested in what Frost thought about poetic art, because his theories obviously affected his practice. He explained many of his ideas in letters to his friends.

Another popular and influential American poet was E. E. Cummings. When Cummings died in 1962, the nation mourned for one of its most original and delightful talents. The obituary which follows is a tribute to Cummings as a young man, and also to the kind of poetry he wrote. His eulogist is Malcolm Cowley, himself a distinguished American critic.

On Poetry: Five Letters

ROBERT FROST

To John Cournos 8 July 1914

My versification seems to bother people more than I should have expected—I suppose because I have been so long accustomed to thinking of it in my own private way. It is as simple as this: there are the very regular preestablished accent and measure of blank verse; and there are the very irregular accent and measure of speaking intonation. I am never more pleased than when I can get these into strained relation. I like to drag and break the intonation across the meter as waves first comb and then break stumbling on the shingle. That's all but it's no mere figure of speech though one can make figures enough about it.

To Louis Untermeyer 1 January 1916

I took the Midnight Horror out of Littleton not long ago, and on the train with me I had about as many good-looking boys and girls as there are great poets in the book. They were of the Lisbon High School which had just beaten at basketball for a second time the Littleton High School. And they were yelling glad. And this is what they kept saying all together and out loud: it came somewhere near expressing my feelings, though at the same time it shocked me: since as you know I am not a swearing man: I couldn't help liking the liberty taken in the rhyme: all the old rhyme pairs are so worn out that I'm ready to permit anything for the sake of a fresh combination: this was a new one to me—it may not be to you: well here goes: I mustn't put you off any longer: this is what the good looking children said:

Lisbon *once*—Lisbon *twice!*
Holy jumping Jesus Christ!

Maybe you don't like me to talk this way. I can see that I am going to make enemies if I keep on. Still that won't be anything new or strange. I had nothing but enemies three years ago this Christmas.

Why go into details? Granted that there are a few good poems in the book—I read yours and liked it because it *says* something, first felt and then unfolded in thought as the poem wrote itself. That's what makes a poem. A poem is never a put-up job so to speak. It begins as a lump in the throat, a sense of wrong, a homesickness, a lovesickness. It is never a thought to begin with. It is at its best when it is a tantalizing vagueness. It finds its thought and succeeds, or doesn't find it and comes to nothing. It finds its thought or makes its thought. I suppose it finds it lying around with others not so much to its purpose in a more or less full mind. That's why it oftener comes to nothing in youth before experience has filled the mind with thoughts. It may be a big big emotion then and yet finds nothing it can embody in. It finds the thought and the thought finds the words. Let's say again: A poem particularly must not begin thought first.

To Sidney Cox 19 September 1929

Poetry is measured in more senses than one: it is measured feet but more important still it is a measured amount of all we could say and we would. We shall be judged finally by the delicacy of our feeling of where to stop short. The right people know, and we artists should know better than they know. There is no greater fallacy going than that art is expression—an undertaking to tell all to the last scrapings of the brain pan. I needn't qualify as a specialist in botany and astronomy for a license to invoke flowers and stars in my poetry. I needn't have scraped those subjects to the point of exhaustiveness. God forbids that I should have to be an authority on anything even the psyche before I can set up for an artist. A little of anything goes a long way in art. I'm never so desperate for material that I have to trench on the confidential for one thing, nor on the private for another nor on the personal, nor in general on the sacred. A little in the fist to manipulate is all I ask. My object is true form—is, was and always will be—form true to any chance bit of true life. Almost any bit will do. I don't naturally trust any other object. I fight to be allowed to sit cross-legged on the old flint pile and flake a lump into an artifact. Or if I don't actually fight myself, the soldiers of my tribe do for me to keep the unsympathetic off me and give me elbow room. The best hour I ever had in the class room was good only for the shape it took. I like an encounter to shape up, unify however roughly. There is such a thing as random talk, but it is to be valued as a scouting expedition for coinable gold. I may say this partly to save myself from being misunderstood; I say it partly too to help you what I can toward your next advance in thought if not in office. You'll find yourself most effective in things people find out by accident you might have said but didn't say. Those are the things that make people take a good reestimating look at you. You have to refrain from saying many things to get credit for refraining from a few. There is a discouraging waste there as everywhere else in life. But never mind: there is a sense of strength gained in not caring. You feel so much in having something to yourself. You have added to the mass of your private in reserve. You are more alluring to your friends and baffling to your foes.

To Kimball Flaccus 26 October 1930

You wish the world better than it is, more poetical. You are that kind of poet. I would rate as the other kind. I wouldn't give a cent to see the world, the United States or even New York made better. I want them left just as they are for me to make poetical on paper. I don't ask anything done to them that I don't do to them myself. I'm a mere selfish artist most of the time. I have no quarrel with the material. The grief will be simply if I can't transmute it into poems. I don't want the world made safer for poetry or easier. To hell with it. That is its own lookout. Let it stew in its own materialism. No, not to Hell with it. Let it hold its position while I do it in art. My whole anxiety is for myself as a performer. Am I any good? That's what I'd like to know and all I need to know. I wonder which kind of poet is more numerous, your kind or my kind. There should have been a question in the census-taking to determine. Not that it should bother us. We can be friends across the difference.

To R. P. T. Coffin 24 February 1938

Poetry is the renewal of words forever and ever. Poetry is that by which we live forever and ever unjaded. Poetry is that by which the world is never old. Even the poetry of trade names gives the lie to the unoriginal who would drag us down in their own powerlessness to originate. Heavy they are but not so heavy that we can't rise under them and throw them off.

Well well well——

Sincerely yours, Robert Frost

FOR DISCUSSION

1. At times it seems to the student of literature that every succeeding generation of poets tries once again (and considers itself unique in trying) to work into poetry the "very irregular accent and measure of speaking intonation." Why would Frost be especially pleased when he got the accent and measure of both blank verse and natural speech "into strained relation"? Why would this kind of tension be a natural goal for the poet to try to achieve?
2. By combining all of the information you get from the letters printed here, formulate Frost's theory of poetry. What poems would have to be judged unsuccessful by his criterion?

FOR COMPOSITION

Write an essay comparing Frost's and Poe's theories of poetry. Point out which assumptions the two men shared, and how their thoughts differ. You might also indicate the strengths and weaknesses of their theories.

A Farewell to the Last Harvard "Dandy"

MALCOLM COWLEY

After the shock of hearing that a great writer is dead, one goes back to his early years, if lucky enough to have known about him then. It is something done partly for solace and partly, if one is a critic, in an effort to place his work in context.

E.E. Cummings' early years were spent in Cambridge, Massachusetts, at home and at Harvard. When he was at Harvard, from 1911 to 1916, a poetic tradition there was drawing to a close, although some of the poets who represented it were still to become famous. The tradition had started about 1890, and it includes such distinguished names as those of Trumbull Stickney—our most neglected major poet—Edwin Arlington Robinson, Wallace Stevens, Conrad Aiken and T. S. Eliot, among a score of others.

It has never been given a name, and an accurate one would be hard to find for a movement that comprehended so many diverse talents, but simply for convenience we might call it the tradition of the Harvard dandies. Of course these poets weren't dandies in the sense that they dressed or acted with any precious sort of refinement. The dandyism went into their poems, which were as proudly discriminating and as free from vulgarity (except of a deliberate sort, introduced for effect) as the costume of a Regency[1] gentleman.

All the Harvard dandies had a cold, dry, sharp New England wit of the kind that stabs you with icicles. As distinguished from other poets of the period, they all had a sense of fact that sometimes became brutal realism. Almost all of them were pagans, in the sense that they invoked Greek deities—especially goat-footed Pan—more often in their poems than they invoked Christian saints, and also in the sense that all except Robinson started as fleshly poets, in revolt against Christian austerity.

Including Robinson this time, they had all received sound classical educations, and almost all of them read and admired modern French poetry. That double pattern of influence, Greek and French, was set by Trumbull Stickney, who was the first American to be awarded a doctorate by the Sorbonne,[2] after writing a thesis in French about axioms in Greek poetry. But they also worshiped the Elizabethans[3] and believed somewhere in their minds that poetic drama was the highest form of art, so that sooner or later they all wrote or tried to write poetic plays.

I mention these men as a group, which they never were, because they help us to recognize the antecedents of another poet. For all his rebellions and innovations, Cummings was, in another sense, the last and youngest of the poets in a rich tradition. He was the last of the dandies because the Great War[4] changed the literary atmosphere at Harvard and elsewhere. The poets who appeared after 1920 had a different set of values and aspirations—some of which, incidentally, they learned from Cummings as his work changed with the years.

I didn't know him when he was in college. By the fall of 1915 Cummings was already a graduate student, outside the horizon of a freshman, but I must have seen him at two or three meetings of the Harvard Poetry Society, which he helped to found later in the academic year. Already he was famous in college literary circles for his wit and his escapades.

[1] *Regency:* early nineteenth-century English

[2] *Sorbonne:* the school of science and letters at the University of Paris

[3] *Elizabethans:* English poets and playwrights of the late sixteenth century, the Age of Shakespeare

[4] *Great War:* World War I

He had taken his degree magna cum[5] in the classics and English, he had quoted Amy Lowell and Gertrude Stein[6] in a commencement address, and, the son of a famous minister, he was in revolt against ministerial standards. On one occasion his father's car, with its clergyman's license plates, was found parked outside a famous joint near Scollay Square,[7] to the embarrassment of the Boston police. Some of the poems he published in the Harvard Monthly, of which he was secretary, had made the Cambridge ladies squirm deliciously with horror.

In those days there were two literary magazines at Harvard, the *Monthly* and the *Advocate*, which were not on good terms with each other. There was a feeling among editors of the *Monthly* that editors of the *Advocate* were clubmen, athletes, journalists, disciples of Teddy Roosevelt, and not truly devoted to the art of letters. The feeling on the *Advocate* was that editors of the *Monthly* were art-for-art's-sakers, long-haired aesthetes, socialists, pacifists, or worse. The daily *Crimson* kept urging them both to amalgamate into one really good literary magazine, but they showed no disposition to follow this apparently sound advice.

As a matter of fact, they gained something from their rivalry. The editors of both magazines, glaring at each other from facing doorways on the dusty third floor of the Harvard Union, were inspired to "show those people over there that we can put out a better paper." The *Advocate* had more success in being liked by undergraduates, but the *Monthly* in Cummings' time had more soon-to-be-famous contributors. Some of his editorial colleagues were Gilbert Seldes, Robert Nathan, John Dos Passos, and Robert Hillyer.[8]

In the winter of 1916-'17, after Cummings had taken his M.A. and moved to New York, the issue that divided the two magazines was that of preparedness and pacifism. The *Advocate* was as hot for preparedness as the most famous of its one-time editors, Theodore Roosevelt. The *Monthly* was

[5]*magna cum:* magna cum laude, with high honors

[6]*Amy Lowell and Gertrude Stein:* American writers considered revolutionary when Cummings was an undergraduate

[7]*Scollay Square:* a square in Boston once noted for its night life

[8]*Seldes, Nathan, Dos Passos, Hillyer:* well-known writers and critics of the 1920's and 1930's

of divided mind or minds: four of the editors were pacifists and four were superpatriots. That division on the staff led to the end of the brilliant but impractical *Monthly* in the spring of 1917, when this country entered the war. In an editorial that didn't mention the war, the editors explained that they were suspending publication on account of "existing circumstances."

But the story of the *Monthly* had a sequel. In January, 1920, a former editor of the magazine, Sibley Watson, and another rich young Harvard graduate named Scofield Thayer brought out the first issue of the monthly *Dial.* It proved to be the most distinguished literary magazine that has so far appeared in this country, and it was also, in some of its aspects, the Harvard *Monthly* revived for readers over the nation. The featured contributor, whose verse and drawings in the first issue caused an almost nation-wide scandal, was E. E. Cummings.

His career from that time was remarkably self-consistent. Except for his painting, carried on over the years, and some brilliant excursions into prose, he applied himself exclusively to writing verse. Of how many other American poets could that be said? There is Conrad Aiken, of course, but how many others, if asked their profession, could truthfully answer "poet," and not teacher, critic, lecturer, anthologist, publisher, or journalist writing poems in his spare time? How many could say that they have never sacrificed their poetry to their public enthusiasm or administrative duties or to the simple desire for getting themselves talked about? Cummings' poems were talked about, and his aberrant[9] punctuation, but not his private life. He spent much of it in poverty, most of it in deliberate obscurity—as regards his person—and all for the sake of getting his work done.

During his later years his one concession to the public, and to the need for earning money, was reading his poems aloud, mostly to college audiences in all parts of the country. It required physical courage, for by that time he was partly crippled by arthritis, wore a brace on his back that jutted out two inches from his shoulder blades, and had to read while

[9] *aberrant:* unusual or non-standard

sitting on a straight-backed kitchen chair. Nevertheless he held and charmed the audience, and I found that students were more familiar with his work than with that of any other contemporary poet except Robert Frost. They all knew Frost, but many of them had learned two or three of Cummings' poems by heart.

One of the last times I saw him was at the University of Michigan in 1957. The hall in which he was reading had eight hundred seats, and it was full long before the reading began. Then the doors were locked, and more than a thousand other students milled about in the streets. It was the first and last time in this country that I heard of students almost rioting to hear a poetry reading, and Cummings must have enjoyed that tribute to the magic of his verse.

FOR DISCUSSION

1. Malcolm Cowley identifies E. E. Cummings with a literary group that flourished at Harvard just before World War I. What characteristics did this diverse group have in common? What leads Cowley to call them the Harvard dandies?
2. What were the issues on which Harvard's literary magazines, the *Monthly* and the *Advocate*, disagreed? With which magazine was Cummings associated?
3. On what evidence does Cowley base his opinion that Cummings' career as a poet was "remarkably self-consistent"?
4. How did Cummings show courage during the last few years of his life?
5. Discuss the important ways in which this "farewell" differed from the usual newspaper obituary. What purpose, or purposes, do you think prompted Cowley to write it? In your opinion, how well does he achieve them?
6. Mr. Cowley is a distinguished author and critic. Discuss the ways in which his literary ability is clearly evident in the knowledge he shares with you and in his style of writing.

FOR COMPOSITION

1. Analyze a poem by E. E. Cummings. If you are not already familiar with his poetry, you are in for some pleasant surprises. His

poems are available in his own collections (*Poems 1923-54* and *95 Poems*, for instance) and in most anthologies of modern verse.

2. Do some research into the life of one of the other poets mentioned as a Harvard dandy and write a brief report on him.

PERKINS AND FAULKNER

One force shaping the literary scene at any time is the editor who works in a position of responsibility. Without adventurous editors, no original or "different" work of literature would ever be published, regardless of its inherent quality. In the 1920's one particular editor, Maxwell Perkins, became associated with the best fiction being published at that time. He brought out the work of Ernest Hemingway, F. Scott Fitzgerald, and Thomas Wolfe, to name only his brightest lights. *The Great Gatsby*, which Perkins edited and which is generally considered Fitzgerald's masterpiece, already ranks as a "classic" of American fiction. The following letter concerning *Gatsby* reveals the highly sensitive and intelligent way in which a great editor approached one of his writers and helped him polish his work to the greatest advantage.

Among the internationally recognized "beautiful people" of the Jazz Age, Scott and Zelda Fitzgerald seemed to embody the glamor and self-destructive energy of the roaring twenties. Another writer who began his work in the 1920's, but whose life was lived in an altogether different style, was William Faulkner. Faulkner's reputation grew slowly. He had none of the flamboyant magnetism of a Fitzgerald or a Hemingway, which could make him famous as a "personality." But after years of neglect, his reputation has grown—especially in France—until many consider him the greatest American writer, and one of the greatest Western writers, of the twentieth century. By the 1950's, people were eager to hear Faulkner's views on writing and art. The interview which follows presents Faulkner's opinions in his characteristically anecdotal style. It provides excellent evidence of the man's personal charm and sheds light on his theories and practice.

A Letter on The Great Gatsby

MAXWELL PERKINS

November 20, 1924

Dear Scott:

I think you have every kind of right to be proud of this book (*The Great Gatsby*). It is an extraordinary book, suggestive of all sorts of thoughts and moods. You adopted exactly the right method of telling it, that of employing a narrator who is more of a spectator than an actor: this puts the reader upon a point of observation on a higher level than that on which the characters stand and at a distance that gives perspective. In no other way could your irony have been so immensely effective, nor the reader have been enabled so strongly to feel at times the strangeness of human circumstance in a vast heedless universe. In the eyes of Dr. Eckleberg[1] various readers will see different significances; but their presence gives a superb touch to the whole thing; great unblinking eyes, expressionless, looking down upon the human scene. It's magnificent!

I could go on praising the book and speculating on its various elements, and means, but points of criticism are more

[1]*the eyes of Dr. Eckleberg:* a billboard, described in *The Great Gatsby*, which consists of an enormous pair of glasses looking out over a dump nicknamed "The Valley of Ashes"

important now. I think you are right in feeling a certain slight sagging in chapters six and seven, and I don't know how to suggest a remedy. I hardly doubt that you will find one and I am only writing to say that I think it does need something to hold up here to the pace set, and ensuing. I have only two actual criticisms:

One is that among a set of characters marvelously palpable and vital—I would know Tom Buchanan if I met him on the street and would avoid him—Gatsby is somewhat vague. The reader's eyes can never quite focus upon him, his outlines are dim. Now everything about Gatsby is more or less a mystery, i.e., more or less vague, and this may be somewhat of an artistic intention, but I think it is mistaken. Couldn't he be physically described as distinctly as the others, and couldn't you add one or two characteristics like the use of that phrase "old sport"—not verbal, but physical ones, perhaps. I think that for some reason or other a reader—this was true of Mr. Scribner[2] and of Louise[3]—gets an idea that Gatsby is a much older man than he is, although you have the writer say that he is little older than himself. But this would be avoided if on his first appearance he was seen as vividly as Daisy and Tom are, for instance—and I do not think your scheme would be impaired if you made him so.

The other point is also about Gatsby: his career must remain mysterious, of course. But in the end you make it pretty clear that his wealth came through his connection with Wolfsheim. You also suggest this much earlier. Now almost all readers numerically are going to be puzzled by his having all this wealth and are going to feel entitled to an explanation. To give a distinct and definite one would be, of course, utterly absurd. It did occur to me, though, that you might here and there interpolate some phrases, and possibly incidents, little touches of various kinds, that would suggest that he was in some active way mysteriously engaged. You do have him called on the telephone, but couldn't he be seen once or twice consulting at his parties with people of some sort of mysterious

[2] *Mr. Scribner:* Charles Scribner, Senior (1854-1930), president of Charles Scribner's Sons

[3] *Louise:* Mrs. Maxwell E. Perkins

significance, from the political, the gambling, the sporting world, or whatever it may be. I know I am floundering, but that fact may help you to see what I mean. The total lack of an explanation through so large a part of the story does seem to me a defect—or not of an explanation, but of the suggestion of an explanation. I wish you were here so I could at least make you understand what I mean. What Gatsby did ought never to be definitely imparted, even if it could be. Whether he was an innocent tool in the hands of somebody else, or to what degree he was this, ought not to be explained. But if some sort of business activity of his were simply adumbrated, it would lend further probability to that part of the story.

There is one other point: in giving deliberately Gatsby's biography, when he gives it to the narrator, you do depart from the method of the narrative in some degree, for otherwise almost everything is told, and beautifully told, in the regular flow of it, in the succession of events or in accompaniment with them. But you can't avoid the biography altogether. I thought you might find ways to let the truth of some of his claims like "Oxford" and his army career come out, bit by bit, in the course of actual narrative. I mention the point anyway, for consideration in this interval before I send the proofs.

The general brilliant quality of the book makes me ashamed to make even these criticisms. The amount of meaning you get into a sentence, the dimensions and intensity of the impression you make a paragraph carry, are most extraordinary. The manuscript is full of phrases which make a scene blaze with life. If one enjoyed a rapid railroad journey I would compare the number and vividness of pictures your living words suggest, to the living scenes disclosed in that way. It seems, in reading, a much shorter book than it is, but it carries the mind through a series of experiences that one would think would require a book of three times its length.

The presentation of Tom, his place, Daisy and Jordan, and the unfolding of their characters is unequaled so far as I know. The description of the valley of ashes adjacent to the lovely country, the conversation and the action in Myrtle's apartment, the marvelous catalogue of those who came to Gatsby's house —these are such things as make a man famous. And all these things, the whole pathetic episode, you have given a place in time and space, for with the help of T. J. Eckleberg and by an occasional glance at the sky, or the sea, or the city, you have imparted a sort of sense of eternity. You once told me you were not a natural writer—my God! You have plainly mastered the craft, of course; but you needed far more than craftsmanship for this.

As ever,—
MAXWELL E. PERKINS

FOR DISCUSSION

1. Maxwell Perkins was one of the most famous editors in American publishing history. He edited the works of Fitzgerald, Hemingway, and Thomas Wolfe, among others. What personal qualities evident in this letter partially explain his great success? What is his attitude toward Fitzgerald? toward *The Great Gatsby* as a work of art? toward himself?
2. From the phrases included in this letter, reconstruct Perkins' standards for excellent fiction. What kind of prose fiction particularly appealed to him? Is this kind of fiction similar to any other form of writing? How?

FOR COMPOSITION

Read *The Great Gatsby* and report on the changes Fitzgerald made at Perkins' direction, and those he did not make. Are any of Perkins' criticisms still applicable? Do you agree with Perkins' assessment of the novel?

An Interview with William Faulkner

This interview took place in New York City, early in 1956.

INTERVIEWER: Mr. Faulkner, you were saying a while ago that you don't like interviews.

FAULKNER: The reason I don't like interviews is that I seem to react violently to personal questions. If the questions are about the work, I try to answer them. When they are about me, I may answer or I may not, but even if I do, if the same question is asked tomorrow, the answer may be different.

INTERVIEWER: How about yourself as a writer?

FAULKNER: If I had not existed, someone else would have written me, Hemingway, Dostoevski,[1] all of us. Proof of that is that there are about three candidates for the authorship of Shakespeare's plays. But what is important is *Hamlet* and *Midsummer Night's Dream*, not who wrote them, but that somebody did. The artist is of no importance. Only what he creates is important, since there is nothing new to be said. Shakespeare, Balzac,[2] Homer have all written about the same things,

[1] *Dostoevski:* Russian novelist (1821-1881)

[2] *Balzac:* French novelist (1799-1850)

and if they had lived one thousand or two thousand years longer, the publishers wouldn't have needed anyone since.

INTERVIEWER: But even if there seems nothing more to be said, isn't perhaps the individuality of the writer important?

FAULKNER: Very important to himself. Everybody else should be too busy with the work to care about the individuality.

INTERVIEWER: And your contemporaries?

FAULKNER: All of us failed to match our dream of perfection. So I rate us on the basis of our splendid failure to do the impossible. In my opinion, if I could write all my work again, I am convinced that I would do it better, which is the healthiest condition for an artist. That's why he keeps on working, trying again; he believes each time that this time he will do it, bring it off. Of course he won't, which is why this condition is healthy. Once he did it, once he matched the work to the image, the dream, nothing would remain but to cut his throat, jump off the other side of that pinnacle of perfection into suicide. I'm a failed poet. Maybe every novelist wants to write poetry first, finds he can't, and then tries the short story, which is the most demanding form after poetry. And, failing at that, only then does he take up novel writing.

INTERVIEWER: Is there any possible formula to follow in order to be a good novelist?

FAULKNER: Ninety-nine per cent talent . . . 90 per cent discipline . . . 99 per cent work. He must never be satisfied with what he does. It never is as good as it can be done. Always dream and shoot higher than you know you can do. Don't bother just to be better than your contemporaries or predecessors. Try to be better than yourself. An artist is a creature driven by demons. He don't know why they choose him and he's usually too busy to wonder why. He is completely amoral in that he will rob, borrow, beg, or steal from anybody and everybody to get the work done.

INTERVIEWER: Do you mean the writer should be completely ruthless?

FAULKNER: The writer's only responsibility is to his art. He will be completely ruthless if he is a good one. He has a dream. It anguishes him so much he must get rid of it. He has no peace until then. Everything goes by the board: honor, pride, decency, security, happiness, all, to get the book written. If a writer has to rob his mother, he will not hesitate; the "Ode on a Grecian Urn"[3] is worth any number of old ladies.

INTERVIEWER: Then could the *lack* of security, happiness, honor, be an important factor in the artist's creativity?

FAULKNER: No. They are important only to his peace and contentment, and art has no concern with peace and contentment.

INTERVIEWER: Then what would be the best environment for a writer?

FAULKNER: Art is not concerned with environment either; it doesn't care where it is. So the only environment the artist needs is whatever peace, whatever solitude, and whatever pleasure he can get at not too high a cost. All the wrong environment will do is run his blood pressure up; he will spend more time being frustrated or outraged. . . .

INTERVIEWER: You mentioned economic freedom. Does the writer need it?

FAULKNER: No. The writer doesn't need economic freedom. All he needs is a pencil and some paper. I've never known anything good in writing to come from having accepted any free gift of money. The good writer never applies to a foundation. He's too busy writing something. If he isn't first rate he fools himself by saying he hasn't got time or economic freedom. Good art can come out of thieves, bootleggers, or horse swipes. People really are afraid to find out just how much hardship and poverty they can stand. They are afraid to find out how tough they are. Nothing can destroy the good writer. The only thing that can alter the good writer is death. Good ones don't have time to bother with success or getting rich. Success is feminine and like a woman; if you cringe before her, she will override you. So the way to treat her is to show her the back of your hand. Then maybe she will do the crawling.

INTERVIEWER: Can working for the movies hurt your own writing?

[3] *"Ode on a Grecian Urn"*: poem by John Keats (1795-1821)

FAULKNER: Nothing can injure a man's writing if he's a first-rate writer. If a man is not a first-rate writer, there's not anything can help it much. The problem does not apply if he is not first rate, because he has already sold his soul for a swimming pool.

INTERVIEWER: Does a writer compromise in writing for the movies?

FAULKNER: Always, because a moving picture is by its nature a collaboration, and any collaboration is compromise because that is what the word means—to give and to take.

INTERVIEWER: Which actors do you like to work with most?

FAULKNER: Humphrey Bogart is the one I've worked with best. He and I worked together in *To Have and Have Not* and *The Big Sleep*.

INTERVIEWER: Would you like to make another movie?

FAULKNER: Yes, I would like to make one of George Orwell's *1984*. I have an idea for an ending which would prove the thesis I'm always hammering at: that man is indestructible because of his simple will to freedom.

INTERVIEWER: How do you get the best results in working for the movies?

FAULKNER: The moving-picture work of my own which seemed best to me was done by the actors and the writer throwing the script away and inventing the scene in actual rehearsal just before the camera turned. If I didn't take, or feel I was capable of taking, motion-picture work seriously, out of simple honesty to motion pictures and myself too, I would not have tried. But I know now that I will never be a good motion-picture writer; so that work will never have the urgency for me which my own medium has.

INTERVIEWER: Would you comment on that legendary Hollywood experience you were involved in?

FAULKNER: I had just completed a contract at MGM and was about to return home. The director I had worked with said, "If you would like another job here, just let me know and I will speak to the studio about a new contract." I thanked him and came home. About six months later I wired my director friend that I would like another job. Shortly after that I received a letter from my Hollywood agent enclosing my first week's paycheck. I was surprised because I had expected first to get an official notice or recall and a contract from the studio. I thought to myself the contract is delayed and will arrive in the next mail. Instead, a week later I got another letter from the agent, enclosing my second-week's paycheck. That began in November 1932 and continued until May 1933. Then I received a telegram from the studio. It said: *William Faulkner, Oxford, Miss. Where are You? MGM Studio.*

I wrote out a telegram: *MGM Studio, Culver City, California. William Faulkner.*

The young lady operator said, "Where is the message, Mr. Faulkner?" I said, "That's it." She said, "The rule book says that I can't send it without a message, you have to say something." So we went through her samples and selected I forget which one—one of the canned anniversary greeting messages. I sent that. Next was a long-distance telephone call from the studio directing me to get on the first airplane, go to New Orleans, and report to Director Browning. I could have got on a train in Oxford and been in New Orleans eight hours later. But I obeyed the studio and went to Memphis, where an airplane did occasionally go to New Orleans. Three days later one did.

I arrived at Mr. Browning's hotel about six p.m. and reported to him. A party was going on. He told me to get a good night's sleep and be ready for an early start in the morning. I asked him about the story. He said, "Oh, yes. Go to room so and so. That's the continuity writer. He'll tell you what the story is."

I went to the room as directed. The continuity writer was sitting in there alone. I told him who I was and asked him about the story. He said, "When you have written the dialogue I'll let you see the story." I went back to Browning's room and told him what had happened. "Go back," he said, "and tell that so and so—never mind, you get a good night's sleep so we can get an early start in the morning."

So the next morning in a very smart rented launch all of us except the continuity writer sailed down to Grand Isle, about a hundred miles away, where the picture was to be shot, reaching there just in time to eat lunch and have time to run the hundred miles back to New Orleans before dark.

That went on for three weeks. Now and then I would worry a little about the story, but Browning always said, "Stop worrying. Get a good night's sleep so we can get an early start tomorrow morning."

One evening on our return I had barely entered my room when the telephone rang. It was Browning. He told me to come to his room at once. I did so. He had a telegram. It said: *Faulkner is fired. MGM Studio.* "Don't worry," Browning said. "I'll call that so and so up this minute and not only make him put you back on the payroll but send you a written apology." There was a knock on the door. It was a page with another telegram. This one said: *Browning is fired. MGM Studio.* So I came back home. I presume Browning went somewhere too. I imagine that continuity writer is still sitting in a room somewhere with his weekly salary check clutched tightly in his hand. They never did finish the film. But they did build a shrimp village—a long platform on piles in the water with sheds built on it something like a wharf. The studio could have bought dozens of them for forty or fifty dollars apiece. Instead, they built one of their own, a false one. That is, a platform with a single wall on it, so that when you opened the door and stepped through it, you stepped right on off to the ocean itself. As they built it, on the first day, the Cajun[4] fisherman paddled up in his narrow tricky pirogue[5] made out of a hollow log. He would sit in it all day long in the broiling sun watching the strange white folks building this strange imitation platform. The next day he was back in the pirogue with his whole family, his wife nursing the baby, and other children, and the mother-in-law, all to sit all that day in the broiling sun to watch this foolish and incomprehensible activity. I was in New Orleans two or three years later and heard that the Cajun people were still coming in for miles to look at that imitation shrimp platform which a lot of white people had rushed in and built and then abandoned.

INTERVIEWER: You say that the writer must compromise in working for the motion pictures. How about his writing? Is he under any obligation to his reader?

[4] *Cajun:* a contraction of *Acadian,* a French peasant group who settled in the coastal plains and swamps of Louisiana. Many still speak a French *patois.*

[5] *pirogue:* small boat

FAULKNER: His obligation is to get the work done the best he can do it; whatever obligations he has left over after that he can spend any way he likes. I myself am too busy to care about the public. I have no time to wonder who is reading me. I don't care about John Doe's opinion on my or anyone else's work. Mine is the standard which has to be met, which is when the work makes me feel the way I do when I read *La Tentation de Saint Antoine*,[6] or the Old Testament. They make me feel good. So does watching a bird make me feel good. You know that if I were reincarnated, I'd want to come back a buzzard. Nothing hates him or envies him or wants him or needs him. He is never bothered or in danger, and he can eat anything.

INTERVIEWER: What technique do you use to arrive at your standard?

FAULKNER: Let the writer take up surgery or bricklaying if he is interested in technique. There is no mechanical way to get the writing done, no short cut. The young writer would be a fool to follow a theory. Teach yourself by your own mistakes; people learn only by error. The good artist believes that nobody is good enough to give him advice. He has supreme vanity. No matter how much he admires the old writer, he wants to beat him.

INTERVIEWER: Then would you deny the validity of technique?

FAULKNER: By no means. Sometimes technique charges in and takes command of the dream before the writer himself can get his hands on it. That is *tour de force*[7] and the finished work is simply a matter of fitting bricks neatly together, since the writer knows probably every single word right to the end before he puts the first one down. This happened with *As I Lay Dying*. It was not easy. No honest work is. It was simple in that all the material was already at hand. It took me just about six weeks in the spare time from a twelve-hour-a-day job at manual labor. I simply imagined a group of people and subjected them to the simple universal natural catastrophes, which are flood and fire, with a simple natural motive to give direction to their progress. But then, when technique does not

[6] *La Tentation de Saint Antoine:* a work by Gustave Flaubert (1821-1880)
[7] *tour de force:* feat of skill

intervene, in another sense writing is easier too. Because with me there is always a point in the book where the characters themselves rise up and take charge and finish the job—say somewhere about page 275. Of course I don't know what would happen if I finished the book on page 274. The quality an artist must have is objectivity in judging his work, plus the honesty and courage not to kid himself about it. Since none of my work has met my own standards, I must judge it on the basis of that one which caused me the most grief and anguish, as the mother loves the child who became the thief or murderer more than the one who became the priest.

INTERVIEWER: What work is that?

FAULKNER: *The Sound and the Fury.* I wrote it five separate times, trying to tell the story, to rid myself of the dream which would continue to anguish me until I did. It's a tragedy of two lost women: Caddy and her daughter. Dilsey is one of my own favorite characters, because she is brave, courageous, generous, gentle, and honest. She's much more brave and honest and generous than me....

INTERVIEWER: Are there any artistic advantages in casting the novel in the form of an allegory, as the Christian allegory you used in *A Fable*?

FAULKNER: Same advantage the carpenter finds in building square corners in order to build a square house. In *A Fable* the Christian allegory was the right allegory to use in that particular story, like an oblong square corner is the right corner with which to build an oblong rectangular house.

INTERVIEWER: Does that mean an artist can use Christianity simply as just another tool, as a carpenter would borrow a hammer?

FAULKNER: The carpenter we are speaking of never lacks that hammer. No one is without Christianity, if we agree on what we mean by the word. It is every individual's individual code of behavior by means of which he makes himself a better human being than his nature wants to be, if he followed his nature only. Whatever its symbol—cross or crescent[8] or whatever—that symbol is man's reminder of his duty inside the human race. Its various allegories are the charts against which

[8] *crescent:* symbol of the Moslem religion

he measures himself and learns to know what he is. It cannot teach man to be good as the textbook teaches him mathematics. It shows him how to discover himself, evolve for himself a moral code and standard within his capacities and aspirations, by giving him a matchless example of suffering and sacrifice and the promise of hope. Writers have always drawn, and always will draw, upon the allegories of moral consciousness, for the reason that the allegories are matchless —the three men in *Moby Dick*, who represent the trinity of conscience: knowing nothing, knowing but not caring, knowing and caring. The same trinity is represented in *A Fable* by the young Jewish pilot officer, who said, "This is terrible. I refuse to accept it, even if I must refuse life to do so"; the old French Quartermaster General, who said, "This is terrible, but we can weep and bear it"; and the English battalion runner, who said, "This is terrible, I'm going to do something about it."

INTERVIEWER: Are the two unrelated themes in *The Wild Palms* brought together in one book for any symbolic purpose? Is it as certain critics intimate a kind of esthetic counterpoint, or is it merely haphazard?

FAULKNER: No, no. That was one story—the story of Charlotte Rittenmeyer and Harry Wilbourne, who sacrificed everything for love, and then lost that. I did not know it would be two separate stories until after I had started the book. When I reached the end of what is now the first section of *The Wild Palms,* I realized suddenly that something was missing, it needed emphasis, something to lift it like counterpoint in music. So I wrote on the "Old Man" story until "The Wild Palms" story rose back to pitch. Then I stopped the "Old Man" story at what is now its first section, and took up "The Wild Palms" story until it began again to sag. Then I raised it to pitch again with another section of its antithesis, which is the story of a man who got his love and spent the rest of the book fleeing from it, even to the extent of voluntarily going back to jail where he would be safe. They are only two stories by chance, perhaps necessity. The story is that of Charlotte and Wilbourne.

INTERVIEWER: How much of your writing is based on personal experience?

FAULKNER: I can't say. I never counted up. Because "how much" is not important. A writer needs three things, experience, observation, and imagination, any two of which, at times any one of which, can supply the lack of the others. With me, a story usually begins with a single idea or memory or mental picture. The writing of the story is simply a matter of working up to that moment, to explain why it happened or what it caused to follow. A writer is trying to create believable people in credible moving situations in the most moving way he can. Obviously he must use as one of his tools the environment which he knows. I would say that music is the easiest means in which to express, since it came first in man's experience and history. But since words are my talent, I must try to express clumsily in words what the pure music would have done better. That is, music would express better and simpler, but I prefer to use words, as I prefer to read rather than listen. I prefer silence to sound, and the image produced by words occurs in silence. That is, the thunder and the music of the prose take place in silence.

INTERVIEWER: Some people say they can't understand your writing, even after they read it two or three times. What approach would you suggest for them?

FAULKNER: Read it four times.

INTERVIEWER: You mentioned experience, observation, and imagination as being important for the writer. Would you include inspiration?

FAULKNER: I don't know anything about inspiration, because I don't know what inspiration is—I've heard about it, but I never saw it.

INTERVIEWER: As a writer you are said to be obsessed with violence.

FAULKNER: That's like saying the carpenter is obsessed with his hammer. Violence is simply one of the carpenter's tools. The writer can no more build with one tool than the carpenter can.

INTERVIEWER: Can you say how you started as a writer?

FAULKNER: I was living in New Orleans, doing whatever kind of work was necessary to earn a little money now and then. I met Sherwood Anderson. We would walk about the city in the afternoon and talk to people. In the evenings we would meet again and sit over a bottle or two while he talked and I listened. In the forenoon I would never see him. He was secluded, working. The next day we would repeat. I decided that if that was the life of a writer, then becoming a writer was the thing for me. So I began to write my first book. At once I found that writing was fun. I even forgot that I hadn't seen Mr. Anderson for three weeks until he walked in my door, the first time he ever came to see me, and said, "What's wrong? Are you mad at me?" I told him I was writing a book. He said, "My God," and walked out. When I finished the book—it was *Soldier's Pay*—I met Mrs. Anderson on the street. She asked how the book was going, and I said I'd finished it. She said, "Sherwood says that he will make a trade with you. If he doesn't have to read your manuscript he will tell his publisher to accept it." I said, "Done," and that's how I became a writer. . . .

INTERVIEWER: You must feel indebted to Sherwood Anderson, but how do you regard him as a writer?

FAULKNER: He was the father of my generation of American writers and the tradition of American writing which our successors will carry on. He has never received his proper evaluation. Dreiser is his older brother and Mark Twain the father of them both.

INTERVIEWER: What about the European writers of that period?

FAULKNER: The two great men in my time were Mann and Joyce. You should approach Joyce's *Ulysses* as the illiterate Baptist preacher approaches the Old Testament: with faith.

INTERVIEWER: How did you get your background in the Bible?

FAULKNER: My Great-Grandfather Murry was a kind and gentle man, to us children anyway. That is, although he was a Scot, he was (to us) neither especially pious nor stern either: he was simply a man of inflexible principles. One of them was, everybody, children on up through all adults present, had to have a verse from the Bible ready and glib at tongue-tip when we gathered at the table for breakfast each morning; if you didn't have your scripture verse ready, you didn't have any breakfast; you would be excused long enough to leave the room and swot one up (there was a maiden aunt, a kind of sergeant-major for this duty, who retired with the culprit and gave him a brisk breezing which carried him over the jump next time).

It had to be an authentic, correct verse. While we were little, it could be the same one, once you had it down good, morning after morning, until you got a little older and bigger, when one morning (by this time you would be pretty glib at it, galloping through without even listening to yourself since you were already five or ten minutes ahead, already among the ham and steak and fried chicken and grits and sweet potatoes and two or three kinds of hot bread) you would suddenly find his eyes on you—very blue, very kind and gentle, and even now not stern so much as inflexible; and next morning you had a new verse. In a way, that was when you discovered that your childhood was over; you had outgrown it and entered the world.

INTERVIEWER: Do you read your contemporaries?

FAULKNER: No, the books I read are the ones I knew and loved when I was a young man and to which I return as you do to old friends: the Old Testament, Dickens, Conrad, Cervantes—*Don Quixote*. I read that every year, as some do the Bible. Flaubert, Balzac—he created an intact world of his own, a bloodstream running through twenty books—Dostoevski, Tolstoi, Shakespeare. I read Melville occasionally, and of the poets Marlowe, Campion, Jonson, Herrick, Donne, Keats, and Shelley. I still read Housman. I've read these books so often that I don't always begin at page one and read on to the end. I just read one scene, or about one character, just as you'd meet and talk to a friend for a few minutes.

INTERVIEWER: And Freud?

FAULKNER: Everybody talked about Freud when I lived in New Orleans, but I have never read him. Neither did Shakespeare. I doubt if Melville did either, and I'm sure Moby Dick didn't.

INTERVIEWER: Do you ever read mystery stories?

FAULKNER: I read Simenon because he reminds me something of Chekhov.

INTERVIEWER: What about your favorite characters?

FAULKNER: My favorite characters are Sarah Gamp—a cruel, ruthless woman, a drunkard, opportunist, unreliable, most of her character was bad, but at least it was character; Mrs. Harris, Falstaff, Prince Hal, Don Quixote, and Sancho of course. Lady Macbeth I always admire. And Bottom, Ophelia, and Mercutio—both he and Mrs. Gamp coped with life, didn't ask any favors, never whined. Huck Finn, of course, and Jim. Tom Sawyer I never liked much—an awful prig. And then I like Sut Lovingood, from a book written by George Harris about 1840 or '50 in the Tennessee mountains. He had no illusions about himself, did the best he could; at certain times he was a coward and knew it and wasn't ashamed; he never blamed his misfortunes on anyone and never cursed God for them.

INTERVIEWER: Would you comment on the future of the novel?

FAULKNER: I imagine as long as people will continue to read novels, people will continue to write them, or vice versa; unless of course the pictorial magazines and comic strips finally atrophy[9] man's capacity to read, and literature really is on its way back to the picture writing in the Neanderthal cave. . . .

INTERVIEWER: Critics claim that blood relationships are central in your novels.

FAULKNER: That is an opinion and, as I have said, I don't read critics. I doubt that a man trying to write about people is any more interested in blood relationships than in the shape of their noses, unless they are necessary to help the story move. If the writer concentrates on what he does need to be interested in, which is the truth and the human heart, he won't have much time left for anything else, such as ideas and facts like the shape of noses or blood relationships, since in my opinion ideas and facts have very little connection with truth.

INTERVIEWER: Critics also suggest that your characters never consciously choose between good and evil.

FAULKNER: Life is not interested in good and evil. Don Quixote was constantly choosing between good and evil, but

[9] *atrophy:* wither from disuse

then he was choosing in his dream state. He was mad. He entered reality only when he was so busy trying to cope with people that he had no time to distinguish between good and evil. Since people exist only in life, they must devote their time simply to being alive. Life is motion, and motion is concerned with what makes man move—which is ambition, power, pleasure. What time a man can devote to morality, he must take by force from the motion of which he is a part. He is compelled to make choices between good and evil sooner or later, because moral conscience demands that from him in order that he can live with himself tomorrow. His moral conscience is the curse he had to accept from the gods in order to gain from them the right to dream....

INTERVIEWER: What happened to you between *Soldier's Pay* and *Sartoris*—that is, what caused you to begin the Yoknapatawpha saga?

FAULKNER: With *Soldier's Pay* I found out writing was fun. But I found out afterward that not only each book had to have a design but the whole output or sum of an artist's work had to have a design. With *Soldier's Pay* and *Mosquitoes* I wrote for the sake of writing because it was fun. Beginning with *Sartoris* I discovered that my own little postage stamp of native soil was worth writing about and that I would never live long enough to exhaust it, and that by sublimating the actual into the apocryphal[10] I would have complete liberty to use whatever talent I might have to its absolute top. It opened up a gold mine of other people, so I created a cosmos of my own. I can move these people around like God, not only in space but in time too. The fact that I have moved my characters around in time successfully, at least in my own estimation, proves to me my own theory that time is a fluid condition which has no existence except in the momentary avatars[11] of individual people. There is no such thing as *was*—only *is*. If *was* existed, there would be no grief or sorrow. I like to think of the world I created as being a kind of keystone in the universe; that, small as that keystone is, if it were ever taken

[10] *apocryphal:* more imaginative than factually accurate
[11] *avatars:* reincarnations or forms

away the universe itself would collapse. My last book will be the Doomsday Book, the Golden Book, of Yoknapatawpha County. Then I shall break the pencil and I'll have to stop.

FOR DISCUSSION

1. In his replies to personal questions, Faulkner emphasizes that he considers a literary work more important than its author. Explain what you think he means when he says, "If I had not existed, someone else would have written me, Hemingway, Dostoevski, all of us."
2. Note that Faulkner describes himself as a "failed poet." He calls the short story "the most demanding form after poetry" and ranks novel-writing as the least demanding of all. What reasons might he have for putting these literary forms in this order? Explain why you do, or do not, agree.
3. What qualities does Faulkner attribute to the true artist? What commonly accepted standards or conditions does he sweep aside as unnecessary for creative work?
4. Writing a movie scenario was a familiar experience for Faulkner. What is his attitude toward this kind of work? What does his experience with MGM illustrate about the ways of Hollywood?
5. Faulkner's discussion of techniques provides some important insights into his own creative processes. What are some of the problems he raises? By what standards does he say the artist must judge his own work?
6. In his comments on *A Fable* he says, "No one is without Christianity, if we agree on what we mean by the word." Look closely again at the entire discussion of this subject, and explain what you think he means by Christianity. What do you think are some of "the allegories of moral consciousness" upon which "writers have always drawn, and always will draw"?
7. Faulkner's account of how *The Wild Palms* developed throws some light on his method of working out his stories. How, and to what extent, did his purposes as a writer determine the method he used?
8. Do you think Faulkner is revealing the whole truth when he tells how he came to be a writer? What more important reasons for becoming a writer does he reveal, directly or indirectly, in his answers to other questions?

9. What was Faulkner's own "literary education"? What does his favorite reading reveal about him?
10. Faulkner concludes the interview with some serious observations that are central to his philosophy. What is his view of the problem of choosing between good and evil? What is his theory of time?

FOR COMPOSITION

1. Although Faulkner claims that a literary work is more important than its creator, during the course of his interview he mentions more than twenty writers who had influenced him. As a class project, draw up a list of these writers and assign one to each student for a brief report on his life and work. The reports might be written, or oral, or both.
2. Perhaps a particular work has been especially important to you, in the way that *Don Quixote*, for instance, was to Faulkner. Tell about your favorite work, analyzing its significance for you personally.

Speech of Acceptance, Nobel Prize for Literature

WILLIAM FAULKNER

William Faulkner delivered this speech December 10, 1950, in Stockholm, Sweden, where he received the Nobel Prize for Literature. He was the fourth American so honored, having been preceded by Sinclair Lewis, Pearl Buck, and Eugene O'Neill. Ernest Hemingway received the award a few years later and was followed, in 1962, by John Steinbeck.

I feel that this award was not made to me as a man but to my work—a life's work in the agony and sweat of the human spirit, not for glory and least of all for profit, but to create out of the materials of the human spirit something which did not exist before. So this award is only mine in trust. It will not be difficult to find a dedication for the money part of it commensurate with the purpose and significance of its origin. But I would like to do the same with the acclaim too, by using this moment as a pinnacle from which I might be listened to by the young men and women already dedicated to the same anguish and travail, among whom is already that one who will some day stand here where I am standing.

Our tragedy today is a general and universal physical fear so long sustained by now that we can even bear it. There are no longer problems of the spirit. There is only the question: when will I be blown up? Because of this, the young man or woman writing today has forgotten the problems of the human heart in conflict with itself which alone can make good writing because only that is worth writing about, worth the agony and the sweat.

He must learn them again. He must teach himself that the basest of all things is to be afraid; and, teaching himself that, forget it forever, leaving no room in his workshop for anything but the old verities[1] and truths of the heart, the old universal truths lacking which any story is ephemeral[2] and doomed—love and honor and pity and pride and compassion and sacrifice. Until he does so he labors under a curse. He writes not of love but of lust, of defeats in which nobody loses anything of value, of victories without hope and worst of all without pity or compassion. His griefs grieve on no universal bones, leaving no scars. He writes not of the heart but of the glands.

Until he relearns these things he will write as though he stood among and watched the end of man. I decline to accept the end of man. It is easy enough to say that man is immortal simply because he will endure; that when the last ding-dong of doom has clanged and faded from the last worthless rock hanging tideless in the last red and dying evening, that even then there will still be one more sound: that of his puny inexhaustible voice, still talking. I refuse to accept this. I believe that man will not merely endure: he will prevail. He is immortal, not because he alone among creatures has an inexhaustible voice, but because he has a soul, a spirit capable of compassion and sacrifice and endurance. The poet's, the writer's, duty is to write about these things. It is his privilege to help man endure by lifting his heart, by reminding him of the courage and honor and hope and pride and compassion and pity and sacrifice which have been the glory of his past. The poet's voice need not merely be the record of man, it can be one of the props, the pillars to help him endure and prevail.

[1] *verities:* truths
[2] *ephemeral:* filmy

FOR DISCUSSION

1. In his speech of acceptance, William Faulkner makes a mature statement that reveals his view of the "human condition" and the role of the writer in today's world. What does he see as "our tragedy today"? How has the young writer been affected by this tragedy?
2. According to Faulkner, what must the writer re-learn to avoid laboring "under a curse"?
3. What does Faulkner think is the destiny of man? What is the writer's duty? What is his privilege?
4. Faulkner has emerged as one of the modern giants of American literature. Why, in your opinion, is this speech dramatic proof—if such were needed—that he merited the distinction of being awarded the Nobel Prize for Literature?

PENN WARREN AND SMITH

Sometimes the twentieth century has been called "the Age of Criticism," not because criticism has been the major type of creative writing produced, but because the volume and quality of the literary criticism has been exceptionally high. In America especially, the critical essay has become an art form with its own particular requirements: it must be illuminating, original, logically organized, soundly reasoned, but also gracefully phrased.

Two kinds of critical essays have been equally typical of the American literary scene. One is the theoretical essay in which the nature of a particular literary type, such as the novel or poetry, is explored. Of course, this kind of theorizing has been written since Aristotle. Many of the major literary figures of the English tradition have contributed such criticism; for example, Sir Philip Sidney, John Dryden, Samuel Johnson, Samuel Taylor Coleridge, Matthew Arnold, and T. S. Eliot. Appropriately, the example of the philosophical essay which follows was written by one of America's distinguished men of letters—an outstanding novelist, poet, and critic, Robert Penn Warren.

Another, and equally interesting, kind of criticism is more easily associated with the present century and examines not the nature of a *genre*, but of a particular work. Here the goal is to explore every significant aspect of the work to determine the importance not only of the work as a whole, but also of its individual facets. Illustrating this kind of critical essay, which has been particularly associated with American scholarship, is Henry Nash Smith's discussion of *Huckleberry Finn.*

Why Do We Read Fiction?

ROBERT PENN WARREN

Why do we read fiction? The answer is simple. We read it because we like it. And we like it because fiction, as an image of life, stimulates and gratifies our interest in life. But whatever interests may be appealed to by fiction, the special and immediate interest that takes us to fiction is always our interest in a story.

A story is not merely an image of life, but of life in motion—specifically, the presentation of individual characters moving through their particular experiences to some end that we may accept as meaningful. And the experience that is characteristically presented in a story is that of facing a problem, a conflict. To put it bluntly: No conflict, no story.

It is no wonder that conflict should be at the center of fiction, for conflict is at the center of life. But why should we, who have the constant and often painful experience of conflict in life and who yearn for inner peace and harmonious relation with the outer world, turn to fiction, which is the image of conflict? The fact is that our attitude toward conflict is ambivalent.[1] If we do find a totally satisfactory adjustment

[1] *ambivalent:* mixed, divided

in life, we tend to sink into the drowse of the accustomed. Only when our surroundings—or we ourselves—become problematic[2] again do we wake up and feel that surge of energy which is life. And life more abundantly lived is what we seek.

So we, at the same time that we yearn for peace, yearn for the problematic. The adventurer, the sportsman, the gambler, the child playing hide-and-seek, the teen-age boys choosing up sides for a game of sandlot baseball, the old grad cheering in the stadium—we all, in fact, seek out or create problematic situations of greater or lesser intensity. Such situations give us a sense of heightened energy, of life. And fiction, too, gives us that heightened awareness of life, with all the fresh, uninhibited opportunity to vent the rich emotional charge—tears, laughter, tenderness, sympathy, hate, love, and irony—that is stored up in us and short-circuited in the drowse of the accustomed. Furthermore, this heightened awareness can be more fully relished now, because what in actuality would be the threat of the problematic is here tamed to mere imagination, and because some kind of resolution of the problem is, owing to the very nature of fiction, promised.

The story promises us a resolution, and we wait in suspense to learn how things will come out. We are in suspense, not only about what will happen, but even more about what the event will mean. We are in suspense about the story in fiction because we are in suspense about another story far closer and more important to us—the story of our own life as we live it. We do not know how that story of our own life is going to come out. We do not know what it will mean. So, in that deepest suspense of life, which will be shadowed in the suspense we feel about the story in fiction, we turn to fiction for some slight hint about the story in the life we live. The relation of our life to the fictional life is what, in a fundamental sense, takes us to fiction.

Even when we read, as we say, to "escape," we seek to escape not from life but to life, to a life more satisfying than our own drab version. Fiction gives us an image of life—

[2]*problematic:* uncertain, having the nature of a problem

sometimes of a life we actually have and like to dwell on, but often and poignantly of one we have had but do not have now, or one we have never had and can never have. The ardent fisherman, when his rheumatism keeps him housebound, reads stories from *Field and Stream.* The baseball fan reads "You Know Me Al," by Ring Lardner. The little co-ed, worrying about her snub nose and her low mark in Sociology 2, dreams of being a debutante out of F. Scott Fitzgerald;[3] and the thin-chested freshman, still troubled by acne, dreams of being a granite-jawed Neanderthal out of Mickey Spillane.[4]

And that is what, for all of us, fiction, in one sense, is—a daydream. It is, in other words, an imaginative enactment. In it we find, in imagination, not only the pleasure of recognizing the world we know and of reliving our past, but also the pleasure of entering worlds we do not know and of experimenting with experiences which we deeply crave but which the limitations of life, the fear of consequences, or the severity of our principles forbid to us. Fiction can give us this pleasure without any painful consequences, for there is no price tag on the magic world of imaginative enactment. But fiction does not give us only what we want; more importantly, it may give us things we hadn't even known we wanted.

In this sense, then, fiction painlessly makes up for the defects of reality. Long ago Francis Bacon[5] said that poetry—which, in his meaning, would include our fiction—is "agreeable to the spirit of man" because it affords "a greater grandeur of things, a more perfect order, and a more beautiful variety" than can "anywhere be found in nature. . . ." More recently we find Freud[6] putting it that the "meagre satisfactions" that man "can extract from reality leave him starving," and John

[3]*F. Scott Fitzgerald (1896-1940):* American author whose novels of the "roaring Twenties" feature many heroines who are rich, beautiful, and vivacious

[4]*Mickey Spillane (1918-   ):* American author of detective stories whose hero, Mike Hammer, is noted for his strength and hardboiled attitude toward life

[5]*Francis Bacon (1561-1626):* English diplomat, scientist, and author famous for his short essays

[6]*Sigmund Freud (1856-1939):* Austrian doctor who founded the branch of medicine known as psychoanalysis, which treats disorders of the mind

Dewey[7] saying that art "was born of need, lack, deprivation, incompleteness." But philosophers aside, we all know entirely too well how much we resemble poor Walter Mitty.[8]

If fiction is—as it clearly is for some readers—merely a fantasy to redeem the liabilities of our private fate, it is flight from reality and therefore the enemy of growth, of the life process. But is it necessarily this? Let us look at the matter in another way.

The daydream which is fiction differs from the ordinary daydream in being publicly available. This fact leads to consequences. In the private daydream you remain yourself—though nobler, stronger, more fortunate, more beautiful than in life. But when the little freshman settles cozily with his thriller by Mickey Spillane, he finds that the granite-jawed hero is not named Slim Willett, after all—as poor Slim, with his thin chest, longs for it to be. And Slim's college instructor, settling down to *For Whom the Bell Tolls*,[9] finds sadly that this other college instructor who is the hero of the famous tale of sleeping bags, bridge demolition, tragic love and lonely valor, is named Robert Jordan.

In other words, to enter into that publicly available daydream which fiction is, you have to accept the fact that the name of the hero will never be your own; you will have to surrender something of your own identity to him, have to let it be absorbed in him. But since that kind of daydream is not exquisitely custom-cut to the exact measure of your secret longings, the identification can never be complete. In fact, only a very naïve reader tries to make it thrillingly complete. The more sophisticated reader plays a deep double game with himself; one part of him is identified with a character—or with several in turn—while another part holds aloof to respond, interpret and judge. How often have we heard some sentimental old lady say of a book: "I just loved the heroine—I mean I just went through everything with her and I knew

[7]*John Dewey (1859-1952):* American philosopher whose theory of education has had an important influence on modern education in America

[8]*Walter Mitty:* the daydreaming hero of a short story by James Thurber

[9]*For Whom the Bell Tolls:* novel by Ernest Hemingway about the Spanish Civil War

exactly how she felt. Then when she died I just cried." The sweet old lady, even if she isn't very sophisticated, is instinctively playing the double game too: She identifies herself with the heroine, but she survives the heroine's death to shed the delicious tears. So even the old lady knows how to make the most of what we shall call her role-taking. She knows that doubleness, in the very act of identification, is of the essence of role-taking: There is the taker of the role and there is the role taken. And fiction is, in imaginative enactment, a role-taking.

For some people—those who fancy themselves hardheaded and realistic—the business of role-taking is as reprehensible as indulgence in a daydream. But in trying to understand our appetite for fiction, we can see that the process of role-taking not only stems from but also affirms the life process. It is an essential part of growth.

Role-taking is, for instance, at the very center of children's play. This is the beginning of the child's long process of adaptation to others, for only by feeling himself into another person's skin can the child predict behavior; and the stakes in the game are high, for only thus does he learn whether to expect the kiss or the cuff. In this process of role-taking we find, too, the roots of many of the massive intellectual structures we later rear—most obviously psychology and ethics, for it is only by role-taking that the child comes to know, to know "inwardly" in the only way that finally counts, that other people really exist and are, in fact, persons with needs, hopes, fears and even rights. So the role-taking of fiction, at the same time that it gratifies our deep need to extend and enrich our own experience, continues this long discipline in human sympathy. And this discipline in sympathy, through the imaginative enactment of role-taking, gratifies another need deep in us: our yearning to enter and feel at east in the human community.

Play when we are children, and fiction when we are grown up, lead us, through role-taking, to an awareness of others. But all along the way role-taking leads us, by the same token, to an awareness of ourselves; it leads us, in fact, to the creation of the self. For the individual is not born with a self. He is born as a mysterious bundle of possibilities which, bit by bit, in a long process of trial and error, he sorts out until he gets some sort of unifying self, the ringmaster self, the official self.

The official self emerges, but the soul, as Plato long ago put it, remains full of "ten thousand opposites occurring at the same time," and modern psychology has said nothing to contradict him. All our submerged selves, the old desires and possibilities, are lurking deep in us, sleepless and eager to have another go. There is knife-fighting in the inner dark. The fact that most of the time we are not aware of trouble does not mean that trouble is any the less present and significant; and fiction, most often in subtly disguised forms, liberatingly reenacts for us such inner conflict. We feel the pleasure of liberation even when we cannot specify the source of the pleasure.

Fiction brings up from their dark, forgotten dungeons our shadowy, deprived selves and gives them an airing in, as it were, the prison yard. They get a chance to participate, each according to his nature, in the life which fiction presents. When in Thackeray's *Vanity Fair* the girl Becky Sharp, leaving school for good, tosses her copy of Doctor Johnson's *Dictionary* out of the carriage, something in our own heart leaps gaily up, just as something rejoices at her later pecuniary adventures in Victorian society, and suffers, against all our sense of moral justice, when she comes a cropper.[10] When Holden Caulfield, of Salinger's *Catcher in the Rye*, undertakes his gallant and absurd little crusade against the "phony" in our world, our own nigh-doused idealism flares up again, for the moment without embarrassment. When in Faulkner's *Light in August* Percy Grimm pulls the trigger of the black, blunt-nosed automatic and puts that tight, pretty little pattern of slugs in the top of the overturned table behind which Joe Christmas cowers, our trigger finger tenses, even while, at the same time, with a strange joy of release and justice satisfied, we feel those same slugs in our heart. When we read Dostoevski's *Crime and Punishment*, something in our nature participates in the bloody deed, and later, something else in us

[10] *comes a cropper:* fails (colloq.)

experiences, with the murderer Raskolnikov, the bliss of repentance and reconciliation.

For among our deprived selves we must confront the redeemed as well as the damned, the saintly as well as the wicked; and strangely enough, either confrontation may be both humbling and strengthening. In having some awareness of the complexity of self we are better-prepared to deal with that self. As a matter of fact, our entering into the fictional process helps to redefine this dominant self—even, as it were, to re-create, on a sounder basis—sounder because better understood—that dominant self, the official "I." As Henri Bergson[11] says, fiction "brings us back into our own presence"—the presence in which we must make our final terms with life and death.

The knowledge in such confrontations does not come to us with intellectual labels. We don't say, "Gosh, I've got 15 percent of sadism in me"—or 13 percent of unsuspected human charity. No, the knowledge comes as enactment; and as imaginative enactment, to use our old phrase, it comes as knowledge. It comes, rather, as a heightened sense of being, as the conflict in the story evokes the conflict in ourselves, evokes it with some hopeful sense of meaningful resolution, and with, therefore, an exhilarating sense of freedom.

Part of this sense of freedom derives, to repeat ourselves, from the mere fact that in imagination we are getting off scot-free with something which we, or society, would never permit in real life; from the fact that our paradoxical relation to experience presented in fiction—our involvement and noninvolvement at the same time—gives a glorious feeling of mastery over the game of life. But there is something more important that contributes to this sense of freedom, the expansion and release that knowledge always brings; and in fiction we are permitted to know in the deepest way, by imaginative participation, things we would otherwise never know—including ourselves. We are free from the Garden curse: We may eat of the Tree of Knowledge, and no angel with flaming sword will appear.

[11]*Henri Bergson* (1859-1941): French philosopher

But in the process of imaginative enactment we have, in another way, that sense of freedom that comes from knowledge. The image that fiction presents is purged of the distractions, confusions and accidents of ordinary life. We can now gaze at the inner logic of things—of a personality, of the consequences of an act or a thought, of a social or historical situation, of a lived life. One of our deepest cravings is to find logic in experience, but in real life how little of our experience comes to us in such a manageable form!

We have all observed how a person who has had a profound shock needs to tell the story of the event over and over again, every detail. By telling it he objectifies it, disentangling himself, as it were, from the more intolerable effects. This objectifying depends, partly at least, on the fact that the telling is a way of groping for the logic of the event, an attempt to make the experience intellectually manageable. If a child—or a man—who is in a state of blind outrage at his fate can come to understand that the fate which had seemed random and gratuitous is really the result of his own previous behavior or is part of the general pattern of life, his emotional response is modified by that intellectual comprehension. What is intellectually manageable is, then, more likely to be emotionally manageable.

This fiction is a "telling" in which we as readers participate and is, therefore, an image of the process by which experience is made manageable. In this process experience is foreshortened, is taken out of the ruck of time, is put into an ideal time where we can scrutinize it, is given an interpretation. In other words, fiction shows, as we have said, a logical structure which implies a meaning. By showing a logical structure, it relieves us, for the moment at least, of what we sometimes feel as the greatest and most mysterious threat of life—the threat of the imminent but "unknowable," of the urgent but "unsayable." Insofar as a piece of fiction is original and not merely a conventional repetition of the known and predictable, it is a movement through the "unknowable" toward the "knowable"—the imaginatively knowable. It says the "unsayable."

This leads us, as a sort of aside, to the notion that fiction sometimes seems to be, for the individual or for society, prophetic. Now looking back we can clearly see how Melville, Dostoevski, James, Proust, Conrad and Kafka[12] tried to deal with some of the tensions and problems which have become characteristic of our time. In this sense they foretold our world —and even more importantly, forefelt it. They even forefelt us.

Or let us remember that F. Scott Fitzgerald and Hemingway did not merely report a period, they predicted it in that they sensed a new mode of behavior and feeling. Fiction, by seizing on certain elements in its time and imaginatively pursuing them with the unswerving logic of projected enactment, may prophesy the next age. We know this from looking back on fiction of the past. More urgently we turn to fiction of our own time to help us envisage the time to come and our relation to it.

But let us turn to more specific instances of that inner logic which fiction may reveal. In *An American Tragedy* Dreiser shows us in what subtle and pitiful ways the materialism of America and the worship of Success can corrupt an ordinary young man and bring him to the death cell. In *Madame Bovary* Flaubert shows us the logic by which Emma's yearning for color and meaning in life leads to the moment when she gulps the poison. In both novels we sense this logic most deeply because we, as we have seen, are involved, are accomplices. We, too, worship Success—as did Dreiser. We, too, have yearnings like Emma's, and we remember that Flaubert said that he himself was Emma Bovary.

We see the logic of the enacted process, and we also see the logic of the end. Not only do we have now, as readers, the freedom that leads to a knowledge of the springs of action; we have also the more difficult freedom that permits us to contemplate the consequences of action and the judgment that may be passed on it. For judgment, even punishment, is the end of the logic we perceive. In our own personal lives, as we well know from our endless secret monologues of extenuation and alibi, we long to escape from judgment; but here, where the price tag is only that of imaginative involvement, we can ac-

[12] *Melville, Dostoevski . . . Kafka:* famous novelists of the nineteenth and twentieth centuries

cept judgment. We are reconciled to the terrible necessity of judgment—upon our surrogate self in the story, our whipping boy and scapegoat. We find a moral freedom in this fact that we recognize a principle of justice, with also perhaps some gratification of the paradoxical desire to suffer.

It may be objected here that we speak as though all stories were stories of crime and punishment. No, but all stories, from the gayest farce to the grimmest tragedy, are stories of action and consequence—which amounts to the same thing. All stories, as we have said, are based on conflict; and the resolution of the fictional conflict is, in its implications, a judgment too, a judgment of values. In the end some shift of values has taken place. Some new awareness has dawned, some new possibility of attitude has been envisaged.

Not that the new value is necessarily "new" in a literal sense. The point, to come back to an old point, is that the reader has, by imaginative enactment, lived through the process by which the values become valuable. What might have been merely an abstraction has become vital, has been lived, and is, therefore, "new"—new because newly experienced. We can now rest in the value as experienced; we are reconciled in it, and that is what counts.

It is what counts, for in the successful piece of fiction, a comic novel by Peter de Vries or a gut-tearing work like Tolstoy's *War and Peace*, we feel, in the end, some sense of reconciliation with the world and with ourselves. And this process of moving through conflict to reconciliation is an echo of our own life process. The life process, as we know it from babyhood on, from our early relations with our parents on to our adult relation with the world, is a long process of conflict and reconciliation. This process of enriching and deepening experience is a pattern of oscillation—a pattern resembling that of the lovers' quarrel: When lovers quarrel, each asserts his special ego against that of the beloved and then in the moment of making up finds more keenly than before the joy of losing the self in the love of another. So in fiction we enter imaginatively a situation of difficulty and estrangement—a problematic situation that, as we said earlier, sharpens our awareness of life—and move through it to a reconciliation which seems fresh and sweet.

Reconciliation—that is what we all, in some depth of being, want. All religion, all philosophy, all psychiatry, all ethics involve this human fact. And so does fiction. If fiction begins in daydream, if it springs from the cramp of the world, if it relieves us from the burden of being ourselves, it ends, if it is good fiction and we are good readers, by returning us to the world and to ourselves. It reconciles us with reality.

Let us pause to take stock. Thus far what we have said sounds as though fiction were a combination of opium addiction, religious conversion without tears, a home course in philosophy and the poor man's psychoanalysis. But it is not; it is fiction.

It is only itself, and that *itself* is not, in the end, a mere substitute for anything else. It is an art—an image of experience formed in accordance with its own laws of imaginative enactment, laws which, as we have seen, conform to our deep needs. It is an "illusion of life" projected through language, and the language is that of some individual man projecting his own feeling of life.

The story, in the fictional sense, is not something that exists of and by itself, out in the world like a stone or a tree. The materials of stories—certain events or characters, for example—may exist out in the world, but they are not fictionally meaningful to us until a human mind has shaped them. We are, in other words, like the princess in one of Hans Christian Andersen's tales; she refuses her suitor when she discovers that the bird with a ravishing song which he has offered as a token of love is only a real bird after all. We, like the princess, want an artificial bird—an artificial bird with a real song. So we go to fiction because it is a *created* thing.

Because it is created by a man, it draws us, as human beings, by its human significance. To begin with, it is an utterance, in words. No words, no story. This seems a fact so obvious, and so trivial, as not to be worth the saying, but it is of fundamental importance in the appeal fiction has for us. We are creatures of words, and if we did not have words we would have no inner life. Only because we have words can we envisage and think about experience. We find our human nature through words. So in one sense we may say that insofar as the language of the story enters into the expressive whole of the story we find the deep satisfaction, conscious or unconscious, of a fulfillment of our very nature.

As an example of the relation of words, of style, to the expressive whole which is fiction, let us take Hemingway. We readily see how the stripped, laconic, monosyllabic style relates to the tight-lipped, stoical ethic, the cult of self-discipline, the physicality and the anti-intellectualism and the other such elements that enter into his characteristic view of the world. Imagine Henry James writing Hemingway's story *The Killers.* The complicated sentence structure of James, the deliberate and subtle rhythms, the careful parentheses—all these things express the delicate intellectual, social and aesthetic discriminations with which James concerned himself. But what in the Lord's name would they have to do with the shocking blankness of the moment when the gangsters enter the lunchroom, in their tight-buttoned identical blue overcoats, with gloves on their hands so as to leave no fingerprints when they kill the Swede?

The style of a writer represents his stance toward experience, toward the subject of his story; and it is also the very flesh of our experience of the story, for it is the flesh of our experience as we read. Only through his use of words does the story come to us. And with language, so with the other aspects of a work of fiction. Everything there—the proportioning of plot, the relations among the characters, the logic of motivation, the speed or retardation of the movement—is formed by a human mind into what it is, into what, if the fiction is successful, is an expressive whole, a speaking pattern, a form. And in recognizing and participating in this form, we find a gratification, though often an unconscious one, as fundamental as any we have mentioned.

We get a hint of the fundamental nature of this gratification in the fact that among primitive peoples decorative patterns are developed long before the first attempts to portray the objects of nature, even those things on which the life of the tribe depended. The pattern images a rhythm of life and intensifies the tribesman's sense of life.

Or we find a similar piece of evidence in psychological studies made of the response of children to comic books.

"It is not the details of development," the researchers tell us, "but rather the general aura which the child finds fascinating." What the child wants is the formula of the accelerating buildup of tension followed by the glorious release when the righteous Superman appears just in the nick of time. What the child wants, then, is a certain "shape" of experience. Is his want, at base, different from our own?

At base, no. But if the child is satisfied by a nearly abstract pattern for the feelings of tension and release, we demand much more. We, too, in the build and shape of experience, catch the echo of the basic rhythm of our life. But we know that the world is infinitely more complicated than the child thinks. We, unlike the child, must scrutinize the details of development, the contents of life and of fiction. So the shaping of experience to satisfy us must add to the simplicity that satisfies the child something of the variety, roughness, difficulty, subtlety and delight which belongs to the actual business of life and our response to it. We want the factual richness of life absorbed into the pattern so that content and form are indistinguishable in one expressive flowering in the process that John Dewey says takes "life and experience in all its uncertainties, mystery, doubt and half-knowledge and turns that experience upon itself to deepen and intensify its own qualities." Only then will it satisfy our deepest need—the need of feeling our life to be, in itself, significant.

FOR DISCUSSION

1. Why does Warren call fiction "an image of life"? How can an image gratify our interest in life? How can fiction make up for "the defects of reality"?
2. If characters decide at the end of a story that their experiences have had no meaning, can the works in which such characters appear still fit the definition of "life in motion" suggested in the second paragraph?
3. Test the maxim: "No conflict, no story." Can you remember or imagine a story which has no conflict? What does Warren mean by conflict?

4. Have you ever felt frustrated because a story which promised to be fascinating ended up seeming to go nowhere? How would Warren explain your frustration?
5. According to Warren, what is the relationship between the reader and the fictional characters about whom he reads? If "role-taking" helps us feel at ease in the community, how might we benefit by taking the role of someone who opposes the assumptions of our community?
6. Warren says that a writer's style represents his stance—or attitude—toward experience. Can you tell anything about Warren's attitude toward experience from his style in this essay?

FOR COMPOSITION

1. Write an essay defending the proposition "We all yearn for the problematic." Try to find examples from your own experience which differ from those Warren uses.
2. Take a book you think is particularly enjoyable and test it to see whether it fits Warren's thesis that good fiction reconciles us with reality by returning us to the world and to ourselves. Write an essay reporting your conclusions about the book.

Mark Twain: The Adventures of Huckleberry Finn

HENRY NASH SMITH

Mark Twain is the most widely read of American authors, living or dead, and *The Adventures of Huckleberry Finn* is by far his most popular book. It was a best seller when it was published in 1885; it has held its audience steadily ever since; and it has been translated into more foreign languages than any other work in our literature. Professor Walter Blair has estimated on the basis of carefully compiled statistics that ten million copies of the book have been printed. For some fifty years after its publication, *Huckleberry Finn* received relatively little attention from the official arbiters of literary taste. But, as Mr. Blair points out, "Beginning in the late 1940's this lack has been remedied with a vengeance. By the end of 1960 critics and scholars [had] published within a fifteen-year period more than a hundred lengthy discussions of the novel." And the critical discussion continues to increase in volume.

How can we account for the unique status of this story told in the language of a fourteen-year-old boy growing up as an outcast in the pre-Civil-War South? Some of the answers to the question are obvious. The book is extremely funny, and its humor seems unfading. Huck's comments that *The Pilgrim's Progress* is "about a man that left his family it didn't say why" and that "The statements was interesting but tough" have a mixture of naïveté and profundity that retains its charm even upon the tenth or the twentieth reading. In addition to its humor, the book has an immense vitality. Mark Twain poured into it his memories of people and places observed during his childhood in Hannibal, Missouri, in the 1840's and his years on the Mississippi as a steamboat pilot in the 1850's. Bernard DeVoto called Huck's story "a faring-forth with inexhaustible delight through the variety of America, the heritage of a nation not unjustly symbolized by the river's flow." Furthermore, the narrative is fully accessible. The author does not seem to be trying to get one-up on the reader. It is a book that can be read with pleasure both by scholars and by people who read nothing else but the newspapers.

These qualities point to a less obvious reason for the fascination the book holds for Americans in all walks of life. It bears upon the long-standing and increasingly urgent problem of the identity of this country and its people. Just at the end of the American War of Independence, in 1782, the naturalized Frenchman St. John de Crèvecoeur had asked in his *Letters from an American Farmer*, "What then is the American, this new man?" He proposed an answer that was shrewd and valid for his day, but the question has had to be asked again and again in the history of our literature. James Fenimore Cooper found a different answer from Crèvecoeur's in his backwoodsman Leatherstocking; Emerson stated yet another, much more philosophical, in his address on "The American Scholar"; Walt Whitman devoted most of his *Leaves of Grass* to defining the ideal American type he believed would emerge as the citizen of "these States." And Mark Twain himself had begun his literary career in 1869 by relating the adventures of a rather philistine[1] American Innocent Abroad confronting history and cultural tradition in Europe and the Holy Land.

Fifteen years later Mark Twain arrived at the more definitive answer represented by his ragged orphan boy floating

[1] *philistine:* uncultured

down the Mississippi River with Jim, the runaway Negro slave. At first glance this story of the 1840's may seem to have no connection with the problems of the Cold War in the mid-twentieth century. Recent discussion of the book, however, has made Huck's story seem directly relevant to our present circumstances. Somewhat bewildered by both their power and their responsibilities, Americans have been impelled to seek in art shared images that can help them become aware of their identity as a people. At least, this is a conclusion that has occurred to more than one observer. Let us take it as a hypothesis,[2] and ask what features of Mark Twain's masterpiece offer a definition of the American character and the American situation in our day.

We notice at once that the book invites its readers to identify themselves with an adolescent protagonist suddenly exposed to novel risks and opportunities. Huck has never before been outside the little river town of St. Petersburg, that is, Hannibal, Missouri; yet now he is launched upon a journey that will take him more than a thousand miles downstream, as the river flows, through a constantly changing panorama of new landscapes, strange characters, unforeseen and unimagined dangers. The voyage of discovery that he did not plan in advance and did not want to make has a suggestive similarity to the role of the United States in the mid-twentieth century.

Equally obvious is the fact that Huck's story is a story of movement. He runs away from St. Petersburg in order to escape from his father's brutality and the well-meaning attempts of the townspeople of St. Petersburg to "sivilize" him. And the outcome of each episode in his story is renewed flight: from Jackson's Island, where he and Jim fear they will be found by slave-hunters; from the wrecked steamboat "Walter Scott" in mid-river on which they encounter a band of robbers and murderers; from the violence and bloodshed of the feud on the Grangerford plantation. This pattern of repeated movement has characterized American history from the beginning. Frederick Jackson Turner's celebrated "frontier hypothesis" maintained that the American character was

[2] *hypothesis:* theory

formed by the experience of advancing westward across the continent. Professor George W. Pierson has included the Turner thesis in a theory which finds Americans ready to move, not only westward, but in every direction. Foreign observers get the impression that Americans are constantly on the road. Certainly no other people has shown such a fondness for the "mobile home" on wheels that can stand for days or months or years in one of the trailer parks lining the highways outside every American city, then can be towed by an automobile to a similar location outside another city across the continent. Take an informal census of a group of Americans anywhere by asking them where they were born. You will find not one in five living close to his birthplace. Huck Finn is like that. He is on the move through most of his narrative, and at the end he is about to set out again, for the Indian Territory.

Huck's impulse to run away when he is faced by a problem he cannot solve is closely related to what W. H. Auden has called his habit of "moral improvisation." What he decides in one crisis, points out Mr. Auden, "tells him nothing about what he should do on other occasions, or what other people should do on other occasions. . . ."[3] Since the problem Huck faces is always a new one, he cannot depend on what he has learned from experience as a guide to action. The present does not seem to him continuous with the past, and he therefore has no reason to believe the future will be continuous with the present. Although Mr. Auden does not make the further inference, Huck's moral improvisation might be regarded as one aspect of his indifference to abstract ideas. He sees no basis for regarding a given situation as an illustration of a general principle. Each one must be faced on its own terms.

The disposition to make up policy as one goes along is sometimes called pragmatism, and in a vague sense I suppose Huck must be considered a pragmatist. But this seems too pedantic a term to describe him; he does not really have a philosophy. It is more accurate to say that he relies on intuition rather than reason. His moral improvisation is largely a

[3]"Huck and Oliver," *The Listener,* L, No. 1283 (October 1, 1953), pp. 540-541.

matter of acting on impulse rather than according to preconceived plan. A good illustration is Huck's behavior when the raft taking him and Jim downstream approaches the mouth of the Ohio River. Jim grows more and more excited because he believes that when he can head up the Ohio he will be out of slave territory, and therefore be free; and Huck for the first time begins to realize that he is actually helping a slave escape. His conscience, formed by the society in which he has grown up, goads him until he decides he will turn Jim in as a runaway slave. He has actually set out for shore in a canoe, "all in a sweat to tell on" Jim, when he encounters a skiff with two men in it searching for five Negroes who have just escaped from a plantation on the shore. They ask Huck whether the man left on his raft is black or white. "I didn't answer up prompt," Huck says.

> I tried to, but the words wouldn't come. I tried, for a second or two, to brace up and out with it, but I warn't man enough—hadn't the spunk of a rabbit. I see I was weakening, so I just give up trying, and up and says—"He's white."

Then, in order to prevent the men from going to see for themselves, Huck improvises an elaborate story that makes them believe there is smallpox on the raft.

When Huck finds himself unable to carry out his preconceived intention, he falls back on impulse. He acts in this way again and again. Eventually, in fact, he even makes his own generalization about his procedure. As he approaches the Phelps plantation far down in Arkansas, where Jim is held prisoner in a log cabin and where the final sequence of the story takes place, Huck says:

> I went right along, not fixing up any particular plan, but just trusting to Providence to put the right words in my mouth when the time come; for I'd noticed that Providence always did put the right words in my mouth, if I left it alone.

A boy—or a nation—that operates like this will give the impression of having no coherent policy, of behaving in an unpredictable and sometimes even treacherous fashion. Such a boy or nation may seem an unreliable ally because no one can infer from past actions how he, or it, will behave in a future situation. American national policy, both foreign and domestic, has often made such an impression on the rest of the world. But both Huck and the American people are more predictable in the long run than in the short run.

The parallel, however, should not be taken too literally. Mark Twain means to demonstrate that the abstract principles Huck is aware of have been implanted in him by a peculiarly corrupt society—the slaveholding culture of the Old South. He has had no chance to arrive at a rational view of slavery as an institution. Until the time when he runs into Jim hiding on Jackson's Island, he has accepted without question the attitude toward slavery prevalent in St. Petersburg. He considers it divinely ordained and he has never imagined a society in which slavery does not exist. But this slave has been a friend of his for a long time; and when Jim reveals the awful fact that he has run away from his mistress, Huck hesitates hardly a moment. "People would call me a low down Abolitionist and despise me for keeping mum," he says, "—but that don't make no difference. I ain't agoing to tell. . . ."

By enlisting himself in Jim's cause, Huck becomes an outlaw. From this point to almost the end of the story he believes himself to be engaged in a criminal undertaking. He goes through two moral crises in which he is denounced by his conscience, but he finally reaches a clear decision to "go to Hell," that is, to defy what he understands to be the laws of God and of man by remaining loyal to Jim. This appeal from revealed or codified law to an intuitive notion of what is right is a very American trait in Huck. We are notoriously not a law-abiding people. Our crime rate and our divorce rate are high. In this sense there is a pronounced strain of anarchism[4] in our culture. From whatever source it may be derived—from our exposure to frontier conditions or from some other influence—our disrespect for the law and its representatives is the dark aspect of our passionate cult of freedom.

Although Huck does not question the legality of slavery, he does not accept the laws as a guide to action. In fact, all estab-

[4]*anarchism:* rejection of all forms of government

lished institutions are alien to him. He has no use for them and by preference no contact with them. He suffers when the Widow Douglas and Miss Watson dress him in conventional clothing, try to teach him table manners and passages from the Bible, and send him to school. The modes of behavior prescribed by custom and tradition seem to him abnormal. In Huck's unreflecting fashion he illustrates Emerson's aphorism[5] that the American people receive their culture from one continent but their duties from another. From the beginning we have faced a continual need to adapt European traditions and conventions to the new circumstances of this continent. As a consequence, we have had to become accustomed to a more than ordinary discontinuity between theory and practice.

This is the state of affairs that Emerson dealt with in such essays as "The American Scholar" and "Self-Reliance." It is perfectly exemplified in one of the most profound passages of Mark Twain's novel—one in which the dominant figure is, to be sure, not Huck but Tom Sawyer, yet one that defines Huck's own situation very well because Tom is making articulate both the demands of convention and the way Americans have often met these demands. The boys are digging a tunnel under the wall of the cabin where Jim is imprisoned on the Phelps plantation. Tom has insisted that they use only case knives for this purpose because that is the implement used by prisoners escaping from European dungeons in the historical romances he has read. But even Tom has to admit at last that the work is going too slowly. They will have to dig the tunnel with picks. "It ain't right, and it ain't moral," he says with regret. "And I wouldn't like it to get out—but there ain't only just the one way; we got to dig him out with the picks, and *let on* it's case-knives." Calling a spade a spade—or a pick a pick—is not the absolute rule in any society, but Americans have had to make more accommodations of this sort than peoples whose traditional culture grows more directly out of their own experience.

Huck's habit of moral improvisation, his antinomian[6] attitude toward established authorities and institutions, his toler-

[5] *aphorism:* truthful statement

[6] *antinomian:* a doctrine which holds that grace frees Christians from moral law; hence, a refusal to recognize laws of any sort

ance of a wide disparity between theory and practice, all derive from the same aspect of his character. In a comment on the book after it was published Mark Twain described Huck as a boy with "a sound heart and a deformed conscience." Although Huck's heart is undisciplined and even the source of subversive impulses, it is nevertheless "sound," that is, not depraved, not wicked, but essentially virtuous. Mark Twain intends for the reader to identify himself with this part of Huck, to feel a thrill of moral exaltation when the ignorant boy decides to go to hell rather than betray his friend. And there can be no doubt of Huck's underlying innocence. He intends harm to no one; he is sickened by the violence of the Kentucky feud and the cynical hypocrisy of the "king" gulling the mourners at Peter Wilks's funeral into taking him for a Christian minister. Huck tries to protect other people from harm, not only his comrade Jim and the orphaned Wilks girls, but even the bloodthirsty bandits on the wrecked "Walter Scott." His deepest emotion is love, most of all of course for Jim. Their comradeship on the raft has been called by one enthusiastic critic, not without some justice, a community of saints; and Mark Twain gives it poetic support by providing for their idyllic moments of solitude a setting of starry sky and quiet water. Nature cherishes them, and the purity of sunrise on the river is an affirmation of both Huck's and Jim's innocence.

Yet this purity is not allowed to endure. The celebrated description of sunrise at the beginning of Chapter XIX ends with a reference to the odor of decaying fish that prepares for the entrance of the rascally "duke" and "king" a page or two later. Huck and Jim can escape only momentarily from the depraved society of the shore. And this society has made an indelible imprint on Huck's character. It has given him the deformed conscience that is at war with his sound heart. His conscience—the voice that condemns him for helping Jim—is the sum total of the fancied obligations, the foolish inhibitions, the perverse constraints imposed on Huck by society. It is thus, by an inevitable extension of mearning, the voice of tradition, of the past, of what Emerson meant by "culture." Huck's innocence is compromised by the only culture he knows, that of the towns along the River, in which slavery has become the focus of moral and legal values, religion is "soul butter and hogwash," honor is expressed in the cowardly ambushes and murders of the feud, and the arts are represented by the comically vulgar ornaments of the Grangerford parlor, or Emmeline Grangerford's doggerel verses, or Tom Sawyer's grotesque "rules" derived from his reading in historical fiction.

The hostile depiction of Huck's conscience is extended further in the story by the characterization of his father and of the women who function as mothers to him. The man who would normally embody for Huck the ideal of wisdom and moral authority is a neurotic drunkard whose beatings actually threaten the boy's life and drive him to flight. The duke and the king, who assume authority over Huck and may therefore be regarded as parodies of the father image, are amusing rascals through the middle section of the narrative, but they are potentially dangerous criminals. As the raft floats farther and farther southward, Huck shows that he understands them fully. He says:

> They took a change, and began to lay their heads together in the wigwam and talk low and confidential two or three hours at a time. . . . Jim and me got uneasy. We didn't like the look of it. We judged they was studying up some kind of worse deviltry than ever.

What they do is to turn Jim in fraudulently, for a reward; and Huck's last encounter with the duke leads to a moment of pure fright. It suddenly occurs to the duke that the boy may represent a danger. "'Looky here,' he says—'do you think *you'd* venture to blow on us? Blamed if I think I'd trust you. Why, if you *was* to blow on us—.'" Huck adds: "He stopped, but I never see the duke look so ugly out of his eyes before." This orphan has no reason at all to consider his fathers, actual or symbolic, as a source of moral authority; they are quite simply the enemy.

The mother figures seem less menacing. Although Miss Watson is hard and angular, with an ignorant bigotry, the Widow Douglas and Aunt Sally Phelps have traces of motherly warmth. Aunt Sally, the substitute mother who is portrayed at greatest length in the story, is allowed for a moment to awaken remorse in Huck. As she sits all night by the window hoping for Tom's return, he says:

> . . . I wished I could do something for her, but I couldn't, only to swear that I wouldn't never do nothing to grieve her any more.

Nevertheless, most of the time Aunt Sally is a comic victim of the boy's pranks. And like Miss Watson and the Widow Douglas, she is determined to subjugate Huck to the mores of a society that Mark Twain has deprived of all moral authority. The celebrated last lines of the story express a hostility toward her which the reader is expected to share:

> . . . I reckon I got to light out for the Territory ahead of the rest, because Aunt Sally she's going to adopt me and sivilize me and I can't stand it. I been there before.

Most of the women in this fictive world are elderly; they are lawgivers rather than sexual partners, actual or potential. Female custody of the arts is represented by poor dead Emmeline Grangerford. Her two sisters—the proud Charlotte and Sophia, "gentle and sweet, like a dove"—are no more than glimpsed. Huck is perhaps too young to take a romantic interest in girls, although he remembers Mary Jane Wilks vividly enough to declare that "she had more sand in her than any girl I ever see." The fact remains that the adventures of this American protagonist are in effect sexless. Critics have debated the significance of Mark Twain's consistent avoidance of a theme that runs through the literature of the world. Professor Leslie Fiedler has pointed out that two other nineteenth-century American literary masterpieces—Cooper's Leatherstocking series and Melville's *Moby Dick*—also pay virtually no attention to the love of man and woman. This remark could hardly be made about American literature of the twentieth century, and Hawthorne's Hester Prynne stands early in our literary history as a powerful and very womanly heroine. But none of these books can compare with *The Adventures of Huckleberry Finn* in appeal to the American public. The subject is complicated; let us leave it with the remark that the American experience of sexual love may well be markedly different from that of any other people in the world. Maybe American males, like Huck, are afraid of women.

We are on firmer ground when we notice the incomparable rendering in this novel of the American dream of a preindustrial, agrarian Eden. Despite its shadows of violence and terror, Huck's story is remembered by most readers for the pastoral interludes in which the raft drifts down the river in a landscape of breath-taking beauty. Amid the industrial cities and the factories and machines of the twentieth century, American literature has continued to cling to an imagined rural simplicity and innocence as a moral norm. The agrarian tradition in our culture still influences—some critics would say, perverts—public policy. Huck's raft, larger than life and distorted as all images are distorted that pass from the pages of a book into the popular imagination, is one of the principal links between the present and the past in our culture.

Much more complex is the revelation of basic American attitudes in the over-all structure of the book. The narrative begins in the near-farcical mood of *The Adventures of Tom Sawyer,* acquires a rich symbolic meaning as Huck's and Jim's quest for freedom becomes the narrative focus, moves toward the tragic recognition that freedom cannot be attained in this or any world, then suddenly veers back toward farce in Tom Sawyer's arrangements for Jim's "Evasion"—which proves in the end to be merely a gigantic hoax. Is not Mark Twain taking refuge from tragedy in a joke? He probably is, and in doing so he is conforming to a notorious American habit. This trait in our national character is by no means wholly bad. One aspect of it is our irreverence, the attitude that makes the Bronx cheer a familiar response to pretentiousness. Our irreverence protects us against the pompousness of our leaders. But it also insulates us against emotions that we do wrong to avoid; it sometimes makes us frivolous about matters that are truly serious. We should not be flattered to realize that our national identity can achieve so nearly complete expression through our identification with an adolescent boy. We cannot hope to escape all our problems by lighting out for the Territory. And if the time comes when we have to stand and face a crisis instead of passing it off with a joke or running away from it, the image of Huck Finn does not offer us much to go on in the way of techniques for dealing frontally with a world of adult problems and adversaries.

The very mixture of traits in Huck's character, however, makes this book a unique possession of the American people. Its curious blend of humor and satire and incipient tragedy; its apparently arbitrary and improvised structure that nevertheless achieves a coherent over-all effect—these resist placement in any literary tradition, although Huck's vernacular language has been one of the principal influences on American prose in the twentieth century. The book is a literary sport rather than the culmination of a coherent development. Yet the fact that it has in a sense no connections with the past, no history, is perhaps one of the qualities that make it most American. And in the end we can take a good deal of satisfaction in the positive qualities of Huck that seem to reflect a recognizable American identity. His sound heart, his freedom from malice, his loyalty to his friends, his revulsion against cruelty and hypocrisy, are traits that even foreign critics usually credit us with. Huck is also characteristic in his resourcefulness in emergencies. He is not easily flustered and he has an admirable toughness and resilience. If he lacks cultivation, he nevertheless has a keen intelligence: he is shrewd, observant, and clear in his processes of thought. And while he is subject to fits of depression because he perhaps too readily feels guilty, he is essentially stable; he tends to be cheerful in adversity. Yet he has no arrogance at all. Not a bad type, everything considered—rather above average, as national types go.

FOR DISCUSSION

1. How does Smith explain the popularity of *Huckleberry Finn*? Can you think of other explanations for the popularity of the novel?
2. According to Smith, how does Huck represent the "typical American"? How fitting a representative do you find him? In what ways is he untypical?

3. Cite current examples of American disrespect for the law and its representatives. What examples can you find of the lighter side of "our passionate cult of freedom"?
4. Do you think American males were once afraid of women? Why might this statement be true? If it is not true, why would nineteenth-century writers have avoided the subject of romantic love?
5. What would be a mature way of "dealing frontally with a world of adult problems and adversaries" such as those Huck Finn faced? How would this mature technique differ from Huck's methods?

FOR COMPOSITION

1. Write an essay tracing the popularity of *Huckleberry Finn* to one cause Smith does not mention. Develop your argument carefully, and give evidence to prove your point.
2. Pick a character other than Huck Finn—from literature, movies, or television—and prove that he is popular because he is a "typical American." Give several reasons for your conclusion.
3. Describe the "typical American" as he sees himself and as others see him. Show why discrepancies exist between these two views.

THE AMERICAN SCENE

MARK TWAIN

In his work, a writer always uses what he is most familiar with, though the landscape or "scene" which to him is most vivid may vary. For one writer, it may be his childhood. For another, it may be the present or contemporary scene. For still another, it may be an imaginary world that is most alive.

The scene in which the public will be most interested at a given time also varies. In different periods, readers have preferred the shadowy forests of Hawthorne and Cooper, or the familiar hearthstones of Howells, or the sordid cities of Crane and Dreiser, or the decaying family plantations of Faulkner.

The meaning of the phrase "the American scene" varies from writer to writer and from decade to decade. But in all periods, writers have struggled to define or describe that scene, because they have known that the definition of the American scene would also be a definition of Americans. The following selections will illustrate a variety of approaches to the American scene, landscape, and environment.

Mark Twain began publishing in the "local-color period" following the Civil War, when Americans were eager for information about the more remote areas of the nation. Local color writers placed great emphasis on geographical setting, and devoted much attention to the speech, dress, mannerisms, and habits peculiar to a certain region. Their readers demanded that this literature be entertaining, informative, and educational; Twain's "local color" fulfilled all of these requirements. His accounts of life in the mining town of Virginia City, Nevada, published in *Roughing It*, and of the experiences of a Mississippi riverboat pilot, published in *Old Times on the Mississippi*, are among the best local-color nonfiction. They are lively, vivid, and full of facts about fascinating places which were unfamiliar to those living along the Eastern coast. The humor in both sketches makes their educational aspect quite palatable; for above all, Twain conveys the fun and excitement to be experienced in a western mining town and on the great river.

Flush Times in Virginia City

MARK TWAIN

In 1859, a second gold rush drew thousands of prospectors to the foothills of the Rockies near Pike's Peak. The same year a new discovery was made on the eastern slopes of the Sierra Nevada, near Lake Tahoe. This was the Comstock Lode, one of the richest veins of silver in the world. Within a year, three roaring towns had sprung up on the barren mountainside in Nevada: Virginia City, Aurora, and Gold City.

Six months after my entry into journalism the grand "flush times" of Silverland began, and they continued with unabated splendor for three years. All difficulty about filling up the "local department" ceased, and the only trouble now was how to make the lengthened columns hold the world of incidents and happenings that came to our literary net every day. Virginia had grown to be the "livest" town, for its age and population, that America had ever produced. The sidewalks swarmed with people—to such an extent, indeed, that it was generally no easy matter to stem the human tide. The streets themselves were just as crowded with quartz wagons, freight teams, and other vehicles. The procession was endless. So great was the pack that buggies frequently had to wait half an hour for an opportunity to cross the principal street. Joy sat on every countenance, and there was a glad, almost fierce, intensity in every eye, that told of the money-getting schemes that were seething in every brain and the high hope that held sway in every heart. Money was as plenty as dust; every individual considered himself wealthy, and a melancholy countenance was nowhere to be seen. There were military companies, fire companies, brass bands, banks, hotels, theaters, "hurdy-gurdy houses," wide-open gambling palaces, political pow-wows, civic processions, street fights, murders, inquests, riots, a whisky mill every fifteen steps, a board of aldermen, a mayor, a city surveyor, a city engineer, a chief of the fire department, with first, second, and third assistants, a chief of police, city marshal, and a large police force, two boards of mining brokers, a dozen breweries, and half a dozen jails and station houses in full operation, and some talk of building a church. The flush times were in magnificent flower! Large fireproof brick buildings were going up in the principal streets, and the wooden suburbs were spreading out in all directions. Town lots soared up to prices that were amazing.

The great Comstock Lode stretched its opulent length straight through the town from north to south, and every mine on it was in diligent process of development. One of these mines alone employed 675 men, and in the matter of elections the adage was, "as the 'Gould & Curry' goes, so goes the city." Laboring men's wages were four and six dollars a day, and they worked in three shifts or gangs, and the blasting and picking and shoveling went on without ceasing, night and day.

The city of Virginia roosted royally midway up the steep side of Mount Davidson, 7200 feet above the level of the sea, and in the clear Nevada atmosphere was visible from a distance of fifty miles! It claimed a population of fifteen thousand to eighteen thousand, and all day long half of this little army swarmed the streets like bees and the other half swarmed among the drifts and tunnels of the Comstock hundreds of feet down in the earth directly under those same streets. Often we felt our chairs jar, and heard the faint boom of a blast down in the interior of the earth under the office.

The mountainside was so steep that the entire town had a slant to it like a roof. Each street was a terrace, and from each to the next street below the descent was forty or fifty feet. The fronts of the houses were level with the street they faced, but their rear first floors were propped on lofty stilts; a man could stand at a rear first-floor window of a C Street house and look down the chimneys of the row of houses below him facing D street.

My salary was increased to forty dollars a week. But I seldom drew it. I had plenty of other resources, and what were two broad twenty-dollar gold pieces to a man who had his pockets full of such, and a cumbersome abundance of bright half dollars besides? (Paper money has never come into use on the Pacific coast.) Reporting was lucrative and every man in the town was lavish with his money and his "feet." The city and all the great mountainside were riddled with mining shafts. There were more mines than miners. True, not ten of these mines were yielding rock worth hauling to a mill, but everybody said, "Wait till the shaft gets down where the ledge comes in solid, and then you will see!" So nobody was discouraged. These were nearly all "wildcat" mines, and wholly worthless, but nobody believed it then. The "Ophir," the "Gould & Curry," the "Mexican," and other great mines on the Comstock lead in Virginia and Gold Hill were turning out huge piles of rich rock every day, and every man believed that his little wildcat claim was as good as any on the "main lead" and would infallibly be worth a thousand dollars a foot when he "got down where it came in solid." Poor fellow! he was blessedly blind to the fact that he never would see that day. So the thousand wildcat shafts burrowed deeper and deeper into the earth day by day, and all men were beside themselves with hope and happiness. How they labored, prophesied, exulted! Surely nothing like it was ever seen before since the world began. Every one of these wildcat mines—not mines, but holes in the ground over imaginary mines—was incorporated and had handsomely engraved "stock" and the stock was salable, too. It was bought and sold with a feverish avidity on the boards every day. You could go up on the mountainside, scratch around and find a ledge (there was no lack of them), put up a "notice" with a grandiloquent name on it, start a shaft, get your stock printed, and with nothing whatever to prove that your mine was worth a straw, you could put your stock on the market and sell out for hundreds and even thousands of dollars. To make money, and make it fast, was as easy as it was to eat your dinner. Every man owned "feet" in fifty different wildcat mines and considered his fortune made. Think of a city with not one solitary poor man in it! One would suppose that when month after month went by and still not a wildcat mine (by wildcat I mean, in general terms, *any* claim not located on the mother vein, *i.e.*, the "Comstock") yielded a ton of rock worth crushing, the people would begin to wonder if they were not putting too much faith in their prospective riches; but there was not a thought of such a thing. They burrowed away, bought and sold, and were happy.

New claims were taken up daily, and it was the friendly custom to run straight to the newspaper offices, give the reporters forty or fifty "feet," and get them to go and examine the mine and publish a notice of it. They did not care a fig what you said about the property so you said something. Consequently we generally said a word or two to the effect that the "indications" were good, or that the ledge was "six feet wide," or that the rock "resembled the Comstock" (and so it did—but as a general thing the resemblance was not startling enough to knock you down). If the rock was moderately promising, we followed the custom of the country, used strong adjectives and frothered at the mouth as if a very marvel in silver discoveries had transpired. If the mine was a "developed" one, and had no pay ore to show (and of course it hadn't), we praised the tunnel; said it was one of the most infatuating tunnels in the land; driveled and driveled about the tunnel till we ran entirely out of ecstasies—but never said a word about the rock. We would squander half a column of adulation on a shaft, or a new wire rope, or a dressed pine windlass, or a fascinating force pump, and close with a burst of admiration of the "gentlemanly and efficient superintendent" of the mine—but never utter a whisper about the rock. And those people were always pleased, always satisfied.

Occasionally we patched up and varnished our reputation for discrimination and stern, undeviating accuracy, by giving some old abandoned claim a blast that ought to have made its dry bones rattle—and then somebody would seize it and sell it on the fleeting notoriety thus conferred upon it.

There was *nothing* in the shape of a mining claim that was not salable. We received presents of "feet" every day. If we needed a hundred dollars or so, we sold some; if not, we hoarded it away, satisfied that it would ultimately be worth a thousand dollars a foot. I had a trunk about half full of "stock." When a claim made a stir in the market and went up to a high figure, I searched through my pile to see if I had any of its stock—and generally found it.

The prices rose and fell constantly; but still a fall disturbed us little, because a thousand dollars a foot was our figure, and so we were content to let it fluctuate as much as it pleased till it reached it. My pile of stock was not all given to me by people who wished their claims "noticed." At least half of it was given me by persons who had no thought of such a thing, and looked for nothing more than a simple verbal "thank you"; and you were not even obliged by law to furnish that. If you are coming up the street with a couple of baskets of apples in your hands, and you meet a friend, you naturally invite him to take a few. That describes the condition of things in Virginia in the "flush times." Every man had his pockets full of stock, and it was the actual *custom* of the country to part with small quantities of it to friends without the asking. Very often it was a good idea to close the transaction instantly, when a man offered a stock present to a friend, for the offer was only good and binding at that moment, and if the price went to a high figure shortly afterward the procrastination was a thing to be regretted. Mr. Stewart (Senator, now, from Nevada) one day told me he would give me twenty feet of "Justis" stock if I would walk over to his office. It was worth five or ten dollars a foot. I asked him to make the offer good for next day, as I was just going to dinner. He said he would not be in town; so I risked it and took my dinner instead of the stock. Within the week the price went up to seventy dollars and afterward to a hundred and fifty, but nothing could make that man yield. I suppose he sold that stock of mine and placed the guilty proceeds in his own pocket. I met three friends one afternoon, who said they had been buying "Overman" stock at auction at eight dollars a foot. One said if I would come up to his office he would give me fifteen feet; another said he would add fifteen; the third said he would do the same. But I was going after an inquest and could not stop. A few weeks afterward they sold all their "Overman" at six hundred dollars a foot and generously came around to tell me about it—and also to urge me to accept of the next forty-five feet of it that people tried to force on me. These are actual facts, and I could make the list a long one and still confine myself strictly to the truth. Many a time friends gave us as much as twenty-five feet of stock that was selling at twenty-five dollars a foot, and they thought no more of it than they would of offering a guest a cigar. These were "flush times" indeed! I thought they were going to last always but somehow I never was much of a prophet.

To show what a wild spirit possessed the mining brain of the community, I will remark that "claims" were actually "located" in excavations for cellars, where the pick had exposed what seemed to be quartz veins—and not cellars in the suburbs, either, but in the very heart of the city; and forthwith stock would be issued and thrown on the market. It was small matter who the cellar belonged to—the "ledge" belonged to the finder, and unless the United States government interfered (inasmuch as the government holds the primary right to mines of the noble metals in Nevada—or at least did then), it was considered to be his privilege to work it. Imagine a stranger staking out a mining claim among the costly shrubbery in your front yard and calmly proceeding to lay waste the ground with pick and shovel and blasting powder! It has been often done in California. In the middle of one of the principal business streets of Virginia, a man "located" a mining claim and began a shaft on it. He gave me a hundred feet of the stock and I sold it for a fine suit of clothes because I was afraid somebody would fall down the shaft and sue for damages. I owned in another claim that was located in the middle of another street; and to show how absurd people can be, that

"East India" stock (as it was called) sold briskly although there was an ancient tunnel running directly under the claim and any man could go into it and see that it did not cut a quartz ledge or anything that remotely resembled one.

One plan of acquiring sudden wealth was to "salt" a wildcat claim and sell out while the excitement was up. The process was simple. The schemer located a worthless ledge, sunk a shaft on it, bought a wagon load of rich "Comstock" ore, dumped a portion of it into the shaft and piled the rest by its side, above ground. Then he showed the property to a simpleton and sold it to him at a high figure. Of course the wagon load of rich ore was all that the victim ever got out of his purchase. A most remarkable case of "salting" was that of the "North Ophir." It was claimed that this vein was a remote "extension" of the original "Ophir," a valuable mine on the "Comstock." For a few days everybody was talking about the rich developments in the "North Ophir." It was said that it yielded perfectly pure silver in small, solid lumps. I went to the place with the owners, and found a shaft six or eight feet deep, in the bottom of which was a badly shattered vein of dull, yellowish, unpromising rock. One would as soon expect to find silver in a grindstone. We got out a pan of the rubbish and washed it in a puddle, and sure enough, among the sediment we found half a dozen black, bullet-looking pellets of unimpeachable "native" silver. Nobody had ever heard of such a thing before; science could not account for such a queer novelty. The stock rose to sixty-five dollars a foot, and at this figure the world-renowned tragedian, McKean Buchanan, bought a commanding interest and prepared to quit the stage once more—he was always doing that. And then it transpired that the mine had been "salted"—and not in any hackneyed way, either, but in a singularly bold, barefaced and peculiarly original and outrageous fashion. On one of the lumps of "native" silver was discovered the minted legend, "TED STATES OF," and then it was plainly apparent that the mine had been "salted" with melted half dollars! The lumps thus obtained had been blackened till they resembled native silver, and were then mixed with the shattered rock in the bottom of the shaft. It is literally true. Of course the price of the stock at once fell to nothing, and the tragedian was ruined. But for this calamity we might have lost McKean Buchanan from the stage.

The "flush times" held bravely on. Something over two years before, Mr. Goodman and another journeyman printer had borrowed forty dollars and set out from San Francisco to try their fortunes in the new city of Virginia. They found the *Territorial Enterprise*, a poverty-stricken weekly journal, gasping for breath and likely to die. They bought it, type, fixtures, good-will, and all, for a thousand dollars, on long time. The editorial sanctum, news-room, press-room, publication office, bed-chamber, parlor, and kitchen were all compressed into one apartment, and it was a small one, too. The editors and printers slept on the floor, a Chinaman did their cooking, and the "imposing-stone" was the general dinner table. But now things were changed. The paper was a great daily, printed by steam; there were five editors and twenty-three compositors; the subscription price was sixteen dollars a year; the advertising rates were exorbitant, and the columns crowded. The paper was clearing from six to ten thousand dollars a month, and the "Enterprise Building" was finished and ready for occupation—a stately fireproof brick. Every day from five all the way up to eleven columns of "live" advertisements were left out or crowded into spasmodic and irregular "supplements."

The "Gould & Curry" company were erecting a monster hundred-stamp mill at a cost that ultimately fell little short of a million dollars. Gould & Curry stock paid heavy dividends—a rare thing, and an experience confined to the dozen or fifteen claims located on the "main lead," the "Comstock." The superintendent of the Gould & Curry lived, rent free, in a fine house built and furnished by the company. He drove a fine pair of horses which were a present from the company, and his salary was twelve thousand dollars a year. The superintendent of another of the great mines traveled in grand state, had a salary of twenty-eight thousand dollars a year, and in a lawsuit in after days claimed that he was to have had one percent of the gross yield of the bullion likewise.

Money was wonderfully plenty. The trouble was, not how

to get it—but how to spend it, how to lavish it, get rid of it, squander it.

FOR DISCUSSION

1. What evidence does Twain give to support his statement that "these were 'flush times' indeed"? Why was making money as easy as eating one's dinner? How do you explain Twain's last sentence "The trouble was, not how to get it—but how to spend it, how to lavish it, get rid of it, squander it"?
2. How did "striking it rich"—or the possibility of it—affect the attitude and behavior of the people of Virginia City? Would people today behave in much the same way? Tell why or why not.
3. At one point in this account Twain says, "Think of a city with not a solitary poor man in it!" At another he says, "These were nearly all 'wildcat' mines, and wholly worthless." How do you explain this seeming contradiction? Who had "real money"? Where did they get it?
4. Twain describes newspaper reporting in Virginia City as "lucrative." What do the "stories" describing new claims reveal about the standards of reporting in those "flush times"? From the information contained in this account, tell what you think the Virginia City newspaper was like and the purpose it served.
5. This account, like all those contained in *Roughing It*, was not written "on the spot" or at the time the events occurred. What techniques does Twain use to give the impression that it was, and that all the information was first-hand and accurate? Why is this account considered literature rather than journalism? Cite evidence from the work itself.

FOR COMPOSITION

1. In a short composition state the impression you gained of the town of Virginia City, its people, and its way of life. Try to convey what you think was the over-all mood of the time and place.
2. Accounts of the Comstock Lode and the part it played in the development of the West appear in most histories and encyclopedias. Read one or more of these accounts. Select the information you found most interesting and present it in two or three paragraphs. You might also present it orally to the class.

Learning the River

MARK TWAIN

Mark Twain began his apprenticeship to a Mississippi pilot in 1857 at the age of twenty-two. He was fairly well acquainted with this country, having worked as a typesetter for various printers and newspapers in most of the large cities. New adventures awaited him in South America, or so he thought.

What with lying on the rocks four days at Louisville and some other delays, the poor old *Paul Jones* fooled away about two weeks in making the voyage from Cincinnati to New Orleans. This gave me a chance to get acquainted with one of the pilots, and he taught me how to steer the boat, and thus made the fascination of river life more potent than ever for me.

It also gave me a chance to get acquainted with a youth who had taken deck passage[1]—more's the pity, for he easily borrowed six dollars of me on a promise to return to the boat and pay it back to me the day after we should arrive. But he probably died or forgot, for he never came. It was doubtless the former, since he had said his parents were wealthy and he only traveled deck passage because it was cooler.

I soon discovered two things. One was that a vessel would not be likely to sail for the mouth of the Amazon under ten or twelve years, and the other was that the nine or ten dollars

[1]*deck passage:* steerage passage

still left in my pocket would not suffice for so impossible an exploration as I had planned, even if I could afford to wait for a ship. Therefore it followed that I must contrive a new career. The *Paul Jones* was now bound for St. Louis. I planned a siege against my pilot, and at the end of three hard days he surrendered. He agreed to teach me the Mississippi River from New Orleans to St. Louis for five hundred dollars, payable out of the first wages I should receive after graduating. I entered upon the small enterprise of "learning" twelve or thirteen hundred miles of the great Mississippi River with the easy confidence of my time of life. If I had really known what I was about to require of my faculties, I should not have had the courage to begin. I supposed that all a pilot had to do was keep his boat in the river, and I did not consider that that could be much of a trick, since it was so wide.

The boat backed out from New Orleans at four in the afternoon, and it was "our watch" until eight. Mr. Bixby, my chief, "straightened her up," plowed her along past the sterns of the other boats that lay at the Levee,[2] and then said, "Here, take her; shave those steamships as close as you'd peel an apple." I took the wheel and my heart went down into my boots; for it seemed to me that we were about to scrape the side off every ship in the line, we were so close. I held my breath and began to claw the boat away from the danger, and I had my own opinion of the pilot who had known no better than to get us into such peril, but I was too wise to express it. In half a minute I had a wide margin of safety intervening between the *Paul Jones* and the ships, and within ten seconds more I was set aside in disgrace and Mr. Bixby was going into danger again and flaying me alive with abuse of my cowardice. I was stung but I was obliged to admire the easy confidence with which my chief loafed from side to side of his wheel and trimmed the ships so closely that disaster seemed ceaselessly imminent. When he had cooled a little he told me that the easy water was close ashore and the current outside, and therefore we must hug the bank up-stream, to get the benefit of the former, and stay well out down-stream, to take advantage of

[2] *Levee:* dike or wall which protects the banks from the flooding river and also serves as dock for ships

the latter. In my own mind I resolved to be a down-stream pilot and leave the up-streaming to people dead to prudence.[3]

Now and then Mr. Bixby called my attention to certain things. Said he, "This is Six-Mile Point." I assented. It was pleasant enough information but I could not see the bearing of it. I was not conscious that it was a matter of any interest to me. Another time he said, "This is Nine-Mile Point." Later he said, "This is Twelve-Mile Point." They were all about level with the water's edge; they all looked about alike to me; they were monotonously unpicturesque. I hoped Mr. Bixby would change the subject. But no, he would crowd up around a point, hugging the shore with affection, and then say: "The slack water ends here, abreast this bunch of China trees; now we cross over." So he crossed over. He gave me the wheel once or twice but I had no luck. I either came near chipping off the edge of a sugar-plantation, or I yawed[4] too far from shore and so dropped back into disgrace again and got abused.

The watch was ended at last, and we took supper and went to bed. At midnight the glare of a lantern shone in my eyes, and the night watchman said:

"Come, turn out!"

And then he left. I could not understand this extraordinary procedure; so I presently gave up trying to and dozed off to sleep. Pretty soon the watchman was back again, and this time he was gruff. I was annoyed. I said:

"What do you want to come bothering around here in the middle of the night for? Now, as like as not, I'll not get to sleep again to-night."

The watchman said:

"Well, if this ain't good, I'm blessed."

The "off-watch" was just turning in and I heard some brutal laughter from them, and such remarks as "Hello, watchman! ain't the new cub turned out yet? He's delicate, likely. Give him some sugar in a rag and send for the chambermaid to sing 'Rock-a-by Baby,' to him."

About this time Mr. Bixby appeared on the scene. Something like a minute later I was climbing the pilot-house steps

[3] *prudence:* common sense
[4] *yawed:* swerved off course

with some of my clothes on and the rest in my arms. Mr. Bixby was close behind, commenting. Here was something fresh—this thing of getting up in the middle of the night to go to work. It was a detail in piloting that had never occurred to me at all. I knew that boats ran all night but somehow I had never happened to reflect that somebody had to get up out of a warm bed to run them. I began to fear that piloting was not quite so romantic as I had imagined it was; there was something very real and worklike about this new phase of it.

It was a rather dingy night, although a fair number of stars were out. The big mate was at the wheel and he had the old tub pointed at a star and was holding her straight up the middle of the river. The shores on either hand were not much more than half a mile apart, but they seemed wonderfully far away and ever so vague and indistinct. The mate said:

"We've got to land at Jones's plantation, sir."

The vengeful spirit in me exulted. I said to myself, "I wish you joy of your job, Mr. Bixby; you'll have a good time finding Mr. Jones's plantation such a night as this, and I hope you never *will* find it as long as you live."

Mr. Bixby said to the mate:

"Upper end of the plantation, or the lower?"

"Upper."

"I can't do it. The stumps there are out of water at this stage. It's no great distance to the lower and you'll have to get along with that."

"All right, sir. If Jones don't like it, he'll have to lump it, I reckon."

And then the mate left. My exultation began to cool and my wonder to come up. Here was a man who not only proposed to find this plantation on such a night but to find either end of it you preferred. I dreadfully wanted to ask a question, but I was carrying about as many short answers as my cargo-room would admit of, so I held my peace. All I desired to ask Mr. Bixby was the simple question whether he was ass enough to really imagine he was going to find that plantation on a night when all plantations were exactly alike and all of the same color. But I held in. I used to have fine inspirations of prudence in those days.

Mr. Bixby made for the shore and soon was scraping it, just the same as if it had been daylight. And not only that but singing:

"Father in heaven, the day is declining," etc.

It seemed to me that I had put my life in the keeping of a peculiarly reckless outcast. Presently he turned on me and said:

"What's the name of the first point above New Orleans?"

I was gratified to be able to answer promptly, and I did. I said I didn't know.

"Don't *know*?"

This manner jolted me. I was down at the foot again, in a moment. But I had to say just what I had said before.

"Well, you're a smart one!" said Mr. Bixby. "What's the name of the *next* point?"

Once more I didn't know.

"Well, this beats anything. Tell me the name of *any* point or place I told you."

I studied awhile and decided that I couldn't.

"Look here! What do you start out from, above Twelve-Mile Point, to cross over?"

"I–I–don't know."

"You–you–don't know?" mimicking my drawling manner of speech. "What *do* you know?"

"I–I–nothing, for certain."

"By the great Cæsar's ghost, I believe you! You're the stupidest dunderhead I ever saw or ever heard of, so help me Moses! The idea of *you* being a pilot–*you*! Why, you don't know enough to pilot a cow down a lane."

Oh, but his wrath was up! He was a nervous man, and he shuffled from one side of his wheel to the other as if the floor was hot. He would boil awhile to himself and then overflow and scald me again.

"Look here! What do you suppose I told you the names of those points for?"

I tremblingly considered a moment and then the devil of temptation provoked me to say:

"Well to–to–be entertaining, I thought."

This was a red rag to the bull. He raged and stormed so (he was crossing the river at the time) that I judged it made him blind, because he ran over the steering-oar of a trading-scow. Of course the traders sent up a volley of red-hot profanity. Never was a man so grateful as Mr. Bixby was, because he was brimful and here were subjects who could *talk back*. He threw open a window, thrust his head out, and such an irruption followed as I never had heard before. The fainter and farther away the scowmen's curses drifted, the higher Mr. Bixby lifted his voice and the weightier his adjectives grew. When he closed the window he was empty. You could have drawn a seine[5] through his system and not caught curses enough to disturb your mother with. Presently he said to me in the gentlest way:

"My boy, you must get a little memorandum-book, and every time I tell you a thing, put it down right away. There's only one way to be a pilot and that is to get this entire river by heart. You have to know it just like ABC."

That was a dismal revelation to me, for my memory was never loaded with anything but blank cartridges. However, I did not feel discouraged long. I judged that it was best to make some allowances, for doubtless Mr. Bixby was "stretching." Presently he pulled a rope and struck a few strokes on the big bell. The stars were all gone now and the night was as black as ink. I could hear the wheels churn along the bank but I was not entirely certain that I could see the shore. The voice of the invisible watchman called up from the hurricane-deck:

"What's this, sir?"

"Jones's plantation."

I said to myself, "I wish I might venture to offer a small bet that it isn't." But I did not chirp. I only waited to see. Mr. Bixby handled the engine-bells and in due time the boat's nose came to the land, a torch glowed from the forecastle, a man skipped ashore, a darky's voice on the bank said: "Gimme de k'yarpet-bag, Mass' Jones," and the next moment we were standing up the river again, all serene. I reflected deeply awhile, and then said—but not aloud—"Well, the finding of that plantation was the luckiest accident that ever happened,

[5] *seine:* net

but it couldn't happen again in a hundred years." And I fully believed it *was* an accident, too.

By the time we had gone seven or eight hundred miles up the river, I had learned to be a tolerably plucky up-stream steersman, in daylight, and before we reached St. Louis I had made a trifle of progress in night work, but only a trifle. I had a note-book that fairly bristled with the names of towns, "points," bars, islands, bends, reaches, etc., but the information was to be found only in the note-book—none of it was in my head. It made my heart ache to think I had only got half of the river set down, for as our watch was four hours off and four hours on, day and night, there was a long four-hour gap in my book for every time I had slept since the voyage began.

My chief was presently hired to go on a big New Orleans boat and I packed my satchel and went with him. She was a grand affair. When I stood in her pilot-house I was so far above the water that I seemed perched on a mountain, and her decks stretched so far away, fore and aft, below me, that I wondered how I could ever have considered the little *Paul Jones* a large craft. There were other differences too. The *Paul Jones's* pilot-house was a cheap, dingy, battered rattletrap, cramped for room, but here was a sumptuous glass temple: room enough to have a dance in; showy red and gold window-curtains, an imposing sofa, leather cushions and a back to the high bench where visiting pilots sit to spin yarns and "look at the river," bright, fanciful "cuspidores" instead of a broad wooden box filled with sawdust, nice new oilcloth on the floor, a hospitable big stove for winter, a wheel as high as my head costly with inlaid work, a wire tiller-rope, bright brass knobs for the bells, and a tidy, white-aproned, black "texas-tender,"[6] to bring up tarts and ices and coffee during mid-watch, day and night. Now this was "something like," and so I began to take heart once more to believe that piloting was a romantic sort of occupation after all. The moment we were under way I began to prowl about the great steamer and fill myself with joy. She was as clean and as dainty as a drawing-room; when I looked down her long, gilded saloon,[7] it was like gazing through a

[6] *"texas-tender"*: attendant for the texas, or pilot-house
[7] *saloon:* main lounge

splendid tunnel; she had an oil-picture, by some gifted sign-painter, on every stateroom door; she glittered with no end of prism-fringed chandeliers; the clerk's office was elegant, the bar was marvelous, and the barkeeper had been barbered and upholstered at incredible cost. The boiler-deck (*i.e.*, the second story of the boat, so to speak) was as spacious as a church, it seemed to me, so with the forecastle, and there was no pitiful handful of deck-hands, firemen, and roustabouts down there but a whole battalion of men. The fires were fiercely glaring from a long row of furnaces and over them were eight huge boilers! This was unutterable pomp. The mighty engines—but enough of this. I had never felt so fine before. And when I found that the regiment of natty servants respectfully "sir'd" me, my satisfaction was complete.

When I returned to the pilot-house St. Louis was gone and I was lost. Here was a piece of river which was all down in my book but I could make neither head nor tail of it: you understand, it was turned around. I had seen it when coming up-stream but I had never faced about to see how it looked when it was behind me. My heart broke again, for it was plain that I had got to learn this troublesome river *both ways*.

The pilot-house was full of pilots, going down to "look at the river." What is called the "upper river" (the two hundred miles between St. Louis and Cairo, where the Ohio comes in) was low, and the Mississippi changes its channel so constantly that the pilots used to always find it necessary to run down to Cairo to take a fresh look when their boats were to lie in port a week, that is, when the water was at a low stage. A deal of this "looking at the river" was done by poor fellows who seldom had a berth and whose only hope of getting one lay in their being always freshly posted and therefore ready to drop into the shoes of some reputable pilot for a single trip, on account of such pilot's sudden illness or some other necessity. And a good many of them constantly ran up and down inspecting the river, not because they ever really hoped to get a berth but because (they being guests of the boat) it was cheaper to "look at the river" than stay ashore and pay board. In time these fellows grew dainty in their tastes and only infested boats that had an established reputation for setting good tables. All visiting pilots were useful, for they were always ready and willing, winter or summer, night or day, to go out in the yawl and help buoy the channel or assist the boat's pilots in any way they could. They were likewise welcomed because all pilots are tireless talkers when gathered together, and as they talk only about the river they are always understood and are always interesting. Your true pilot cares nothing about anything on earth but the river, and his pride in his occupation surpasses the pride of kings.

We had a fine company of these river inspectors along this trip. There were eight or ten, and there was abundance of room for them in our great pilot-house. Two or three of them wore polished silk hats, elaborate shirt-fronts, diamond breast-pins, kid gloves, and patent-leather boots. They were choice in their English, and bore themselves with a dignity proper to men of solid means and prodigious reputation as pilots. The others were more or less loosely clad, and wore upon their heads tall felt cones that were suggestive of the days of the Commonwealth.

I was a cipher in this august company and felt subdued, not to say torpid. I was not even of sufficient consequence to assist at the wheel when it was necessary to put the tiller hard down in a hurry; the guest that stood nearest did that when occasion required—and this was pretty much all the time, because of the crookedness of the channel and the scant water. I stood in a corner, and the talk I listened to took the hope all out of me. One visitor said to another:

"Jim, how did you run Plum Point, coming up?"

"It was in the night there, and I ran it the way one of the boys on the *Diana* told me; started out about fifty yards above the woodpile on the false point and held on the cabin under Plum Point till I raised the reef—quarter less twain[8]—then straightened up for the middle bar till I got well abreast the old one-limbed cottonwood in the bend, then got my stern on the cottonwood and head on the low place above the point, and came through a-booming—nine and a half."

[8] *quarter less twain:* the depth of the water at that point. On a sounding, or lead, line, used to measure depth, bits of leather called marks are placed at intervals. The first of these, which indicates two fathoms, is called mark twain.

"Pretty square crossing, ain't it?"

"Yes, but the upper bar's working down fast."

Another pilot spoke up and said:

"I had better water than that and ran it lower down; started out from the false point—mark twain—raised the second reef abreast the big snag in the bend and had quarter less twain."

One of the gorgeous ones remarked:

"I don't want to find fault with your leadsmen[9] but that's a good deal of water for Plum Point, it seems to me."

There was an approving nod all around as this quiet snub dropped on the boaster and "settled" him. And so they went on talk-talk-talking. Meantime, the thing that was running in my mind was, "Now, if my ears hear right, I have not only to get the names of all the towns and islands and bends, and so on by heart, but I must even get up a warm personal acquaintanceship with every old snag and one-limbed cottonwood and obscure wood-pile that ornaments the banks of this river for twelve hundred miles; and more than that, I must actually know where these things are in the dark, unless these guests are gifted with eyes that can pierce through two miles of solid blackness. I wish the piloting business was in Jericho and I had never thought of it."

At dusk Mr. Bixby tapped the big bell three times (the signal to land) and the captain emerged from his drawing-room in the forward end of the "texas," and looked up, inquiringly. Mr. Bixby said:

"We will lay up here all night, captain."

"Very well, sir."

That was all. The boat came to shore and was tied up for the night. It seemed to me a fine thing that the pilot could do as he pleased, without asking so grand a captain's permission. I took my supper and went immediately to bed, discouraged by my day's observations and experiences. My late voyage's note-booking was but a confusion of meaningless names. It had tangled me all up in a knot every time I had looked at it in the daytime. I now hoped for respite in sleep, but no, it reveled all through my head till sunrise again, a frantic and tireless nightmare.

[9] *leadsmen:* men who measure water depth

Next morning I felt pretty rusty and low-spirited. We went booming along, taking a good many chances, for we were anxious to "get out of the river" (as getting out to Cairo was called) before night should overtake us. But Mr. Bixby's partner, the other pilot, presently grounded the boat and we lost so much time getting her off that it was plain the darkness would overtake us a good long way above the mouth. This was a great misfortune, especially to certain of our visiting pilots, whose boats would have to wait for their return, no matter how long that might be. It sobered the pilot-house talk a good deal. Coming up-stream, pilots did not mind low water or any kind of darkness; nothing stopped them but fog. But down-stream work was different; a boat was too nearly helpless with a stiff current pushing behind her, so it was not customary to run down-stream at night in low water.

There seemed to be one small hope, however: if we could get through the intricate and dangerous Hat Island crossing before night, we could venture the rest, for we would have plainer sailing and better water. But it would be insanity to attempt Hat Island at night. So there was a deal of looking at watches all the rest of the day and a constant ciphering upon the speed we were making; Hat Island was the eternal subject; sometimes hope was high and sometimes we were delayed in a bad crossing and down it went again. For hours all hands lay under the burden of this suppressed excitement; it was even communicated to me and I got to feeling so solicitous about Hat Island, and under such an awful pressure of responsibility, that I wished I might have five minutes on shore to draw a good, full, relieving breath and start over again. We were standing no regular watches. Each of our pilots ran such portions of the river as he had run when coming up-stream, because of his greater familiarity with it, but both remained in the pilot-house constantly.

An hour before sunset Mr. Bixby took the wheel and Mr. W. stepped aside. For the next thirty minutes every man held his watch in his hand and was restless, silent, and uneasy. At last somebody said, with a doomful sigh:

"Well, yonder's Hat Island—and we can't make it."

All the watches closed with a snap, everybody sighed and muttered something about its being "too bad, too bad—ah, if we could *only* have got there half an hour sooner!" and the place was thick with the atmosphere of disappointment. Some started to go out but loitered, hearing no bell-tap to land. The sun dipped behind the horizon, the boat went on. Inquiring looks passed from one guest to another, and one who had his hand on the door-knob and had turned it, waited, then presently took away his hand and let the knob turn back again. We bore steadily down the bend. More looks were exchanged and nods of surprised admiration—but no words. Insensibly the men drew together behind Mr. Bixby, as the sky darkened and one or two dim stars came out. The dead silence and sense of waiting became oppressive. Mr. Bixby pulled the cord and two deep, mellow notes from the big bell floated off on the night. Then a pause, and one more note was struck. The watchman's voice followed, from the hurricane-deck:

"Labboard[10] lead, there! Stabboard[11] lead!"

The cries of the leadsmen began to rise out of the distance and were gruffly repeated by the word-passers on the hurricane-deck.

"M-a-r-k three! M-a-r-k three! Quarter-less-three! Half twain! Quarter twain! M-a-r-k twain! Quarter-less—"

Mr. Bixby pulled two bell-ropes and was answered by faint jinglings far below in the engine-room, and our speed slackened. The steam began to whistle through the gauge-cocks. The cries of the leadsmen went on—and it is a weird sound, always, in the night. Every pilot in the lot was watching now, with fixed eyes, and talking under his breath. Nobody was calm and easy but Mr. Bixby. He would put his wheel down and stand on a spoke, and as the steamer swung into her (to me) utterly invisible marks—for we seemed to be in the midst of a wide and gloomy sea—he would meet and fasten her there. Out of the murmur of half-audible talk one caught a coherent sentence now and then—such as:

"There; she's over the first reef all right!"

After a pause, another subdued voice:

[10]*Labboard:* (larboard) the port or left side of the ship as one faces the bow (front end)

[11]*Stabboard:* (starboard) the right side of the ship as one faces the bow

"Her stern's coming down just *exactly* right, by *George*! Now she's in the marks; over she goes!"

Someone else muttered:

"Oh, it was done beautiful—*beautiful*!"

Now the engines were stopped altogether and we drifted with the current. Not that I could see the boat drift, for I could not, the stars being all gone by this time. This drifting was the dismalest work; it held one's heart still. Presently I discovered a blacker gloom than that which surrounded us. It was the head of the island. We were closing right down upon it. We entered its deeper shadow, and so imminent seemed the peril that I was likely to suffocate, and I had the strongest impulse to do *something*, anything, to save the vessel. But still Mr. Bixby stood by his wheel, silent, intent as a cat, and all the pilots stood shoulder to shoulder at his back.

"She'll not make it!" somebody whispered.

The water grew shoaler[12] and shoaler by the leadsman's cries, till it was down to:

"Eight-and-a-half! E-i-g-h-t feet! E-i-g-h-t feet! Seven-and—"

Mr. Bixby said warningly through his speaking-tube to the engineer:

"Stand by, now!"

"Ay, ay, sir!"

"Seven-and-a-half! Seven feet! *Six*-and—"

We touched bottom! Instantly Mr. Bixby set a lot of bells ringing, shouted through the tube, "*Now*, let her have it—every ounce you've got!" then to his partner, "Put her hard down! snatch her! snatch her!" The boat rasped and ground her way through the sand, hung upon the apex of disaster a single tremendous instant, and then over she went! And such a shout as went up at Mr. Bixby's back never loosened the roof of a pilot-house before!

There was no more trouble after that. Mr. Bixby was a hero that night, and it was some little time, too, before his exploit ceased to be talked about by river-men.

Fully to realize the marvelous precision required in laying the great steamer in her marks in that murky waste of water,

[12]*shoaler:* shallower

one should know that not only must she pick her intricate way through snags and blind reefs, and then shave the head of the island so closely as to brush the overhanging foliage with her stern, but at one place she must pass almost within arm's reach of a sunken and invisible wreck that would snatch the hull timbers from under her if she should strike it—and destroy a quarter of a million dollars' worth of steamboat and cargo in five minutes, and maybe a hundred and fifty human lives into the bargain.

The last remark I heard that night was a compliment to Mr. Bixby, uttered in soliloquy[13] and with unction[14] by one of our guests. He said:

"By the Shadow of Death, but he's a lightning pilot!"

[13] *soliloquy:* a speech made to oneself
[14] *unction:* pronounced reverence

FOR DISCUSSION

1. Before Twain began to "learn the River" he thought of it as a small enterprise. Why? Years later he wrote, "If I had really known what I was about to require of my faculties, I should not have had the courage to begin." What faculties were required of a good riverboat pilot a hundred years ago? How does Twain's attitude toward the River and toward the pilots change during the course of his first lesson?
2. On the trip up-river, what does Twain do and say that arouses the scorn of the crew and the wrath of Mr. Bixby? By the time the boat reaches St. Louis, what impression do you gain of the character of Mr. Bixby and of his cub pilot, Twain? When Twain considers his notebook, why does it make his heart ache?
3. In the boom years before the Civil War, a luxury cruise on the Mississippi was as fashionable as an ocean cruise today. What features of the New Orleans boat impress Twain as "unutterable pomp"? How would they impress a modern traveler?
4. On the trip down-river, why does Twain have no choice but to stand in a corner? What picture does he create of the "august company" of pilots in the pilot-house? Why are they making the

trip? Why are they always welcome? When the boat ties up the first night, how does Twain feel? What causes him to feel that way?

5. The high point of this trip is the "intricate and dangerous Hat Island crossing." Why couldn't it be attempted at night? Discuss the difficulties and risks that Mr. Bixby faces, how they affect the pilots and the crew, and how Mr. Bixby proves himself a "lightning pilot."
6. Whether Twain was writing about real or imaginary people, he always dramatized them in such a way that they vividly revealed themselves. Discuss the ways in which he dramatizes Mr. Bixby. Point out not only the incidents which Twain includes but also the language he uses to describe Bixby or to make an observation about him.
7. Twain was the first American writer to use the vernacular at the level of art, as in sentences like this: "You could have drawn a seine through his system and not caught curses enough to disturb your mother with." Find other examples which represent the everyday language of the region and time and, in addition, contribute to the artistic effect of the entire literary work.

FOR COMPOSITION

At the end of his first trip from New Orleans to St. Louis and back, Twain had a great respect for Mr. Bixby. In a short composition point out the faculties which Mr. Bixby possessed and which you think Twain most admired.

STEFFENS AND MENCKEN

By 1880, the American scene had changed. It was now dominated by industry instead of agriculture; and with the expanded industrialism came accompanying urban evils, such as slums, sweat shops, starvation wages, and child labor. By the turn of the century, many Americans realized that nothing in the nation's history had adequately prepared her leaders to deal with these new problems of the overcrowded cities, where political corruption, filth, and squalor were familiar aspects of daily life for millions of citizens. Many of the more fortunate reacted in horror to these conditions and refused to face the fact that the quality and nature of the American environment had changed radically, that the old solutions of rural communities no longer applied to the new problems.

Before the problems could be attacked, however, they had to be identified. The job of pointing out where the major problems lay was assumed by a group of reporters soon derisively labeled the *muckrakers*. Foremost among the muckrakers was Lincoln Steffens, a belligerent reformer who made it his business to examine political corruption in the nation's cities. His discussion of Philadelphia is representative of his methods. The selection is taken from his famous study, *The Shame of the Cities*.

H. L. Mencken, whose major work appeared some twenty years after Steffens', seemed, like Steffens, a menace to self-satisfied Americans. Mencken attacked and ridiculed some of their most precious ideas and institutions; but he often delighted the many readers he did not scandalize. His vitriolic abuse was so extreme that few sophisticated readers found it necessary to identify themselves with the caricatures Mencken set up to knock over. Many, on the other hand, found his rhetoric exhilarating. In his way, he performed the useful function of shaking a few people out of their smugness and complacency.

Both Mencken and Steffens illustrate one way of coming to grips with the American scene. Finding the reality hopelessly inferior to the ideal, they sharply criticize existing conditions. Thus the idealistic element in their criticism should be recognized. The man who treasures ideals most fervently is the one who also objects most strenuously when reality does not match his vision. One way of paying homage to the ideal American scene is to attack the corrupted version of that ideal which the world of fact sometimes proves to be.

Philadelphia: Corrupt and Contented

LINCOLN STEFFENS

Other American cities, no matter how bad their own condition may be, all point with scorn to Philadelphia as worse—"the worst-governed city in the country." St. Louis, Minneapolis, Pittsburg submit with some patience to the jibes of any other community; the most friendly suggestion from Philadelphia is rejected with contempt. The Philadelphians are "supine," "asleep"; hopelessly ring-ruled, they are "complacent." "Politically benighted," Philadelphia is supposed to have no light to throw upon a state of things that is almost universal.

This is not fair. Philadelphia is, indeed, corrupt; but it is not without significance. Every city and town in the country can learn something from the typical experience of this great representative city. New York is excused for many of its ills because it is the metropolis, Chicago because of its forced development; Philadelphia is our "third largest" city and its growth has been gradual and natural. Immigration has been blamed for our municipal conditions; Philadelphia, with 47 per cent of its population native-born of native-born parents, is the most American of our greater cities. It is "good," too, and intelligent. I don't know just how to measure the intelligence of a community, but a Pennsylvania college professor who declared to me his belief in education for the masses as a way out of political corruption, himself justified the "rake-off" of preferred contractors on public works on the ground of a "fair business profit." Another plea we have made is that we are too busy to attend to public business, and we have promised, when we come to wealth and leisure, to do better. Philadelphia has long enjoyed great and widely distributed prosperity; it is the city of homes; there is a dwelling house for every five persons – men, women, and children, – of the population; and the people give one a sense of more leisure and repose than any community I have ever dwelt in. Some Philadelphians account for their political state on the ground of their ease and comfort. There is another class of optimists whose hope is in an "aristocracy" that is to come by and by; Philadelphia is surer that it has a "real aristocracy" than any other place in the world, but its aristocrats, with few exceptions, are in the ring, with it, or of no political use. Then we hear that we are a young people and that when we are older and "have traditions," like some of the old countries, we also will be honest. Philadelphia is one of the oldest of our cities and treasures for us scenes and relics of some of the noblest traditions of "our fair land." Yet I was told once, "for a joke," a party of boodlers[1] counted out the "divvy"[2] of their graft in unison with the ancient chime of Independence Hall.

Philadelphia is representative. This very "joke," told, as it was, with a laugh, is typical. All our municipal governments are more or less bad, and all our people are optimists. Philadelphia is simply the most corrupt and the most contented. Minneapolis has cleaned up, Pittsburg has tried to, New York fights every other election, Chicago fights all the time. Even St. Louis has begun to stir (since the elections are over), and at its worst was only shameless. Philadelphia is proud; good people there defend corruption and boast of their machine. My college professor, with his philosophic view of "rake-

[1] *boodlers:* those receiving bribes or taking money by graft
[2] *"divvy":* dividing the graft money

offs,"[3] is one Philadelphia type. Another is the man, who, driven to bay with his local pride, says: "At least you must admit that our machine is the best you have ever seen."

Disgraceful? Other cities say so. But I say that if Philadelphia is a disgrace, it is a disgrace not to itself alone, nor to Pennsylvania, but to the United States and to American character. For this great city, so highly representative in other respects, is not behind in political experience, but ahead, with New York. Philadelphia is a city that has had its reforms. Having passed through all the typical stages of corruption, Philadelphia reached the period of miscellaneous loot with a boss for chief thief, under James McManes and the Gas Ring 'way back in the late sixties and seventies. This is the Tweed stage of corruption from which St. Louis, for example, is just emerging. Philadelphia, in two inspiring popular revolts, attacked the Gas Ring, broke it, and in 1885 achieved that dream of American cities—a good charter. The present condition of Philadelphia, therefore, is not that which precedes, but that which follows reform, and in this distinction lies its startling general significance. What has happened since the Bullitt Law or charter went into effect in Philadelphia may happen in any American city "after reform is over."

For reform with us is usually revolt, not government, and is soon over. Our people do not seek, they avoid self-rule, and "reforms" are spasmodic efforts to punish bad rulers and get somebody that will give us good government or something that will make it. A self-acting form of government is an ancient superstition. We are an inventive people, and we think that we shall devise some day a legal machine that will turn out good government automatically. The Philadelphians have treasured this belief longer than the rest of us and have tried it more often. Throughout their history they have sought this wonderful charter and they thought they had it when they got the Bullitt Law, which concentrates in the mayor ample power, executive and political, and complete responsibility. Moreover it calls for very little thought and action on the part of the people. All they expected to have to do when the Bullitt Law went into effect was to elect as mayor a good business

[3] *"rake-offs"*: money taken illegally from city funds

man, who, with his probity and common sense, would give them that good business administration which is the ideal of many reformers.

The Bullitt Law went into effect in 1887. A committee of twelve—four men from the Union League, four from business organizations, and four from the bosses—picked out the first man to run under it on the Republican ticket, Edwin H. Fitler, an able, upright business man, and he was elected. Strange to say, his administration was satisfactory to the citizens, who speak well of it to this day, and to the politicians also; Boss McManes (the ring was broken, not the boss) took to the next national convention from Philadelphia a delegation solid for Fitler for President of the United States. It was a farce, but it pleased Mr. Fitler, so Matthew S. Quay, the State boss, let him have a complimentary vote on the first ballot. The politicians "fooled" Mr. Fitler, and they "fooled" also the next business mayor, Edwin S. Stuart, likewise a most estimable gentleman. Under these two administrations the foundation was laid for the present government of Philadelphia, the corruption to which the Philadelphians seem so reconciled, and the machine which is "at least the best you have ever seen."

The Philadelphia machine isn't the best. It isn't sound, and I doubt if it would stand in New York or Chicago. The enduring strength of the typical American political machine is that it is a natural growth—a sucker, but deep-rooted in the people. The New Yorkers vote for Tammany Hall. The Philadelphians do not vote; they are disfranchised,[4] and their disfranchisement is one anchor of the foundation of the Philadelphia organization.

This is no figure of speech. The honest citizens of Philadelphia have no more rights at the polls than the negroes down South. Nor do they fight very hard for this basic privilege. You can arouse their Republican ire by talking about the black Republican votes lost in the Southern States by white Democratic intimidation, but if you remind the average Philadelphian that he is in the same position, he will look

[4] *disfranchised:* denied the vote

startled, then say, "That's so, that's literally true, only I never thought of it in just that way." And it is literally true.

The machine controls the whole process of voting, and practices fraud at every stage. The assessor's list is the voting list, and the assessor is the machine's man. "The assessor of a division kept a disorderly house; he padded his list with fraudulent names registered from his house; two of these names were used by election officers. . . . The constable of the division kept a disreputable house; a policeman was assessed as living there. . . . The election was held in the disorderly house maintained by the assessor. . . . The man named as judge had a criminal charge for a life offense pending against him. . . . Two hundred and fifty-two votes were returned in a division that had less than one hundred legal votes within its boundaries." These extracts from a report of the Municipal League suggest the election methods. The assessor pads the list with the names of dead dogs, children, and non-existent persons. One newspaper printed the picture of a dog, another that of a little four-year-old negro boy, down on such a list. A ring orator in a speech resenting sneers at his ward as "low down" reminded his hearers that that was the ward of Independence Hall, and, naming the signers of the Declaration of Independence, he closed his highest flight of eloquence with the statement that "these men, the fathers of American liberty, voted down here once. And," he added, with a catching grin, "they vote here yet." Rudolph Blankenburg, a persistent fighter for the right and the use of the right to vote (and, by the way, an immigrant), sent out just before one election a registered letter to each voter on the rolls of a certain selected division. Sixty-three per cent were returned marked "not at," "removed," "deceased," etc. From one four-story house where forty-four voters were addressed, eighteen letters came back undelivered; from another of forty-eight voters, came back forty-one letters; from another sixty-one out of sixty-two; from another forty-four out of forty-seven. Six houses in one division were assessed at one hundred and seventy-two voters, more than the votes cast in the previous election in any one of two hundred entire divisions.

The repeating is done boldly, for the machine controls the election officers, often choosing them from among the fraudulent names; and when no one appears to serve, assigning the heeler ready for the expected vacancy. The police are forbidden by law to stand within thirty feet of the polls, but they are at the box and they are there to see that the machine's orders are obeyed and that repeaters whom they help to furnish are permitted to vote without "intimidation" on the names they, the police, have supplied. The editor of an anti-machine paper who was looking about for himself once told me that a ward leader who knew him well asked him into a polling place. "I'll show you how it's done," he said, and he had the repeaters go round and round voting again and again on the names handed them on slips.

FOR DISCUSSION

1. Steffens charges that Americans do not seek, but rather try to avoid, self-rule. Do you agree or disagree? Why? In Steffens' terms, how would those who really seek self-rule behave?
2. What reaction do you think greeted this article? In Philadelphia, at least, citizens were outraged at Steffens. If they were being systematically disfranchized, why would they be angry at the man who pointed out this fact?

FOR COMPOSITION

1. Do some research at city hall and then write an essay on voting procedures in your town. What safeguards exist to prevent corruption? What voting inequities exist in your town?
2. Write an "exposé" of some aspect of life in your home town. Remember that you must have *facts* to back up your statements. You may have to do some interviewing or research. For ideas, look through speeches delivered in your last mayoral or city council elections.

On Being an American

H. L. MENCKEN

It is, for example, one of my firmest and most sacred beliefs, reached after an inquiry extending over a score of years and supported by incessant prayer and meditation, that the government of the United States, in both its legislative arm and its executive arm, is ignorant, incompetent, corrupt, and disgusting—and from this judgment I except no more than twenty living lawmakers and no more than twenty executioners of their laws. It is a belief no less piously cherished that the administration of justice in the Republic is stupid, dishonest, and against all reason and equity[1]—and from this judgment I except no more than thirty judges, including two upon the bench of the Supreme Court of the United States. It is another that the foreign policy of the United States—its habitual manner of dealing with other nations, whether friend or foe—is hypocritical, disingenuous,[2] knavish, and dishonorable—and from this judgment I consent to no exceptions whatever, either recent or long past. And it is my fourth (and, to avoid too depressing a bill, final) conviction that the American

[1] *equity:* impartiality or fairness
[2] *disingenuous:* lacking innocence

people, taking one with another, constitute the most timorous, sniveling, poltroonish,[3] ignominious[4] mob of serfs and goose-steppers ever gathered under one flag in Christendom since the end of the Middle Ages, and that they grow more timorous, more sniveling, more poltroonish, more ignominious every day....

All of which may be boiled down to this: that the United States is essentially a commonwealth of third-rate men—that distinction is easy here because the general level of culture, of information, of taste and judgment, of ordinary competence is so low. No sane man, employing an American plumber to repair a leaky drain, would expect him to do it at the first trial, and in precisely the same way no sane man, observing an American Secretary of State in negotiation with Englishmen and Japanese, would expect him to come off better than second best. Third-rate men, of course, exist in all countries, but it is only here that they are in full control of the state, and with it of all the national standards. The land was peopled, not by the hardy adventurers of legend, but simply by incompetents who could not get on at home, and the lavishness of nature that they found here, the vast ease with which they could get livings, confirmed and augmented their native incompetence. No American colonist, even in the worst days of the Indian wars, ever had to face such hardships as ground down the peasants of Central Europe during the Hundred Years' War, nor even such hardships as oppressed the English lower classes during the century before the Reform Bill of 1832. In most of the colonies, indeed, he seldom saw any Indians at all: the one thing that made life difficult for him was his congenital dunderheadedness. The winning of the West, so rhetorically celebrated in American romance, cost the lives of fewer men than the single battle of Tannenberg, and the victory was much easier and surer. The immigrants who have come in since those early days have been, if anything, of even lower grade than their forerunners. . . .

The American Republic, as nations go, has led a safe and easy life, with no serious enemies to menace it, either within or without, and no grim struggle with want. Getting a living

[3] *poltroonish:* cowardly
[4] *ignominious:* humiliating, contemptible

here has always been easier than anywhere else in Christendom; getting a secure foothold has been possible to whole classes of men who would have remained submerged in Europe, as the character of our plutocracy, and no less of our *intelligentsia* so brilliantly shows. The American people have never had to face such titanic assaults as those suffered by the people of Holland, Poland and half a dozen other little countries; they have not lived with a ring of powerful and unconscionable[5] enemies about them, as the Germans have lived since the Middle Ages; they have not been torn by class wars, as the French, the Spaniards and the Russians have been torn; they have not thrown their strength into far-flung and exhausting colonial enterprises, like the English. All their foreign wars have been fought with foes either too weak to resist them or too heavily engaged elsewhere to make more than a half-hearted attempt. The combats with Mexico and Spain were not wars; they were simply lynchings. Even the Civil War, compared to the larger European conflicts since the invention of gunpowder, was trivial in its character and transient in its effects. The population of the United States, when it began, was about 31,500,000 – say 10 per cent under the population of France in 1914. But after four years of struggle, the number of men killed in action or dead of wounds, in the two armies, came to but 200,000 – probably little more than a sixth of the total losses of France between 1914 and 1918. Nor was there any very extensive destruction of property. In all save a small area in the North there was none at all, and even in the South only a few towns of any importance were destroyed. The average Northerner passed through the four years scarcely aware, save by report, that a war was going on. In the South the breath of Mars blew more hotly, but even there large numbers of men escaped service, and the general hardship everywhere fell a great deal short of the hardships suffered by the Belgians, the French of the North, the Germans of East Prussia, and the Serbians and Rumanians in the world war. The agonies of the South have been much exaggerated in popular romance; they were probably more severe during Reconstruction, when they were chiefly psychical,

[5] *unconscionable:* conscienceless

than they were during the actual war. Certainly General Robert E. Lee was in a favorable position to estimate the military achievement of the Confederacy. Well, Lee was of the opinion that his army was very badly supported by the civil population, and that its final disaster was largely due to that ineffective support. . . .

Turn, now, to politics. Consider, for example, a campaign for the Presidency. Would it be possible to imagine anything more uproariously idiotic—a deafening, nerve-wracking battle to the death between Tweedledum and Tweedledee, Harlequin and Sganarelle, Gobbo and Dr. Cook—the unspeakable, with fearful snorts, gradually swallowing the inconceivable? I defy any one to match it elsewhere on this earth. In other lands, at worst, there are at least intelligible issues, coherent ideas, salient[6] personalities. Somebody says something, and somebody replies. But what did Harding say in 1920, and what did Cox reply? Who was Harding, anyhow, and who was Cox? Here, having perfected democracy, we lift the whole combat to symbolism, to transcendentalism, to metaphysics. Here we load a pair of palpably tin cannon with blank cartridges charged with talcum powder, and so let fly. Here one may howl over the show without any uneasy reminder that it is serious, and that some one may be hurt. I hold that this elevation of politics to the plane of undiluted comedy is peculiarly American, that nowhere else on this disreputable ball has the art of the sham-battle been developed to such fineness. Two experiences are in point. During the Harding-Cox combat of bladders an article of mine, dealing with some of its more melodramatic phases, was translated into German and reprinted by a Berlin paper. At the head of it the editor was careful to insert a preface explaining to his readers, but recently delivered to democracy, that such contests were not taken seriously by intelligent Americans, and warning them solemnly against getting into sweats over politics. At about the same time I had dinner with an Englishman. From cocktails to Bromo-Seltzer he bewailed the political lassitude of the English populace—its growing in-

[6]*salient:* prominent

difference to the whole partisan harlequinade. Here were two typical foreign attitudes: the Germans were in danger of making politics too harsh and implacable, and the English were in danger of forgetting politics altogether. Both attitudes, it must be plain, make for bad shows. Observing a German campaign, one is uncomfortably harassed and stirred up; observing an English campaign (at least in times of peace), one falls asleep. In the United States the thing is done better. Here politics is purged of all menace, all sinister quality, all genuine significance, and stuffed with such gorgeous humors, such inordinate farce that one comes to the end of a campaign with one's ribs loose, and ready for "King Lear," or a hanging, or a course of medical journals.

FOR DISCUSSION

1. What is your reaction to Mencken's first sentence? Readers who grow annoyed with Steffens' articles find Mencken's both entertaining and amusing. Can you tell from the opening sentence why this might be so?
2. What pose does Mencken assume in this essay; that is, what kind of man does he seem to be? How does your opinion of him affect your opinion of what he says?
3. Do you see any truth in what Mencken says? Boil down Mencken's attacks into a well-considered, sane, objective statement of facts. Which would you rather read, his statements or the objective ones? Why?
4. What are the characteristics of Mencken's prose? What kind of vocabulary does he use? What kind of sentence structure does he favor? How is his writing organized?

FOR COMPOSITION

Pick an aspect of American life—or of your own life or routine—which particularly annoys you. Write a Menckenesque attack against it, remembering that your invective should depend for its force on a sophisticated, polysyllabic vocabulary, not on coarse abuse.

WOLFE AND THURBER

For some, the most vivid scenes of life remain those of childhood or adolescence, when a person responds with immediate and sensuous delight to the sights and sounds and tastes and smells which surround him. Such a man was Thomas Wolfe, who strove restlessly, until his death, to capture on paper all the marvels and sensations he remembered from his youth.

For others, such as James Thurber, childhood, adolescence, and even college were essentially painful times in which an awkward boy or adolescent struggled to survive with a shred of dignity. Fortunately, many learn to cope with such trials through a protective sense of humor. Fortunately for America, Thurber learned to express his sense of humor in writing, becoming one of the great American humorists.

Both Thurber and Wolfe define the American scene in terms of impressions they received when they were young. The scenes which are "typically American" are those in which they themselves played out the role of typical American boy, or typical American student. Their particular experiences, therefore, become representative of the experiences of most Americans.

Circus at Dawn

THOMAS WOLFE

There were times in early autumn—in September—when the greater circuses would come to town—the Ringling Brothers, Robinson's, and Barnum and Bailey shows, and when I was a route-boy on the morning paper, on those mornings when the circus would be coming in, I would rush madly through my route in the cool and thrilling darkness that comes just before break of day, and then I would go back home and get my brother out of bed.

Talking in low excited voices we would walk rapidly back toward town under the rustle of September leaves, in cool streets just grayed now with that still, that unearthly and magical first light of day which seems suddenly to rediscover the great earth out of darkness, so that the earth emerges with an awful, a glorious sculptural stillness, and one looks out with a feeling of joy and disbelief, as the first men on this earth must have done, for to see this happen is one of the things that men will remember out of life forever and think of as they die.

At the sculptural still square where at one corner, just emerging into light, my father's shabby little marble shop stood with a ghostly strangeness and familiarity, my brother and I would "catch" the first streetcar of the day bound for the "depot" where the circus was—or sometimes we would meet someone we knew, who would give us a lift in his automobile.

Then, having reached the dingy, grimy, and rickety depot section, we would get out, and walk rapidly across the tracks of the station yard, where we could see great flares and steamings from the engines, and hear the crash and bump of shifting freight cars, the swift sporadic thunders of a shifting engine, the tolling of bells, the sounds of great trains on the rails.

And to all these familiar sounds, filled with their exultant prophecies of flight, the voyage, morning, and the shining cities—to all the sharp and thrilling odors of the trains—the smell of cinders, acrid smoke, of musty, rusty freight cars, the clean pine-board of crated produce, and the smells of fresh stored food—oranges, coffee, tangerines and bacon, ham, and flour and beef—there would be added now, with an unforgettable magic and familiarity, all the strange sounds and smells of the coming circus.

The gay yellow sumptuous-looking cars in which the star performers lived and slept, still dark and silent, heavily and powerfully still, would be drawn up in long strings upon the tracks. And all around them the sounds of the unloading circus would go on furiously in the darkness. The receding gulf of lilac and departing night would be filled with the savage roar of the lions, the murderously sudden snarling of great jungle cats, the trumpeting of the elephants, the stamp of the horses, and with the musty, pungent, unfamiliar odor of the jungle animals: the tawny camel smells, and the smells of panthers, zebras, tigers, elephants, and bears.

Then, along the tracks, beside the circus trains, there would be the sharp cries and oaths of the circus men, the magical swinging dance of lanterns in the darkness, the sudden heavy rumble of the loaded vans and wagons as they were pulled along the flats[1] and gondolas,[2] and down the runways to the

[1] *flats:* flatcars

[2] *gondolas:* railroad cars with sides and ends, but without tops

ground. And everywhere, in the thrilling mystery of darkness and awakening light, there would be the tremendous conflict of a confused, hurried, and yet orderly movement.

The great iron-gray horses, four and six to a team, would be plodding along the road of thick white dust to a rattling of chains and traces and the harsh cries of their drivers. The men would drive the animals to the river which flowed by beyond the tracks, and water them; and as first light came, one could see the elephants wallowing in the familiar river and the big horses going slowly and carefully down to drink.

Then, on the circus grounds, the tents were going up already with the magic speed of dreams. All over the place (which was near the tracks and the only space of flat land in the town that was big enough to hold a circus) there would be this fierce, savagely hurried, and yet orderly confusion. Great flares of gaseous circus light would blaze down on the seared and battered faces of the circus toughs as, with the rhythmic precision of a single animal—a human riveting machine—they swung their sledges at the stakes, driving a stake into the earth with the incredible instancy of accelerated figures in a motion picture. And everywhere, as light came, and the sun appeared, there would be a scene of magic, order, and of violence. The drivers would curse and talk their special language to their teams, there would be the loud, gasping, and uneven labor of a gasoline engine, the shouts and curses of the bosses, the wooden riveting of driven stakes, and the rattle of heavy chains.

Already in an immense cleared space of dusty beaten earth, the stakes were being driven for the main exhibition tent. And an elephant would lurch ponderously to the field, slowly lower his great swinging head at the command of a man who sat perched upon his skull, flourish his gray, wrinkled snout a time or two, and then solemnly wrap it around a tent pole big as the mast of a racing schooner. Then the elephant would back slowly away, dragging the great pole with him as if it were a stick of matchwood. . . .

Meanwhile, the circus food tent—a huge canvas top without concealing sides—had already been put up, and now we could see the performers seated at long trestled tables underneath the tent, as they ate breakfast. And the savor of the food they ate—mixed as it was with our strong excitement, with the powerful but wholesome smells of the animals, and with all the joy, sweetness, mystery, jubilant magic and glory of the morning and the coming of the circus—seemed to us to be of the most maddening and appetizing succulence of any food that we had ever known or eaten.

We could see the circus performers eating tremendous breakfasts, with all the savage relish of their power and strength: they ate big fried steaks, pork chops, rashers[3] of bacon, a half-dozen eggs, great slabs of fried ham and great stacks of wheat cakes which a cook kept flipping in the air with the skill of a juggler, and which a husky-looking waitress kept rushing to their tables on loaded trays held high and balanced marvelously on the fingers of a brawny hand. And above all the maddening odors of the wholesome and succulent food, there brooded forever the sultry and delicious fragrance—that somehow seemed to add a zest and sharpness to all the powerful and thrilling life of morning—of strong boiling coffee, which we could see sending off clouds of steam from an enormous polished urn, and which the circus performers gulped down, cup after cup.

And the circus men and women themselves—these star performers—were such fine-looking people, strong and handsome, yet speaking and moving with an almost stern dignity and decorum, that their lives seemed to us to be as splendid and wonderful as any lives on earth could be. There was never anything loose, rowdy, or tough in their comportment. . . .

Rather, these people in an astonishing way seemed to have created an established community which lived an ordered existence on wheels, and to observe with a stern fidelity unknown in towns and cities the decencies of family life. There would be a powerful young man, a handsome and magnificent young woman with blond hair and the figure of an Amazon,[4]

[3]*rashers:* thin slices

[4]*Amazon:* a member of a legendary race of women warriors; used generally to describe a woman of great strength or size

and a powerfully built, thickset man of middle age, who had a stern, lined, responsible-looking face and a bald head. They were probably the members of a trapeze team – the young man and woman would leap through space like projectiles, meeting the grip of the older man and hurtling back again upon their narrow perches, catching the swing of their trapeze in mid-air, and whirling thrice before they caught it, in a perilous and beautiful exhibition of human balance and precision.

But when they came into the breakfast tent, they would speak gravely yet courteously to other performers, and seat themselves in a family group at one of the long tables, eating their tremendous breakfast with an earnest concentration, seldom speaking to one another, and then gravely, seriously, and briefly.

And my brother and I would look at them with fascinated eyes; my brother would watch the man with the bald head for a while and then turn toward me, whispering:

"D-d-do you see that f-f-fellow there with the bald head? W-w-well, he's the heavy man," he whispered knowingly. "He's the one that c-c-c-catches them! That f-f-fellow's got to know his business! You know what happens if he m-m-misses, don't you?" said my brother.

"What?" I would say in a fascinated tone.

My brother snapped his fingers in the air.

"Over!" he said. "D-d-done for! W-w-why, they'd be d-d-d-dead before they knew what happened. Sure!" he said, nodding vigorously. "It's a f-f-f-fact! If he ever m-m-m-misses it's all over! That boy has g-g-g-got to know his s-s-s-stuff!" my brother said. "W-w-w-why," he went on in a low tone of solemn conviction, "it w-w-w-wouldn't surprise me at all if they p-p-p-pay him s-s-seventy-five or a hundred dollars a week! It's a fact!" my brother cried vigorously.

And we would turn our fascinated stares again upon these splendid and romantic creatures, whose lives were so different from our own, and whom we seemed to know with such familiar and affectionate intimacy. And at length, reluctantly, with full light come and the sun up, we would leave the circus grounds and start for home.

And somehow the memory of all we had seen and heard that glorious morning, and the memory of the food tent with its wonderful smells, would waken in us the pangs of such a ravenous hunger that we could not wait until we got home to eat. We would stop off in town at lunchrooms and, seated on tall stools before the counter, we would devour ham-and-egg sandwiches, hot hamburgers, red and pungent at their cores with coarse, spicy, sanguinary[5] beef, coffee, glasses of foaming milk, and doughnuts, and then go home to eat up everything in sight upon the breakfast table.

[5] *sanguinary:* rare

FOR DISCUSSION

1. Many readers admire Thomas Wolfe's prose because he continually finds universal significance in ordinary, everyday events. He therefore makes the things a boy might notice seem extremely important and, by extension, makes all boys (or all people) important, too. Where in his selection can you find examples of this technique?
2. What other characteristics of Wolfe's prose do you notice? How, and where, does he use adjectives? Where do you find catalogues of articles? Why would Wolfe include such catalogues? Where does he evoke with particular vividness the sensual sensations of the boys?
3. What mood pervades "Circus at Dawn"? How does Wolfe sustain this mood? What attitude toward the circus does he convey?

FOR COMPOSITION

Describe a childhood scene you particularly like to remember. Try to convey a sense of the colors, sounds, and smells which you associate with the scene.

University Days

JAMES THURBER

I passed all the other courses that I took at my University, but I could never pass botany. This was because all botany students had to spend several hours a week in a laboratory looking through a microscope at plant cells, and I could never see through a microscope. I never once saw a cell through a microscope. This used to enrage my instructor. He would wander around the laboratory pleased with the progress all the students were making in drawing the involved and, so I am told, interesting structure of flower cells, until he came to me. I would just be standing there. "I can't see anything," I would say. He would begin patiently enough, explaining how anybody can see through a microscope, but he would always end up in a fury, claiming that I could *too* see through a microscope but just pretended that I couldn't. "It takes away from the beauty of flowers anyway," I used to tell him. "We are not concerned with beauty in this course," he would say. "We are concerned solely with what I may call the *mechanics* of flars." "Well," I'd say, "I can't see anything." "Try it just once again," he'd say, and I would put my eye to the microscope and see nothing at all, except now and again a nebulous[1] milky substance—a phenomenon of maladjustment. You were supposed to see a vivid, restless clockwork of sharply defined plant cells. "I see what looks like a lot of milk," I would tell him. This, he claimed, was the result of my not having adjusted the microscope properly, so he would re-adjust it for me, or rather, for himself. And I would look again and see milk.

I finally took a deferred pass, as they called it, and waited a year and tried again. (You had to pass one of the biological sciences or you couldn't graduate.) The professor had come back from vacation brown as a berry, bright-eyed, and eager to explain cell-structure again to his classes. "Well," he said to me, cheerily, when we met in the first laboratory hour of the semester, "we're going to see cells this time, aren't we?" "Yes, sir," I said. Students to right of me and to left of me and in front of me were seeing cells; what's more, they were quietly drawing pictures of them in their notebooks. Of course, I didn't see anything.

"We'll try it," the professor said to me, grimly, "with every adjustment of the microscope known to man. As God is my witness, I'll arrange this glass so that you see cells through it or I'll give up teaching. In twenty-two years of botany, I—" He cut off abruptly for he was beginning to quiver all over, like Lionel Barrymore, and he genuinely wished to hold onto his temper; his scenes with me had taken a great deal out of him.

So we tried it with every adjustment of the microscope known to man. With only one of them did I see anything but blackness or the familiar lacteal[2] opacity, and that time I saw, to my pleasure and amazement, a variegated constellation of flecks, specks, and dots. These I hastily drew. The instructor, noting my activity, came back from an adjoining desk, a smile on his lips and his eyebrows high in hope. He looked at my cell drawing. "What's that?" he demanded, with a hint of a squeal in his voice. "That's what I saw," I said. "You didn't,

[1] *nebulous:* formless
[2] *lacteal:* milk-like

you didn't, you *did*n't!" he screamed, losing control of his temper instantly, and he bent over and squinted into the microscope. His head snapped up. "That's your eye!" he shouted. "You've fixed the lens so that it reflects! You've drawn your eye!"

Another course that I didn't like, but somehow managed to pass, was economics. I went to that class straight from the botany class, which didn't help me any in understanding either subject. I used to get them mixed up. But not as mixed up as another student in my economics class who came there direct from a physics laboratory. He was a tackle on the football team; named Bolenciecwcz. At that time Ohio State University had one of the best football teams in the country, and Bolenciecwcz was one of its outstanding stars. In order to be eligible to play it was necessary for him to keep up in his studies, a very difficult matter, for while he was not dumber than an ox he was not any smarter. Most of his professors were lenient and helped him along. None gave him more hints, in answering questions, or asked him simpler ones than the economics professor, a thin, timid man named Bassum. One day when we were on the subject of transportation and distribution, it came Bolenciecwcz's turn to answer a question. "Name one means of transportation," the professor said to him. No light came into the big tackle's eyes. "Just any means of transportation," said the professor. Bolenciecwcz sat staring at him. "That is," pursued the professor, "any medium, agency, or method of going from one place to another." Bolenciecwcz had the look of a man who is being led into a trap. "You may choose among steam, horse-drawn, or electrically propelled vehicles," said the instructor. "I might suggest the one which we commonly take in making long journeys across land." There was a profound silence in which everybody stirred uneasily, including Bolenciecwcz and Mr. Bassum. Mr. Bassum abruptly broke this silence in an amazing manner. "Choo-choo-choo," he said, in a low voice, and turned instantly scarlet. He glanced appealingly around the room. All of us, of course, shared Mr. Bassum's desire that Bolenciecwcz should stay abreast of the class in economics, for the Illinois game, one of the hardest and most important of the season, was only a week off. "Toot, toot, too-tooooooot!" some student with a deep voice moaned, and we all looked encouragingly at Bolenciecwcz. Somebody else gave a fine imitation of a locomotive letting off steam. Mr. Bassum himself rounded off the little show. "Ding, dong, ding, dong," he said, hopefully. Bolenciecwcz was staring at the floor now, trying to think, his great brow furrowed, his huge hands rubbing together, his face red.

"How did you come to college this year, Mr. Bolenciecwcz?" asked the professor. "*Chuff*a chuffa, *chuff*a chuffa."

"M'father sent me," said the football player.

"What on?" asked Bassum.

"I git an 'lowance," said the tackle, in a low, husky voice, obviously embarrassed.

"No, no," said Bassum. "Name a means of transportation. What did you *ride* here on?"

"Train," said Bolenciecwcz.

"Quite right," said the professor. "Now, Mr. Nugent, will you tell us——"

If I went through anguish in botany and economics—for different reasons—gymnasium work was even worse. I don't even like to think about it. They wouldn't let you play games or join in the exercises with your glasses on and I couldn't see with mine off. I bumped into professors, horizontal bars, agricultural students, and swinging iron rings. Not being able to see, I could take it but I couldn't dish it out. Also, in order to pass gymnasium (and you had to pass it to graduate) you had to learn to swim if you didn't know how. I didn't like the swimming pool, I didn't like swimming, and I didn't like the swimming instructor, and after all these years I still don't. I never swam but I passed my gym work anyway, by having another student give my gymnasium number (978) and swim across the pool in my place. He was a quiet, amiable blonde youth, number 473, and he would have seen through a microscope for me if we could have got away with it, but we couldn't get away with it. Another thing I didn't like about gymnasium work was that they made you strip the day you registered. It is impossible for me to be happy when I am stripped and being asked a lot of questions. Still, I did better than a lanky agricultural student who was cross-examined just before I was.

Springfield rifles and studied the tactics of the Civil War even though the World War[3] was going on at the time. At 11 o'clock each morning thousands of freshmen and sophomores used to deploy over the campus, moodily creeping up on the old chemistry building. It was good training for the kind of warfare that was waged at Shiloh but it had no connection with what was going on in Europe. Some people used to think there was German money behind it, but they didn't dare say so or they would have been thrown in jail as German spies. It was a period of muddy thought and marked, I believe, the decline of higher education in the Middle West.

As a soldier I was never any good at all. Most of the cadets were glumly indifferent soldiers, but I was no good at all. Once General Littlefield, who was commandant of the cadet corps, popped up in front of me during regimental drill and snapped, "You are the main trouble with this university!" I think he meant that my type was the main trouble with the university but he may have meant me individually. I was mediocre at drill, certainly—that is, until my senior year. By that time I had drilled longer than anybody else in the Western Conference, having failed at military at the end of each preceding year so that I had to do it all over again. I was the only senior still in uniform. The uniform which, when new, had made me look like an inter-urban railway conductor, now that it had become faded and too tight made me look like Bert Williams in his bellboy act. This had a definitely bad effect on my morale. Even so, I had become by sheer practise little short of wonderful at squad manoeuvres.

One day General Littlefield picked our company out of the whole regiment and tried to get it mixed up by putting it through one movement after another as fast as we could execute them: squads right, squads left, squads on right into line, squads right about, squads left front into line etc. In about three minutes one hundred and nine men were marching in one direction and I was marching away from them at an angle of forty degrees, all alone. "Company, halt!" shouted General Littlefield, "That man is the only man who has it right!" I was made a corporal for my achievement.

[3] World War I

The next day General Littlefield summoned me to his office. He was swatting flies when I went in. I was silent and he was silent too, for a long time. I don't think he remembered me or why he had sent for me, but he didn't want to admit it. He swatted some more flies, keeping his eyes on them narrowly before he let go with the swatter. "Button up your coat!" he snapped. Looking back on it now I can see that he meant me although he was looking at a fly, but I just stood there. Another fly came to rest on a paper in front of the general and began rubbing its hind legs together. The general lifted the swatter cautiously. I moved restlessly and the fly flew away. "You startled him!" barked General Littlefield, looking at me severely. I said I was sorry. "That won't help the situation!" snapped the General, with cold military logic. I didn't see what I could do except offer to chase some more flies toward his desk, but I didn't say anything. He stared out the window at the faraway figures of co-eds crossing the campus toward the library. Finally, he told me I could go. So I went. He either didn't know which cadet I was or else he forgot what he wanted to see me about. It may have been that he wished to apologize for having called me the main trouble with the university; or maybe he had decided to compliment me on my brilliant drilling of the day before and then at the last minute decided not to. I don't know. I don't think about it much any more.

FOR DISCUSSION

1. The dialogue between Thurber and his botany instructor represents an age-old argument (one you may have participated in yourself) between the spokesmen for intuition and emotion, and the advocates of analysis and intellect. When reduced to an extreme, each point of view about the flower is equally shortsighted. What justification can you find for each position?
2. Assuming for the sake of argument that the sources of humor are usually either a desire for revenge or a need to assert one's superiority over another person, decide which motive dominates the narrator in this selection. Which dominates the reader? Did you find the piece amusing? If so, why? If not, why not?

3. The last sentence suggests the type of personality Thurber pretends to have in this essay, because the sentence is so pathetically and obviously untrue. What "image" of himself does Thurber project here? Why would this image be effective for the narrator of a humorous essay?

FOR COMPOSITION

Describe a flower, a poem, or a person from two viewpoints, each equally narrow and exclusive. First describe your object as the intuitive dreamer would, and then as the analytical, fact-dominated, scientific researcher would.

STEINBECK, BALDWIN, AND BUCKLEY

Scene is a vague word. It can suggest either a physical environment or a dominating psychological atmosphere. Thus, we readily speak of the literary scene, or the social scene, or the political scene. Writers who have discussed the "American scene" have by no means limited themselves to natural landscapes. They have also been interested in the landscape of the mind, and in determining whether, in particular regions, such a mental landscape is shared in common.

John Steinbeck tries in "The Texas of the Mind" to analyze the elements to be found in the image of the Texan. Because the Texan himself often believes in a stereotype of what Texans are like, the symbol of the Texan is powerful enough to control the behavior of Texans. Steinbeck attempts to explore the landscape of the Texas mind.

The scene James Baldwin explores in "My Dungeon Shook" is altogether different. Baldwin's concern is with the kind of scene created by prejudice, injustice, and discrimination. His concern is also to help his nephew cope with such forces. If Baldwin's observations are true, then the suggestions he offers his nephew can benefit anyone who has met injustice of any kind. The avenues to freedom which he describes can profitably be traveled by all. But if injustice, particularly racial discrimination, has been permitted to exist in America since the nation began, then the resentments and frustrations which result from such injustice remain an integral part of the American scene.

Another part of the American social scene is determined by American traditions. William F. Buckley, Jr., bewails the existence of one particular tradition—the assumption that a gentleman never calls attention to himself in public, particularly by making an unpleasant scene. Even on the revered subject of national tradition, it is possible in America to hear negative views. Perhaps such opposition is one of the better aspects of the American scene.

The Texas of the Mind

JOHN STEINBECK

Writers facing the problem of Texas find themselves floundering in generalities, and I am no exception. Texas is a state of mind. Texas is an obsession. Above all, Texas is a nation in every sense of the word. And there's an opening covey of generalities. A Texan outside of Texas is a foreigner. My wife refers to herself as the Texan that got away, but that is only partly true. She has virtually no accent until she talks to a Texan, when she instantly reverts. You would not have to scratch deep to find her origin. She says such words as yes, air, hair, guess, with two syllables—yayus, ayer, hayer, gayus. And sometimes in a weary moment the word ink becomes ank. Our daughter, after a stretch in Austin, was visiting New York friends. She said, "Do you have a pin?"

"Certainly, dear," said her host. "Do you want a straight pin or a safety pin?"

"Aont a fountain pin," she said.

I've studied the Texas problem from many angles and for many years. And of course one of my truths is inevitably canceled by another. Outside their state I think Texans are a little frightened and very tender in their feelings, and these qualities cause boasting, arrogance, and noisy complacency—the outlets of shy children. At home Texans are none of these things. The ones I know are gracious, friendly, generous, and quiet. In New York we hear them so often bring up their treasured uniqueness. Texas is the only state that came into the Union by treaty. It retains the right to secede at will. We have heard them threaten to secede so often that I formed an enthusiastic organization—The American Friends for Texas Secession. This stops the subject cold. They want to be able to secede but they don't want anyone to want them to.

Like most passionate nations Texas has its own private history based on, but not limited by, facts. The tradition of the tough and versatile frontiersman is true but not exclusive. It is for the few to know that in the great old days of Virginia there were three punishments for high crimes—death, exile to Texas, and imprisonment, in that order. And some of the deportees must have descendants.

Again—the glorious defense to the death of the Alamo against the hordes of Santa Anna is a fact. The brave bands of Texans did indeed wrest their liberty from Mexico, and freedom, liberty, are holy words. One must go to contemporary observers in Europe for a non-Texan opinion as to the nature of the tyranny that raised need for revolt. Outside observers say the pressure was twofold. The Texans, they say, didn't want to pay taxes and, second, Mexico had abolished slavery in 1829, and Texas, being part of Mexico, was required to free its slaves. Of course there were other causes of revolt, but these two are spectacular to a European, and rarely mentioned here.

I have said that Texas is a state of mind, but I think it is more than that. It is a mystique closely approximating a religion. And this is true to the extent that people either passionately love Texas or passionately hate it and, as in other religions, few people dare to inspect it for fear of losing their bearings in mystery and paradox. Any observations of mine can be quickly canceled by opinion or counter-observation. But I think there will be little quarrel with my feeling that Texas is one thing. For all its enormous range of space, climate, and physical appearance, and for all the internal squabbles, contentions, and strivings, Texas has a tight cohesiveness perhaps stronger than any other section of America. Rich, poor, Panhandle, Gulf, city, country, Texas is the obsession, the proper study, and the passionate possession of all Texans. Some years ago, Edna Ferber wrote a book about a very tiny group of very rich Texans. Her description was accurate, so far as my knowledge extends, but the emphasis was one of disparagement.[1] And instantly the book was attacked by Texans of all groups, classes, and possessions. To attack one Texan is to draw fire from all Texans. The Texas joke, on the other hand, is a revered institution, beloved and in many cases originating in Texas.

The tradition of the frontier cattleman is as tenderly nurtured in Texas as is the hint of Norman blood in England. And while it is true that many families are descended from contract colonists not unlike the present-day braceros, all hold to the dream of the longhorn steer and the unfenced horizon. When a man makes his fortune in oil or government contracts, in chemicals or wholesale groceries, his first act is to buy a ranch, the largest he can afford, and to run some cattle. A candidate for public office who does not own a ranch is said to have little chance of election. The tradition of the land is deep fixed in the Texas psyche. Businessmen wear heeled boots that never feel a stirrup, and men of great wealth who have houses in Paris and regularly shoot grouse in Scotland refer to themselves as little old country boys. It would be easy to make sport of their attitude if one did not know that in this way they try to keep their association with the strength and simplicity of the land. Instinctively they feel that this is the source not only of wealth but of energy. And the energy of Texans is boundless and explosive. The successful man with his traditional ranch, at least in my experience, is no absentee owner. He works at it, oversees his herd and adds to it. The energy, in a climate so hot as to be staggering, is also staggering. And the tradition of hard work is maintained whatever the fortune or lack of it.

The power of an attitude is amazing. Among other tendencies to be noted, Texas is a military nation. The armed

[1] *disparagement:* disapproval

forces of the United States are loaded with Texans and often dominated by Texans. Even the dearly loved spectacular sports are run almost like military operations. Nowhere are there larger bands or more marching organizations, with corps of costumed girls whirling glittering batons. Sectional football games have the glory and the despair of war, and when a Texas team takes the field against a foreign state, it is an army with banners.

If I keep coming back to the energy of Texas, it is because I am so aware of it. It seems to me like that thrust of dynamism which caused and permitted whole peoples to migrate and to conquer in earlier ages. The land mass of Texas is rich in recoverable spoil. If this had not been so, I think I believe the relentless energy of Texans would have moved out and conquered new lands. This conviction is somewhat borne out in the restless movement of Texas capital. But now, so far, the conquest has been by purchase rather than by warfare. The oil deserts of the Near East, the opening lands of South America have felt the thrust. Then there are new islands of capital conquest: factories in the Middle West, food-processing plants, tool and die works, lumber and pulp. Even publishing houses have been added to the legitimate twentieth-century Texas spoil. There is no moral in these observations, nor any warning. Energy must have an outlet and will seek one.

In all ages, rich, energetic, and successful nations, when they have carved their place in the world, have felt hunger for art, for culture, even for learning and beauty. The Texas cities shoot upward and outward. The colleges are heavy with gifts and endowments. Theaters and symphony orchestras sprout overnight. In any huge and boisterous surge of energy and enthusiasm there must be errors and miscalculations, even breach of judgment and taste. And there is always the non-productive brotherhood of critics to disparage and to satirize, to view with horror and contempt. My own interest is attracted to the fact that these things are done at all. There will doubtless be thousands of ribald failures, but in the world's history artists have always been drawn where they are welcome and well treated.

By its nature and its size Texas invites generalities, and the generalities usually end up as paradox—the "little ol' country boy" at a symphony, the booted and blue-jeaned ranchman in Neiman-Marcus, buying Chinese jades.

Politically Texas continues its paradox. Traditionally and nostalgically it is Old South Democrat, but this does not prevent its voting conservative Republican in national elections while electing liberals to city and county posts. My opening statement still holds—everything in Texas is likely to be canceled by something else.

Most areas in the world may be placed in latitude and longitude, described chemically in their earth, sky, and water, rooted and fuzzed over with identified flora and peopled with known fauna, and there's an end to it. Then there are others where fable, myth, preconception, love, longing, or prejudice step in and so distort a cool, clear appraisal that a kind of high-colored magical confusion takes permanent hold. Greece is such an area, and those parts of England where King Arthur walked. One quality of such places as I am trying to define is that a very large part of them is personal and subjective. And surely Texas is such a place.

I have moved over a great part of Texas and I know that within its borders I have seen just about as many kinds of country, contour, climate, and conformation as there are in the world saving only the Arctic, and a good north wind can even bring the icy breath down. The stern horizon-fenced plains of the Panhandle are foreign to the little wooded hills and sweet streams in the Davis Mountains. The rich citrus orchards of the Rio Grande valley do not relate to the sagebrush grazing of South Texas. The hot and humid air of the Gulf Coast has no likeness in the cool crystal in the northwest of the Panhandle. And Austin on its hills among the bordered lakes might be across the world from Dallas.

What I am trying to say is that there is no physical or geographical unity in Texas. Its unity lies in the mind. And this is not only in Texans. The word Texas becomes a symbol to everyone in the world. There's no question that this Texas-of-the-mind fable is often synthetic, sometimes untruthful, and frequently romantic, but that in no way diminishes its strength as a symbol.

FOR DISCUSSION

1. When you read about a character who speaks in dialect, what attitude do you take toward him? Why? What attitude toward Texas does Steinbeck convey in his first paragraph, when he concentrates on the Texas dialect? What does the fact suggest about dialect stories or jokes?
2. On which elements of the popular stereotype of Texans (and of Southerners) does Steinbeck rely in his essay? Why are stereotypes always unfair, even when they involve good qualities? Why do all of us accept some stereotypes without thinking? What are the advantages to be gained from using stereotypes? In this essay, is Steinbeck aware of the dangers, as well as the advantages, of stereotyping people? How do you know?
3. Steinbeck ends his essay by stating that the Texas-of-the-mind fable is a powerful symbol. How is the power of a symbol revealed? What is a symbol strong enough to do? Why is it necessary to recognize the symbols we respond to?

FOR COMPOSITION

Linguists assert that every individual, family, class, and neighborhood has its own dialect; dialects include not only a special pronunciation but also a particular vocabulary. How does your dialect differ from standard American? (Standard American is spoken only by radio and television broadcasters. Outside the studio, it usually sounds affected or pretentious.) Write a dialogue between yourself and your favorite television news commentator. Write your conversation in your own dialect.

My Dungeon Shook: Letter to My Nephew

JAMES BALDWIN

Dear James:

I have begun this letter five times and torn it up five times. I keep seeing your face, which is also the face of your father and my brother. Like him, you are tough, dark, vulnerable, moody —with a very definite tendency to sound truculent[1] because you want no one to think you are soft. You may be like your grandfather in this, I don't know, but certainly both you and your father resemble him very much physically. Well, he is dead, he never saw you, and he had a terrible life; he was defeated long before he died because, at the bottom of his heart, he really believed what white people said about him. This is one of the reasons that he became so holy. I am sure that your father has told you something about all that. Neither you nor your father exhibit any tendency towards holiness: you really *are* of another era, part of what happened when the Negro left the land and came into what the late E. Franklin Frazier called "the cities of destruction." You can only be destroyed

[1] *truculent:* ready to fight

by believing that you really are what the white world calls a *nigger.* I tell you this because I love you, and please don't you ever forget it.

I have known both of you all your lives, have carried your Daddy in my arms and on my shoulders, kissed and spanked him and watched him learn to walk. I don't know if you've known anybody from that far back; if you've loved anybody that long, first as an infant, then as a child, then as a man, you gain a strange perspective on time and human pain and effort. Other people cannot see what I see whenever I look into your father's face, for behind your father's face as it is today are all those other faces which were his. Let him laugh and I see a cellar your father does not remember and a house he does not remember and I hear in his present laughter his laughter as a child. Let him curse and I remember him falling down the cellar steps, and howling, and I remember, with pain, his tears, which my hand or your grandmother's so easily wiped away. But no one's hand can wipe away those tears he sheds invisibly today, which one hears in his laughter and in his speech and in his songs. I know what the world has done to my brother and how narrowly he has survived it. And I know, which is much worse, and this is the crime of which I accuse my country and my countrymen, and for which neither I nor time nor history will ever forgive them, that they have destroyed and are destroying hundreds of thousands of lives and do not know it and do not want to know it. One can be, indeed one must strive to become, tough and philosophical concerning destruction and death, for this is what most of mankind has been best at since we have heard of man. (But remember: *most* of mankind is not *all* of mankind.) But it is not permissible that the authors of devastation should also be innocent. It is the innocence which constitutes the crime.

Now, my dear namesake, these innocent and well-meaning people, your countrymen, have caused you to be born under conditions not very far removed from those described for us by Charles Dickens in the London of more than a hundred years ago. (I hear the chorus of the innocents screaming, "No! This is not true! How *bitter* you are!"—but I am writing this letter to *you*, to try to tell you something about how to handle *them*, for most of them do not yet really know that you exist. I *know* the conditions under which you were born, for I was there. Your countrymen were *not* there, and haven't made it yet. Your grandmother was also there, and no one has ever accused her of being bitter. I suggest that the innocents check with her. She isn't hard to find. Your countrymen don't know that *she* exists, either, though she has been working for them all their lives.)

Well, you were born, here you came, something like fifteen years ago; and though your father and mother and grandmother, looking about the streets through which they were carrying you, staring at the walls into which they brought you, had every reason to be heavyhearted, yet they were not. For here you were, Big James, named for me—you were a big baby, I was not—here you were: to be loved. To be loved, baby, hard, at once, and forever, to strengthen you against the loveless world. Remember that: I know how black it looks today, for you. It looked bad that day, too, yes, we were trembling. We have not stopped trembling yet, but if we had not loved each other none of us would have survived. And now you must survive because we love you, and for the sake of your children and your children's children.

This innocent country set you down in a ghetto in which, in fact, it intended that you should perish. Let me spell out precisely what I mean by that, for the heart of the matter is here, and the root of my dispute with my country. You were born where you were born and faced the future that you faced because you were black and *for no other reason*. The limits of your ambition were, thus, expected to be set forever. You were born into a society which spelled out with brutal clarity, and in as many ways as possible, that you were a worthless human being. You were not expected to aspire to excellence: you were expected to make peace with mediocrity. Wherever you have turned, James, in your short time on this earth, you have been told where you could go and what you could do (and *how* you could do it) and where you could live and whom you could marry. I know your countrymen do not agree with me about this, and I hear them saying, "You exaggerate." They do not know Harlem, and I do. So do you. Take no one's word for anything, including mine—but trust your experience. Know whence you came. If you know whence you came, there is really no limit to where you can go. The details and symbols of your life have been deliberately constructed to make you believe what white people say about you. Please try to remember that what they believe, as well as what they do and cause you to endure, does not testify to your inferiority but to their inhumanity and fear. Please try to be clear, dear James, through the storm which rages about your youthful head today, about the reality which lies behind the words *acceptance* and *integration.* There is no reason for you to try to become like white people and there is no basis whatever for their impertinent assumption that *they* must accept *you.* The really terrible thing, old buddy, is that *you* must accept *them.* And I mean that very seriously. You must accept them and accept them with love. For these innocent people have no other hope. They are, in effect, still trapped in a history which they do not understand; and until they understand it, they cannot be released from it. They have had to believe for many years, and for innumerable reasons, that black men are inferior to white men. Many of them, indeed, know better, but, as you will discover, people find it very difficult to act on what they know. To act is to be committed, and to be committed is to be in danger. In this case, the danger, in the minds of most white Americans, is the loss of their identity. Try to imagine how you would feel if you woke up one morning to find the sun shining and all the stars aflame. You would be frightened because it is out of the order of nature. Any upheaval in the universe is terrifying because it so profoundly attacks one's sense of one's own reality. Well, the black man has functioned in the white man's world as a fixed star, as an immovable pillar: and as he moves out of his place, heaven and earth are shaken to their foundations. You, don't be afraid. I said that it was intended that you should perish in the ghetto, perish by never being allowed to go behind the white man's definitions, by never being allowed to spell your proper name. You have, and many of us have, defeated this intention; and, by a terrible law, a terrible paradox, those innocents who believed that your imprisonment made them safe are losing their grasp of reality. But these men are your brothers—your lost, younger brothers. And if the word *integration* means anything, this is what it means: that we, with love, shall force our brothers to see themselves as they are, to cease fleeing from reality and begin to change it. For this is your home, my friend, do not be driven from it; great men have done great things here, and will again, and we can make America what America must become. It will be hard, James, but you come from sturdy, peasant stock, men who picked cotton and dammed rivers and built railroads, and, in the teeth of the most terrifying odds, achieved an unassailable and monumental dignity. You come from a long line of great poets, some of the greatest poets since Homer. One of them said, *The very time I thought I was lost, My dungeon shook and my chains fell off.*

You know, and I know, that the country is celebrating one hundred years of freedom one hundred years too soon. We cannot be free until they are free. God bless you, James, and Godspeed.

Your uncle,

James

FOR DISCUSSION

1. This public letter which Baldwin wrote to his nephew mentions some of the destructive elements of stereotypes. Why would accepting a negative stereotype about himself destroy an individual? Besides the stereotype of the Negro, what other negative racial, class, regional, or religious stereotypes are widely accepted in the United States? Do any of these stereotypes affect you? How?
2. Is it true that America has destroyed hundreds of thousands of lives which it doesn't want to know about? Why does "the innocence constitute the crime"? What kind of innocence is Baldwin referring to, and what kind of crime?
3. What does the line of poetry Baldwin quotes at the end of his letter mean? Do you detect a biblical allusion in this line? What dungeon does he refer to? What shakes the dungeon?

4. Test the epigram, "to act is to be committed, and to be committed is to be in danger." To what commitments could this epigram apply? Is it ever untrue? Is anyone ever completely uncommitted to anything? Is being completely uncommitted dangerous?
5. Why does Baldwin state that "we cannot be free until they are free"? Who does he mean by *we* and *they*? Why are the freedoms of the two groups dependent on each other?

FOR COMPOSITION

Write an essay analyzing the dangers and rewards of your strongest commitment.

Why Don't We Complain?

WILLIAM F. BUCKLEY, JR.

It was the very last coach and the only empty seat on the entire train, so there was no turning back. The problem was to breathe. Outside, the temperature was below freezing. Inside the railroad car the temperature must have been about 85 degrees. I took off my overcoat, and a few minutes later my jacket, and noticed that the car was flecked with the white shirts of the passengers. I soon found my hand moving to loosen my tie. From one end of the car to the other, as we rattled through Westchester County, we sweated; but we did not moan.

I watched the train conductor appear at the head of the car. "Tickets, all tickets, please!" In a more virile age, I thought, the passengers would seize the conductor and strap him down on a seat over the radiator to share the fate of his patrons. He shuffled down the aisle, picking up tickets, punching commutation cards. *No one addressed a word to him.* He approached my seat, and I drew a deep breath of resolution. "Conductor," I began with a considerable edge to my voice. . . . Instantly the doleful eyes of my seatmate turned tiredly from his newspaper to fix me with a resentful stare: what question could be so important as to justify my sibilant[1] intrusion into his stupor? I was shaken by those eyes. I am incapable of making a discreet fuss, so I mumbled a question about what time we were due in Stamford (I didn't even ask whether it would be before or after dehydration could be expected to set in), got my reply, and went back to my newspaper and to wiping my brow.

The conductor had nonchalantly walked down the gauntlet of eighty sweating American freemen, and not one of them had asked him to explain why the passengers in that car had been consigned to suffer. There is nothing to be done when the temperature *outdoors* is 85 degrees, and indoors the air conditioner has broken down; obviously when that happens there is nothing to do, except perhaps curse the day that one was born. But when the temperature outdoors is below freezing, it takes a positive act of will on somebody's part to set the temperature *indoors* at 85. Somewhere a valve was turned too far, a furnace overstocked, a thermostat maladjusted: something that could easily be remedied by turning off the heat and allowing the great outdoors to come indoors. All this is so obvious. What is not obvious is what has happened to the American people.

It isn't just the commuters, whom we have come to visualize as a supine[2] breed who have got on to the trick of suspending their sensory faculties twice a day while they submit to the creeping dissolution of the railroad industry. It isn't just they who have given up trying to rectify irrational vexations. It is the American people everywhere.

A few weeks ago at a large movie theatre I turned to my wife and said, "The picture is out of focus." "Be quiet," she answered. I obeyed. But a few minutes later I raised the point again, with mounting impatience. "It will be all right in a minute," she said apprehensively. (She would rather lose her eyesight than be around when I make one of my infrequent scenes.) I waited. It was *just* out of focus—not glaringly out, but out. My vision is 20-20, and I assume that is the vision, adjusted, of most people in the movie house. So, after hector-

[1] *sibilant:* hissed
[2] *supine:* passive

ing[3] my wife throughout the first reel, I finally prevailed upon her to admit that it *was* off, and very annoying. We then settled down, coming to rest on the presumption that: a) someone connected with the management of the theatre must soon notice the blur and make the correction; or b) that someone seated near the rear of the house would make the complaint in behalf of those of us up front; or c) that—any minute now—the entire house would explode into catcalls and foot stamping, calling dramatic attention to the irksome distortion.

What happened was nothing. The movie ended, as it had begun, *just* out of focus, and as we trooped out, we stretched our faces in a variety of contortions to accustom the eye to the shock of normal focus.

I think it is safe to say that everybody suffered on that occasion. And I think it is safe to assume that everyone was expecting someone else to take the initiative in going back to speak to the manager. And it is probably true even that if we had supposed the movie would run right through the blurred image, someone surely would have summoned up the purposive indignation to get up out of his seat and file his complaint.

But notice that no one did. And the reason no one did is because we are all increasingly anxious in America to be unobtrusive, we are reluctant to make our voices heard, hesitant about claiming our rights; we are afraid that our cause is unjust, or that if it is not unjust, that it is ambiguous; or if not even that, that it is too trivial to justify the horrors of a confrontation with Authority; we will sit in an oven or endure a racking headache before undertaking a head-on, I'm-here-to-tell-you complaint. That tendency to passive compliance, to a heedless endurance, is something to keep one's eyes on—in sharp focus.

I myself can occasionally summon the courage to complain, but I cannot, as I have intimated, complain softly. My own instinct is so strong to let the thing ride, to forget about it—to expect that someone will take the matter up, when the grievance is collective, in my behalf—that it is only when the provocation is at a very special key, whose vibrations touch

[3] *hectoring:* annoying

simultaneously a complexus[4] of nerves, allergies, and passions, that I catch fire and find the reserves of courage and assertiveness to speak up. When that happens, I get quite carried away. My blood gets hot, my brow wet, I become unbearably and unconscionably sarcastic and bellicose;[5] I am girded for a total showdown.

Why should that be? Why could not I (or anyone else) on that railroad coach have said simply to the conductor, "Sir"— I take that back: that sounds sarcastic—"Conductor, would you be good enough to turn down the heat? I am extremely hot. In fact, I tend to get hot every time the temperature reaches 85 degr—" Strike that last sentence. Just end it with the simple statement that you are extremely hot, and let the conductor infer the cause.

Every New Year's Eve I resolve to do something about the Milquetoast in me and vow to speak up, calmly, for my rights, and for the betterment of our society, on every appropriate occasion. Entering last New Year's Eve I was fortified in my resolve because that morning at breakfast I had had to ask the waitress three times for a glass of milk. She finally brought it— after I had finished my eggs, which is when I don't want it any more. I did not have the manliness to order her to take the milk back, but settled instead for a cowardly sulk, and ostentatiously refused to drink the milk—though I later paid for it— rather than state plainly to the hostess, as I should have, why I had not drunk it, and would not pay for it.

So by the time the New Year ushered out the Old, riding in on my morning's indignation and stimulated by the gastric juices of resolution that flow so faithfully on New Year's Eve, I rendered my vow. Henceforward I would conquer my shyness, my despicable disposition to supineness. I would speak out like a man against the unnecessary annoyances of our time.

Forty-eight hours later, I was standing in line at the ski repair store in Pico Peak, Vermont. All I needed, to get on with my skiing, was the loan, for one minute, of a small screwdriver, to tighten a loose binding. Behind the counter in the workshop were two men. One was industriously engaged in servicing the complicated requirements of a young lady at the head

[4]*complexus:* an intricate compound
[5]*bellicose:* war-like

of the line, and obviously he would be tied up for quite a while. The other—"Jiggs," his workmate called him—was a middle-aged man, who sat in a chair puffing a pipe, exchanging small talk with his working partner. My pulse began its telltale acceleration. The minutes ticked on. I stared at the idle shopkeeper, hoping to shame him into action, but he was impervious to my telepathic reproof and continued his small talk with his friend, brazenly insensitive to the nervous demands of six good men who were raring to ski.

Suddenly my New Year's Eve resolution struck me. It was now or never. I broke from my place in line and marched to the counter. I was going to control myself. I dug my nails into my palms. My effort was only partially successful:

"If you are not too busy," I said icily, "would you mind handing me a screwdriver?"

Work stopped and everyone turned his eyes on me, and I experienced that mortification I always feel when I am the center of centripetal shafts of curiosity, resentment, perplexity.

But the worst was yet to come. "I am sorry, sir," said Jiggs deferentially, moving the pipe from his mouth. "I am not supposed to move. I have just had a heart attack." That was the signal for a great whirring noise that descended from heaven. We looked, stricken, out the window, and it appeared as though a cyclone had suddenly focused on the snowy courtyard between the shop and the ski lift. Suddenly a gigantic army helicopter materialized, and hovered down to a landing. Two men jumped out of the plane carrying a stretcher, tore into the ski shop, and lifted the shopkeeper onto the stretcher. Jiggs bade his companion good-by, was whisked out the door, into the plane, up to the heavens, down—we learned—to a near-by army hospital. I looked up manfully—into a score of man-eating eyes. I put the experience down as a reversal.

As I write this, on an airplane, I have run out of paper and need to reach into my briefcase under my legs for more. I cannot do this until my empty lunch tray is removed from my lap. I arrested the stewardess as she passed empty-handed down the aisle on the way to the kitchen to fetch the lunch trays for the passengers up forward who haven't been served yet. "Would you please take my tray?" "Just a *moment*, sir!" she said, and marched on sternly. Shall I tell her that since she is headed for the kitchen *anyway,* it could not delay the feeding of the other passengers by more than two seconds necessary to stash away my empty tray? Or remind her that not fifteen minutes ago she spoke unctuously into the loudspeaker the words undoubtedly devised by the airline's highly paid public relations counselor: "If there is anything I or Miss French can do for you to make your trip more enjoyable, *please* let us—" I have run out of paper.

I think the observable reluctance of the majority of Americans to assert themselves in minor matters is related to our increased sense of helplessness in an age of technology and centralized political and economic power. For generations, Americans who were too hot, or too cold, got up and did something about it. Now we call the plumber, or the electrician, or the furnace man. The habit of looking after our own needs obviously had something to do with the assertiveness that characterized the American family familiar to readers of American literature. With the technification of life goes our direct responsibility for our material environment, and we are conditioned to adopt a position of helplessness not only as regards the broken air conditioner, but as regards the overheated train. It takes an expert to fix the former, but not the latter; yet these distinctions, as we withdraw into helplessness, tend to fade away.

Our notorious political apathy is a related phenomenon. Every year, whether the Republican or the Democratic Party is in office, more and more power drains away from the individual to feed vast reservoirs in far-off places; and we have less and less say about the shape of events which shape our future. From this alienation of personal power comes the sense of resignation with which we accept the political dispensations of a powerful government whose hold upon us continues to increase.

An editor of a national weekly news magazine told me a few years ago that as few as a dozen letters of protest against an editorial stance of his magazine was enough to convene a plenipotentiary[6] meeting of the board of editors to review policy. "So few people complain, or make their voices heard,"

[6]*plenipotentiary:* attended by all members

he explained to me, "that we assume a dozen letters represent the inarticulated views of thousands of readers." In the past ten years, he said, the volume of mail has noticeably decreased, even though the circulation of his magazine has risen.

When our voices are finally mute, when we have finally suppressed the natural instinct to complain, whether the vexation is trivial or grave, we shall have become automatons, incapable of feeling. When Premier Khrushchev first came to this country late in 1959 he was primed, we are informed, to experience the bitter resentment of the American people against his tyranny, against his persecutions, against the movement which is responsible for the great number of American deaths in Korea, for billions in taxes every year, and for life everlasting on the brink of disaster; but Khrushchev was pleasantly surprised, and reported back to the Russian people that he had been met with overwhelming cordiality (read: apathy), except, to be sure, for "a few fascists who followed me around with their wretched posters, and should be horsewhipped."

I may be crazy, but I say there would have been lots more posters in a society where train temperatures in the dead of winter are not allowed to climb to 85 degrees without complaint.

FOR DISCUSSION

1. Buckley cites two amusingly effective examples of a widespread American desire to be indistinguishable from everybody else. How widespread is this desire? Would commuters or theatergoers in Westchester County (a wealthy suburban area near New York City) feel this need any more acutely than others throughout the nation? How does the need manifest itself in your community?
2. Although essays deriding conformity are read by school children at almost every level, why do you think people continue to conform? Is there anything good to be said for conformity? for refusing to complain?

3. What is the other side of the coin Buckley describes? Do any people try desperately *not* to be like everybody else? What kinds of people try conscientiously to protest indignities they find around them? What do you think of such protesters?

HARRINGTON AND CARSON

There are other parts of the American scene that must evoke a deep sense of dissatisfaction. We know that our society, like every other society in history, has its defects and failures. This is no reason for discouragement or cynicism but rather for a determination to do better. But first we must know where, how, and why the failures have occurred.

Michael Harrington introduces us to a *social* disaster. The scene is New York City's Bowery, where human derelicts, most of them alcoholics, plumb the depths of degradation and self-destructiveness. Every sizable American city has its own Bowery, or "skid row," where men who have been defeated by life congregate. Harrington is one of the few well-known writers with the courage and compassion to explore this underworld at our very doorsteps and to describe unflinchingly what he has seen there. The following selection is a chapter from his book, *The Other America.*

Rachel Carson deals with another kind of disaster—the *destruction of the natural environment,* through ignorance, greed, or indifference. As much as any other writer of this generation, she has helped to awaken Americans to the disaster that awaits this nation unless we learn to live with our natural environment, instead of adopting the "easy" expedients of destroying, polluting, and upsetting the balance of nature. In this brief selection, taken from her book *Silent Spring,* Rachel Carson describes the havoc caused by the indiscriminate use of plant-killing chemicals on the sagebrush lands of our high western plains and the lower slopes of the adjoining Rocky Mountains.

The Poverty of the Bowery

MICHAEL HARRINGTON

Perhaps the bitterest, most physical and obvious poverty that can be seen in an American city exists in skid row among the alcoholics.

During 1951 and 1952, I lived on Chrystie Street, one block from the Bowery in New York. I was a member of the Catholic Worker group that had a house there. Beds were given out on a "first come, first served" basis; we had a bread line in the early morning that provided coffee and rich brown bread, and a soup line at noon; and hand-me-down clothes that readers of the newspaper sent in were distributed. Those of us who came to live at the Worker house accepted a philosophy of voluntary poverty. We had no money and received no pay. We shared the living conditions of the people whom we were helping: alcoholics and the mentally ill. We did not participate in the living hell of that area, for we were not tortured by alcoholism and we had chosen our lot. But we were close, very close, to that world. We could see its horror every day.

The Bowery today does not look as it did then. The elevated tracks of the Third Avenue El[1] have been dismantled,

[1]*El:* elevated train, part of the city subway system

and in time skid row may be driven to some other part of the city, particularly if the Third Avenue property values keep going up. Thus, some of the places I describe no longer exist. Yet that is mere detail, for the essential world of these impressions is still very much with us.

The Third Avenue El gave the Bowery a sort of surrealist character. A dirty, hulking structure, it was as derelict as the men who acted out their misery beneath it. Along both sides of the street were flophouses where a man could get a bed for a night. Each morning, someone had to go through, checking to see if anyone had died during the night. The liquor stores were there, of course, specializing in cheap wine.

The men and women of the Bowery usually drank wine, or sometimes beer or shots of cheap whisky. For those in the direst straits, obsessed by the need for alcohol, there was always canned heat. It is liquid alcohol, and it can be drunk after it is strained through a handkerchief or a stale piece of bread. It has the reputation of knocking a man out before doing serious damage to his nervous system. It is, I am told, tasteless, a method of reaching oblivion and not much else.

There were other businesses around. The second-hand stores were there so that the men could sell whatever they could scavenge or steal (sometimes from one another). They preyed on the misery of the place, and they were indispensable to it. There were a couple of restaurants where at night the derelicts fought to keep their eyes open so that they would not be thrown out; these were most depressing, garishly lighted places. And there were missions, called by some "Three Sixteens" because they so often had the scriptural quotation from John 3:16 over the door: "For God so loved the world that He sent His only begotten son. . . ." In warm weather the "Sallies"—Salvation Army lassies and men—would be out on the avenue.

Over the whole place there hung the smell of urine. The men lived out of doors when they didn't have money for a flop. Sometimes, in the winter, they passed out in the snow or crawled into a doorway. In the summer the stench from some of the favorite haunts was all but overpowering.

There is an almost typical face of the Bowery, or so it seemed to me. The men are dirty, and often their faces are caked with blood after a particularly terrible drunk. They wake up without knowing how they were hurt. Their clothes are ragged, ill-fitting, incongruous. Their trousers stink of the streets and of dried urine. And the human look is usually weak and afraid of direct and full contact with someone else's eyes.

In the summer the Bowery is at its best, if one can use such a word to describe a place of incredible physical and moral desolation. The men sit together and talk, or lounge along the walk in groups. They are capable of stripping the clothes from another alcoholic when he is passed out, yet their drinking is hardly ever solitary. If one of them is lucky enough to panhandle his way to a bottle, he will seek out friends and share his good fortune . . . .

Winter is a catastrophe. Life on skid row is lived out of doors, and the cold and the snow bring with them intense suffering. The men often get drunk enough to lie in the streets in the midst of a storm. The first time one sees a body covered with a light blanket of snow, stretched out on the sidewalk, the sight comes as a shock and a dilemma. Is the man dead or just drunk? Or worse, the habitués are so obsessed and driven that stealing goes on in the dead of winter, and a man who needs a drink will take the shoes of a fellow alcoholic in the middle of January.

The result, of course, is disease. There is a sort of war between the Bowery and the city hospitals. The ambulance drivers and attendants become cynical and inured to the sufferings of those who seem to seek their own hurt so desperately. The administrative staffs must worry about someone from skid row who wants a bed for a couple of nights and who tries to simulate delirium tremens.[2] The officials become angry when these men sell their blood in order to get enough money to drink—and then turn up in the hospital and need blood transfusions.

The end of the line for the Bowery is the hospital and potter's field. Indeed, the Emergency Room of a public hospital like Bellevue could be a study in itself. I remember a

[2]*delirium tremens:* hallucinations caused by the body's inability to absorb a large amount of alcohol

not untypical scene when I was up there with one of the men from the Catholic Worker. There were the alcoholics, the dazed old people, a Negro woman whose lip was hanging by a thread, the little children. One cannot blame the doctors or the administrators for the sickening, depressing atmosphere. That responsibility belongs to the city, whose charity is inadequately financed, maddening in its slowness, and bureaucratically inexplicable to the uneducated poor.

Who are the men and women of the Bowery?

They are different from almost all the other poor people, for they come from every social class, every educational background to be found in the United States. At the Catholic Worker I met newspapermen, a dentist, priests, along with factory workers and drifters from the countryside. This is the one place in the other America where the poor are actually the sum total of misfits from all of the social classes.

Yet there are some strange factors at work in producing the subculture of alcoholism. One met quite a few men of Irish-American extraction (a clear majority, it seemed to me), some Polish-Americans, some Negroes (skid row is not ideologically integrated, but it is usually too drunk to care about race), a few Italians. In the two years that I spent on the Bowery, meeting some hundreds of men and women, I don't think I ran into a single Jew.

When they "dried out," the alcoholics from the middle class used to talk about themselves much as the amateur, college-educated psychologist would speak. They understood their condition as having deep roots in their personal problems and attitudes. But the ones who came from working-class or farm backgrounds were, like the mentally disturbed poor generally, mystified by what had happened to them. If they were religious—and a good many we met at the Worker were Catholic—this meant that sobering up usually involved frantic self-accusation.

I remember talking to an elderly man whom I got to know at the Worker. He was neat, hard-working, and with a great deal of self-respect whenever he was sober. He would stay off alcohol for long periods, sometimes up to three months. During that time he would lead an orderly life marked by careful religious observances. Then, suddenly, he would go on a drinking bout for two or three weeks. Sometimes we would hear about him when he had been taken into a hospital. He would come back then, and the whole process would begin anew.

I was talking to him one evening about alcoholism. I tried to say that it was not something a man chose, that it was related to deep problems, and that it could not be banished by a mere act of the will, no matter how courageous an individual was. He was frantic in his disagreement with me. "We are this way because we want to be," he said. "We are committing a mortal sin by doing it, and we are going to Hell because of it."

Sometimes this self-hatred turned toward others. One day a man stumbled in off the street. He was a physical mess: there was caked blood on his face, his clothes stank, and he wore the semi-human, possessed look that comes at the end of a long, terrible drunk. He lurched in, and I went to help him. We got him bathed and shaved and DDT'd. (The battle against lice and bedbugs was never won at the Worker, but we tried.) In a couple of days, with sleep and regular food and some new hand-me-down clothes, he was in pretty good shape.

Two or three evenings after he came in, he was standing next to me, waiting to go in for dinner. A man came in from the street, his double of two or three days earlier. There were the same blood and clothes and obsessed face. When I went to help the newcomer, the first man said to me, "Why give a hand to that bum?" In his voice there was the passion of genuine self-hatred. When the Bowery sobers up for a day or two, it promises, it sobs, it recriminates against[3] itself. And so it goes, on and on.

Sometimes all this repressed emotion breaks out into a fist fight on the Bowery. If they were not so tragic, they might be funny. The violence is a ballet of mistakes, of drunken, sweeping, impossible punches. The men cannot really hurt each other with any calculation. The real danger is that a

[3]*recriminates against:* accuses

man will throw himself off balance when one of his roundhouse blows miscarries. The weakness and ineffectualness of the Bowery are summed up in these fights.

But then there come periods when the endless nights and days of drinking stop for a while. The sobering up is almost as horrible as the drunkenness itself. Sometimes at the Catholic Worker a man would wake with the shakes. His whole body would be trembling uncontrollably, and his face would be crumpled as if on the verge of tears. He would plead for one shot of whisky, just one, to get over the morning. It was a random risk, completely unpredictable, to answer his plea. There was no way of knowing when that one shot would actually work to tranquilize and make a day of sobriety possible, or when it would drive him out onto the street, and send him back to the world of drunkenness he had begun to flee.

Sometimes, the drying-out process would last for a week. I remember a woman who had been drunk, more or less continuously, for about three months. When she stopped and made it across the line of trembling and shaking, she was still like a caged tiger. She could not bear to sit still for more than a moment. She roamed the house for days on end.

Once they come back to the world of sobriety, the alcoholic poor face the problem of eating. Until then, their obsession is drink, and only drink. They subsist in the period of drunkenness off anything they can scavenge, including the waste in garbage cans, on food from missions, or from the cheap fare in one of the grimy restaurants of the neighborhood. When they become sober, there is a world to face, at least until the next drunk.

For the ones from middle-class families, there is the possibility of money from relatives or even of returning to a job. One of the men at the Catholic Worker when I was there is a successful magazine writer; I have seen his by-line over the years in some of the better publications. But for most of them, their working lives have been ruined by their drinking lives. They exist as a source of cheap labor for the dirty, casual jobs in the economic underworld.

"He went to the mountains" was one of the standard refrains on the Bowery. It meant that a man had taken a job as a dishwasher or janitor in one of the Catskill resorts. Employment agencies, quick to market human desperation, always had openings for such work. Usually, the job would last a couple of weeks, perhaps for a summer. Sometimes a man would stay off the bottle for the whole time. But he would find his way back to the Bowery with a pocketful of money and he would buy drinks for his cronies for a couple of days. And then he would be exactly where he started.

One of the most tragic of these stories was told to me by the late brilliant cameraman who filmed *On the Bowery.* One of the "stars" of that picture was a Bowery habitué who had been around the Catholic Worker when I was there. During the filming of the movie he stayed off alcohol. Finally, when it was over, he had to be paid. The people who produced the film knew what might happen when he got the money—and they also knew that a doctor had told the man that one more serious binge and he would probably die. Yet he had worked, and they had no choice but to pay him. He took the money, drank, and died.

Though all this takes place in the middle of New York City, it is hardly noticed. It is a form of poverty, of social disintegration, that does not attract sympathy. People get moral when they talk about alcoholics, and the very language is loaded against such unfortunates. (I have not used the word "bum" since I went to the Catholic Worker; it is part of the vocabulary of not caring.) And since alcoholic poverty is so immediately and deeply a matter of personality, dealing with it requires a most massive effort. One hardly knows where to begin.

But, of course, nothing is being done, really. For sheer callousness and cynicism, I have never seen anything to rival the attitudes of the tourists and the police. Just below Houston on the Bowery was a place called Sammy's Bowery Follies (I don't know if it is still there; I hope not). It has been written up in magazines, and it is designed for tourists. The gimmick is that it is an old-fashioned Bowery Bar with Nineties bartenders and laughing, painted women who are fixtures of the place. On an evening, well-dressed tourists would arrive there, walking through a couple of rows of human misery, sometimes responding to a panhandler's plea with *noblesse oblige*. They were within a few feet of desperation and degradation, yet they seemed to find it "interesting" and "quaint." This is a small, if radical, case of the invisibility of the poor.

But even more vicious was the police pickup.

I never understood how the exact number to be arrested was computed, but there must have been some method to this social madness. The paddy wagon would arrive on the Bowery; the police would arrest the first men they came to, at random; and that was that. At night, in the drama of dereliction and indifference called Night Court in New York, the alcoholics would be lined up. Sometimes they were still drunk. The magistrate would tell them of their legal rights; they would usually plead guilty, and they would be sentenced. Some of the older men would have been through this time and time again. It was a social ritual, having no apparent effect on anything. It furnished, I suppose, statistics to prove that the authorities were doing their duty, that they were coping with the problem.

These alcoholics will probably be left to themselves for a long while. Though their spiritual torment is well known by most Americans, what is not understood is the grim, terrible, physically debilitating life of the alcoholic: the fact that these people are poor.

Let me end this description with a sad incident, for this is the proper note for an impression such as this.

About six months after I had left the Catholic Worker, I had come back one evening to see some friends and to talk. I had a job, and had begun to build up the wardrobe that had been stolen from me when I first came to Chrystie Street. (The voluntary poverty of the Worker is made real by the fact that if you stay for six months, all your property will be taken anyway.) I had on a fairly decent suit, and I was standing in the back yard with a couple of men I knew from the Bowery. One of them said to me, while the other nodded agreement: "We wondered when you would wise up, Mike. Hanging around here, helping us, that's nothing. Only nuts would do it. It's good you're wised up and going someplace." They were happy that I had left. They couldn't understand why anyone would want to care for them.

FOR DISCUSSION

1. What factors might give rise to alcoholism? Why might one race or nationality be more prone to alcoholism than another?
2. Why would a habitual alcoholic rather think he had committed a mortal sin and was bound for Hell than think that alcoholism is a deep-seated emotional problem which cannot be solved through an act of will or courage? Why is the latter a much more awful suggestion to him than the former?
3. Harrington remarks on the self-hatred of the Bowery drunks. What causes might lie behind such self-loathing? Could a community or a society ever cause these emotions in an individual? Could a community or society prevent them? Where should the responsibility lie for such emotional tragedies?
4. What do you think Harrington means by "the invisibility of the poor"? What does the phrase suggest about the wealthy?
5. This article makes clear that the police are ineffectual in dealing with the problems of the Bowery. Why? What course of action do you think might be more promising?
6. What do you think of Harrington's last anecdote? Why would anyone want to care for the alcoholics?

FOR COMPOSITION

Write an essay explaining why you think it does, or does not, matter what happens to alcoholics.

Earth's Green Mantle

RACHEL CARSON

Water, soil, and the earth's green mantle of plants make up the world that supports the animal life of the earth. Although modern man seldom remembers the fact, he could not exist without the plants that harness the sun's energy and manufacture the basic foodstuffs he depends on for life. Our attitude toward plants is a singularly narrow one. If we see any immediate utility in a plant we foster it. If for any reason we find its presence undesirable or merely a matter of indifference, we may condemn it to destruction forthwith.[1] Besides the various plants that are poisonous to man or his livestock, or crowd out food plants, many are marked for destruction merely because according to our narrow view, they happen to be in the wrong place at the wrong time. Many others are destroyed merely because they happen to be associates of the unwanted plants.

The earth's vegetation is part of a web of life in which there are intimate and essential relations between plants and the earth, between plants and other plants, between plants

[1] *forthwith:* immediately

and animals. Sometimes we have no choice but to disturb these relationships, but we should do so thoughtfully, with full awareness that what we do may have consequences remote in time and place. But no such humility marks the booming "weed killer" business of the present day, in which soaring sales and expanding uses mark the production of plant-killing chemicals.

One of the most tragic examples of our unthinking bludgeoning[2] of the landscape is to be seen in the sagebrush lands of the West, where a vast campaign is on to destroy the sage and to substitute grasslands. If ever an enterprise needed to be illuminated with a sense of the history and meaning of the landscape, it is this. For here the natural landscape is eloquent of the interplay of forces that have created it. It is spread before us like the pages of an open book in which we can read why the land is what it is, and why we should preserve its integrity. But the pages lie unread.

The land of the sage is the land of the high western plains and the lower slopes of the mountains that rise above them, a land born of the great uplift of the Rocky Mountain system many millions of years ago. It is a place of harsh extremes of climate: of long winters when blizzards drive down from the mountains and snow lies deep on the plains, of summers whose heat is relieved by only scanty rains, with drought biting deep into the soil, and drying winds stealing moisture from leaf and stem.

As the landscape evolved, there must have been a long period of trial and error in which plants attempted the colonization of this high and windswept land. One after another must have failed. At last one group of plants evolved which combined all the qualities needed to survive. The sage—low-growing and shrubby—could hold its place on the mountain slopes and on the plains, and within its small gray leaves it could hold moisture enough to defy the thieving winds. It was no accident, but rather the result of long ages of experimentation by nature, that the great plains of the West became the land of the sage.

2 *bludgeoning:* violent, unthinking attack

Along with the plants, animal life, too, was evolving in harmony with the searching requirements of the land. In time there were two as perfectly adjusted to their habitat as the sage. One was a mammal, the fleet and graceful pronghorn antelope. The other was a bird, the sage grouse—the "cock of the plains" of Lewis and Clark.[3]

The sage and the grouse seem made for each other. The original range of the bird coincided with the range of the sage, and as the sagelands have been reduced, so the populations of grouse have dwindled. The sage is all things to these birds of the plains. The low sage of the foothill ranges shelters their nests and their young; the denser growths are loafing and roosting areas; at all times the sage provides the staple food of the grouse. Yet it is a two-way relationship. The spectacular courtship displays of the cocks help loosen the soil beneath and around the sage, aiding invasion by grasses which grow in the shelter of sagebrush.

The antelope, too, have adjusted their lives to the sage. They are primarily animals of the plains, and in winter when the first snows come those that have summered in the mountains move down to the lower elevations. There the sage provides the food that tides them over the winter. Where all other plants have shed their leaves, the sage remains evergreen, the gray-green leaves—bitter, aromatic, rich in proteins, fats, and needed minerals—clinging to the stems of the dense and shrubby plants. Though the snows pile up, the tops of the sage remain exposed, or can be reached by the sharp, pawing hoofs of the antelope. Then grouse feed on them too, finding them on bare and windswept ledges or following the antelope to feed where they have scratched away the snow.

And other life looks to the sage. Mule deer often feed on it. Sage may mean survival for winter-grazing livestock. Sheep graze many winter ranges where the big sagebrush forms almost pure stands. For half the year it is their principal forage, a plant of higher energy value than even alfalfa hay.

[3] *Lewis and Clark:* leaders of an epoch-making expedition that explored the Louisiana Territory, from the Mississippi to the Rocky Mountains, and then pushed westward to the Pacific (1804-06)

The bitter upland plains, the purple wastes of sage, the wild, swift antelope, and the grouse are then a natural system in perfect balance. Are? The verb must be changed—at least in those already vast and growing areas where man is attempting to improve on nature's way. In the name of progress the land management agencies have set about to satisfy the insatiable[4] demands of the cattlemen for more grazing land. By this they mean grassland—grass without sage. So in a land which nature found suited to grass growing mixed with and under the shelter of sage, it is now proposed to eliminate the sage and create unbroken grassland. Few seem to have asked whether grasslands are a stable and desirable goal in this region. Certainly nature's own answer was otherwise. The annual precipitation in this land where the rains seldom fall is not enough to support good sod-forming grass; it favors rather the perennial bunch-grass that grows in the shelter of the sage.

Yet the program of sage eradication has been under way for a number of years. Several government agencies are active in it; industry has joined with enthusiasm to promote and encourage an enterprise which creates expanded markets not only for grass seed but for a large assortment of machines for cutting and plowing and seeding. The newest addition to the weapons is the use of chemical sprays. Now millions of acres of sagebrush lands are sprayed each year.

What are the results? The eventual effects of eliminating sage and seeding with grass are largely conjectural.[5] Men of long experience with the ways of the land say that in this country there is better growth of grass between and under the sage than can possibly be had in pure stands, once the moisture-holding sage is gone.

But even if the program succeeds in its immediate objective, it is clear that the whole closely knit fabric of life has been ripped apart. The antelope and the grouse will disappear along with the sage. The deer will suffer, too, and the

[4] *insatiable:* incapable of being satisfied
[5] *conjectural:* arrived at by surmise or guesswork

land will be poorer for the destruction of the wild things that belong to it. Even the livestock which are the intended beneficiaries will suffer; no amount of lush green grass in summer can help the sheep starving in the winter storms for lack of the sage and bitterbrush and other wild vegetation of the plains.

These are the first and obvious effects. The second is of a kind that is always associated with the shotgun approach to nature: the spraying also eliminates a great many plants that were not its intended target. Justice William O. Douglas, in his recent book *My Wilderness: East to Katahdin,* has told of an appalling example of ecological destruction wrought by the United States Forest Service in the Bridger National Forest in Wyoming. Some 10,000 acres of sagelands were sprayed by the Service, yielding to pressure of cattlemen for more grasslands. The sage was killed, as intended. But so was the green, life-giving ribbon of willows that traced its way across these plains, following the meandering streams. Moose had lived in these willow thickets, for willow is to the moose what sage is to the antelope. Beaver had lived there, too, feeding on the willows, felling them and making a strong dam across the tiny stream. Through the labor of the beavers, a lake backed up. Trout in the mountain streams seldom were more than six inches long; in the lake they thrived so prodigiously[6] that many grew to five pounds. Waterfowl were attracted to the lake, also. Merely because of the presence of the willows and the beavers that depended on them, the region was an attractive recreational area with excellent fishing and hunting.

But with the "improvement" instituted by the Forest Service, the willows went the way of the sagebrush, killed by the same impartial spray. When Justice Douglas visited the area in 1959, the year of the spraying, he was shocked to see the shriveled and dying willows—the "vast, incredible damage." What would become of the moose? Of the beavers and the little world they had constructed? A year later he re-

[6] ***prodigiously:*** on a very large scale

turned to read the answers in the devastated landscape. The moose were gone and so were the beaver. Their principal dam had gone out for want of attention by its skilled architects, and the lake had drained away. None of the large trout were left. None could live in the tiny creek that remained, threading its way through a bare, hot land where no shade remained. The living world was shattered.

FOR DISCUSSION

1. Give examples of the author's statement that we tend to destroy any plant which "according to our narrow view (happens) to be in the wrong place at the wrong time."
2. The web of life is one of the basic concepts of biology. What does it mean? Why does the author think that we might disturb such a relationship only when it is absolutely necessary and then with great care and awareness of the possible consequences?
3. Explain how the sagebrush is naturally adapted to the conditions prevailing in the high western plains of the United States.
4. The author mentions two animals that are beautifully adapted to the sagebrush environment. What are they? Explain the nature of the adaptation in each case.
5. How have people been disturbing the "natural system in perfect balance" represented by the sagebrush and the animals that live in this environment?
6. The author refers to the use of chemical sprays as a "shotgun approach" to the control of nature. What does she mean?
7. Explain how even the organisms that are seen as the intended beneficiaries of the sagebrush destruction may suffer in the long run.
8. The author refers to an "appalling example of ecological destruction" in Wyoming. Ecology (together with its derivatives) has become a vogue word in recent years. Exactly what does the word mean? How would you express the basic interest or point of view of an ecologist such as Rachel Carson?
9. Do the principles of ecology apply only to wild areas, or do they also have significance for densely populated urban areas? Explain.

FOR COMPOSITION

1. People such as Rachel Carson, deeply concerned with the preservation of the natural environment, are often referred to as environmentalists. The word is sometimes used in a critical sense to suggest an unbalanced or fanatical point of view. Are environmentalists really fanatical? Write an essay in which you present your opinion on this question. (You will probably have to do some research beyond the reading given here.)
2. The ecological gains made in the 1960's and early 1970's may be threatened by the energy crisis. Why should this be so? Can anything be done to reconcile the two sets of needs? Try to provide answers to these and related questions in an essay entitled "Ecology and the Energy Crisis."

About the Authors

Henry Brooks Adams (1838-1918) was born into one of the most eminent families in American history. Great-grandson of President John Quincy Adams, and son of Charles Francis Adams, United States Minister to England during the Civil War, Adams was always aware of the power of tradition. After study at Harvard and Dresden and some European travel, Adams became his father's secretary during the 1860-61 session of Congress. Later in 1861, he accompanied his father to London.

From 1870-1877, Adams was an assistant professor of history at Harvard and head of the *North American Review.* He became convinced that the concept of evolution could be applied to human history. Adams's unique and influential book *Mont-Saint-Michel and Chartres* both establishes a dynamic theory of history and interprets medieval life, art, and thought. His nine-volume work, *History of the United States,* established him as an eminent historian. He is perhaps best known, however, for *The Education of Henry Adams,* both an autobiography and a study of the diversity of modern life.

Maya Angelou (1927-) spent most of her early years in rural Arkansas. As a very young woman, she studied dance in San Francisco and then toured Europe and Africa for the State Department in *Porgy and Bess.* She taught dance in Rome and in Tel Aviv (Israel). Then, turning to the stage, she collaborated with Godfrey Cambridge in producing, directing, and appearing in *Cabaret for Freedom* in New York City. She also starred in Jean Genet's drama *The Blacks.* At the personal request of Dr. Martin Luther King, Jr., Ms. Angelou served as Northern Coordinator for the Southern Christian Leadership Conference. Then she went to Africa, where she worked for newspapers in Egypt and Ghana. She has written and produced a ten-part TV series on African traditions in American life. She now lives in New York City.

James Baldwin (1924-), a "native son" of Harlem, New York City, is one of the most articulate, influential, and prolific literary spokesmen for black Americans. At the heart of Baldwin's thesis is the conviction that the deprived status of blacks is not a "black problem" but rather a symptom of a profound sickness of American society. He sees blacks, because of their peculiar history, as racked with self-hate, and believes that they must learn to overcome this by rejecting the "white American myths" that foster such self-hate. Baldwin has written many novels, essay collections and plays. His novels include *Go Tell It on the Mountain, Giovanni's Room,* and *Another Country.* Among his essays are *Notes of a Native Son, Nobody Knows My Name,* and *The Fire Next Time.* Probably his best-known play is *Blues for Mr. Charlie.* He has received the Award of the National Institute of Arts and Letters and has been a member of the Institute since 1964.

William Bradford (1590-1657) was one of the most able and remarkable of the Pilgrim Fathers. Born in Yorkshire, England, he joined a Puritan congregation at the age of twelve and, in 1609, moved with it to Holland. When, ten years later, the group decided to emigrate to the New World, Bradford helped to organize the *Mayflower* expedition. At the end of the voyage, he was one of the men to explore Cape Cod and to make the famous landing on Plymouth Rock in the snowstorm. In 1621, he was elected governor of the Plymouth colony, a post to which he was re-elected thirty times. His decisive leadership was largely responsible for the colony's survival and growth. During his years in office, he wrote *The History of Plimmoth Plantation,* which has provided subsequent generations with invaluable information about the roots of American history.

William F. Buckley, Jr. (1925-) was born in New York City. An editor, author, free-lance writer, and lecturer, Buckley has contributed articles to such magazines as *Esquire, Saturday Review, Harper's* and *The Atlantic Monthly,* and has served in an editorial capacity on *The American Mercury* and *The National Review.* "On the Right," his weekly column, has been syndicated nationally since 1962. A spokesman for conservatism, Buckley expresses his views in numerous speeches and television appearances. In addition, he is the author of books such as *God and Man at Yale* and *Up from Liberalism.*

Rachel Carson (1907-1964) was born in Springdale, Pennsylvania. In her career, she combined two interests—a desire to write and a great love of nature. From 1936 to 1952, she was on the staff of the U.S. Fish and Wildlife Service as a biologist and editor. Meanwhile, she began her literary career, with the appearance of *Under the Sea-Wind* in 1941. In 1951, she published *The Sea Around Us,* which has been translated into some 30 languages and has won many prizes, including the coveted National Book Award for Nonfiction. In 1962, Rachel Carson's *Silent Spring* was published. All of her professional writing has been well characterized as a "protest in behalf of life."

Malcolm Cowley (1898-), American critic and editor, was born in Belsana, Pennsylvania. Graduated from Harvard in 1919, he went to Paris where he lived for several years.

One of his best-known books is *Exile's Return* (revised in 1951), a "literary odyssey of the 1920's" describing both Cowley's experiences as an expatriate in Paris, and his return to America. Another well-known book of his, *The Lost Generation,* is a study of the writers of the 1920's such as Ernest Hemingway. Cowley has translated much from the French, has edited several important editions of contemporary works, and, as an editor of *The New Republic,* has exerted a strong influence upon literary trends. He is credited with being a major force in reviving the critical reputation of William Faulkner in the 1940's.

Hector St. John de Crèvecoeur (1735-1813), a Frenchman from Normandy, settled in Orange County, New York, and became a frontier farmer. He led an idyllic life observing nature and society until the Revolution, when, suspected by both sides, he was imprisoned by the British and later permitted to sail to France. After the Revolution he returned to America, only to find that his wife was dead, his children dispersed, and his property destroyed. He returned to France and lived there until his death. His *Letters from an American Farmer* (1782) gives an outstanding description of American rural life at that time.

Frederick Douglass (1817-1905), abolitionist, was born Frederick Augustus Washington Bailey in Tuckahoe, Maryland. Assuming the name of Douglass upon his escape from slavery in 1838, Douglass married a free Negro, Anna Murray, and moved to New Bedford, Massachusetts. Influenced by William Lloyd Garrison's *Liberator,* Douglass made his first speech before the Massachusetts Antislavery Society in 1841, thereupon becoming its agent. Fearing that the publication of his autobiography, *The Narrative of the Life of Frederick Douglass, an American Slave* (1845), would lead to his eventual recapture, Douglass traveled to England where, for the first time in his life, he was treated by the English liberals as an equal and a man of worth. Douglass began to perceive that freedom is not limited to physical emancipation; it extends to the more important spheres of social, economic, and psychological equality. Returning to America in 1847, Douglass founded and edited for seventeen years the abolitionist *North Star* in Rochester, New York. With the outbreak of the Civil War, the former slave lectured frequently on slavery and recruited Negroes for two regiments which included his two sons. Douglass served as Assistant Secretary of the Santo Domingo Commission in 1871, and as Minister to Haiti from 1889-1891. A staunch exponent of equality in every form, Douglass lectured not only on the subject of abolition, but also, in his later years, on women's suffrage.

Jonathan Edwards (1703-1758) was the only son of a Connecticut minister with ten daughters. Of a studious nature, he wrote a scientific treatise at the age of twelve and was graduated from Yale at seventeen. In 1727, he became the minister of the large and influential Northampton Church, from whose pulpit he delivered many of the sermons for which he is famous. During the 1730's and 1740's, he played an important role in the religious revival known as the Great Awakening, but eventually his emphasis on the importance of personal feeling brought him into conflict with his congregation and, in 1750, he was dismissed from his post. With his family, he spent the next six years doing missionary work in an Indian settlement in Massachusetts. It was here that he wrote his most important book, *The Freedom of the Will.* In 1757, he became the second President of the College of New Jersey (now Princeton), but he died of smallpox shortly after he had assumed office.

Ralph Waldo Emerson (1803-1882) was descended from a long line of Boston "Brahmins." After his graduation from Harvard, he studied at Harvard Divinity School and, in 1829, was appointed pastor of the Second Church (Unitarian) in Boston. He resigned his ministry in 1832, when he could not reconcile a conflict within himself about the sacrament of the Lord's Supper. He went to Europe to meet with Carlyle, Wordsworth, and Coleridge, but they were unable to help him resolve his spiritual crisis. Settling in Concord, Massachusetts, in 1835, he began his career as a lecturer and writer of essays and helped form the Transcendental Club. Failing health did not prevent Emerson from lecturing or writing many volumes of essays and poems. He traveled throughout the country virtually every year and made several trips to Europe. Prior to the Civil War, he joined other New Englanders in supporting the abolitionist movement.

William Faulkner (1891-1962) was born and spent most of his life in Oxford, Mississippi. This area became the model for Yoknapatawpha County, the fictional locale of his best novels. Having attended Oxford University in England and the University of Mississippi, Faulkner served in the Canadian Flying Corps and in the British Royal Air Force during World War I. A newspaper reporter in New Orleans, he later traveled for the State Department and toward the end of his life, became Writer-in-Residence at the University of Virginia. In 1949, Faulkner was awarded the Nobel Prize for Literature; in 1954, he received the Pulitzer Prize for his novel, *A Fable.* Among Faulkner's best-known novels are *The Sound and The Fury, As I Lay Dying, Sanctuary, Light in August,* and *Absalom, Absalom!*

Benjamin Franklin (1706-1790), the son of a Boston candlemaker, was apprenticed to his father at the age of ten, after attending school for only two years. He so disliked his father's business that at twelve he was apprenticed to his brother James, a printer. When Franklin was seventeen he ran away to Philadelphia; a year later he went to London, where he worked as a printer for two years to earn his passage back to Philadelphia. Upon his return, he bought the *Pennsylvania Gazette,* which, under his management, became an extremely popular publication. At this time he also began to publish the famous *Poor Richard's Almanac.*

Franklin's financial success as a publisher and journalist enabled him to devote much of his time to civic affairs and to his scientific interests. He founded the Philadelphia Public Library (the first circulating library in America), the Philadelphia Fire Company, the Pennsylvania Hospital, the Junto Club (an educational and humanitarian society), and the Philadelphia Academy, which later became the University of Pennsylvania. He also initiated such public services as a city police force, a street sanitation department, and a postal system. As a man of science, Franklin left to his fellow men such inventions as the Franklin stove, the lightning rod, the Franklin clock, bifocal glasses, and a map of the Gulf Stream.

Franklin devoted his later years almost entirely to the service of the emerging new country. Sent to England in 1757 to negotiate tax concessions, he remained there until 1774 as agent for Pennsylvania, New Jersey, Georgia, and Massachusetts. After coming back to America to help frame the Declaration of Independence, he returned to France to secure aid for the American Revolution. There he remained as plenipotentiary until 1785, becoming one of the most honored and beloved men in all France. Shortly thereafter, he was chosen a member of the Constitutional Convention. His last public act was to sign a petition to Congress asking for the abolition of slavery. Franklin died in Philadelphia, having lived to see the inauguration of the government he was so instrumental in shaping.

Robert Frost (1875-1963), who fashioned poetry from rural New England life, was born in San Francisco. After the death of his father, young Robert and his mother moved to Lawrence, Massachusetts, where they lived with his father's parents. When he graduated from high school, he shared the honor of being co-valedictorian with Elinor Miriam White, who became his wife in 1895. He spent a few months at Dartmouth College and two years at Harvard University, but left without taking a degree. (In 1957 he was awarded honorary degrees by both Oxford and Cambridge.) For a time, Frost tried varied occupations: farming, shoemaking, teaching, reporting—all of them to support his family. Regularly, he sent his poems to the leading magazines of that time and just as regularly they were rejected.

In 1912, Frost went to England with his wife and children. Here, for the first time, he lived in a literary atmosphere, a friend of many well-established poets. When *A Boy's Will,* Frost's first volume of poems, was published in England in 1913, it attracted some attention. The second volume, *North of Boston,* increased his reputation. However, it was not until this volume was republished in the United States that Frost began to be widely known in his own country.

When Frost returned to America in 1915, he combined farming with college and university teaching. In later years he was in great demand as a lecturer and a reader of his poems. Each new volume of poems, including *In the Clearing,* has added to his reputation and today he is recognized as one of America's great poets. He received the Pulitzer Prize in poetry four times: for *New Hampshire* (1924), *Collected Poems* (1931), *A Further Range* (1937), and *A Witness Tree* (1943).

Michael Harrington (1928-) is perhaps best known for his book *The Other America,* which helped establish support for the Johnson Administration's War on Poverty. Harrington was born in St. Louis, Missouri, and was graduated from Holy Cross College and the Yale Law School. He also received a Master of Arts degree in English from the University of Chicago. An associate editor of the *Catholic Worker* from 1951 to 1953, Harrington then became organizational secretary for the Workers Defense League. He was co-editor of *Labor in a Free Society* and has contributed articles to such publications as *Commentary*, *Commonweal*, and *Partisan Review*. A free-lance writer, Harrington is also a frequent and popular speaker at political symposia and discussions of social problems.

Ernest Hemingway (1899-1961), one of America's major 20th century novelists, pursued an active career that furnished him with exciting themes for his books. Born near Chicago, the teenage Hemingway left his job on a newspaper to serve as an ambulance driver in World War I. Badly wounded in Italy, he turned again to professional writing and subsequent literary fame. Through the years, he has also been noted as a formidable big game hunter, bullfight fan, sport fisherman, and war correspondent. This preoccupation with physical violence—whether in dangerous sport or deadly war—dominates Hemingway's fiction. His heroes are men trapped by danger, failure, or disaster, who try to maintain an outward indifference to fate, who seek comfort in physical pleasure, and are seldom troubled by intellectual matters. His most famous works include *The Sun Also Rises, A Farewell to Arms*, and *For Whom the Bell Tolls*.

Hemingway forged a simple, bare style that has been highly praised and has had a strong influence on modern American literature. His distinctive talent was singled out for attention when, in 1952, he received the Pulitzer Prize for *The Old Man and the Sea* and, in 1954, the Nobel Prize for Literature.

John Hersey (1914-) was born in Tientsin, China, and moved to the United States in 1924. He was graduated from Yale University in 1936 and studied at Cambridge University. In 1937 he worked as a private secretary to Sinclair Lewis. Hersey was a correspondent for *Time* and *Life* magazines on both fronts during World War II and was responsible for some of the best reporting of the war. Out of his war experiences he also created several novels that have been extremely popular. His earliest novels were based on events he witnessed on Bataan and Guadalcanal. In *A Bell for Adano*, for which he was awarded the Pulitzer Prize in 1945, he drew upon the campaign in Italy, having himself accompanied American invasion forces to Sicily.

In 1950, Hersey next wrote a far more ambitious book, *The Wall*, which is a "documentary" novel about the Polish Jews in Warsaw's Ghetto under the Nazi occupation. His more recent novels include

A Single Pebble, Too Far to Walk, and *Under the Eye of the Storm.* Among his nonfiction works, *Hiroshima*, the deeply moving story of what happened to six people when the first atomic bomb was dropped on the Japanese city, stands out as a classic of modern reporting.

Oliver Wendell Holmes (1809-1894), the son of a Cambridge minister, was reared in the tradition of New England gentility. He wrote the popular poem, "Old Ironsides," while attending the Harvard Law School. In 1831 he transferred from law to medicine, studying at private schools, at Harvard, and for two years in Europe. He began his medical career as a physician, but gradually shifted to the academic aspects of medicine, serving as a professor of anatomy at Dartmouth and as Dean of the Harvard Medical School.

Holmes joined Lowell and Longfellow in the "Saturday Club" and helped found *The Atlantic Monthly*. His writings include poems, reviews, memorials, essays, and important scientific publications. While he devoted his life to science and medicine, he won fame as an essayist, poet, and humorist.

William Dean Howells (1837-1920), unofficial "dean of American literature" until 1920, was born in Ohio. Although Howells attended neither high school nor college, he exhibited an early passion for the world of *belles lettres*. In 1871, he became editor-in-chief of *The Atlantic Monthly*, and retained that position for fifteen years, publishing some of the best young writers of the time. Also a writer of fiction, Howells wrote novels of manners in the earlier part of his career. Later, under the influence of Tolstoy, he became a primary exponent of realism. Among his best known realistic works are *A Modern Instance* and *A Hazard of New Fortunes.* His greatest novel is generally considered to be *The Rise of Silas Lapham*. A major literary critic of his age, Howells provides a good source for information about his literary contemporaries. His biographical works include *Literary Friends and Acquaintances*, and *My Mark Twain*.

Washington Irving (1783-1859), the son of a wealthy merchant, was born and reared in New York City. Because of his poor health, he did not follow his older brothers to college, but read for the law in several New York firms. Although he was admitted to the bar in 1806, Irving rarely practiced law, preferring to write and travel.

He spent many years in Europe and, from 1842 to 1845, was the American Minister to Spain. He spent his last thirteen years at Sunnyside, his country estate near Tarrytown, New York. Irving is most famous for his comic *Knickerbocker's History of New York* and for *The Sketch Book.*

Thomas Jefferson (1743-1826), third President of the United States, was born in Goochland County, Virginia, and was reared as a Southern gentleman and farmer. Remembered chiefly as the author of the Declaration of Independence, Jefferson also served as a cabinet minister during Washington's Administration. Jefferson was elected President in 1801, the first Chief Executive to be inaugurated in Washington, D. C. While Jefferson's Embargo Act of 1807 may have indirectly precipitated the War of 1812, his accomplishments as President and as a person far outnumber his errors. A true humanitarian, he believed that the object of knowledge is to further the happiness of man. Accordingly, he firmly supported a state system of education and was uniquely influential in the incorporation and direction of the University of Virginia at Charlottesville. Jefferson compiled a list of basic books in every field of intellectual endeavor, and went so far as to sell his extensive library to the government after the burning of Washington in the War of 1812. This collection served as the basic core of the Library of Congress. It was during his administration that the United States bought from Napoleon a huge tract of land known as the Louisiana Purchase, which increased the national domain by about 140 per cent. Jefferson died on July 4, 1826, the fiftieth anniversary of the Declaration of Independence.

Sarah Kemble Knight (1666-1727), a native of Boston, was well known throughout Massachusetts as a talented, industrious woman. She amassed her considerable knowledge of the law from her employment by the Massachusetts courts to assist in the recording and witnessing of public documents. She also kept a writing school which Benjamin Franklin was said to have attended. In 1714 Mrs. Knight moved to Connecticut, where she prospered by speculating in Indian lands, managing several farms, and keeping a shop. Her famous *Private Journal of a Journey from Boston to New York in the Year 1704* (published in 1825) is a source of information on colonial customs and conditions.

Abraham Lincoln (1809-1866), sixteenth President of the United States, was born near Hodgen's Mill, Hardin County, Kentucky.

After a difficult pioneer childhood in Kentucky and Indiana, in 1831 Lincoln moved to New Salem, Illinois, where he remained until 1837, serving in the various capacities of storekeeper, county surveyor, and spare time student of law. Licensed as an attorney in 1836, Lincoln began his political career in the Illinois legislature from 1834-1841. As a Whig member to the United States House of Representatives from 1847-1849, Lincoln firmly opposed the Mexican War. Joining the young Republican Party in 1856, Lincoln was its unsuccessful 1858 Republican nominee for the United States Senate in opposition to Stephen A. Douglas. The highlight of this notable campaign was the Lincoln-Douglas debates.

As a result of a schism within the Democratic Party, Lincoln became the victorious Republican candidate for the United States Presidency in 1860. Immediately thereafter, the Confederate states formed in direct opposition to Lincoln's election. His earlier prophetic words, "a house divided against itself cannot stand," became the reality of the Civil War. Upon the siege of Fort Sumter, in April, 1861, he called for volunteers to preserve the Union. While Lincoln's Emancipation Proclamation (January 1863), and his Gettysburg Address (July 1863) are the literary legacies of the war, his Inaugural Address in 1865, which included the memorable words, "With malice toward none, with charity for all," became the cornerstone of his reconstruction policy. Before he could bring his policies to fruition, Lincoln was assassinated by John Wilkes Booth at Ford's Theatre, Washington, D. C., on April 14, 1865.

James Russell Lowell (1819-1891) was born in Cambridge, Massachusetts, where he spent his formative years surrounded by books and scholars. Following his graduation from Harvard, he set up practice as a lawyer but soon found this career unsatisfactory. His decision to give up law and pursue a literary career was prompted by his wife, Maria White, a gifted woman who wrote poetry and was active in reform movements. In the years that followed, Lowell wrote two volumes of poetry and served as both writer and editor for reform journals. In 1855, Lowell's versatility and skill with language won for him the Smith professorship of modern languages at Harvard. He resumed his editorial career when he assumed the editorship of *The Atlantic Monthly* in 1857 and the *North American Review* in 1863. Because of his interest in political affairs, Lowell was appointed Minister to Spain in 1877. After three years in Madrid, he was made Minister to England, where he served with distinction until 1885. Lowell achieved success as a poet, teacher, editor, and diplomat, but attained his greatest eminence as a literary critic.

Herman Melville (1819-1891) was born and educated in New York City and claimed that whaling ships were his "Yale and Harvard." After the failure of his father's importing business, Melville groped around on land and sea for a vocation. He worked as a clerk, a farmhand, and shipped before the mast, all before he was twenty. On his first return from sea, he taught school, but soon left this position to join the crew of the *Acushnet* on a long whaling voyage to the South Seas. His experiences in that part of the world were as exciting and colorful as those he later wrote about in such books as *Typee, Omoo,* and *Moby Dick*. With a friend, he deserted ship in the Marquesas Islands, lived among cannibals, escaped on an Australian whaler, mutinied, was set ashore at Tahiti, and drifted through the South Seas. In 1843 he enlisted on an American frigate at Honolulu and returned to the United States, where he was honorably discharged. Shortly after his return home, Melville began to write stories of his adventures in the South Seas and to establish his reputation. He was not recognized as one of America's major literary figures, however, until the 1920's.

Henry Louis Mencken (1880-1956), American editor and essayist, began his journalistic career in his native Baltimore. Early in his career, Mencken became the editor of the *Baltimore Morning Herald.* He then worked on the *Baltimore Sun*, and from 1924 to the end of 1933 was editor of *The American Mercury*. Mencken opposed Puritanism and valued the unorthodox and anarchistic. He has been called many things by many men. His enemies asserted that he endangered all things holy, precious and important to "the American tradition." Louis Kronenberger deemed Mencken "an 'advanced' individualist" who had a "superb gift for communication." He was also known as "the censor-baiting, freedom-roaring Mencken of 1920." Mencken is noted for his scholarly study, *The American Language*, and for helping writers such as Theodore Dreiser and Sinclair Lewis achieve public recognition.

Thomas Paine (1737-1809) came to America from England at the age of thirty-seven. Like his hero and benefactor, Benjamin Franklin, he arrived in Philadelphia with little more than the clothes upon his back, but within a few years his writings had made him one of the most widely known men in the colonies. After serving as an editor for the *Pennsylvania Magazine*, he published, in January of 1776, *Common Sense*, a short pamphlet which forcefully presented the case for American independence, and which, more than any other factor, crystallized American sentiment for independence and helped to bring about the Revolution. A year later, Paine's pamphlet *The Crisis* inspired the American forces to win a crucial victory at the Battle of Trenton.

In the 1780's, he published *The Rights of Man* in England, for which Paine was accused of treason and forced to flee the country. In France, he was an early supporter of the Revolution, but as it became increasingly violent he counseled moderation, and was imprisoned for opposing the execution of Louis XVI. Back in America, Paine published *The Age of Reason* (1796). A forceful statement of Paine's religious beliefs, the book earned its author many enemies because of its sharp criticism of organized religion. His death at the age of seventy-two was unlamented in the land whose independence he had helped to achieve.

Maxwell Perkins (1884-1947) was born in New York City and was graduated from Harvard College in 1907. His career as reporter, editor, and publisher began with his position on the reportorial staff of *The New York Times* from 1907 to 1910. Associated with Charles Scribner's Sons from 1910 until his death, Perkins was one of the most famous editors of his time, and encouraged some of the leading writers of the first half of the twentieth century.

Edgar Allan Poe (1809-1849) lived a life of hardship, frustration, and success marred by dissipation. He was born in Boston, the son of actor parents. When his mother died in 1811, he was taken into the home of Mr. and Mrs. John Allan, who gave him an excellent education in both Richmond, Virginia, and Stoke Newington, England. His relationship with the Allans started to deteriorate when Poe left the University of Virginia because of gambling debts. Eventually, he broke with the Allans, fled to Boston, and started to write poetry. Aided once again by John Allan, Poe was admitted to West Point, but he provoked his own discharge by neglecting his duties. His story, "MS. Found in a Bottle" won him a writing prize and also a position as editor of the *Southern Literary Messenger*. Elated by his success, he married his young cousin and brought her and her mother to Richmond. His articles were soon commanding national attention, but within a year he left this position and went North. While working for various magazines in New York and Philadelphia, he was able to complete his *Tales of the Grotesque and*

Arabesque. His detective story, "Murders in the Rue Morgue" and his volume of poems, *The Raven and Other Poems,* published in 1845, brought him wide critical acclaim. With the death of his wife, Poe collapsed. Gradually recovering his health, he wrote two of his best works, the poem, "Ulalume," and the essay, "The Poetic Principle." He was described by Lowell as "the most discriminating critic in America." He died in a Baltimore hospital in 1849 after being found unconscious in the street.

Ernest Taylor Pyle (1900-1945), journalist, was born on a farm near Dana, Indiana. At Indiana University he became editor of the student daily, and received his first glimpse into the newspaper world. He worked on a number of newspapers in Indiana, Washington, D.C., and New York City, developing the skill of presenting the personal and warm side of human events. Most memorable of these human interest articles are his accounts of a leper colony at Molokai and of Devil's Island off French Guiana. His 1941 account of the London air bombardment by the Nazis received such acclaim that it was considered the "best column of the year."

After America entered World War II, Pyle joined the combined American and British forces in North Africa, sharing their rations and every aspect of their living conditions. His *Here Is Your War* is a compendium of his African dispatches. As a voice for the common soldier, Pyle so awakened the social consciousness of the nation that Congress passed the "Ernie Pyle" bill to raise the base pay of combat soldiers. Pyle remained in France until after the liberation of Paris, and then joined in the United States Navy effort in the Pacific, only to be killed by Japanese gunfire on Ie Shima. He won the respect and love not only of soldiers and his readers, but of governments and scholars as well. Awarded the Pulitzer Prize for distinguished correspondence in 1944, he received the United States Medal of Merit posthumously.

Carl Sandburg (1878-1967) was the son of poor Swedish immigrants. As a youth, he worked more than he attended school. He drove a milk wagon, swept floors in a barbershop, shifted scenery in a theater, and operated a truck at a brick kiln. At the age of seventeen he headed west, working when he had to, but mostly listening to the men talk and learning the songs people sing. After serving in the Sixth Illinois Infantry in the Spanish-American War, he attended Lombard College, where he first acquired his interest in writing. He did not, however, make writing a career until 1909, when he became a reporter and, later, a journalist. The publication of *Chicago Poems* in 1915 established him as a significant American poet. Later volumes added to his reputation, among them storybooks for children and the first comprehensive collection of musical Americana, *The American Songbag.* The last was the fruit of years of collecting and traveling about the country, reciting his poems and singing to the accompaniment of his guitar. In 1926 he published the first of a six-volume biography of Abraham Lincoln, which was awarded the Pulitzer Prize in history. For his *Complete Poems* (1950), he received the Pulitzer Prize in literature.

Arthur Schlesinger, Jr. (1917-), American historian, is Schweitzer Professor of the Humanities at the City University of New York, a position he has held since 1966. Schlesinger was born in Columbus, Ohio, but grew up in the academic environment of Cambridge, Massachusetts, where his father was a professor of American history at Harvard. Since then, Schlesinger has never been far from a center of intellectual activity. Graduating *summa cum laude* from Harvard in 1938, Schlesinger first taught at Cambridge University, in England, and then became a professor of history at Harvard (1946-1961). For his book, *The Age of Jackson*, Schlesinger was awarded the Pulitzer Prize for history in 1945. Pre-eminent among Schlesinger's non-academic activities was his term as Special Assistant to the President, 1961-1965, an ideal position for gathering material for his best seller, *A Thousand Days: John F. Kennedy in the White House*, which won him the Pulitzer Prize for biography in 1966. He is also the author of the four-volume *The Age of Roosevelt* which he completed in 1962.

Henry Nash Smith (1906-), professor of English at the University of California at Berkeley, was born in Dallas, Texas. He received his A.B. from Southern Methodist University and his Ph.D. from Harvard. From 1927-1941 he ascended the academic ladder from instructor to professor of English at Southern Methodist University. Smith has also been a professor of English at the Universities of Texas, Minnesota, and California. He has been a visiting lecturer at Harvard University, as well as a Huntington Library Fellow. As literary editor of the Mark Twain estate since 1953, Smith has also edited the two-volume *Mark Twain–Howells Letters.*

John Smith (1580-1631), before he was twenty-seven, had served in the English army, had fought with the Austrians against the Turks, and had been captured, enslaved, and sent as far as Russia. His next adventure, in 1607, was to sail from England with a group of colonists to establish the Jamestown settlement. In 1608 Smith's enemies secured temporary control of the colony and sentenced him to hang, but once again his life was saved. After his return to England, he made several more adventurous trips to America, including one to New England.

Lincoln Steffens (1866-1936), American journalist, was born in San Francisco and spent his boyhood on a ranch in Sacramento. He was graduated from the University of California in 1889. Associated successively with the New York *Evening Post*, the New York *Commercial Advertiser*, and *McClure's Magazine*, Steffens made the acquaintance of Jacob Riis and Theodore Roosevelt, both of whom kindled his interest in social reform. Along with Ida Tarbell and other muckrakers, Steffens aroused the social consciousness of the nation with his many articles which were later collected and published in his book, *The Shame of the Cities*. Because, like an outspoken, tactless child, he shocked people with the truth, Steffens has been called an *enfant terrible* of the twentieth century. His method of questioning everyone and everything with ostensible naiveté in order to ferret out the truth has won Steffens the title of "Socrates of the Sanctum." Steffens is best known to students for his *Autobiography*.

John Steinbeck (1902-) is invariably identified with his saga of the Joad family in *The Grapes of Wrath*, though he has written many other fine works, several of particular appeal to high school students. One of his best is *The Red Pony*, a short novel about a boy's experiences while growing up on a California ranch. Another successful book, *The Pearl*, tells the tragic tale of what happened to a poor Mexican Indian, his family, and the community, when he found a pearl of great value. In *Tortilla Flat* and *Cannery Row*, Steinbeck created a crew of raffish characters who enjoyed living more than they enjoyed working for a living. Between these humorous works, he wrote *The Moon Is Down*, a serious account of the Nazi invasion of Norway. *Travels with Charley* recounts his impressions of present-day America. Charley is Steinbeck's dog.

Steinbeck was born in Salinas County, California. He attended Stanford University and worked as a laborer and as a reporter in

New York and California. He received the Pulitzer Prize for *The Grapes of Wrath* in 1939 and was awarded the Nobel Prize for Literature in 1962.

Henry David Thoreau (1817-1862), the only native of Concord in the Transcendentalist group, was graduated from Harvard in 1837 but refused to accept his bachelor's degree. To support himself he taught school with his brother John for four years, worked in his father's pencil factory, and surveyed his neighbors' lands. From 1841 to 1843, he lived in the Emerson household and, under Emerson's influence, became a confirmed Transcendentalist. A vehement abolitionist as well, he went to jail in 1845 for refusing to pay a poll tax which, he felt, was being used to support a war with Mexico to extend the slave territory. In 1845, Thoreau conducted his famous experiment of living alone in a cabin beside Walden Pond; his expenses there were sixteen dollars for two years. His best-known book is *Walden* (1854), an account of this experience. After this interlude, he returned to Concord to spend the rest of his life. Thoreau is recognized today as a devoted naturalist, a powerful social critic, and a prose writer of stature.

James Thurber (1894-1961) was born in Columbus, Ohio, and attended Ohio State University. A meticulous craftsman, he frequently rewrote a story or article ten to twenty-five times before he was satisfied with it. His smoothly flowing style and seemingly spontaneous wit have found favor with a wide audience of readers who consider him the foremost humorist in contemporary American literature. In some books, such as *My Life and Hard Times*, he recreated hilariously funny episodes from his family life in Columbus. In others, such as *Fables for Our Time*, he used fantasy to satirize human foibles in a society that, to him, was "more mad than bad." T. S. Eliot once described Thurber's humor as "also a way of saying something serious."

Another facet of Thurber's genius is revealed in his drawings, which he called "a form of nervous relaxation." He wrote, and in several instances illustrated, two dozen books, including such favorites as *Men, Women and Dogs, The Beast in Me and Other Animals*, and *Thurber Country*.

From the vantage point of his long association with *The New Yorker*, Thurber wrote a biography of its founder, *The Years with Ross*, a book which gives an intimate insight into the life of a magazine and its editor. Exhibiting his versatility in still other ways,

Thurber produced both highly successful children's stories and sophisticated plays such as *The Male Animal* and *A Thurber Carnival.*

Mark Twain (1835-1910), born Samuel Langhorne Clemens in the frontier village of Florida, Missouri, grew up in the little town of Hannibal on the banks of the Mississippi River. When his father died, Twain, a boy of twelve, left school to work as a printer's apprentice on his brother's newspaper. In two of his most famous novels, *The Adventures of Tom Sawyer* and *The Adventures of Huckleberry Finn*, he describes the life and people he remembered so well from his boyhood in Hannibal.

Leaving Hannibal in 1853, Twain worked as a printer in different cities until, on a Mississippi River trip, he decided to become a steamboat pilot. Although the Civil War put an end to his piloting career, his years on the river provided him with rich source material for the stories published first as *Old Times on the Mississippi*, and later as *Life on the Mississippi.*

After spending a few weeks as a Confederate soldier, Twain made the journey by stagecoach to Nevada. *Roughing It* describes the years he spent there as a journalist, prospector, and speculator. At the same time he was establishing his reputation as a humorous lecturer and writer. By 1870, Twain had made several trips abroad, had married Olivia Langdon, and had settled in Hartford, Connecticut. *Innocents Abroad*, a humorous account of his travels, was tremendously successful, and the author was soon lionized wherever he went, in this country and abroad.

Financial troubles and family tragedies darkened Twain's later years. Though not legally responsible for debts he had incurred in a business failure, Twain determined to pay them off. He succeeded by means of an exhausting world lecture tour. The death of two daughters, his wife, and his brother made his private life bitter and lonely. In public life, however, he remained a popular idol until his death.

Robert Penn Warren (1905-) has achieved distinction as a novelist, poet, and literary critic. Born in Kentucky, Warren helped to stimulate the Southern "literary renaissance" of the 1930's and 1940's by founding and editing *The Southern Review.* He has taught English at Louisiana State University, the University of Minnesota, and Yale University. As the co-author of such books as *Understanding Poetry* and *Understanding Fiction*, he has influenced the teaching of literature in high schools and colleges throughout the country. He has twice received the Pulitzer Prize: in 1947, for his novel *All the King's Men,* and in 1958, for *Promises: Poems 1954-56.* He was also awarded the coveted Bollingen Prize for poetry.

Noah Webster (1758-1843) was born in Hartford, Connecticut. Exhibiting an early affinity for books, Webster was admitted to Yale in 1774. His lifelong career began in 1782, when, while teaching at Goshen, New York, he prepared an elementary spelling book which appeared as the first part of *A Grammatical Institute of the English Language.* To this first part, Webster later added a grammar, the forerunner of modern day grammars, and a primer, all three of which were to be used by school children. Webster's *The American Spelling Book* and *An American Selection of Lessons in Reading and Spelling* were instrumental in the unique American standardization of spelling and pronunciation. However, it is as a lexicographer that Webster is best remembered. The first of his lexicographical activities was his *A Compendious Dictionary of the English Language.* With this as a beginning, Webster worked on a larger, two-volume edition, *An American Dictionary of the English Language,* which appeared in 1828.

Elwyn Brooks White (1899-   ), American humorist, has been praised for thinking "in terms of the wide and simple fact of our common humanity." White was born in Mt. Vernon, New York, and received his A.B. from Cornell University in 1928. Known for his writing most of the "Talk of the Town" for *The New Yorker* magazine and "One Man's Meat" for *Harper's Magazine,* White believes that humor "plays close to the big, hot fire which is truth and the reader often feels the heat." He is often praised for his style which *Time* magazine called "a kind of precocious offhand humming." In addition, he juxtaposes the clever with the profound in his poetry. His best-known works include *A Subtreasury of American Humor* (with K. S. White), *Is Sex Necessary?* (with James Thurber), and his fantasies, *Stuart Little* and *Charlotte's Web.*

Walt Whitman (1819-1892), born in West Hills, Long Island, went to school in Brooklyn. He became a printer's apprentice at the age of twelve and, during the next two decades, worked as a printer, itinerant school teacher, and journalist. In 1848 he went to New Orleans to work on a newspaper but returned to Brooklyn three months later. This journey, which took him along the Mississippi River and through the Great Lakes, gave him an opportunity to learn about the western part of America. In 1855 Whitman published *Leaves of Grass*, a collection of his poems. Though this volume was largely ignored by his contemporaries, he continued throughout his life to revise and expand it.

The Civil War had a profound effect upon Whitman. He nursed his brother on a battlefield and later, in Washington, volunteered to tend the wounded in hospitals. These experiences in the war, as well as his sorrow at the death of Lincoln, inspired him to write *Drum Taps*, a collection of war poems, and "When Lilacs Last in the Dooryard Bloom'd," one of the great elegies in the English language. Suffering a stroke in 1873, Whitman was left a semi-invalid. He retired from his clerkship in Washington and lived the rest of his life in a cottage in Camden, New Jersey.

Thomas Wolfe (1900-1938) once acknowledged "an almost insane hunger to devour the entire body of human experience." This feverish intensity characterized his entire life. He was born in Asheville, North Carolina and, influenced by his father's love of and reverence for poetry, he later entered the University of North Carolina, where he received his A.B. In 1924 he received his M.A. from Harvard. As an instructor at Washington Square College, New York University, Wolfe taught all day and wrote feverishly all night. His first novel, *Look Homeward, Angel*, published in 1929, brought him immediate fame. Largely autobiographical, it aroused violent feelings among citizens of Asheville, many of whom recognized themselves thinly disguised in the book. The novels that followed—*Of Time and the River, The Web and the Rock*, and *You Can't Go Home Again*—were also fictionalized accounts of his life, even though he changed his hero's name in the last two works. He died of a brain tumor at the age of thirty-nine.

Glossary of Literary Terms

allusion: a reference to some person, place, or event with literary, historical, or geographical significance.

analogy: a comparison of ideas or objects which are essentially different but which are alike in one significant way; for example, the analogy between the tortoise in the fable, and the persevering man who triumphs over his more talented but overconfident rival.

anecdote: a short narrative, usually of an entertaining nature, which is meant to illustrate an idea.

aphorism: a brief statement of a general truth; for example, "Idle hands are the devil's workshop." In present-day usage an aphorism is synonymous with a maxim oı proverb.

autobiography: an account of a person's life written by himself.

biography: an account of a person's life w.itten by someone else.

caricature: exaggeration by means of deliberate simplification and often gross distortion of a person's appearance or traits of character; for example, Scrooge in Charles Dickens' *A Christmas Carol* is a caricature of a greedy and ill-natured man.

cliché: an expression used so often that it has lost its freshness and effectiveness.

coincidence: the chance occurrence of two events which take place at the same time.

connotation: the implied or suggested meaning of a word or expression.

contrast: the bringing together of ideas, images, or characters to show how they differ.

denotation: the precise, literal meaning of a word or expression

dialect: the speech that is characteristic of a particular region or of a class or group of people.

didactic: morally instructive or intended to be so.

essay: a fairly short nonfiction selection in which the author expresses his thoughts and feelings on any subject he chooses to discuss. A *formal essay* is one in which the primary purpose of the author is to make clear the subject being discussed and, at times, its particular meaning or significance. The style of writing is serious and dignified. An *informal essay* is one in which the primary purpose of the author is to reveal himself through his reactions to, and treatment of, his subject. The style of writing is usually casual and conversational.

euphemism: a mild, inoffensive word or expression used in place of one that is harsh or unpleasant; for example, "to pass away" is a euphemism for "to die."

figure of speech: the general term for a number of literary and poetic devices in which words or groups of words are used to create a vivid mental picture or to make a comparison. For specific figures of speech, see *simile, metaphor, hyperbole, irony.*

hyperbole: a figure of speech employing obvious exaggeration; for example, "He died a thousand deaths."

idiom: the language or manner of speaking that is typical of a particular region or group of people.

image: a general term for any representation of a particular thing with its attendant and evocative detail. It may be a metaphor, a simile, or a straightforward description. An image may also have a symbolic meaning.

irony: a mode of expression in which the author says one thing and means the opposite. The term also applies to a situation, or to the outcome of an event (or series of events), that is contrary to what is naturally hoped for or expected.

metaphor: a figure of speech in which two things are compared without the use of *like* or *as*; for example, "The ship plowed the sea."

mood: the frame of mind or state of feeling created by a piece of writing; for example, the *eerie* mood of a story by Poe.

moral: the lesson taught by a literary work.

narration: an account of an event or series of events, whether true or imaginary.

paradox: a statement which seems on the surface to be contradictory, yet actually involves an element of truth; for example, "The country is mobilizing for peace."

personal reminiscence: a recollection of a past experience or impression, which is narrated by the author usually in an informal style.

rhetorical question: a question that is asked for its dramatic effect but to which no answer is expected.

satire: a piece of writing which criticizes manners, individuals, or political and social institutions by holding them up to ridicule.

simile: a figure of speech in which a comparison is made between two objects essentially unlike but resembling each other in one or more respects. This comparison is always introduced by *like* or *as*; for example, "Our dog was as powerful as a wrestler."

style: the distinctive manner in which the writer uses language: his choice and arrangement of words.

symbol: an object that stands for, or represents an idea, belief, superstition, social or political institution, etc.; for example, a pair of scales is often used as a symbol for justice.

theme: the idea, general truth, or commentary on life or people brought out through a literary work.

tone: the feeling conveyed by the author's attitude towards his subject and by the particular way in which he writes about it.